Expert C++

Become a proficient programmer by learning coding best practices with C++17 and C++20's latest features

Marcelo Guerra Hahn

Araks Tigranyan

John Asatryan

Vardan Grigoryan

Shunguang Wu

BIRMINGHAM—MUMBAI

Expert C++

Group Product Manager: Kunal Sawant
Publishing Product Manager: Akash Sharma
Book Project Manager: Manisha Singh
Senior Editor: Kinnari Chohan
Technical Editor: Jubit Pincy
Copy Editor: Safis Editing
Proofreader: Safis Editing
Indexer: Pratik Shirodkar
Production Designer: Shyam Sundar Korumilli
DevRel Marketing Coordinator: Rayyan Khan and Sonia Chauhan

First published: April 2020

Second edition: August 2023

Production reference: 1280723

Published by Packt Publishing Ltd.
Grosvenor House
11 St Paul's Square
Birmingham
B3 1RB, UK.

ISBN 978-1-80461-783-0

www.packtpub.com

Contributors

About the authors

Marcelo Guerra Hahn, a seasoned expert with 18+ years of experience in software development and data analysis, excels in C++, C#, and Azure. Currently Engineering Manager at Microsoft C++ Team and former leader at SoundCommerce, his passion for data-driven decision-making is evident. He shares his wisdom as a lecturer at prestigious institutions like Lake Washington Institute of Technology and University of Washington. In this book, Marcelo empowers readers with advanced C++ techniques, honed through real-world experience, fostering proficiency in programming and data analysis.

Araks Tigranyan is a passionate software engineer who works at Critical Techworks, specializing in C++ with two years of experience overall. Her love for programming, particularly in C++, is evident in her dedication to crafting efficient and innovative solutions. With an insatiable curiosity for the ever-evolving tech world, Araks consistently stays at the cutting edge of the industry.

John Asatryan is the Head of Code Republic Lab at Picsart Academy. Armed with a Bachelor's degree in International Economic Relations from the Armenian State University of Economics, he has ventured into the realms of technology and education. John's commitment to empowering aspiring developers shines through, adding to his expertise in the field with a passion for coding.

Vardan Grigoryan is a senior backend engineer and C++ developer with more than 9 years of experience. Vardan started his career as a C++ developer and then moved to the world of server-side backend development. While being involved in designing scalable backend architectures, he always tries to incorporate the use of C++ in critical sections that require the fastest execution time. Vardan loves tackling computer systems and program structures on a deeper level. He believes that true excellence in programming can be achieved by means of a detailed analysis of existing solutions and by designing complex systems.

Shunguang Wu is a senior professional staff at Johns Hopkins University Applied Physics Laboratory, and received his PhDs in theoretical physics and electrical engineering from Northwestern University (China) and Wright State University (USA), respectively. He published about 50 reviewed journal papers in the area of nonlinear dynamics, statistical signal processing and computer vision in his early career. His professional C++ experience started with teaching undergraduate courses in the late 1990s. Since then he has been designing and developing lots of R&D and end-user application software using C++ in world-class academic and industrial laboratories. These projects span both the Windows and Linux platforms.

About the reviewers

Sergio Guidi Tabosa Pessoa is a software engineer with more than 30 years of experience with software development and maintenance; from complex enterprise software projects to modern mobile applications. In the early days he was working primarily with the Microsoft stack, but soon he discovered the power of the UNIX and Linux operating systems. Even though he has worked with many languages throughout these years, C and C++ remain his favorite languages for their power and speed.

He has a bachelor's degree in Computer Science, an MBA in IT Management, and is currently working on a Professional Certificate on Cybersecurity at MIT. He is always hungry to learn new technologies, breaking code and learning from his mistakes. He currently lives in Brazil with his wife, three Yorkshires and two cockatiels.

Sam Johnson is an Electrical Engineering student at Western Washington University. He has experience as a programming tutor at a college level. With an interest in the electronics and software inside consumer devices, Sam has focused on acquiring an understanding of all levels of programming.

Serban Stoenescu is a software developer specialized in C++. He is currently working for Porsche on an autonomous driving project called Highway Pilot Supervisor.

In his past jobs he worked on OpenCV applications, a CAD project with OpenCASCADE, Big Data projects in Java and in telecom. He was also a trainer, he used to teach Rational ROSE. He is the co-author of *Towards the Impact of Design Flaws on the Resources Used by an Application*, a paper at ARMS-CC 2014. Currently, he is also a Udemy instructor, his most popular course being *C++ Unit Testing: Google Test and Google Mock*. His other courses are *CMake from Zero to Hero* and *C++ Machine Learning Algorithms Inspired by Nature*.

Naseef Chowdhury is a C++ Software Developer with more than 10 years of experience. He is currently working as a Senior Software Engineer at HP Inc. Previously, he has working in Poly/Polycom Inc., IPvision Soft Limited, Kona Software Lab Limited, and Eyeball Networks. He has completed his MS in Computer Science from New Mexico Tech and he did his bachelors from Chittagong University of Engineering & Technology, Bangladesh. He is passionate about clean code, design patterns, architecture and system design, and the modern features of C++.

Table of Contents

Part 1: Under the Hood of C++ Programming

1

Building C++ Applications   3

2

Beyond Object-Oriented Programming   53

3

Understanding and Designing Templates   133

4

Template Meta Programming   167

5

Memory Management and Smart Pointers   205

Part 2: Designing Robust and Efficient Applications

6

Digging into Data Structures and Algorithms in STL   247

7

Advanced Data Structures   281

8

Functional Programming   329

9

Concurrency and Multithreading   357

10

Designing Concurrent Data Structures   391

11

Designing World-Ready Applications   417

12

Incorporating Design Patterns in C++ Applications   435

13

Networking and Security   451

14

Debugging and Testing   469

15

Large-Scale Application Design   493

Part 3: C++ in the AI World

16

17

18

Preface

Welcome to *Expert C++!* If you are an experienced C++ developer eager to elevate your skills and explore the full potential of C++20, you've come to the right place.

In this expert guide, we have meticulously crafted a learning journey to empower you with advanced programming techniques and practical knowledge that goes beyond traditional object-oriented programming. Whether you aspire to design high-performance applications, work with cutting-edge data structures, or master multithreading and concurrency, this book is your ultimate companion.

We will take you through the intricacies of designing templates, including the powerful realm of template metaprogramming. Memory management and smart pointers will become your allies as you tackle complex projects with confidence. Delve into the realm of data structures using the Standard Template Library (STL) containers, and then push the boundaries further with advanced data structures in C++. Discover the elegance of functional programming and the intricacies of concurrency and multithreading, all while learning to design concurrent data structures.

As you progress, we will guide you through the process of creating world-ready applications, incorporating essential design patterns, and understanding networking and security principles. The book's culmination will be your enlightenment on debugging and testing, followed by a profound exploration of large-scale application design.

Whether you aspire to develop enterprise-level software or cutting-edge projects, this book is designed to empower you to become a proficient C++ programmer. So, waste no time and embark on this transformative journey.

Happy coding!

Who this book is for

The primary target audience consists of experienced C++ developers who are eager to elevate their skills and create professional-grade applications. Whether you wish to master complex programming concepts, improve application performance, or explore advanced techniques, this book will serve as a valuable resource in your journey.

The secondary target audience encompasses software engineers and computer science students with an interest in learning advanced C++ programming techniques and discovering real-world applications of the language. By delving into the content of this book, you can expand your knowledge and develop practical expertise in utilizing C++ for various projects and challenges.

Regardless of your background or experience level, "Expert C++" aims to empower you with valuable insights and practical knowledge, guiding you towards becoming a proficient and capable C++ programmer.

What this book covers

Chapter 1, Building C++ Applications, will touch upon topics such as the application-building process in C++ and the low-level details of C++ applications

Chapter 2, Beyond Object-Oriented Programming, dives deeply into the design of OOP

Chapter 3, Understanding and Designing Templates, talks about the syntax of function and class templates, their instantiations, and their specializations.

Chapter 4, Template Meta Programming, provides you with the knowledge and skills you need to master template metaprogramming.

Chapter 5, Memory Management and Smart Pointers, illuminates the mystery behind memory and proper memory management techniques.

Chapter 6, Digging into Data Structures and Algorithms in STL, covers a wide range of data structures and algorithms.

Chapter 7, Advanced Data Structures, dives even deeper into what data structures there are, some of which you may have never heard about before.

Chapter 8, Functional Programming, talks about the fundamental blocks of functional programming, as well as ranges.

Chapter 9, Concurrency and Multithreading, introduces you to concurrency and multithreading fundamentals in C++ and the best practices for concurrent code design.

Chapter 10, Designing Concurrent Data, will help you picture problems with data races and acquire the basic knowledge needed to design concurrent algorithms and data structures.

Chapter 11, Designing World-Ready Applications, addresses common design ideas that will help prevent errors and write world-ready applications.

Chapter 12, Incorporating Design Patterns in C++ Applications, we will analyze examples of using design patterns in C++ applications in various different areas.

Chapter 13, Networking and Security, discuss the standard networking extension and see what is needed to implement networking-supported programs.

Chapter 14, Debugging and Testing, describes the analysis of a software defect, the use of the GNU Debugger (GDB) tool to debug a program, and the use of tools to automatically analyze software.

Chapter 15, Large-Scale Application Design, discusses the practices behind building data-intensive applications and explores data partitioning, replication, caching, and data flow optimization.

Chapter 16, Understanding and Using C++ in Machine Learning Tasks, introduce the concepts of AI and ML and also provides examples of tasks in ML. We are going to implement them and give you a basic idea of how you should research and move forward with solving more complex tasks.

Chapter 17, Using C++ in Data Science, explains why C++ can be used in the data science industry and how it makes it possible.

Chapter 18, Designing and Implementing a Data Analysis Framework, explores the basic steps of building a complex data analysis program using C++.

To get the most out of this book

The g++ compiler with the option -std=c++2a is used to compile the examples throughout the book.

Software/hardware covered in the book	Operating system requirements
g++ compiler	Ubuntu Linux is a plus, but not a requirement

Basic C++ experience, including a familiarity with memory management, object-oriented programming, and basic data structures and algorithms, will be a big plus.

If you are using the digital version of this book, we advise you to type the code yourself or access the code from the book's GitHub repository (a link is available in the next section). Doing so will help you avoid any potential errors related to the copying and pasting of code.

Download the example code files

You can download the example code files for this book from GitHub at `https://github.com/PacktPublishing/Expert-C-2nd-edition`. If there's an update to the code, it will be updated in the GitHub repository.

We also have other code bundles from our rich catalog of books and videos available at `https://github.com/PacktPublishing/`. Check them out!

Conventions used

There are a number of text conventions used throughout this book.

`Code in text`: Indicates code words in text, database table names, folder names, filenames, file extensions, pathnames, dummy URLs, user input, and Twitter handles. Here is an example: "We sort the numericalData vector and calculate the median based on size and values"

A block of code is set as follows:

```
#include <iostream>
#include <vector>
#include <algorithm>
#include <map>
```

Any command-line input or output is written as follows:

```
std::unique_ptr<Base> ptr =      std::make_unique_default_init<Derived>
();

ptr->test();
```

> **Tips or important notes**
> Appear like this.

Get in touch

Feedback from our readers is always welcome.

General feedback: If you have questions about any aspect of this book, email us at customercare@ packtpub.com and mention the book title in the subject of your message.

Errata: Although we have taken every care to ensure the accuracy of our content, mistakes do happen. If you have found a mistake in this book, we would be grateful if you would report this to us. Please visit www.packtpub.com/support/errata and fill in the form.

Piracy: If you come across any illegal copies of our works in any form on the internet, we would be grateful if you would provide us with the location address or website name. Please contact us at copyright@packt.com with a link to the material.

If you are interested in becoming an author: If there is a topic that you have expertise in and you are interested in either writing or contributing to a book, please visit authors.packtpub.com.

Share Your Thoughts

Once you've read *Expert C++, 2nd edition*, we'd love to hear your thoughts! Scan the QR code below to go straight to the Amazon review page for this book and share your feedback.

https://packt.link/r/1804617830

Your review is important to us and the tech community and will help us make sure we're delivering excellent quality content.

Download a free PDF copy of this book

Thanks for purchasing this book!

Do you like to read on the go but are unable to carry your print books everywhere? Is your eBook purchase not compatible with the device of your choice?

Don't worry, now with every Packt book you get a DRM-free PDF version of that book at no cost.

Read anywhere, any place, on any device. Search, copy, and paste code from your favorite technical books directly into your application.

The perks don't stop there, you can get exclusive access to discounts, newsletters, and great free content in your inbox daily

Follow these simple steps to get the benefits:

1. Scan the QR code or visit the link below

https://packt.link/free-ebook/9781804617830

2. Submit your proof of purchase
3. That's it! We'll send your free PDF and other benefits to your email directly

Part 1: Under the Hood of C++ Programming

In this part, you will learn the details of C++ program compilation, linking, and dive into the details of OOP, templates and memory management.

This part has the following chapters:

- Chapter 1, Building C++ Applications
- Chapter 2, Beyond Object-Oriented Programming
- Chapter 3, Understanding and Designing Templates
- Chapter 4, Template Meta Programming
- Chapter 5, Memory Management and Smart Pointers

1

Building C++ Applications

In the world of C++, where precision meets creativity, programmers are building extraordinary applications that will change the lives of people forever. We hope that this book will help you become an inseparable part of that community.

In this chapter, you will go through a crash course in C++ basics. We will touch upon topics such as the application-building process in C++ and the low-level details of C++ applications, and be provided a quick introduction to essential object-oriented programming techniques.

The following topics will be discussed in this chapter:

- Introduction to C++ and its latest standard
- Under the hood of the source code's compilation, preprocessing, and linking
- The process of loading and running an executable file
- Intricacies behind the function call and recursion
- Data types, memory segments, and addressing fundamentals
- Pointers, arrays, and control structures
- Essentials of OOP
- Class relationships, inheritance, and polymorphism

Let's begin!

Technical requirements

The g++ compiler with the `-std=c++2a` option has been used to compile the examples throughout this chapter. You can find the source files that have been used in this chapter in the GitHub repository for this book at `https://github.com/PacktPublishing/Expert-C-2nd-edition`.

Building C++ applications

You can use any text editor to write code, because, ultimately, code is just text. To write code, you are free to choose between simple text editors such as **Vim**, or an advanced **integrated development environment** (**IDE**) such as **MS Visual Studio**. The only difference between a love letter and source code is that the latter might be interpreted by a special program called a **compiler** (while the love letter cannot be compiled into a program, it might give you butterflies in your stomach).

To mark the difference between a plain text file and source code, a special file extension is used. C++ operates with the `.cpp` and `.h` extensions (you may also occasionally encounter `.cxx` and `.hpp` as well). Before getting into the details, think of the compiler as a tool that translates the source code into a runnable program, known as an executable file or just an executable. The process of making an executable from the source code is called compilation. Compiling a C++ program is a sequence of complex tasks that results in machine code generation. Machine code is the native language of the computer – that's why it's called machine code.

Typically, a C++ compiler parses and analyzes the source code, then generates intermediate code, optimizes it, and, finally, generates machine code in a file called an object file. You may have already encountered object files; they have individual extensions – `.o` in Linux and `.obj` in Windows. The created object file contains more than just machine code that can be run by the computer. Compilation usually involves several source files, and compiling each source file produces a separate object file. These object files are then linked together by a tool called a **linker** to form a single executable file. This linker uses additional information stored in object files to link them properly (linking will be discussed later in this chapter).

The following diagram depicts the program-building phases:

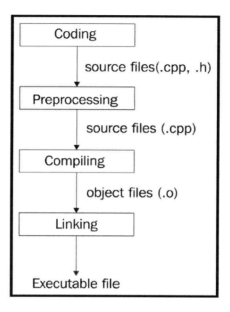

Figure 1.1: The compilation phases of a typical C++ program

The C++ application-building process consists of three major steps:

1. **Preprocessing**
2. **Compiling**
3. **Linking**

All of these steps are done using different tools, but modern compilers encapsulate them in a single tool, thereby providing a single and more straightforward interface for programmers.

The generated executable file persists on the hard drive of the computer. To run it, it should be copied to the main memory, the RAM. The copying is done by another tool, named the **loader**. The loader is a part of the **operating system** (**OS**) and knows what and where should be copied from the contents of the executable file. After loading the executable file into the main memory, the original executable file won't be deleted from the hard drive.

A program is loaded and run by the OS. The OS manages the execution of the program, prioritizes it over other programs, unloads it when it's done, and so on. The running copy of the program is called a **process**. A process is an instance of an executable file.

Preprocessing

A **preprocessor** is intended to process source files to make them ready for compilation. A preprocessor works with preprocessor **directives**, such as #define, #include, and so on. Directives don't represent program statements, but they are commands for the preprocessor, telling it what to do with the text of the source file. The compiler cannot recognize those directives, so whenever you use preprocessor directives in your code, the preprocessor resolves them accordingly before the actual compilation of the code begins.

For example, the following code will be changed before the compiler starts to compile it:

```
#define NUMBER 41
int main() {
    int a = NUMBER + 1;
    return 0;
}
```

Everything that is defined using the #define directive is called a **macro**. After preprocessing, the compiler gets the transformed source in this form:

```
int main() {
    int a = 41 + 1;
    return 0;
}
```

It is dangerous to use macros that are syntactically correct but have logical errors:

```
#define SQUARE_IT(arg) (arg * arg)
```

The preprocessor will replace any occurrence of SQUARE_IT(arg) with (arg * arg), so the following code will output 16:

```
int st = SQUARE_IT(4);
std::cout << st;
```

The compiler will receive this code as follows:

```
int st = (4 * 4);
std::cout << st;
```

Problems arise when we use complex expressions as a macro argument:

```
int bad_result = SQUARE_IT(4 + 1);
std::cout << bad_result;
```

Intuitively, this code will produce 25, but the truth is that the preprocessor doesn't do anything but text processing, and in this case, it replaces the macro like this:

```
int bad_result = (4 + 1 * 4 + 1);
std::cout << bad_result; // prints 9, instead of 25
```

To fix the macro definition, surround the macro argument with additional parentheses:

```
#define SQUARE_IT(arg) ((arg) * (arg))
```

Now, the expression will take this form:

```
int bad_result = ((4 + 1) * (4 + 1));
```

> **Tip**
>
> As a rule of thumb, avoid using macro definitions. Macros are error-prone and C++ provides a set of constructs that make the use of macros obsolete.

The preceding example would be type-checked and processed at compile time if we used a `constexpr` function:

```
constexpr int double_it(int arg) { return arg * arg; }
int bad_result = double_it(4 + 1);
```

Use the `constexpr` specifier to make it possible to evaluate the return value of the function (or the value of a variable) at compile time.

Header files

The most common use of the preprocessor is the `#include` directive, which intends to include header files in the source code. Header files contain definitions for functions, classes, and so on:

```
// file: main.cpp
#include <iostream>
#include "rect.h"
int main() {
    Rect r(3.1, 4.05);
    std::cout << r.get_area() << std::endl;
}
```

After the preprocessor examines `main.cpp`, it replaces the `#include` directives with corresponding contents of `iostream` and `rect.h`.

C++17 introduces the __has_include preprocessor constant expression, which evaluates to 1 if the file with the specified name is found and 0 if not:

```
#if __has_include("custom_io_stream.h")
#include "custom_io_stream.h"
#else
#include <iostream>
#endif
```

When declaring header files, it's strongly advised to use so-called **include guards** (#ifndef, #define, and #endif) to avoid double declaration errors.

Using modules

Modules fix header files with annoying include-guard issues. We can now get rid of preprocessor macros. Modules incorporate two keywords – import, and export. To use a module, we import it. To declare a module with its exported properties, we use export. Before we list the benefits of using modules, let's look at a simple usage example.

The following code declares a module:

```
export module test;
export int square(int a) { return a * a; }
```

The first line declares the module named test. Next, we declared the square() function and set it to export. This means that we can have functions and other entities that are not exported, so they will be private outside of the module. By exporting an entity, we set it to public for module users. To use module, we must import it, as shown in the following code:

```
import test;
int main() {
    square(21);
}
```

The following features make modules better compared to regular header files:

- A **module** is imported only once, similar to precompiled headers supported by custom language implementations. This reduces the compile time drastically. Non-exported entities do not affect the translation unit that imports the module.

- Modules allow us to express the logical structure of code by allowing us to select which units should be exported and which should not. Modules can be bundled together into bigger modules.

- We can get rid of workarounds such as include guards, as described earlier. We can import modules in any order. There are no more concerns for macro redefinitions.

Modules can be used together with header files. We can both import and include headers in the same file, as demonstrated in the following example:

```
import <iostream>;
#include <vector>
int main() {
    std::vector<int> vec{1, 2, 3};
    for (int elem : vec) std::cout << elem;
}
```

When creating modules, you are free to export entities in the interface file of the module and move the implementations to other files. The logic is the same as it is for managing .h and .cpp files.

Compiling

The C++ compilation process consists of several phases. Some of the phases are intended to analyze the source code, while others generate and optimize the target machine code.

The following diagram shows the phases of compilation:

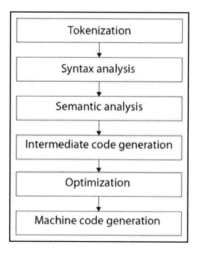

Figure 1.2: C++ compilation phases

Let's look at some of these phases in detail.

Syntax analysis

When speaking about programming language compilation, we usually differentiate two terms – syntax and semantics:

- The **syntax** is the structure of the code; it defines the rules by which combined tokens make structural sense. For example, *day nice* is a syntactically correct phrase in English because it doesn't contain errors in either of the tokens.

- **Semantics**, on the other hand, concerns the actual meaning of the code – that is, *day nice* is semantically incorrect and should be corrected to *nice day*.

Syntax analysis is a crucial part of source analysis because tokens will be analyzed syntactically and semantically – that is, as to whether they bear any meaning that conforms to the general grammar rules.

Let's take a look at the following example:

```
int b = a + 0;
```

This may not make sense to us, since adding zero to the variable won't change its value, but the compiler doesn't look at logical meaning here – it looks for the **syntactic correctness** of the code (a missing semicolon, a missing closing parenthesis, and more). Checking the syntactic correctness of the code is done in the syntax analysis phase of compilation. The lexical analysis part divides the code into tokens; syntax analysis checks for syntactic correctness, which means that the aforementioned expression will produce a syntax error if we have missed a semicolon:

```
int b = a + 0
```

g++ will complain with the expected ' ; ' at the end of the declaration error.

Optimization

Generating intermediate code helps the compiler make optimizations in the code. Compilers try to optimize code a lot. Optimizations are done in more than one pass. For example, take a look at the following code:

```
int a = 41;
int b = a + 1;
```

During compilation, the preceding code will be optimized into the following:

```
int a = 41;
int b = 41 + 1;
```

This, again, will be optimized into the following:

```
int a = 41;
int b = 42;
```

Some programmers do not doubt that, nowadays, compilers code better than programmers.

Machine code generation

Compiler optimizations are done in both intermediate code and generated machine code. The compiler usually generates object files containing a lot of other data besides the machine code.

The structure of an object file depends on the platform; for example, in **Linux**, it is represented in **Executable and Linkable Format** (**ELF**). A **platform** is an environment in which a program is executed. In this context, by platform, we mean the combination of the computer architecture (more specifically, the **instruction set architecture**) and the OS. Hardware and OSs are designed and created by different teams and companies. Each of them has different solutions to design problems, which leads to major differences between platforms. Platforms differ in many ways, and those differences are projected onto the executable file format and structure as well. For example, the executable file format in Windows systems is **Portable Executable** (**PE**), which has a different structure, number, and sequence of sections than ELF in Linux.

An object file is divided into **sections**. The most important ones for us are the code sections (marked as `.text`) and the data section (`.data`). The `.text` section holds the program's instructions, while the `.data` section holds the data used by instructions. Data itself may be split into several sections, such as **initialized**, **uninitialized**, and **read-only** data.

An important part of object files, in addition to the `.text` and `.data` sections, is the **symbol table**. The symbol table stores the mappings of strings (symbols) to locations in the object file. In the preceding example, the compiler-generated output had two portions, the second portion of which was marked as `information:`, which holds the names of the functions used in the code and their relative addresses. This `information:` is the abstract version of the actual symbol table of the object file. The symbol table holds both symbols defined in the code and symbols used in the code that need to be resolved. This information is then used by the linker to link the object files together to form the final executable file.

Linking

Let's take a look at the following project structure:

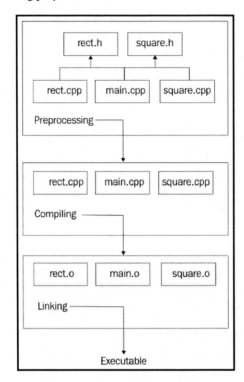

Figure 1.3: A sample project structure with several .h and .cpp files

The compiler will compile each unit separately. Compilation units, also known as source files, are *independent* of each other in some way.

When the compiler compiles main.cpp, which has a call to the get_area() function in Rect, it does not include the get_area() implementation in main.cpp. Instead, it is just sure that the function is implemented somewhere in the project. When the compiler gets to rect.cpp, it does not know that the get_area() function is used somewhere. Here's what the compiler gets after main.cpp passes the preprocessing phase:

```cpp
// contents of the iostream
struct Rect {
private:
    double side1_;
    double side2_;
public:
```

```
    Rect(double s1, double s2);
    const double get_area() const;
};
struct Square : Rect {
    Square(double s);
};
int main() {
    Rect r(3.1, 4.05);
    std::cout << r.get_area() << std::endl;
    return 0;
}
```

After analyzing `main.cpp`, the compiler generates the following intermediate code (many details have been omitted to simply express the idea behind compilation):

```
struct Rect {
    double side1_;
    double side2_;
};

void _Rect_init_(Rect* this, double s1, double s2);
double _Rect_get_area_(Rect* this);

struct Square {
    Rect _subobject_;
};

void _Square_init_(Square* this, double s);

int main() {
    Rect r;
    _Rect_init_(&r, 3.1, 4.05);
    printf("%d\n", _Rect_get_area_(&r));
    // we've intentionally replace cout with printf for
    // brevity and
    // supposing the compiler generates a C intermediate
    // code
    return 0;
}
```

The compiler will remove the `Square` struct with its constructor function (we named it `_Square_init_`) while optimizing the code because it was never used in the source code.

At this point, the compiler operates with main.cpp only, so it sees that we called the _Rect_init_ and _Rect_get_area_ functions but did not provide their implementation in the same file. However, as we did provide their declarations beforehand, the compiler trusts us and believes that those functions are implemented in other compilation units. Based on this trust and the minimum information regarding the function signature (its return type, name, and the number and types of its parameters), the compiler generates an object file that contains the working code in main.cpp and somehow marks the functions that have no implementation but are trusted to be resolved later. This resolution is done by the linker.

In the following example, we have the simplified variant of the generated object file, which contains two sections – code and information. The code section has addresses for each instruction (the hexadecimal values):

```
code:
0x00 main
0x01 Rect r;

 0x02 _Rect_init_(&r, 3.1, 4.05);

0x03 printf("%d\n", _Rect_get_area(&r));
information:

 main: 0x00
_Rect_init_: ????
printf: ????
_Rect_get_area_: ????
```

Take a look at the information section. The compiler marks all the functions used in the code section that were not found in the same compilation unit with ????. These question marks will be replaced by the actual addresses of the functions found in other units by the linker. Finishing with main.cpp, the compiler starts to compile the rect.cpp file:

```
// file: rect.cpp
   struct Rect {
      // #include "rect.h" replaced with the contents
      // of the rect.h file in the preprocessing phase
      // code omitted for brevity
   };
   Rect::Rect(double s1, double s2)
      : side1_(s1), side2_(s2)
   {}
   const double Rect::get_area() const {
      return side1_ * side2_;
}
```

Following the same logic here, the compilation of this unit produces the following output (don't forget, we're still providing abstract examples):

```
code:
 0x00 _Rect_init_
 0x01 side1_ = s1
 0x02 side2_ = s2
 0x03 return
 0x04 _Rect_get_area_
0x05 register = side1_
0x06 reg_multiply side2_
0x07 return
information:
_Rect_init_: 0x00
_Rect_get_area_: 0x04
```

This output has all the addresses of the functions in it, so there is no need to wait for some functions to be resolved later.

The task of the linker is to combine these object files into a single object file. Combining files results in relative address changes; for example, if the linker puts the rect.o file after main.o, the starting address of rect.o becomes 0x04 instead of the previous value of 0x00:

```
code:
 0x00 main
 0x01 Rect r;
 0x02 _Rect_init_(&r, 3.1, 4.05);
 0x03 printf("%d\n", _Rect_get_area(&r)); 0x04 _Rect_init_
 0x05 side1_ = s1
 0x06 side2_ = s2
 0x07 return
 0x08 _Rect_get_area_
 0x09 register = side1_
 0x0A reg_multiply side2_
 0x0B return
information (symbol table):
main: 0x00
 _Rect_init_: 0x04
printf: ????
_Rect_get_area_: 0x08
_Rect_init_: 0x04
_Rect_get_area_: 0x08
```

Correspondingly, the linker updates the symbol table addresses (the information: section in our example). As mentioned previously, each object file has a symbol table, which maps the string name of the symbol to its relative location (address) in the file. The next step of linking is to resolve all the unresolved symbols in the object file.

Now that the linker has combined `main.o` and `rect.o`, it knows the relative location of unresolved symbols because they are now located in the same file. The `printf` symbol will be resolved the same way, except this time, it will link the object files with the standard library. Once all the object files have been combined (we omitted the linking of `square.o` for brevity), all the addresses have been updated, and all the symbols have been resolved, the linker outputs the one final object file that can be executed by the OS. As discussed earlier in this chapter, the OS uses a tool called the loader to load the contents of the executable file into memory.

Linking libraries

A library is similar to an executable file, with one major difference: it does not have a `main()` function, which means that it cannot be invoked as a regular program. Libraries are used to combine code that might be reused with more than one program. You already linked your programs with the standard library by including the `<iostream>` header, for example.

Libraries can be linked with the executable file either as **static** or **dynamic** libraries. When you link them as a static library, they become a part of the final executable file. A dynamically linked library should also be loaded into memory by the OS to provide your program with the ability to call its functions. Let's suppose we want to find the square root of a function:

```
int main() {
    double result = sqrt(49.0);
}
```

The C++ standard library provides the `sqrt()` function, which returns the square root of its argument. If you compile the preceding example, it will produce an error insisting that the `sqrt` function has not been declared. We know that to use the standard library function, we should include the corresponding `<cmath>` header. But the header file does not contain the implementation of the function; it just declares the function (in the `std` namespace), which is then included in our source file:

```
#include <cmath>
int main() {
    double result = std::sqrt(49.0);
}
```

The compiler marks the address of the `sqrt` symbol as unknown, and the linker should resolve it in the linking stage. The linker will fail to resolve it if the source file is not linked with the standard library implementation (the object file containing the library functions). The final executable file generated by the linker will consist of both our program and the standard library if the linking was static. On the other hand, if the linking is dynamic, the linker marks the `sqrt` symbol to be found at runtime.

Now, when we run the program, the loader also loads the library that was dynamically linked to our program. It loads the contents of the standard library into the memory as well and then resolves the actual location of the sqrt() function in memory. The same library that has already been loaded into memory can be used by other programs as well.

Low-level programming with C++

Initially, C++ was perceived as the successor of the C language; however, since then, it has evolved into something big, sometimes scary, and even untamable. With recent language updates, it now represents a complex beast that requires time and patience to tame. We will start this chapter by covering the basic constructs that almost every language supports, such as data types, conditional and loop statements, pointers, structs, and functions. We will look at those constructs from the perspective of a low-level systems programmer, curious about how even a simple instruction can be executed by the computer. A deep understanding of these basic constructs is mandatory to build a solid base for more advanced and abstract topics such as **object-oriented programming (OOP)**.

Functions

Program execution starts with the main() function, which is the *designated start of the program*, as stated in the standard. A simple program outputting the Hello, World! message will look like this:

```
#include <iostream.h>
int main() {
    std::cout << "Hello, World!" << std::endl;
    return 0;
}
```

You may have encountered or used the arguments of the main() function in your passwords. It has two arguments, argc and argv, that allow strings to be passed from the environment. These are usually referred to as **command-line arguments**.

The names argc and argv are conventional and can be replaced with anything you want. The argc argument holds the number of command-line arguments passed to the main() function; the argv argument holds the necessary arguments (you can find the example code at https:// github.com/PacktPublishing/Expert-C-2nd-edition/tree/main/Chapter%20 01/2_argc_and_argv_usage.cpp).

For example, we can compile and run the preceding example with the following arguments:

```
$ my-program argument1 hello world --some-option
```

This will output the following to the screen:

```
The number of passed arguments is: 5
```

```
Arguments are:
argument1
hello
world
--some-option
```

When you look at the number of arguments, you'll notice that it is 5. The first argument is always the name of the program; that's why we skipped it in this example by starting the loop from number 1.

> **Note**
>
> Rarely, you may see a widely supported but not standardized third argument, most commonly named envp. The type of envp is an array of char pointers and it holds the environment variables of the system.

The program can contain lots of functions, but the execution of the program always starts with the main() function, at least from the programmer's perspective. Let's try to compile the following code:

```
#include<iostream>
    void foo() {
    std::cout << "Risky foo" << std::endl;
}
// trying to call the foo() outside of the main() function
foo();
int main() {
    std::cout << "Calling main" << std::endl;
    return 0;
}
```

g++ raises an error on the foo(); call – that is, C++ requires a type specifier for all declarations. The call was parsed as a declaration rather than an instruction to execute. The way we tried to call a function before main() might seem silly for seasoned developers, so let's try another way. What if we declare something that calls a function during its initialization? In the example at https://github.com/PacktPublishing/Expert-C-2nd-edition/tree/main/Chapter%2001/3_before_main.cpp, we defined a BeforeMain struct with a constructor printing a message, and then declared an object of the BeforeMain type in the global scope.

The example successfully compiles and the program outputs the following:

```
Constructing BeforeMain
Calling main()
```

What if we add a member function to BeforeMain and try to call it? See the following code to understand this:

```
struct BeforeMain {
 // constructor code omitted for brevity
   void test() {
       std::cout << "test function" << std::endl;
   }
};

BeforeMain b;
b.test(); // compiler error

int main() {
     // code omitted for brevity
}
```

The call to `test()` won't be successful. So, we cannot call a function before `main()` but we can declare variables – objects that would be initialized by default. So, there is something that performs *initialization* before `main()` is called. It turns out that the `main()` function is not the true starting point of a program. The actual starting function of the program prepares the environment – that is, it collects the arguments that were passed to the program and then calls the `main()` function. This is required because C++ supports global and static objects that need to be initialized before the program begins, which means before the `main()` function is called. In the Linux world, this function is referred to as `__libc_start_main`. The compiler augments the generated code with the call of `__libc_start_main`, which, in turn, may or may not call other initialization functions before the `main()` function gets called. Going abstract, just imagine that the preceding code will be altered to something similar to the following:

```
void __libc_start_main() {
    BeforeMain b;
    main();
}
__libc_start_main(); // call the entry point
```

Recursion

Another special property of `main()` is that it cannot be called recursively. From the perspective of the OS, the `main()` function is the entry point of the program, so calling it again would mean starting everything over; therefore, it is prohibited. However, calling a function recursive just because it calls itself is partially correct. For example, the `print_number()` function calls itself and never stops:

```
void print_number(int num) {
    std::cout << num << std::endl;
    print_number(num + 1); // recursive call
}
```

Calling the `print_number(1)` function will output numbers 1, 2, 3, and so on. This is more like a function that calls itself infinitely rather than a correct recursive function. We should add a couple more properties to make the `print_number()` function a useful recursive one. First of all, the recursive function must have a base case, a scenario when a further function calls stop, which means the recursion stops propagating. We can make such a scenario for the `print_number()` function if, for example, we want to print numbers up to 100:

```cpp
void print_number(int num) {
    if (num > 100) return; // base case
    std::cout << num << std::endl;
    print_number(num + 1); // recursive call
}
```

There is one more property for a function to be recursive: solving smaller problems that will eventually lead to the base case. In the preceding example, we already had this by solving a smaller problem for the function – that is, by printing one number. After printing one number, we move to the next small problem: printing the next number. Finally, we get to the base case and we are done. There isn't any magic in a function calling itself; think of it as a function calling a different function with the same implementation. What's interesting is how a recursive function affects the program's execution overall. Let's take a look at a simple example of calling a function from another function at https://github.com/PacktPublishing/Expert-C-2nd-edition/tree/main/Chapter%20 01/5_calculate.cpp.

When a function is called, memory space is allocated for its arguments and local variables. The program starts with the `main()` function, which in this example simply calls the `calculate()` function by passing the 11 and 22 literal values. Control *jumps* to the `calculate()` function and the `main()` function is kind of *on hold*; it waits until the `calculate()` function returns to continue its execution. The `calculate()` function has two arguments, a and b; although we named `sum()`, `max()`, and `calculate()` differently, we could use the same names in all the functions. Memory space is allocated for these two arguments. Let's suppose that an int takes 4 bytes of memory, so a minimum of 8 bytes are required for the `calculate()` function to be executed successfully. After allocating 8 bytes, 11 and 22 should be copied to the corresponding locations (see the following diagram for details):

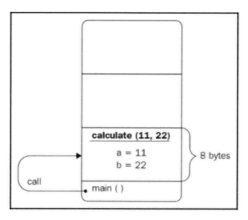

Figure 1.4: The calculate() function call

The calculate() function calls the sum() and max() functions and passes its argument values to them. Correspondingly, it waits for both functions to be executed sequentially to form the value to return to main(). The sum() and max() functions are not called simultaneously. First, sum() is called, which leads to the values of the a and b variables being copied from the locations that were allocated for the arguments of sum(), named n and m, which again take 8 bytes in total. Take a look at the following diagram to understand this better:

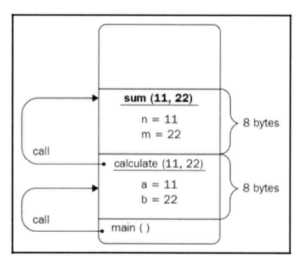

Figure 1.5: The calculate() function calls the sum() function

Their sum is calculated and returned. After the function is done and it returns a value, the memory space is freed. This means that the n and m variables are not accessible anymore and their locations can be reused.

After sum() has returned a value, the max() function is called. It follows the same logic: memory is allocated to the x and y arguments, as well as to the res variable. We intentionally store the result of the ternary operator, (?:), in the res variable to make the max() function allocate more space for this example. So, 12 bytes are allocated to the max() function in total. At this point, the x main() function is still on hold and waits for calculate(), which, in turn, is on hold and waits for the max() function to complete (see the following diagram for details):

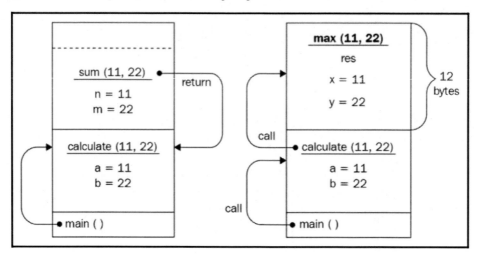

Figure 1.6: The max() function call after the sum() function is returned

When max() is done, the memory that's allocated to it is freed and its return value is used by calculate() to form a value to return. Similarly, when calculate() returns, the memory is freed and the main() function's local variable result will contain the value returned by calculate().

The main() function then finishes its work and the program exits – that is, the OS frees the memory allocated for the program and can reuse it later for other programs. The described process of allocating and freeing memory (deallocating it) for functions is done using a concept called a stack.

Note

A stack is a data structure adapter, which has rules to insert and access the data inside of it. In the context of function calls, the stack usually means a memory segment provided to the program that automatically manages itself while following the rules of the stack data structure adapter. We will discuss this in more detail later in this chapter.

Going back to recursion, when the function calls itself, memory should be allocated to the newly called function's arguments and local variables (if any). The function calls itself again, which means the stack will continue to grow (to provide space for the new functions). It doesn't matter that we call the same function; from the stack's perspective, each new call is a call to a completely different function, so it allocates space for it with a serious look on its face while whistling its favorite song. Take a look at the following diagram:

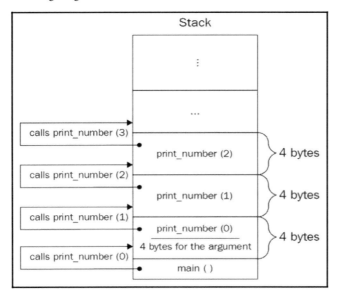

Figure 1.7: Illustration of a recursive function call inside the stack

The first call of the recursive function is on hold and waits for the second call of the same function, which, in turn, is on hold, and waits for the third call to finish and return a value, which, in turn, is on hold, and so on. If there is a bug in the function or the recursion base is difficult to reach, sooner or later, the stack will overgrow, which will lead to a program crash. This is known as **stack overflow**.

Though recursion provides more elegant solutions to a problem, try to avoid recursion in your programs and use the iterative approach (loops). In mission-critical system development guidelines such as the navigation system of a Mars rover, using recursion is completely prohibited.

Data and memory

When we refer to computer memory, we consider **Random Access Memory** (**RAM**) by default. Also, RAM is a general term for either SRAM or DRAM; we will mean DRAM by default unless stated otherwise. To clear things out, let's take a look at the following diagram, which illustrates the memory hierarchy:

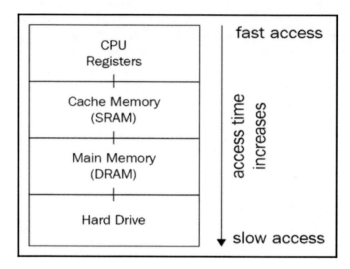

Figure 1.8: Illustration of a memory hierarchy

When we compile a program, the compiler stores the final executable file in the hard drive. To run the executable file, its instructions are loaded into the RAM and are then executed by the CPU one by one. This leads us to the conclusion that any instruction required to be executed should be in the RAM. This is partially true. The environment that is responsible for running and monitoring programs plays the main role.

The programs we write are executed in a hosted environment, which is in the OS. The OS loads the contents of the program (its instructions and data – that is, the process) not directly into the RAM, but into the **virtual memory**, a mechanism that makes it possible both to handle processes conveniently and to share resources between processes. Whenever we refer to the memory that a process is loaded into, we mean the virtual memory, which, in turn, *maps* its contents to the RAM.

Let's begin with an introduction to the memory structure and then investigate data types within the memory.

Virtual memory

Memory consists of lots of boxes, each of which can store a specified amount of data. We will refer to these boxes as *memory cells*, considering that each cell can store 1 byte representing 8 bits. Each memory cell is unique, even if they store the same value. This uniqueness is achieved by addressing the cells so that each cell has its unique address in memory. The first cell has the address **0**, the second cell **1**, and so on.

The following diagram illustrates an excerpt of the memory, where each cell has a unique address and ability to store 1 byte of data:

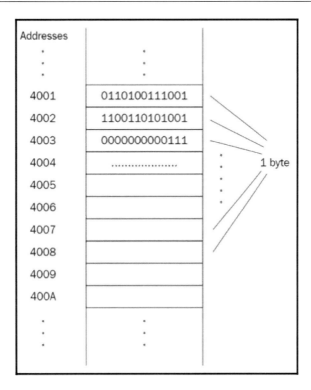

Figure 1.9: Illustration of a memory cell

The preceding diagram can be used to abstractly represent both physical and virtual memories. The point of having an additional layer of abstraction is the ease of managing processes and providing more functionality than with physical memory. For example, OSs can execute programs greater than physical memory. Take a computer game as an example of a program that takes almost 2 GB of space and a computer with a physical memory of 512 MB. Virtual memory allows the OS to load the program portion by portion by unloading old parts from the physical memory and mapping new parts.

Virtual memory also better supports having more than one program in memory, thus supporting parallel (or pseudo-parallel) execution of multiple programs. This also provides efficient use of shared code and data, such as dynamic libraries. Whenever two different programs require the same library to work with, a single instance of the library could exist in memory and be used by both programs without them knowing about each other.

Let's take a look at the following diagram, which depicts three programs loaded into memory:

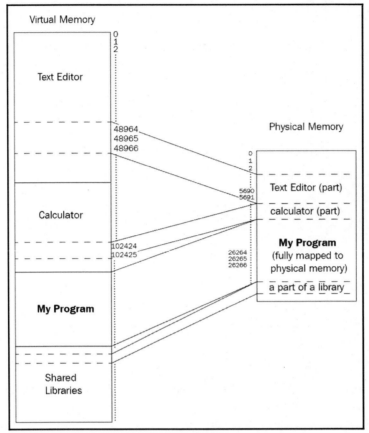

Figure 1.10: Illustration of three different programs that have been loaded into memory

There are three running programs in the preceding diagram; each of the programs takes up some space in virtual memory. **My Program** is fully contained in the physical memory. while the **Calculator** and **Text Editor** are partially mapped to it.

Addressing

As mentioned earlier, each memory cell has a unique **address**, which guarantees the uniqueness of each cell. An address is usually represented in a *hexadecimal* form because it's shorter and it's faster to convert into **binary** rather than decimal numbers. A program that is loaded into virtual memory operates and sees *logical* addresses. These addresses, also called virtual addresses, are *fake* and provided by the OS, which *translates* them into physical addresses when needed. To optimize the translation, the CPU provides a **translation lookaside buffer**, a part of its **memory management unit** (**MMU**).

The translation lookaside buffer caches recent translations of virtual addresses to physical addresses. So, efficient address translation is a software/hardware task. We will dive into the address' structure and translation details in *Chapter 5*, *Memory Management and Smart Pointers*.

The length of the address defines the total size of memory that can be operated by the system. When you encounter statements such as a 32-bit system or a 64-bit system, this means the length of the address – that is, the address is 32 bits or 64 bits long. The longer the address, the bigger the memory. To make things clear, let's compare an 8-bit long address with a 32-bit long one. As agreed earlier, each memory cell can store 1 byte of data and has a unique address. If the address length is 8 bits, the address of the first memory cell is all zeros – 0000 0000. The address of the next cell is greater by one – that is, it's 0000 0001 – and so on.

The biggest value that can be represented by 8 bits is 1111 1111. So, how many memory cells can be represented with an address length of 8 bits? This question is worth answering in more detail. How many different values can be represented by 1 bit? Two! Why? Because 1 bit can represent either 1 or 0. How many different values can be represented by 2 bits? Well, 00 is one value, 01 is another value, and then there's 10, and, finally, 11. So, four different values in total can be represented by 2 bits.

Let's make a table:

number of bits	number of values	values
1 bit	2	0, 1
2 bit	4	00, 01, 10, 11
3 bit	8	000, 001, 010, 100, ...
4 bit	16	0000, 0001, 0010, ...
......	......	......

We can see a pattern here. Each position (each bit) in a number can have two values, so we can calculate the number of different values represented by N bits by finding 2^N; therefore, the number of different values represented by 8 bits is *256*. This means that an 8-bit system can address up to 256 memory cells. On the other hand, a 32-bit system can address *2^32 = 4 294 967 296* memory cells, each storing 1 byte of data – that is, storing *4294967296 * 1 byte = 4 GB* of data.

Data types

What's the point of having data types at all? Why can't we program in C++ using some var keyword to declare variables and forget about variables such as short, long, int, char, wchar, and so on? Well, C++ does support a similar construct, known as the auto keyword, which we used previously in this chapter, a so-called *placeholder type specifier*. It's named a placeholder because it is, indeed, a placeholder. We cannot (and we must not ever be able to) declare a variable and then change its type during runtime. The following code might be valid JavaScript code, but it is not valid C++ code:

```
var a = 12;
a = "Hello, World!";
a = 3.14;
```

Imagine the C++ compiler could compile this code. How many bytes of memory should be allocated for the a variable? When declaring var a = 12;, the compiler could deduce its type to int and specify 4 bytes of memory space, but when the variable changes its value to Hello, World!, the compiler has to reallocate the space or invent a new hidden variable named a1 of the std::string type. Then, the compiler tries to find every way to access the variable in the code that accesses it as a string and not as an integer or a double and replaces the variable with the hidden a1 variable. The compiler might just quit and start to ask itself the meaning of life.

We can declare something similar to the preceding code in C++ as follows:

```
auto a = 12;
auto b = "Hello, World!";
auto c = 3.14;
```

The difference between the previous two examples is that the second example declares three different variables of three different types. The previous non-C++ code declared just one variable and then assigned values of different types to it. You can't change the type of a variable in C++, but the compiler allows you to use the auto placeholder and deduces the type of the variable by the value assigned to it.

It is crucial to understand that the type is deduced at compile time, while languages such as JavaScript allow you to deduce the type at runtime. The latter is possible because such programs are run in environments such as virtual machines, while the only environment that runs the C++ program is the OS. The C++ compiler must generate a valid executable file that could be copied into memory and run without a support system. This forces the compiler to know the actual size of the variable beforehand. Knowing the size is important to generate the final machine code because accessing a variable requires its address and size, and allocating memory space to a variable requires the number of bytes that it should take.

The C++ type system classifies types into two major categories:

- **Fundamental types** (int, double, char, void)
- **Compound types** (pointers, arrays, classes)

The language even supports special type traits, std::is_fundamental and std::is_compound, to find out the category of a type. Here is an example:

```
#include <iostream>
#include <type_traits>
```

```
struct Point {
    float x;
    float y; };
int main() {

std::cout << std::is_fundamental_v<Point> << " "
<< std::is_fundamental_v<int> << " "



<< std::is_compound_v<Point> << " "



<< std::is_compound_v<int> << std::endl;
}
```

Most of the fundamental types are arithmetic types such as `int` or `double`; even the `char` type is arithmetic. It holds a number rather than a character, as shown here:

```
char ch = 65;
std::cout << ch; // prints A
```

A `char` variable holds 1 byte of data, which means it can represent 256 different values (because 1 byte is 8 bits, and 8 bits can be used in 2^8 ways to represent a number). What if we use one of the bits as a *sign* bit, for example, allowing the type to support negative values as well? That leaves us with 7 bits for representing the actual value. Following the same logic, it allows us to represent 2^7 different values – that is, 128 (including 0) different values of positive numbers and the same amount of negative values. Excluding 0 gives us a range of -127 to +127 for the signed `char` variable. This signed versus unsigned representation applies to almost all integral types.

So, whenever you encounter that, for example, the size of an int is 4 bytes, which is 32 bits, you should already know that it is possible to represent the numbers 0 to 2^{32} in an unsigned representation, and the values -2^{31} to $+2^{31}$ in a signed representation.

Pointers

C++ is a unique language in the way that it provides access to low-level details such as addresses of variables. We can take the address of any variable declared in the program using the & operator, as shown here:

```
int answer = 42;
std::cout << &answer;
```

This code will output something similar to this:

```
0x7ffee1bd2adc
```

Notice the hexadecimal representation of the address. Although this value is just an integer, it is used to store it in a special variable called a pointer. A pointer is just a variable that can store address values and supports the * operator (dereferencing), allowing us to find the actual value stored at the address.

For example, to store the address of the variable answer in the preceding example, we can declare a pointer and assign the address to it:

```
int* ptr = &answer;
```

The variable answer is declared as int, which usually takes 4 bytes of memory space. We already agreed that each byte has a unique address. Can we conclude that the answer variable has four unique addresses? Well, yes and no. It does acquire four distinct but contiguous memory bytes, but when the address operator is used against the variable, it returns the address of its first byte. Let's take a look at a portion of code that declares a couple of variables and then illustrate how they are placed in memory:

```
int ivar = 26;
char ch = 't';
double d = 3.14;
```

The size of a data type is implementation-defined, though the C++ standard states the minimum supported range of values for each type. Let's suppose the implementation provides 4 bytes for int, 8 bytes for double, and 1 byte for char. The memory layout for the preceding code should look like this:

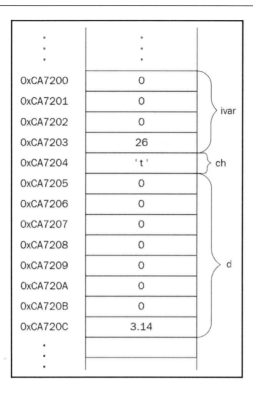

Figure 1.11: Variables in memory

Pay attention to `ivar` in the memory layout; it resides in four contiguous bytes.

Whenever we take the address of a variable, whether it resides in a single byte or more than 1 byte, we get the address of the first byte of the variable. If the size doesn't affect the logic behind the address operator, then why do we have to declare the type of the pointer? To store the address of `ivar` in the preceding example, we should declare the pointer as `int *`:

```
int* ptr = &ivar;
char* pch = &ch;
double* pd = &d;
```

The preceding code is depicted in the following diagram:

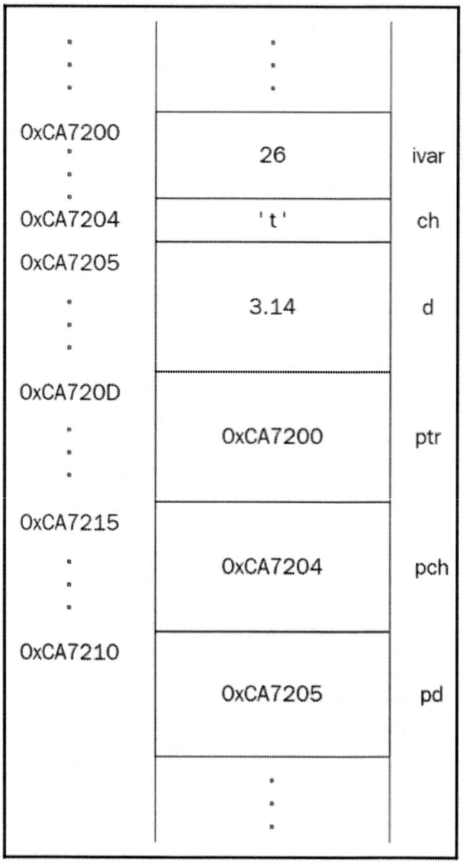

Figure 1.12: Illustration of a piece of memory that holds pointers that point to other variables

It turns out that the type of the pointer is crucial in accessing the variable using that very pointer. C++ provides the dereferencing operator for this (the * symbol before the pointer name):

```
std::cout << *ptr; // prints 26
```

It works like this:

1. It reads the contents of the pointer.

2. It finds the address of the memory cell that is equal to the address in the pointer.

3. It returns the value that is stored in that memory cell.

The question is, what if the pointer points to the data that resides in more than one memory cell? That's where the pointer's type comes in. When dereferencing the pointer, its type is used to determine how many bytes it should read and return, starting from the memory cell that it points to.

Now that we know that a pointer stores the address of the first byte of the variable, we can read any byte of the variable by moving the pointer forward. We should remember that the address is just a number, so adding or subtracting another number from it will produce another address. What if we point to an integer variable with a char pointer?

```
int ivar = 26;
char* p = (char*)&ivar;
```

When we try to dereference the p pointer, it will return only the first byte of ivar.

Now, if we want to move to the next byte of ivar, we can add 1 to the char pointer:

```
// the first byte
*p;
// the second byte
*(p + 1);
// the third byte
*(p + 2);
// dangerous stuff, the previous byte
*(p - 1);
```

Take a look at the following diagram; it clearly shows how we access bytes of the ivar integer:

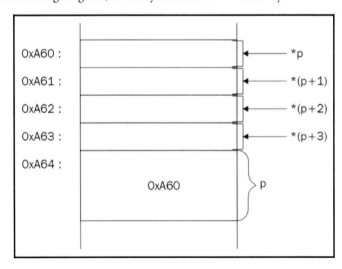

Figure 1.13 Illustration of accessing the ivar integer's bytes

If you want to read the first or the last two bytes, you can use a short pointer:

```
short* sh = (short*)&ivar;
// print the value in the first two bytes of ivar
std::cout << *sh;
// print the value in the last two bytes of ivar
std::cout << *(sh + 1);
```

> **Note**
>
> You should be careful with pointer arithmetics since adding or subtracting a number will move the pointer by the defined size of the data type. Adding 1 to an `int` pointer will add `sizeof(int) * 1` to the actual address.

What about the size of a pointer? As mentioned previously, a pointer is just a variable that is special in the way that it can store a memory address and provide a dereferencing operator that returns the data located at that address. So, if the pointer is just a variable, it should reside in memory as well. We might consider that the size of a `char` pointer is less than the size of an `int` pointer just because the size of `char` is less than the size of `int`.

Here's the catch: the data that is stored in the pointer has nothing to do with the type of data the pointer points to. Both the `char` and `int` pointers store the address of the variable, so to define the size of the pointer, we should consider the size of the address. The size of the address is defined by the system we work in. For example, in a 32-bit system, the address size is 32 bits long, and in a 64-bit system, the address size is 64 bits long. This leads us to a logical conclusion: the size of the pointer is the same regardless of the type of data it points to:

```
std::cout << sizeof(ptr) << " = "
    << sizeof(pch) << " = " << sizeof(pd);
```

It will output 4 = 4 = 4 in a 32-bit system and 8 = 8 = 8 in a 64-bit system.

Stack and the heap

The memory consists of segments and the program segments are distributed through these memory segments during loading. These are artificially divided ranges of memory addresses that make it easier to manage the program using the OS. A binary file is also divided into segments, such as code and data. We previously mentioned code and data as sections. Sections are the divisions of a binary file that are needed for the linker, which uses the sections that are meant for the linker to work and combines the sections that are meant for the loader into segments.

When we discuss a binary file from the runtime's perspective, we mean segments. The data segment contains all the data required and used by the program, and the code segment contains the actual instructions that process the very same data. However, when we mention data, we don't mean every single piece of data used in the program. Let's take a look at this example:

```
#include <iostream>
int max(int a, int b) { return a > b ? a : b; }
int main() {
    std::cout << "The maximum of 11 and 22 is: " <<
        max(11, 22);
}
```

The code segment of the preceding program consists of the instructions of the main() and max() functions, where main() prints the message using the cout object's operator<< and then calls the max() function. What data resides in the data segment? Does it contain the a and b arguments of the max() function? As it turns out, the only data that is contained in the data segment is the The maximum of 11 and 22 is: string, along with other static, global, or constant data. We didn't declare any global or static variables, so the only data is the mentioned message.

The interesting thing comes with the 11 and 22 values. These are literal values, which means they have no address; therefore, they are not located anywhere in memory. If they are not located anywhere, the only logical explanation of how they are located within the program is that they reside in the code segment. They are a part of the max() call instruction.

What about the a and b arguments of the max() function? This is where the segment in virtual memory that is responsible for storing variables that have automatic storage duration comes in – the stack. As mentioned previously, the stack automatically handles allocating/deallocating memory space for local variables and function arguments. The a and b arguments will be located in the stack when the max() function is called. In general, if an object is said to have an automatic storage duration, the memory space will be allocated at the beginning of the enclosing block. So, when the function is called, its arguments are pushed into the stack:

```
int max(int a, int b) {
// allocate space for the "a" argument
 // allocate space for the "b" argument return a > b ? a :
 // b;
 // deallocate the space for the "a" argument // deallocate
 // the space for the "b" argument
 }
```

When the function is done, the automatically allocated space will be freed at the end of the enclosing code block.

It's said that the arguments (or local variables) are popped out of the stack. **Push** and **pop** are terms that are used within the context of the stack. You insert data into the stack by *pushing* it, and you retrieve (and remove) data out of the stack by *popping* it. You might have encountered the term **last in, first out** (**LIFO**). This perfectly describes the push and pop operations of the stack.

When the program is run, the OS provides the fixed size of the stack. The stack can grow in size and if it grows to the extent that no more space is left, it crashes because of the stack overflow.

We described the stack as a manager of variables with *automatic storage duration*. The word *automatic* suggests that programmers shouldn't care about the actual memory allocation and deallocation. Automatic storage duration can only be achieved if the size of the data or a collection of the data is known beforehand. This way, the compiler is aware of the number and type of function arguments and local variables. At this point, it seems more than fine, but programs tend to work with dynamic data – data of unknown size. We will study dynamic memory management in detail in *Chapter 5, Memory Management and Smart Pointers*; for now, let's look at a simplified diagram of memory segments and find out what the heap is used for:

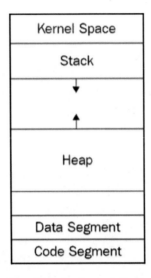

Figure 1.14: Simplified diagram of memory segments

The program uses the heap segment to request more memory space than has been required before. This is done at runtime, which means the memory is allocated dynamically during the program execution. The program requests the OS for new memory space whenever required. The OS doesn't know whether the memory is required for an integer, for a user-defined Point, or even for an array of user-defined Point. The program requests the memory by passing the actual size of bytes that it requires. For example, to request a space for an object of the Point type, the malloc() function can be used, as follows:

```cpp
#include <cstdlib>
struct Point {
    float x;
    float y;
};
int main() {
    std::malloc(sizeof(Point));
}
```

The `malloc()` function allocates a contiguous memory space of `sizeof(Point)` bytes – let's say 8 bytes. It then returns the address of the first byte of that memory as it is the only way to provide access to space. And the thing is, `malloc()` doesn't know whether we requested memory space for a `Point` object or `int`, and it simply returns `void*`. `void*` stores the address of the first byte of allocated memory, but it definitely cannot be used to fetch the actual data by dereferencing the pointer, simply because `void` does not define the size of the data. Take a look at the following diagram; it shows that `malloc` allocates memory on the heap:

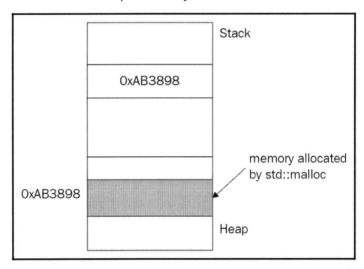

Figure 1.15: Memory allocation on the heap

To use the memory space, we need to cast the `void` pointer to the desired type:

```
Point* p = static_cast<Point*>(std::malloc(sizeof(Point)));
```

C++ solves this headache with the `new` operator, which automatically fetches the size of the memory space to be allocated and converts the result into the desired type:

```
Point* p = new Point;
```

Control flow

It's hard to imagine a program that doesn't contain a conditional statement. It's almost a habit to check the input arguments of functions to secure their safe execution. For example, the `divide()` function takes two arguments, divides one by the other, and returns the result. It's pretty clear that we need to make sure that the divisor is not zero:

```
int divide(int a, int b) {
    if (b == 0) {
```

```
        throw std::invalid_argument("The divisor is zero");
    }
    return a / b;
}
```

Conditionals are at the core of programming languages; after all, a program is a collection of actions and decisions. For example, the code at https://github.com/PacktPublishing/Expert-C-2nd-edition/tree/main/Chapter%2001/6_max.cpp uses conditional statements to find the maximum value out of two input arguments.

The preceding example is oversimplified on purpose to express the usage of the if-else statement as-is. However, what interests us the most is the implementation of such a conditional statement. What does the compiler generate when it encounters an if statement? The CPU executes instructions sequentially one by one, and instructions are simple commands that do exactly one thing. We can use complex expressions in a single line in a high-level programming language such as C++, while the assembly instructions are simple commands that can do only one simple operation in one cycle: move, add, subtract, and so on.

The CPU fetches the instruction from the code memory segment, decodes it to find out what it should do (move data, add numbers, or subtract them), and executes the command.

To run at its fastest, the CPU stores the operands and the result of the execution in storage units called **registers**. You can think of registers as temporary variables of the CPU. Registers are physical memory units that are located within the CPU so that access is much faster compared to the RAM. To access the registers from an assembly language program, we use their specified names, such as rax, rbx, rdx, and so on. The CPU commands operate on registers rather than the RAM cells; that's why the CPU has to copy the contents of the variable from the memory to registers, execute operations and store the results in a register, and then copy the value of the register back to the memory cell.

For example, the following C++ expression takes just a single line of code:

```
a = b + 2 * c - 1;
```

This would look similar to the following assembly representation (comments are added after semicolons):

```
mov rax, b; copy the contents of "b"
  ; located in the memory to the register rax
mov rbx, c
; the same for the "c" to be able to calculate 2 * c
mul rbx, 2
; multiply the value of the rbx register with
; immediate value 2 (2 * c)
add rax, rbx; add rax (b) with rbx (2*c) and store back in the rax sub
rax, 1; subtract 1 from rax
mov a, rax
; copy the contents of rax to the "a" located in the memory
```

A conditional statement suggests that a portion of the code should be skipped. For example, calling max(11, 22) means the if block will be omitted. To express this in the assembly language, the idea of jumps is used. We compare two values and, based on the result, we jump to a specified portion of the code. We label the portion to make it possible to find the set of instructions. For example, to skip adding 42 to the rbx register, we can jump to the portion labeled UNANSWERED using the unconditional jump instruction, jpm, as shown here:

```
mov rax, 2
 mov rbx, 0
 jmp UNANSWERED
 add rbx, 42; will be skipped UNANSWERED:
     add rax, 1
     ; ...
```

The jmp instruction performs an unconditional jump; this means it starts executing the first instruction at a specified label without any condition check. The good news is that the CPU provides conditional jumps as well. The body of the max() function will translate into the following assembly code (simplified), where the jg and jle commands are interpreted as jump if greater than and jump if less than or equal, respectively (based on the results of the comparison using the cmp instruction):

```
mov rax, max; copy the "max" into the rax register
 mov rbx, a
 mov rdx, b
 cmp rbx, rdx; compare the values of rbx and rdx (a and b)
 jg GREATER; jump if rbx is greater than rdx (a > b)
 jl LESSOREQUAL; jump if rbx is lesser than GREATER:
mov rax, rbx; max = a LESSOREQUAL:
 mov rax, rdx; max = b
```

In the preceding code, the GREATER and LESSOREQUAL labels represent the if and else clauses of the max() function we implemented earlier.

Replacing conditionals with function pointers

Previously, we looked at memory segments, and one of the most important segments is the code segment (also called a text segment). This segment contains the program image, which is the instructions for the program that should be executed. Instructions are usually grouped into functions, which provide us with a unique name that allows us to call them from other functions. Functions reside in the code segment of the executable file.

A function has its own address. We can declare a pointer that takes the address of the function and then use it later to call that function:

```
int get_answer() { return 42; }
```

```
int (*fp)() = &get_answer;
// int (*fp)() = get_answer; same as &get_answer
```

The function pointer can be called the same way as the original function:

```
get_answer(); // returns 42
fp(); // returns 42
```

Let's suppose we are writing a program that takes two numbers and a character from the input and executes an arithmetic operation on the numbers. The operation is specified by the character, whether it's +, -, *, or /. We implement four functions, add(), subtract(), multiply(), and divide(), and call one of them based on the value of the character's input.

Instead of checking the value of the character in a bunch of if statements or a switch statement, we will map the type of the operation to the specified function using a hash table (you can find the code at https://github.com/PacktPublishing/Expert-C-2nd-edition/tree/main/Chapter%2001/7_calculating_with_hash_table.cpp).

As you can see, std::unordered_map maps char to a function pointer defined as (*) (int, int). That is, it can point to any function that takes two integers and returns an integer.

Details of OOP

C++ supports OOP, a paradigm that is built upon dissecting entities into objects that exist in a web of close intercommunication. Imagine a simple scenario in the real world where you pick a remote to change the TV channel. At least three different objects take part in this action: the remote, the TV, and, most importantly, you. To express these real-world objects and their relationship using a programming language, we aren't forced to use classes, class inheritance, abstract classes, interfaces, virtual functions, and so on. These features and concepts make the process of designing and coding a lot easier as they allow us to express and share ideas elegantly, but they are not mandatory. As the creator of C++, Bjarne Stroustrup, says, *"Not every program should be object-oriented."* To understand the high-level concepts and features of the OOP paradigm, we will try to look behind the scenes. Throughout this book, we will dive into the design of object-oriented programs. Understanding the essence of objects and their relationship, and then using them to design object-oriented programs, is one of the goals of this book.

Most of the time, we operate with a collection of data grouped under a certain name, thus making an **abstraction**. Variables such as is_military, speed, and seats don't make much sense if they're perceived separately. Grouping them under the name Spaceship changes the way we perceive the data stored in the variables. We now refer to the many variables packed as a single object. To do so, we use abstraction; that is, we collect the individual properties of a real-world object from the perspective of the observer. An abstraction is a key tool in the programmer's toolchain as it allows them to deal with complexity. The C language introduced struct as a way to aggregate data, as shown in the following code:

```
struct Spaceship {
bool is_military;
int speed;
int seats;
};
```

Grouping data is somewhat necessary for OOP. Each group of data is referred to as an object.

C++ does its best to support compatibility with the C language. While C structs are just tools that allow us to aggregate data, C++ makes them equal to classes, allowing them to have constructors, virtual functions, inherit other structs, and so on. The only difference between struct and class is the default visibility modifier: public for structs and private for classes. There is usually no difference in using structs over classes or vice versa. OOP requires more than just data aggregation. To fully understand OOP, let's find out how we would incorporate the OOP paradigm if we have only simple structs providing data aggregation and nothing more.

The central entity of an e-commerce marketplace such as Amazon or Alibaba is Product, which we represent in the following way:

```
struct Product {
    std::string name;
    double price;
    int rating;
    bool available;
};
```

We will add more members to Product if necessary. The memory layout of an object of the Product type can be depicted like this:

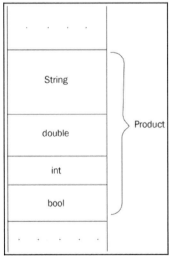

Figure 1.16: The memory layout of a Product object

Declaring a `Product` object takes `sizeof(Product)` space in memory while declaring a pointer or a reference to the object takes the space required to store the address (usually 4 or 8 bytes). See the following code block:

```
Product book;
Product tshirt;
Product* ptr = &book;
Product& ref = tshirt;
```

We can depict the preceding code as follows:

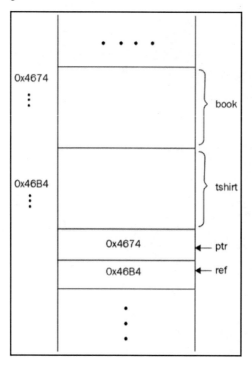

Figure 1.17: Illustration of the Product pointer and the Product reference in memory

Let's start with the space the `Product` object takes in memory. We can calculate the size of the `Product` object by summing the sizes of its member variables. The size of a `boolean` variable is 1 byte. The exact size of `double` or `int` is not specified in the C++ standard. In 64-bit machines, a `double` variable usually takes 8 bytes and an `int` variable takes 4 bytes.

The implementation of `std::string` is not specified in the standard, so its size depends on the library implementation. `string` stores a pointer to a character array, but it might also store the number of allocated characters to efficiently return it when `size()` is called. Some implementations of std::string take 8, 24, or 32 bytes of memory, but we will stick to 24 bytes in our example. By summing it up, the size of Product will be as follows:

```
24 (std::string) + 8 (double) + 4 (int) + 1 (bool) = 37 bytes.
```

Printing the size of Product outputs a different value:

```
std::cout << sizeof(Product);
```

It outputs 40 instead of the calculated 37 bytes. The reason behind the redundant bytes is the padding of the struct, a technique practiced by the compiler to optimize access to individual members of the object. The **central processing unit** (**CPU**) reads the memory in fixed-size words. The size of the word is defined by the CPU (usually, it's 32 or 64 bits long). The CPU can access the data at once if it's starting from a word-aligned address. For example, the boolean data member of Product requires 1 byte of memory and can be placed right after the rating member. As it turns out, the compiler aligns the data for faster access. Let's suppose the word size is 4 bytes. This means that the CPU will access a variable without redundant steps if the variable starts from an address that's divisible by 4. The compiler augments the struct earlier with additional bytes to align the members to word-boundary addresses.

High-level details of objects

We deal with objects as entities representing the result of abstraction. We have already mentioned the role of the observer – that is, the programmer who defines the object based on the problem domain. The way the programmer defines this represents the process of abstraction. Let's take an example of an eCommerce marketplace and its products. Two different teams of programmers might have different views of the same product. The team that implements the website cares about the properties of the object that are essential to website visitors: buyers. The properties that we showed earlier in the Product struct are mostly meant for website visitors, such as the selling price, the rating of the product, and so on. Programmers that implement the website touch the problem domain and verify the properties that are essential to defining a Product object.

The team that implements the online tools that help manage the products in the warehouse cares about the properties of the object that are essential in terms of product placement, quality control, and shipment. This team shouldn't care about the **rating** of the product or even its **price**. This team mostly cares about the **weight**, **dimensions**, and **conditions** of the product. The following illustration shows the properties of interest:

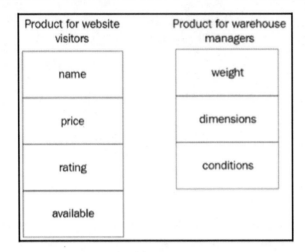

Figure 1.18: The properties of interest for website visitors and warehouse managers

The first thing that programmers should do when starting the project is to analyze the problem and gather the requirements. In other words, they should get familiar with the *problem domain* and define the *project requirements*. The process of analyzing leads to defining objects and their types, such as the Product we discussed earlier. To get proper results from analyzing, we should think in objects, and, by thinking in objects, we mean considering the three main properties of objects: **state**, **behavior**, and **identity**.

Each object has a state that may or may not differ from the state of other objects. We've already introduced the Product struct, which represents an abstraction of a physical (or digital) product. All the members of a Product object collectively represent the state of the object. For example, Product contains members such as available, which is a Boolean; it equals true if the product is in stock. The values of the member variables define the state of the object. If you assign new values to the object member, its state will change:

```
Product cpp_book; // declaring the object
...
 // changing the state of the object cpp_book
cpp_book.available = true;
cpp_book.rating = 5;
```

The state of the object is the combination of all of its properties and values.

Identity is what differentiates one object from another. Even if we try to declare two physically indistinguishable objects, they will still have different names for their variables – that is, different identities:

```
Product book1;
book1.rating = 4;
book1.name = "Book";
```

```
Product book2;
book2.rating = 4;
book2.name = "Book";
```

The objects in the preceding example have the same state, but they differ by the names we refer to them by – that is, book1 and book2. Let's say we could somehow create objects with the same name, as shown in the following code:

```
Product prod;
Product prod; // won't compile, but still "what if?"
```

If this was the case, they would still have different addresses in memory:

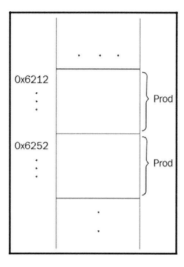

Figure 1.19: Illustration of a piece of memory that would hold
variables with the same name if it was possible

In the previous examples, we assigned 5 and then 4 to the rating member variable. We can easily make things unexpectedly wrong by assigning invalid values to the object, like so:

```
cpp_book.rating = -12;
```

-12 is invalid in terms of the rating of a product and will confuse users if it's allowed to. We can control the behavior of the changes made to the object by providing **setter** functions:

```
void set_rating(Product* p, int r) {
    if (r >= 1 && r <= 5) {
        p->rating = r;
    }
    // otherwise ignore
```

```
    }
...
  set_rating(&cpp_book, -12); // won't change the state
```

An object acts and reacts to requests from other objects. The requests are performed via function calls, which otherwise are called **messages**: an object passes a message to another. In the preceding example, the object that passed the corresponding `set_rating` message to the `cpp_book` object represents the object that we call the `set_rating()` function in. In this case, we suppose that we call the function from `main()`, which doesn't represent any object at all. We could say it's the global object, the one that operates the `main()` function, though there is not an entity like that in C++.

We distinguish the objects conceptually rather than physically. That's the main point of thinking in terms of objects. The physical implementation of some concepts of OOP is not standardized, so we can name the `Product` struct as a class and claim that `cpp_book` is an **instance** of `Product` and that it has a member function called `set_rating()`. The C++ implementation almost does the same: it provides syntactically convenient structures (classes, visibility modifiers, inheritance, and so on) and translates them into simple structs with global functions such as `set_rating()` in the preceding example. Now, let's dive into the details of the C++ object model.

Working with classes

Classes make things a lot easier when dealing with objects. They do the simplest necessary thing in OOP: they combine data with functions for manipulating data. Let's rewrite the example of the `Product` struct using a class and its powerful features (you can find the code at `https://github.com/PacktPublishing/Expert-C-2nd-edition/tree/main/Chapter%2001/8_product.h`).

The class declaration seems more organized, even though it exposes more functions than we use to define a similar struct. Here's how we should illustrate the class:

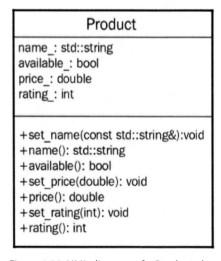

Figure 1.20: UML diagram of a Product class

The preceding figure is somewhat special. As you can see, it has organized sections, signs before the names of functions, and so on. This type of diagram is called a **unified modeling language** (**UML**) class diagram. UML is a way to standardize the process of illustrating classes and their relationship. The first section is the name of the class (in bold), next comes the section for member variables, and then the section for member functions. The + (plus) sign in front of a function's name means that the function is public. Member variables are usually private, but, if you need to emphasize this, you can use the - (minus) sign.

Initialization, destruction, copying, and moving

As shown previously, creating an object is a two-step process: memory allocation and initialization. Memory allocation is a result of an object declaration. C++ doesn't care about the initialization of variables; it allocates the memory (whether it is automatic or manual) and it's done. The actual initialization should be done by the programmer, which is why we have a constructor in the first place.

The same logic follows for the destructor. If we skip the declarations of the default constructor or destructor, the compiler should generate them implicitly; it will also remove them if they are empty (to eliminate redundant calls to empty functions). The default constructor will not be generated by the compiler if any constructor with parameters is declared, including the copy constructor. We can force the compiler to implicitly generate the default constructor:

```
class Product {
public:
    Product() = default;
// ...
};
```

We also can force it not to generate the compiler by using the delete specifier, as shown here:

```
class Product {
public:
    Product() = delete;
// ...
};
```

This will prohibit default-initialized object declarations – that is, Product p; won't compile.

Object initialization happens when the object is created. Destruction usually happens when the object is no longer accessible. The latter may be tricky when the object is allocated on the heap. Take a look at the following code; it declares four Product objects in different scopes and segments of memory:

```
static Product global_prod; // #1
Product* foo() {
  Product* heap_prod = new Product(); // #4 heap_prod->name
                                      // = "Sample";
```

```
   return heap_prod;
}
int main() {
 Product stack_prod; // #2 if (true) {
Product tmp; // #3
      tmp.rating = 3;
    }
     stack_prod.price = 4.2;
foo();
}
```

`global_prod` has a static storage duration and is placed in the global/static section of the program; it is initialized before `main()` is called. When `main()` starts, `stack_prod` is allocated on the stack and will be destroyed when `main()` ends (the closing curly brace of the function is considered as its end). Though the conditional expression looks weird and too artificial, it's a good way to express the block scope.

The `tmp` object will also be allocated on the stack, but its storage duration is limited to the scope it has been declared in: it will be automatically destroyed when the execution leaves the `if` block. That's why variables on the stack have *automatic storage duration*. Finally, when the `foo()` function is called, it declares the `heap_prod` pointer, which points to the address of the `Product` object allocated on the heap.

The preceding code contains a memory leak because the `heap_prod` pointer (which itself has an automatic storage duration) will be destroyed when the execution reaches the end of `foo()`, while the object allocated on the heap won't be affected. Don't mix the pointer and the actual object it points to: the pointer just contains the address of the object, but it doesn't represent the object.

When the function ends, the memory for its arguments and local variables, which is allocated on the stack, will be freed, but `global_prod` will be destroyed when the program ends – that is, after the `main()` function finishes. The destructor will be called when the object is about to be destroyed.

There are two kinds of copying: *deep* copying and *shallow* copying objects. The language allows us to manage copy-initialization and assigning objects with the **copy constructor** and the **assignment operator**. This is a necessary feature for programmers because we can control the semantics of copying. Take a look at the following example:

```
Product p1;
Product p2;
p2.set_price(4.2);
p1 = p2; // p1 now has the same price Product p3 = p2;
// p3 has the same price
```

The `p1 = p2;` line is a call to the assignment operator, while the last line is a call to the copy constructor. The equals sign shouldn't confuse you regarding whether it's an assignment or a copy constructor call.

Each time you see a declaration followed by an assignment, consider it a copy construction. The same applies to the new initializer syntax (`Product p3{p2};`).   *If declared, even the equal sign still copy constructor!*

The compiler will generate the following code:

```
Product p1;
 Product p2;
Product_set_price(p2, 4.2);
operator=(p1, p2);
 Product p3;
Product_copy_constructor(p3, p2);
```

Temporary objects are everywhere in code. Most of the time, they are required to make the code work as expected. For example, when we add two objects together, a temporary object is created to hold the return value of `operator+`:

```
Warehouse small;
 Warehouse mid;
 // ... some data inserted into the small and mid objects
Warehouse large{small + mid}; // operator+(small, mid)
```

Let's take a look at the implementation of the `operator+()` global for `Warehouse` objects:

```
// considering declared as friend in the Warehouse class Warehouse
operator+(const Warehouse& a, const Warehouse& b) {
    Warehouse sum; // temporary
    sum.size_ = a.size_ + b.size_;
    sum.capacity_ = a.capacity_ + b.capacity_;
    sum.products_ = new Product[sum.capacity_];
    for (int ix = 0; ix < a.size_; ++ix) {
       sum.products_[ix] = a.products_[ix];
    }
    for (int ix = 0; ix < b.size_; ++ix) {
       sum.products_[a.size_ + ix] = b.products_[ix];
    }
    return sum;
 }
```

The preceding implementation declares a temporary object and returns it after filling it with necessary data. The call in the previous example could be translated into the following:

```
Warehouse small;
 Warehouse mid;
 // ... some data inserted into the small and mid objects
Warehouse tmp{operator+(small, mid)};
 Warehouse large;
```

```
Warehouse_copy_constructor(large, tmp);
__destroy_temporary(tmp);
```

Move semantics, which was introduced in C++11, allow us to skip the temporary creation by *moving* the return value into the `Warehouse` object. To do so, we should declare a **move constructor** for `Warehouse`, which can *distinguish* between temporaries and treat them efficiently:

```
class Warehouse {
public:
Warehouse(); // default constructor
Warehouse(const Warehouse&); // copy constructor
Warehouse(Warehouse&&); // move constructor
 // code omitted for brevity
};
```

Class relationships

Object intercommunication is at the heart of object-oriented systems. The relationship is the logical link between objects. The way we can distinguish or set up a proper relationship between classes of objects defines both the performance and quality of the system design overall. Consider the `Product` and `Warehouse` classes; they are in a relationship called aggregation because `Warehouse` contains products – that is, `Warehouse` aggregates `Product`:

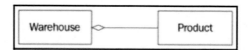

Figure 1.21: A UML diagram that depicts aggregation between Warehouse and Product

There are several kinds of relationships in terms of pure OOP, such as association, aggregation, composition, instantiation, generalization, and others.

Aggregation and composition

We encountered aggregation in the example of the `Warehouse` class. The `Warehouse` class stores an array of products. In more general terms, it can be called an *association*, but to strongly emphasize the exact containment, we use the term *aggregation* or *composition*. In the case of aggregation, the class that contains an instance or instances of other classes could be instantiated without the aggregate. This means that we can create and use a `Warehouse` object without necessarily creating `Product` objects contained in `Warehouse`. Another example of aggregation is `Car` and `Person`. A `Car` object can contain a `Person` object (as a driver or passenger) since they are associated with each other, but the containment is not strong. We can create a `Car` object without a `Driver` object in it (you can find the code at `https://github.com/PacktPublishing/Expert-C-2nd-edition/tree/main/Chapter%2001/9_car_person_aggregation.h`).

Strong containment is expressed by **composition**. For the Car example, an object of the Engine class is required to make a complete Car object. In this physical representation, the Engine member is automatically created when a Car object is created.

The following is the UML representation of aggregation and composition:

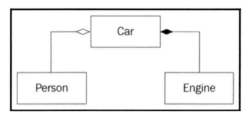

Figure 1.22: A UML diagram that demonstrates examples of aggregation and composition

When designing classes, we have to decide on their relationship. The best way to define the composition between the two classes is the *has-a* relationship test. A Car object has-a Engine member because a car has an engine. Any time you can't decide whether the relationship should be expressed in terms of composition, ask the *has-a* question. **Aggregation** and **composition** are somewhat similar; they just describe the strength of the connection. For aggregation, the proper question would be *can have a*; for example, a Car object can have a Driver object (of the Person type); that is, the containment is weak.

'can have' vs 'must have'
aggregation   composition

Inheritance

Inheritance is a programming concept that allows us to reuse classes. Programming languages provide different implementations of inheritance, but the general rule always stands: the class relationship should answer the *is-a* question. For example, a Car object is-a Vehicle class, which allows us to inherit Car from Vehicle:

```
class Vehicle {
  public:
    void move();
  };
class Car : public Vehicle { public: Car();
// ...
};
```

Car now has the move() member function derived from Vehicle. Inheritance itself represents a generalization/specialization relationship, where the parent class (Vehicle) is the generalization and the child class (Car) is the specialization.

You should only consider using inheritance if it is necessary. As we mentioned earlier, classes should satisfy the *is-a* relationship, and sometimes, this is a bit tricky.

Summary

In this chapter, we touched on a few of the many new features of C++20 and are now ready to dive deeper into the language. We discussed the process of building a C++ application and its compilation phases. This includes analyzing the code to detect syntactical and grammatical errors, generating intermediate code to make optimizations, and, finally, generating the object file that will be linked with other generated object files to form the final executable file.

In the next chapter, we will learn more about OOP, including the inner workings of the language object model. We will dive into the details of virtual functions and learn how to use polymorphism.

2

Beyond Object-Oriented Programming

The complexity of a software project affects how difficult it is to develop, implement, and maintain the project. The procedural approach, or procedural programming paradigm, might be used to create a straightforward calculator, but a bank account management system would be too difficult to develop in this way.

The **object-oriented programming (OOP)** paradigm, which is supported by C++, is based on breaking down entities into objects that coexist in a web of close intercommunication. Imagine a simple situation where you use the remote to switch the TV station in the real world. The remote control, the TV, and, most importantly, you, are all involved in this activity. To express real-world objects and their relationship using a programming language, we aren't forced to use classes, class inheritance, abstract classes, interfaces, virtual functions, and so on. While not necessary, the aforementioned capabilities and concepts make the process of designing and coding much simpler by enabling us to communicate and share ideas elegantly. *"Not every program should be object-oriented,"* as C++'s creator, Bjarne Stroustrup, puts it. To understand high-level concepts and features of the OOP paradigm, we will try to look behind the scenes. We shall go deeply into the design of OOP throughout this book. One of the objectives of this book is to comprehend the fundamental nature of objects and their relationships, before applying them to the creation of object-oriented applications.

In this chapter, we'll study in-depth information about the following subjects:

- An introduction to OOP and the C++ object model
- Under the hood of inheritance and polymorphism
- Classical design patterns
- Design principles
- More UML in project design

Technical requirements

The g++ compiler with the -std=c++20 option is used to compile the examples throughout this chapter.

You can find the source files for this chapter at https://github.com/PacktPublishing/Expert-C-2nd-edition/tree/main/Chapter02.

An introduction to OOP and the C++ object model

When writing a book about C++, you just have to talk about OOP because a) C++ is an object-oriented language, and b) OOP is at the heart of C++, which is also known by its original name – "C with classes." OOP is one of the many paradigms that exist in the programming world. Its main purpose is to make the life of a programmer easier by allowing them to represent everything that exists in the real world with the help of objects.

Understanding objects

The majority of the time, we work with a set of data grouped together with a name, thus creating an abstraction. When viewed separately, variables such as is_military, speed, and seats don't make much sense. We see the information stored in the variables differently when we group them together under the term spaceship. The multiple variables that are packed together are now referred to as one object. In order to accomplish this, we employ abstraction, which entails collecting the individual properties of a real-world object from the perspective of the observer. Abstraction is a key tool in the programmer's toolchain, as it allows them to deal with complexity. The C language introduced struct as a way to aggregate data, as shown in the following code:

```
struct spaceship {
bool is_military;
int speed;
int seats;
};
```

Grouping data is somewhat necessary for OOP. Each group of data is referred to as an object's blueprint.

Low-level details of objects

C++ does its best to support compatibility with the C language. While C structs are only a mechanism to aggregate data, C++ elevates them to the status of classes by enabling them to have constructors, virtual functions, the ability to inherit from other structs, and so on. The only difference between a struct and a class is the default visibility modifier – public for structs and private for classes. Typically, there is no difference between using structs instead of classes or vice versa. OOP requires more than just data aggregation. Let's investigate how we would use the OOP paradigm if we had only basic structs that provided data aggregation and nothing else in order to properly comprehend OOP. A central entity of an e-commerce marketplace such as Amazon or Alibaba is `Product`, which we represent in the following way:

```
struct Product {
std::string name;
double price;
int rating;
bool available;
};
```

We will add more members to `Product` if necessary. The memory layout of an object of the `Product` type can be depicted like this:

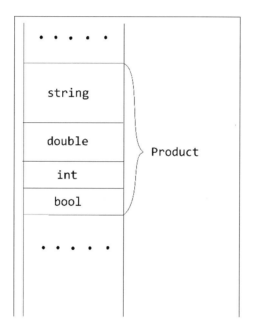

Figure 2.1 – The memory layout of the Product object

Declaring a `Product` object takes `sizeof(Product)` space in memory, while declaring a pointer or a reference to the object takes the space required to store the address. If the computer we use has a 32-bit operating system, the size of the space required to store the address is going to be 4 bytes, and if it has a 64-bit operating system, the size is 8 bytes (which is the most common nowadays). See the following code block:

```
Product book;
Product tshirt;
Product* ptr = &book;
Product& ref = tshirt;
```

The previous code can be illustrated as follows:

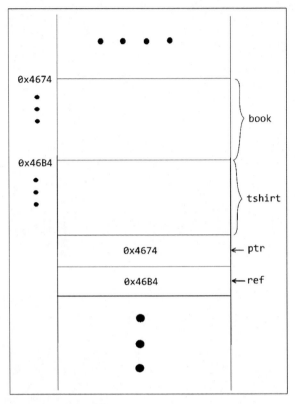

Figure 2.2 – Memory space taken by the Product object versus the Product pointer

Let's start with how much memory the `Product` object consumes. By adding up the sizes of each of its member variables, we can determine the size of the `Product` object. A `boolean` variable is 1 byte in size. The C++ standard does not specify the precise size of a `double` or `int` variable. `Double` variables typically take up 8 bytes on 64-bit computers, while `int` variables take up 4 bytes.

The size of `std::string` depends on the library implementation, as the implementation is not specified in the standard. In addition to storing a reference as a character array, `string` can also store the total number of characters allocated so that `size()` can return the value quickly. Some implementations of `std::string` take 8, 24, 32, or other completely different bytes of memory, but we will stick to 24 bytes in our example. By summing it all up, the size of `Product` will be as follows:

```
24 (std::string) + 8 (double) + 4 (int) + 1 (bool) = 37 bytes
```

Printing the size of `Product` outputs a different value:

```
std::cout << sizeof(Product);
```

Instead of the predicted 37 bytes, it outputs 40. The reason behind the redundant bytes is the padding of the struct, a technique practiced by the compiler to optimize access to individual members of the object. The **Central Processing Unit (CPU)** reads the memory in fixed-size words. The CPU defines the word size, which is typically 32 or 64 bits. If the CPU beings from a word-aligned address, it may access the data all at once. For instance, the `Product` object's Boolean data member only needs 1 byte of memory and can be placed right after the rating member. It turns out that the data is aligned by the compiler for quicker access. Assume that each word takes up 4 bytes. This means that if a variable starts at an address that is divisible by four, the CPU will access the variable without repeating steps. The compiler augments the struct earlier with additional bytes to align the members to word-boundary addresses.

High-level details of objects

We deal with objects as entities, representing the result of abstraction. We have already mentioned the role of the observer – that is, the programmer who defines the object based on the problem domain. The programmer's definition of this illustrates the abstraction process. Let's use an online store and its products as an example. The same product could be seen differently by two separate programming teams. The website implementation team is concerned with the characteristics of the item that is crucial to website visitors – buyers. The selling price, the product's rating, and other attributes that we previously displayed in the `Product` struct are primarily intended for website visitors. Programmers that implement the website touch the problem domain and verify the properties that are essential to defining a `Product` object.

The team that implements the online tools that help manage the products in a warehouse cares about the properties of the object that are essential in terms of product placement, quality control, and shipment. The product's rating or even its price shouldn't matter to this team. The product's weight, size, and conditions are of primary concern to them. The following diagram shows the properties of interest:

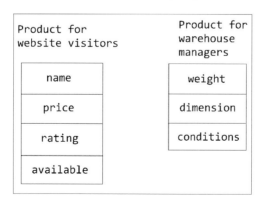

Figure 2.3 – The properties of interest of a product for two different teams

The first thing that programmers should do when starting the project is to analyze the problem and gather the requirements. In other words, they should get familiar with the *problem domain* and define the *project requirements*. The process of analyzing leads to defining objects and their types, such as the product we discussed earlier. To get proper results from analyzing, we should think in terms of objects, and by thinking in terms of objects, we mean considering the three main properties of objects – state, behavior, and identity. However, before talking about those three properties, let's understand what the C++ object model looks like.

C++ object model

When we refer to an object model, we mean the underlying mechanisms that are used to construct and work with an object. Let us consider what object models there are, based on simple examples. We will start with a `Rectangle` class. First of all, let's express `Rectangle` with the help of the C language. In the C language, `Rectangle` would be constructed with the help of a struct. The following is an example of a `Rectangle` struct in the C language, which we will transform into a C++ class:

```
typedef struct Rectangle {
int length;
int width;
} Rectangle;
```

And if we want to calculate the perimeter of a rectangle, we can write a function that takes the address of a `Rectangle` object and calculates it. An example can be seen here:

```
int rect_perimeter (const Rectangle* rect)
{
return 2 * (rect->length + rect->width);
}
```

As we know, in C there is no support for a relationship between data and functions that operate on it, which is why the functions are declared separately in C. In C++, the same example can be expressed in the following way:

```
class Rectangle {
public:
    Rectangle (int length = 0, int width = 0) :
                                m_length( length ),
                                m_width(width) {};
    int get_length() { return m_length; }
    int get_width() { return m_width; }
    void set_length(int length) { m_length = length; }
    void set_width(int width) { m_width = width; }
    int perimeter()
    {
        return 2 * (m_length + m_width);
```

```
    }
private:
    int m_length;
    int m_width;
};
```

As we can see in the C++ `Rectangle` class, we also have functions that help us to work with data members – for example, for setting and getting the necessary values. Seeing these many functions, the question arises whether the object is going to take up more space in memory than its identical object written in C. The question can be answered by considering the object model that C++ uses to construct objects. Many people have different approaches to this problem, which is why we are going to introduce some of these approaches and then go with the one that seems more realistic and logical. The first approach is the one that says that functions, in fact, affect the size of an object. If we consider that each object has function pointers to every function the class has, then the object of the class below will occupy 56 bytes of memory (considering that the size of a pointer is 8 bytes and an integer is 4 bytes).

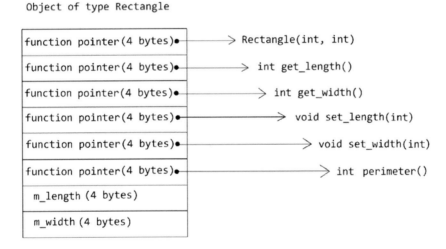

Figure 2.4 – An object model where the object contains pointers to all of its member functions

In this case, the size of the object can be considered consistent in some way, as it will always be the size of the pointer multiplied by the number of functions, plus the size of the data declared in the class. We can make it even more consistent if we use the model where data members and functions are all kept outside the object, and it only contains pointers to everything declared inside the class. In the case of our `Rectangle` object, the size won't differ between the two models described, but if the class contains large sizes of arrays and also other large ADTs, the model that keeps only pointers will come in handy.

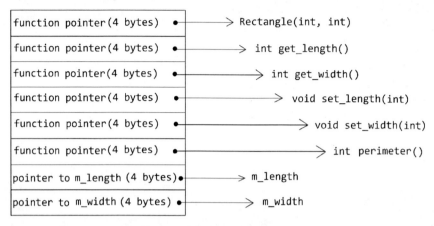

Figure 2.5 – An object model where the object contains pointers
to all of its data members and member functions

The two aforementioned models are not as space-efficient as the one we will talk about next. The concept of the third model is to make an object take up less space than it did in the previous models, and for that reason, the object in the third model holds only two pointers, no matter how many data members and functions are declared. There are also two tables – one that holds the data members, which are declared inside a class, and another that holds the addresses of the functions, which are also declared inside a class. The two pointers that take up space point to the two corresponding tables.

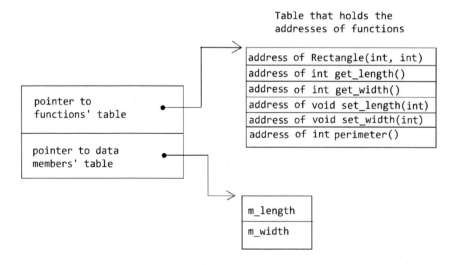

Figure 2.6 – An object model where the object contains only two pointers

In this case, the object takes up less space but takes more time to run, so it's not that efficient.

As we move closer to a more realistic object model, there is a need to talk about not only the classes *Static* that have simple data structures and functions but also all types of data and functions that can be *non- static* declared in a class. When it comes to data members, a class can have two types, static and non-static, *virtual* and when it comes to functions, a class can have static, non-static, and virtual types. According to the last model, which is the more realistic one, only the non-static data members are allocated directly within a class. Static data members, static and non-static functions, and virtual functions are allocated outside the object of the class. However, in this case, when it comes to virtual functions, there are some tricky aspects. The class has to know how to deal with virtual functions and what one it has to deal with exactly, and as virtual functions are called at runtime, there is a need for the object to have something that has access to that exact virtual function. For that reason, the object holds a pointer, a so-called virtual pointer, which points to a table, also known as the virtual table, the fields of which *v-table* hold the addresses of virtual functions. The first slot of the virtual table is usually RTTI information about the object. So, let us change our class so that it contains all types of data and functions, but note that it's done only as an example, and it's definitely not the right way to implement a `Rectangle` class:

```cpp
class Rectangle {
public:
    Rectangle(int length = 0, int width = 0) {
    m_length = length;
    m_width = width;
    }
    static int get_length() { return m_length; }
    int get_width() { return m_width; }
    virtual void set_length(int length) { m_length = length; }
    virtual void set_width(int width) { m_width = width; }
    int perimeter()
    {
        return 2 * (m_length + m_width);
    }
private:
    static int m_length;
    int m_width;
};
```

Now that our class contains all types of functions and data members, our object model looks as follows and is based on the description we gave previously.

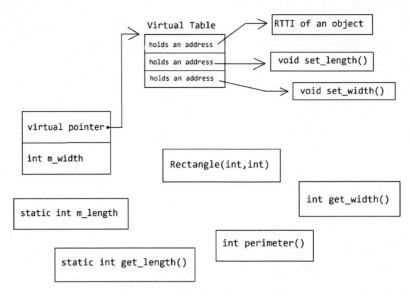

Figure 2.7 – The C++ object model

So, as we can see, the last model is some kind of combination of the last models. It is the most logical one, and we are going to stick with this one as the final C++ object model.

State

There is a state for each object, which might or might not be different from other objects' states. We've already introduced the `Product` struct, which represents an abstraction of a physical (or digital) product. All the members of a `Product` object collectively represent the state of the object. `Product`, for instance, has a member called `available`, a Boolean that equals `true` if the product is in stock. The state of the object is determined by the values of the member variables. The state of the object member will change if new values are assigned to it:

```
Product cpp_book; // declaring the object
...
// changing the state of the object cpp_book
cpp_book.available = true;
cpp_book.rating = 5;
```

The state of the object is the combination of all of its properties and values.

Identity

One thing that sets an object apart from other objects is its identity. Even if we try to declare two physically indistinguishable objects, they will still have different names for their variables – that is, different identities:

```
Product book1;
book1.rating = 4;
book1.name = "Book";
Product book2;
book2.rating = 4;
book2.name = "Book";
```

The objects in the previous example have the same state, but book1 and book2 are the different names we use to refer to them. Suppose we could somehow construct objects with the same name, as can be seen in the following block of code:

```
Product prod;
Product prod; // won't compile, but still "what if?"
```

If this was the case, they would still have different addresses in memory:

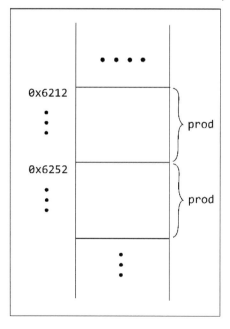

Figure 2.8 – Objects with the same name taking different addresses in the memory

Identity is a fundamental property of an object and is one of the reasons why we can't create empty objects, such as the following:

```
struct Empty {};
int main() {
    Empty e;
    std::cout << sizeof(e);
}
```

The preceding code will not output 0 as intended. A standard does not specify the size of an empty object. Compiler developers often allocate 1 byte for such objects; however, you may also come across 4 or 8 bytes as well. The compiler must ensure that objects will occupy at least 1 byte of memory, since two or more instances of Empty should have distinct addresses in memory.

Behavior

In previous examples, we assigned 5 and then 4 to the rating member variable. We can easily make things unexpectedly wrong by assigning invalid values to the object, like so:

```
cpp_book.rating = -12;
```

-12 is invalid in terms of a product's rating and will perplex users. By providing setter methods, we can regulate how the object reacts to changes made to it:

```
void set_rating(Product* p, int r) {
    if (r >= 1 && r <= 5) {
        p->rating = r;
    }
// otherwise ignore
}
...
set_rating(&cpp_book, -12); // won't change the state
```

An object acts and reacts to requests from other objects. Function calls – also called messages – are used to carry out the requests; one object transmits a message to another. In the preceding example, the object that passed the corresponding set_rating message to the cpp_book object represents the object that we call the set_rating() function. In this case, we assume that we could call the function from main(), which doesn't actually represent any object at all. We could say it's the global object, the one that operates the main() function, though there is not an entity like that in C++.

We distinguish the objects conceptually rather than physically. That's the main thing to consider when thinking about objects. The physical implementation of some concepts of OOP is not standardized, so we can name the Product struct as a class and claim that cpp_book is an instance of Product, and that it has a member function called `set_rating()`. The C++ implementation essentially accomplishes the same thing – it offers syntactically useful structures (classes, visibility modifiers, inheritance, and so on) and converts them into simple structs with global functions, such as `set_rating()` in the previous example.

Mimicking a class

A struct allows us to group variables, name them, and create objects. The idea of a class is to include the corresponding operations in the object, grouping both data and operations that are applicable to that particular data. For example, for the object of the `Product` type, it is natural to call the `set_rating()` function on the object directly, rather than having a separate global function that takes a `Product` object via a pointer and modifies it. However, as we opted to use structs in the C manner, we can't afford to have member functions. To mimic a class using a C struct, we have to declare functions that work with the `Product` object as global functions, as shown in the following code:

```cpp
struct Product {
    std::string name;
    double price;
    int rating;
    bool available;
};
void initialize(Product* p) {
    p->price = 0.0;
    p->rating = 0;
    p->available = false;
}
void set_name(Product* p, const std::string& name) {
    p->name = name;
}
std::string get_name(Product* p) {
    return p->name;
}
void set_price(Product* p, double price) {
    if (price < 0 || price > 9999.42) return;
    p->price = price;
}
double get_price(Product* p) {
    return p->price;
}
// code omitted for brevity
```

To use the struct as a class, we should manually call the functions in the proper order. For example, to use the object with properly initialized default values, we have to call the `initialize()` function first:

```cpp
int main() {
    Product cpp_book;
    initialize(&cpp_book);
    set_name(&cpp_book, "Mastering C++ Programming");
    std::cout << "Book title is: " << get_name(&cpp_book);
    // ...
}
```

This seems doable, but the preceding code will quickly turn into an unorganized mess if new types are added. For example, consider the `Warehouse` struct that keeps track of products:

```cpp
struct Warehouse {
    Product* products;
    int capacity;
    int size;
};
void initialize_warehouse(Warehouse* w) {
    w->capacity = 1000;
    w->size = 0;
    w->products = new Product[w->capacity];
    for (int ix = 0; ix < w->capacity; ++ix) {
    initialize(&w->products[ix]); // initialize each
                                  // Product object
    }
}
void set_size(int size) { ... }
// code omitted for brevity
```

The first obvious issue is the naming of functions. We had to name the initializer function of `Warehouse` `initialize_warehouse` to avoid conflict with the already declared `initialize()` function for `Product`. We might consider renaming the functions for the `Product` type to avoid possible conflicts in the future. Next comes the mess with functions. Now, we have a bunch of global functions, which will increase in number as we add new types. It will be even more unmanageable if we add some hierarchy of types.

Though compilers tend to translate classes into structs with global functions, as we showed earlier, C++ and other high-level programming languages solve these issues, and others that have not been mentioned, by introducing classes with smooth mechanisms and organizing them into hierarchies. Conceptually, keywords (`class`, `public`, and `private`) and mechanisms (inheritance and polymorphism) are there for developers to conveniently organize their code, but it won't make the life of a compiler any easier.

Working with classes

Classes make things a lot easier when dealing with objects. They do the simplest necessary thing in OOP – they combine data with functions to manipulate data. Let's rewrite the example of the Product struct using a class and its powerful features:

```cpp
class Product {
public:
    Product() = default; // default constructor
    Product(const Product&); // copy constructor
    Product(Product&&); // move constructor
    Product& operator=(const Product&) = default;
    Product& operator=(Product&&) = default;
// destructor is not declared, should be generated by the
// compiler
public:
    void set_name(const std::string&);
    std::string name() const;
    void set_availability(bool);
    bool available() const;
// code omitted for brevity
private:
    std::string name_;
    double price_;
    int rating_;
    bool available_;
};
std::ostream& operator<<(std::ostream&, const Product&);
std::istream& operator>>(std::istream&, Product&);
```

The class declaration seems more organized, even though it exposes more functions than we use to define a similar struct. Here's how we should illustrate the class:

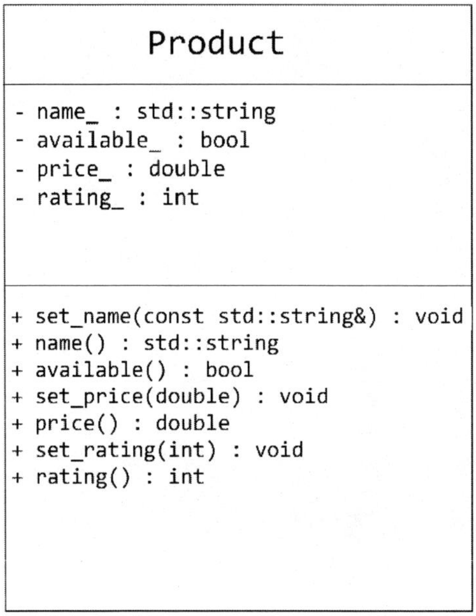

```
┌─────────────────────────────────────────┐
│               Product                    │
├─────────────────────────────────────────┤
│ - name_  : std::string                   │
│ - available_ : bool                      │
│ - price_ : double                        │
│ - rating_ : int                          │
│                                          │
│                                          │
├─────────────────────────────────────────┤
│ + set_name(const std::string&) : void    │
│ + name() : std::string                   │
│ + available() : bool                     │
│ + set_price(double) : void               │
│ + price() : double                       │
│ + set_rating(int) : void                 │
│ + rating() : int                         │
│                                          │
│                                          │
│                                          │
└─────────────────────────────────────────┘
```

Figure 2.9 – A UML diagram of the Product class

The preceding diagram is somewhat special. As you can see, it has organized sections, signs before the names of functions, and so on. This type of diagram is called a **Unified Modeling Language** (**UML**) class diagram. UML is a way to standardize the process of illustrating classes and their relationships. The first section is the name of the class (in bold), followed by the section for member variables, and then the section for member functions. The + (plus) sign in front of a function name means that the function is public. Member variables are usually private, but, if you need to emphasize this, you can use the – (minus) sign. We can omit all the details by simply illustrating the class, as shown in the following UML diagram:

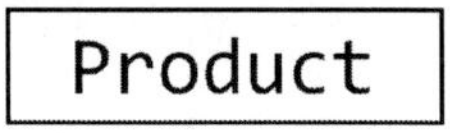

```
┌─────────────────┐
│     Product     │
└─────────────────┘
```

Figure 2.10 – A UML diagram of the Product class without data members and member functions

We will use UML diagrams throughout this book and introduce new types of diagrams as needed. Before dealing with initializing, copying, moving, default and deleted functions, and, of course, operator overloading, let's clear a couple of things up.

Classes from a compiler perspective

First of all, no matter how monstrous the class from earlier may seem in comparison to the previously introduced struct, a compiler will translate it into the following code (we have slightly modified it for the sake of simplicity):

```cpp
struct Product {
    std::string name_;
    bool available_;
    double price_;
    int rating_;
};
// we forced the compiler to generate the default
// constructor
void Product_constructor(Product&);
void Product_copy_constructor(Product& this, const Product&);
void Product_move_constructor(Product& this, Product&&);
// default implementation
Product& operator=(Product& this, const Product&);
// default implementation
Product& operator=(Product& this, Product&&);

void Product_set_name(const std::string&);
// takes const because the method was declared as const
std::string Product_name(const Product& this);
void Product_set_availability(Product& this, bool b);
bool Product_availability(const Product& this);
std::ostream& operator<<(std::ostream&, const Product&);
std::istream& operator>>(std::istream&, Product&);
```

Basically, the compiler generates the same code that we introduced earlier as a way to mimic class behavior using a simple struct. Though compilers vary in techniques and methods to implement the C++ object model, the preceding example is one of the popular approaches practiced by compiler developers. It balances the space and time efficiency in accessing object members (including member functions).

Next, we should consider when a compiler edits our code by augmenting and modifying it. The following code declares the global `create_apple()` function, which creates and returns a `Product` object with values specific to an apple. It also declares a book object in the `main()` function:

```cpp
Product create_apple() {
    Product apple;
    apple.set_name("Red apple");
    apple.set_price("0.2");
    apple.set_rating(5);
    apple.set_available(true);
    return apple;
```

```
}
int main() {
    Product red_apple = create_apple();
    Product book;
    Product* ptr = &book;
    ptr->set_name("Alice in Wonderland");
    ptr->set_price(6.80);
    std::cout << "I'm reading " << book.name()
        << " and I bought an apple for " << red_apple.price()
        << std::endl;
}
```

We already know that the compiler modifies the class to translate it into a struct and moves member functions to the global scope, each of which takes the reference (or a pointer) to the class as its first parameter. To support those modifications in the client code, it should also modify all access to the objects.

> **Tip**
>
> A line or lines of code that declare or use already declared class objects are referred to as client code.

Here's how we will assume that a compiler modifies the preceding code (we use the word *assume* because we're trying to introduce a compiler-abstract rather than a compiler-specific approach):

```
void create_apple(Product& apple) {
    Product_set_name(apple, "Red apple");
    Product_set_price(apple, 0.2);
    Product_set_rating(apple, 5);
    Product_set_available(apple, true);
    return;
}
int main() {
    Product red_apple;
    Product_constructor(red_apple);
    create_apple(red_apple);
    Product book;
    Product* ptr;
    Product_constructor(book);
    Product_set_name(*ptr, "Alice in Wonderland");
    Product_set_price(*ptr, 6.80);
    std::ostream os = operator<<(std::cout, "I'm reading ");
    os = operator<<(os, Product_name(book));
    os = operator<<(os, " and I bought an apple for ");
    os = operator<<(os, Product_price(red_apple));
```

```
    operator<<(os, std::endl);
    // destructor calls are skipped because the compiler
    // will remove them as empty functions to optimize
    // the code
    // Product_destructor(book);
    // Product_destructor(red_apple);
}
```

The compiler also optimized the call to the `create_apple()` function to prevent temporary object creation. We will discuss the invisible temporaries that were generated by the compiler later in this chapter.

Initialization and destruction

As shown previously, the creation of an object is a two-step process – memory allocation and initialization. Memory allocation is a result of an object declaration. C++ doesn't care about the initialization of variables; it allocates the memory (whether it is automatic or manual) and it's done. The actual initialization should be done by the programmer, which is why we have a constructor in the first place.

The same logic follows for the destructor. If we skip the declarations of the default constructor or destructor, a compiler should generate them implicitly, which it would also remove if they are empty (to eliminate redundant calls to empty functions). The default constructor will not be generated by the compiler if any constructor with parameters is declared, including the copy constructor. We can force the compiler to implicitly generate the default constructor:

```
class Product {
public:
    Product() = default;
    // ...
};
```

We also can force it not to generate the compiler by using the `delete` specifier, as shown here:

```
class Product {
public:
    Product() = delete;
    // ...
};
```

This will prohibit default-initialized object declarations – that is, `Product p;` won't compile.

Here's a tip – destructors are called in the order opposite to object declarations because the automatic memory allocation is managed by a stack, which is a data structure adapter that follows the **last in, first out** (**LIFO**) rule.

Object initialization happens on its creation. Destruction usually happens when an object is no longer accessible. The latter may be tricky when the object is allocated to the heap. Take a look at the following code; it declares four `Product` objects in different scopes and segments of memory:

```
static Product global_prod; // #1
Product* foo() {
    Product* heap_prod = new Product(); // #4
    heap_prod->name = "Sample";
    return heap_prod;
}
int main() {
    Product stack_prod; // #2
    if (true) {
    Product tmp; // #3
    tmp.rating = 3;
    }
    stack_prod.price = 4.2;
    foo();
}
```

`global_prod` has a static storage duration and is placed in the global/static section of the program; it is initialized before `main()` is called. When `main()` starts, `stack_prod` is allocated on the stack and will be destroyed when `main()` ends (the closing curly brace of the function is considered as its end). Though the conditional expression looks weird and too artificial, it's a good way to express the block scope.

The `tmp` object will also be allocated on the stack, but its storage duration is limited to the scope it has been declared in; it will be automatically destroyed when the execution leaves the `if` block. That's why variables on the stack have automatic storage duration. Finally, when the `foo()` function is called, it declares the `heap_prod` pointer, which points to the address of the `Product` object allocated on the heap.

The preceding code contains a memory leak because the `heap_prod` pointer (which itself has an automatic storage duration) will be destroyed when the execution reaches the end of `foo()`, while the object allocated on the heap won't be affected. Don't mix the pointer and the actual object it points to; the pointer contains the value of the object, but it doesn't represent it.

When the function ends, the memory for its arguments and the local variables allocated on the stack will be freed, but `global_prod` will be destroyed when the program ends – that is, after the `main()` function finishes. The destructor will be called when the object is about to be destroyed.

Copying objects

There are two kinds of copying – a *deep* copy and a *shallow* copy of objects. The language allows us to manage copy initialization and the assignment of objects with the copy constructor and the assignment operator. This is a necessary feature for programmers because we can control the semantics of copying. Take a look at the following example:

```
Product p1;
Product p2;
p2.set_price(4.2);
p1 = p2; // p1 now has the same price
Product p3 = p2; // p3 has the same price
```

The line `p1 = p2;` is a call to the assignment operator, while the last line is a call to the copy constructor. The equals sign shouldn't confuse you in terms of whether it's an assignment or a copy constructor call. Each time you see a declaration followed by an assignment, consider it a copy construction – `Product p3 = p2;`.

The compiler will generate the following code:

```
Product p1;
Product p2;
Product_set_price(p2, 4.2);
operator=(p1, p2);
Product p3;
Product_copy_constructor(p3, p2);
```

The default implementation of the copy constructor (and assignment operator) performs a member-wise copy of objects, as shown in the following diagram:

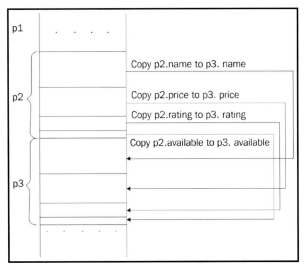

Figure 2.11 – A member-wise copy of objects

Custom implementation is required if the member-wise copy produces invalid copies. For example, consider the following copy of the `Warehouse` objects:

```
class Warehouse {
public:
    Warehouse()
    : size_{0}, capacity_{1000}, products_{nullptr}
    {
        products_ = new Products[capacity_];
    }
    ~Warehouse() {
        delete [] products_;
    }
public:
    void add_product(const Product& p) {
    if (size_ == capacity_) { /* resize */ }
    products_[size_++] = p;
    }
    // other functions omitted for brevity
private:
    int size_;
    int capacity_;
    Product* products_;
};
int main() {
    Warehouse w1;
    Product book;
    Product apple;
    // ...assign values to products (omitted for brevity)
    w1.add_product(book);
    Warehouse w2 = w1; // copy
    w2.add_product(apple);
    // something somewhere went wrong...
}
```

The preceding code declares two `Warehouse` objects, and two different products are then added to the warehouses. Although this example is somewhat unnatural, it shows the dangers of the default implementation of copying. The following diagram shows us what went wrong in the code:

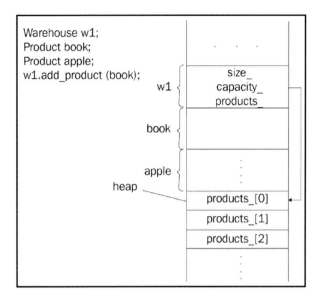

Figure 2.12 – The representation of objects declared on the left in memory

Assigning w1 to w2 leads to the following structure:

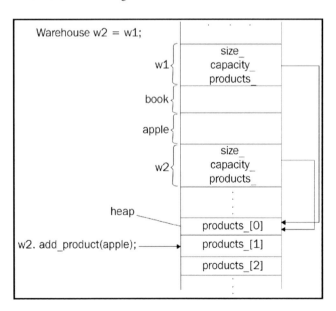

Figure 2.11 – The result of a default copy constructor called on
an object that allocates memory on the heap

The default implementation simply copies each member of w1 to w2. After copying, both the products_ members of w1 and w2 point to the same location on the heap. When we add a new product to w2, the array pointed to by w1 is affected. It's a logical error that could lead to undefined behavior in the program. We need a *deep* rather than a *shallow* copy – that is, we need to actually create a new array of products that has a copy of w1 object's array.

A custom implementation of the copy constructor and the assignment operator solves this issue of shallow copying:

```cpp
class Warehouse {
public:
    // ...
    Warehouse(const Warehouse& rhs) {
        size_ = rhs.size_;
        capacity_ = rhs.capacity_;
        products_ = new Product[capacity_];
        for (int ix = 0; ix < size_; ++ix) {
        products_[ix] = rhs.products_[ix];
        }
    }
// code omitted for brevity
};
```

The custom implementation of the copy constructor creates a new array. Then, it copies the source objects' array elements one by one, thus preventing the product_ pointer from pointing to the wrong memory address. In other words, we implemented a deep copy of Warehouse objects by creating a new array.

Moving objects

Temporary objects are everywhere in code. Most of the time, they are required to make the code work as expected. For example, when we add two objects together, a temporary object is created to hold the return value of operator+:

```cpp
Warehouse small;
Warehouse mid;
// ... some data inserted into the small and mid objects
Warehouse large{small + mid}; // operator+(small, mid)
```

Let's take a look at the implementation of the global operator+() for Warehouse objects:

```cpp
// considering declared as friend in the Warehouse class
Warehouse operator+(const Warehouse& a, const Warehouse& b) {
    Warehouse sum; // temporary
    sum.size_ = a.size_ + b.size_;
```

```
    sum.capacity_ = a.capacity_ + b.capacity_;
    sum.products_ = new Product[sum.capacity_];
    for (int ix = 0; ix < a.size_; ++ix)
        { sum.products_[ix] = a.products_[ix]; }
    for (int ix = 0; ix < b.size_; ++ix)
        { sum.products_[a.size_ + ix] = b.products_[ix]; }
    return sum;
}
```

The preceding implementation declares a temporary object and returns it after filling it with necessary data. The call in the previous example could be translated into the following:

```
Warehouse small;
Warehouse mid;
// ... some data inserted into the small and mid objects
Warehouse tmp{operator+(small, mid)};
Warehouse large;
Warehouse_copy_constructor(large, tmp);
__destroy_temporary(tmp);
```

Move semantics, which was introduced in C++11, allows us to skip the temporary creation by *moving* the return value into the `Warehouse` object. To do so, we should declare a move constructor for *Warehouse*, which can *distinguish* between temporaries and treat them efficiently:

```
class Warehouse {
public:
    Warehouse(); // default constructor
    Warehouse(const Warehouse&); // copy constructor
    Warehouse(Warehouse&&); // move constructor
    // code omitted for brevity
};
```

The parameter of the move constructor is `rvalue reference (&&)`.

An lvalue reference

Before explaining why `rvalue` references were introduced in the first place, let's clear things up regarding `lvalues`, references, and lvalue references. When a variable is an lvalue, it can be addressed and pointed to and has a scoped storage duration:

```
double pi{3.14}; // lvalue
int x{42}; // lvalue
int y{x}; // lvalue
int& ref{x}; // lvalue-reference
```

`ref` is an `lvalue` reference, a synonym for a variable that can be treated as a `const` pointer:

```
int * const ref = &x;
```

Besides the ability to modify objects by a reference, we can pass heavy objects to functions by reference in order to optimize and avoid redundant object copies. For example, `operator+` for `Warehouse` takes two objects *by reference*, thus making it copy the addresses of objects rather than full objects.

`lvalue` references optimize code in terms of function calls, but to optimize temporaries, we should move on to rvalue references.

Rvalue references

We cannot bind `lvalue` references to temporaries. The following code won't compile:

```
int get_it() {
    int it{42};
    return it;
}
...
int& impossible{get_it()}; // compile error
```

We need to declare an `rvalue` reference to be able to bind to temporaries (including literal values):

```
int&& possible{get_it()};
```

`rvalue` references allow us to skip a generation of temporaries as much as possible. For example, a function that takes a result as an `rvalue` reference runs faster by eliminating temporary objects:

```
void do_something(int&& val) {
    // do something with the val
}
// the return value of the get_it is moved to do_something
// rather than copied
do_something(get_it());
```

To consider the effect of moving, imagine that the preceding code is translated into the following (just to get the full idea of moving):

```
int val;
void get_it() {
    val = 42;
}
void do_something() {
    // do something with the val
}
do_something();
```

Before moving was introduced, the preceding code would look like this (with some compiler optimization):

```
int tmp;
void get_it() {
    tmp = 42;
}
void do_something(int val) {
    // do something with the val
}
do_something(tmp);
```

The move constructor, along with the move operator, = (), has the effect of copying without actually carrying out a copy operation when the input argument represents rvalue. That's why we should also implement these new functions in the class – so that we can optimize code wherever it makes sense. The move constructor can grab the source object instead of copying it, as shown here:

```
class Warehouse {
public:
    // constructors omitted for brevity
    Warehouse(Warehouse&& src)
    : size_{src.size_}, capacity_{src.capacity_},
    products_{src.products_}
    {
        src.size_    = 0;
        src.capacity_ = 0;
        src.products_ = nullptr;
    }
};
```

Instead of creating a new array of capacity_ size and then copying each element of the products_ array, we just grabbed the pointer to the array. We know that the src object is an rvalue and that it will soon be destroyed, which means the destructor will be called and delete the allocated array. Now, we point to the allocated array from the newly created Warehouse object, which is why we cannot let the destructor delete the source array. Due to this, we assign nullptr to it to make sure the destructor will miss the allocated object. So, the following code will be optimized because of the move constructor:

```
Warehouse large = small + mid;
```

The result of the + operator will be moved rather than copied. Take a look at the following diagram:

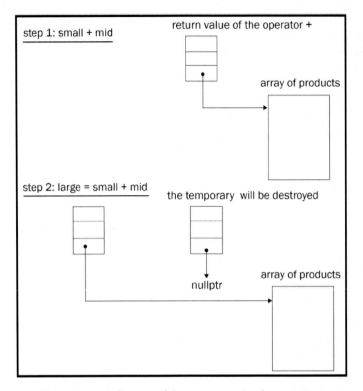

Figure 2.14 – A diagram of the + operator implementation

The preceding diagram demonstrates how the temporary is moved to the large object.

Notes on operator overloading

C++ provides a powerful mechanism to overload operators for custom types. It's much better to calculate the sum of two objects using the + operator, rather than calling a member function. Calling a member function also involves remembering its name before calling it. It might be add, calculateSum, calculate_sum, or something else. Operator overloading allows for a consistent approach in class design. On the other hand, overloading operators increases unnecessary verbosity in code. The following snippet represents a list of comparison operators being overloaded, along with addition and subtraction for the Money class. The functions are marked as constexpr in the examples that follow. The constexpr specifier declares that the value of the function can be evaluated at compile time. The same definition applies to variables as well. The name itself consists of const and expression. This is a useful feature because it allows you to optimize your code to the fullest:

```
constexpr bool operator<(const Money& a, const Money& b) {
    return a.value_ < b.value_;
}
constexpr bool operator==(const Money& a, const Money& b) {
```

```
        return a.value_ == b.value_;
    }
    constexpr bool operator<=(const Money& a, const Money& b) {
        return a.value_ <= b.value_;
    }
    constexpr bool operator!=(const Money& a, const Money& b) {
        return !(a == b);
    }
    constexpr bool operator>(const Money& a, const Money& b) {
        return !(a <= b);
    }
    constexpr bool operator>=(const Money& a, const Money& b) {
        return !(a < b);
    }
    constexpr Money operator+(const Money& a, const Money& b) {
        return Money{a.value_ + b.value_};
    }
    constexpr Money operator-(const Money& a, const Money& b) {
        return Money{a.value_ - b.value_};
    }
```

As you can see, most of the preceding functions directly access the value member of the Money instance. To make it work, we should declare them as friends for Money. Here's what Money will look like:

```
class Money
{
public:
    Money() {}
    explicit Money(double v) : value_{v} {}
    // construction/destruction functions omitted for
    // brevity
public:
    friend constexpr bool operator<(const Money&, const Money&);
    friend constexpr bool operator==(const Money&, const Money&);
    friend constexpr bool operator<=(const Money&, const Money&);
    friend constexpr bool operator!=(const Money&, const Money&);
    friend constexpr bool operator>(const Money&, const Money&);
    friend constexpr bool operator>=(const Money&, const Money&);
    friend constexpr bool operator+(const Money&, const Money&);
    friend constexpr bool operator-(const Money&, const Money&);
private:
    double value_;
};
```

The class looks monstrous. C++20 introduces the spaceship operator, which allows us to skip the definition of comparison operators. `operator<=>()`, also known as the three-way comparison operator, requests the compiler to generate relational operators. For the `Money` class, we can use the default `operator<=>()`, as shown here:

```
class Money
{
// code omitted for brevity
    friend auto operator<=>(const Money&, const Money&) = default;
};
```

The compiler will generate the `==`, `!=`, `<`, `>`, `<=`, and `>=` operators. The `spaceship` operator reduces the redundant definitions for operators and also provides a way to implement a generic behavior for all the generated operators. When implementing a custom behavior for the `spaceship` operator, we should note the return value type of the operator. It can be one of the following:

- `std::strong_ordering`

- `std::weak_ordering`

- `std::partial_ordering`

- `std::strong_equality`

- `std::weak_equality`

All of them are defined in the `<compare>` header. The compiler generates operators based on the return type of the three-way operator.

Encapsulation and the public interface

Encapsulation is a key concept in OOP. It allows us to hide the implementation details of objects from the client code. Take, for example, a computer keyboard – it has keys for letters, numbers, and symbols, each of which acts if we press them. Its usage is simple and intuitive, and it hides a lot of low-level details that only a person familiar with electronics would be able to handle. Imagine a keyboard without keys – one that has a bare board with unlabeled pins. You would have to guess which one to press to achieve the desired key combination or text input. Now, imagine a keyboard without pins – you have to send proper signals to the corresponding sockets to get the key-pressed event of a particular symbol. Users could be confused by the absence of labels, and they also could use it incorrectly by pressing or sending signals to invalid sockets. The keyboard as we know it solves this issue by encapsulating the implementation details – the same way programmers encapsulate objects so that they don't load the user with redundant members, and to make sure users won't use objects in the wrong way.

Visibility modifiers serve that purpose in the class by allowing us to define the accessibility level of any member. The private modifier prohibits any use of the `private` member from the client code. This allows us to control the modification of the `private` member by providing corresponding member functions. A `mutator` function, familiar to many as a setter function, modifies the value of a `private` member after testing the value against specified rules for that particular class. An example of this can be seen in the following code:

```cpp
class Warehouse {
public:
    // rather naive implementation
    void set_size(int sz) {
    if (sz < 1) throw std::invalid_argument("Invalid size");
    size_ = sz;
    }
    // code omitted for brevity
private:
    int size_;
};
```

Modifying a data member through a `mutator` function allows us to control its value. The actual data member is private, which makes it inaccessible from the client code, while the class itself provides public functions to update or read the contents of its private members. These functions, along with the constructors, are often referred to as the *public interface* of the class. Programmers strive to make the class' public interface user-friendly.

Take a look at the following class, which represents a quadratic equation solver – an equation of the form $ax2 + bx + c = 0$. One of the solutions is finding a discriminant using the formula $D = b2 - 4ac$ and then calculating the value of x, based on the value of the discriminant (D). The following class provides five functions – to set the values of a, b, and c respectively, to find the discriminant, and to solve and return the value of x:

```cpp
class QuadraticSolver {
public:
    QuadraticSolver() = default;
    void set_a(double a);
    void set_b(double b);
    void set_c(double c);
    void find_discriminant();
    double solve(); // solve and return the x
private:
    double a_;
    double b_;
    double c_;
    double discriminant_;
};
```

The public interface includes the aforementioned four functions and the default constructor. To solve the equation *2x2 + 5x - 8 = 0*, we should use `QuadraticSolver` like so:

```
QuadraticSolver solver;
solver.set_a(2);
solver.set_b(5);
solver.set_c(-8);
solver.find_discriminant();
std::cout << "x is: " << solver.solve() << std::endl;
```

The public interface of the class should be designed wisely; the preceding example shows signs of bad design. A user must know the protocol – that is, the exact order to call the functions. If the user misses the call to find_discriminant(), the result will be undefined or invalid. The public interface forces the user to learn the protocol and call functions in the proper order – that is, setting the values of a, b, and c, calling the find_discriminant() function, and finally, calling the solve() function to get the desired value of x. A good design should provide an easy public interface. We can overwrite QuadraticSolver so that it only has one function that takes all the necessary input values, calculates the discriminant and returns the solution:

```
class QuadtraticSolver {
public:
    QuadraticSolver() = default;
    double solve(double a, double b, double c);
};
```

The preceding design is more intuitive than the previous one. The following code demonstrates the usage of QuadraticSolver to find the solution to the equation $22 + 5x - 8 = 0$:

```
QuadraticSolver solver;
std::cout << solver.solve(2, 5, -8) << std::endl;
```

The last thing to consider here is the idea that a quadratic equation can be solved in more than one way. The one we introduced is solved by finding the discriminant. We should consider that, in the future, we could add further implementation methods to the class. Changing the name of the function may increase the readability of the public interface and secure future updates to the class. We should also note that the solve() function in the preceding example takes a, b, and c as arguments, and we don't need to store them in the class, since the solution is calculated directly in the function.

It's obvious that declaring an object of `QuadraticSolver` just to be able to access the `solve()` function seems to be a redundant step. The final design of the class will look like this:

```cpp
class QuadraticSolver {
public:
    QuadraticSolver() = delete;
    static double solve_by_discriminant(double a,
        double b, double c);
    // other solution methods' implementations can be
    // prefixed by "solve_by_"
};
```

We renamed the `solve()` function to `solve_by_discriminant()`, which also exposes the underneath method of the solution. We also made the function *static*, thus making it available to a user without declaring an instance of the class. However, we also marked the default constructor as *deleted*, which, again, forces the user not to declare an object:

```cpp
std::cout << QuadraticSolver::solve_by_discriminant(2, 5, -8) <<
std::endl;
```

The client code now spends less effort using the class.

Class relationships

Object intercommunication is at the heart of object-oriented systems. The relationship is the logical link between objects. The way we can distinguish or set up a proper relationship between classes of objects defines both the performance and quality of a system design overall. Consider the `Product` and `Warehouse` classes; they are in a relationship called aggregation because `Warehouse` contains `Products` – that is, `Warehouse` aggregates `Products`:

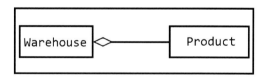

Figure 2.15 – A UML diagram of the relationship between the Warehouse and Product classes

There are several kinds of relationships in terms of pure OOP, such as association, aggregation, composition, instantiation, generalization, and others.

Aggregation and composition

We encountered aggregation in the Warehouse class example. The Warehouse class stores an array of Products. In more general terms, it can be called an *association*, but to strongly emphasize the exact containment, we use the terms *aggregation* or *composition*. In the case of aggregation, the class that contains an instance or instances of other classes can be instantiated without the aggregate. This means that we can create and use a Warehouse object without necessarily creating Product objects contained in Warehouse.

Another example of aggregation is Car and Person. A Car object can contain a Person object (as a driver or passenger), since they are associated with each other, but the containment is not strong. We can create a Car object without a Driver object in it, as follows:

```cpp
class Person; // forward declaration
class Engine { /* code omitted for brevity */ };
class Car {
public:
    Car();
    // ...
private:
    Person* driver_; // aggregation
    std::vector<Person*> passengers_; // aggregation
    Engine engine_; // composition
// ...
};
```

The strong containment is expressed by **composition**. For the Car example, an object of the Engine class is required to make a complete Car object. In this physical representation, the Engine member is automatically created when Car is created.

The following is the UML representation of aggregation and composition:

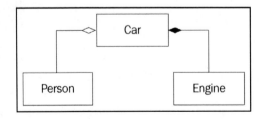

Figure 2.16 – An example of aggregation and composition expressed in a UML diagram

When designing classes, we have to decide on their relationship. The best way to define the composition between the two classes is the *has-a* relationship test. Car has Engine because a car has an engine. Anytime you can't decide whether a relationship should be expressed in terms of composition, ask the *has-a* question. Aggregation and composition are somewhat similar; they just describe the strength of the connection. For aggregation, the proper phrase would be *can have a*. For example, Car can have a driver (of the Person type) – that is, the containment is weak.

Another type of relationship that connects objects with each other is inheritance, and when talking about inheritance, we should also talk about polymorphism, as they go hand in hand.

Under the hood of inheritance and polymorphism

Inheritance and polymorphism are two of the four main principles that OOP has. The four principles are as follows:

- Abstraction
- Encapsulation
- Inheritance
- Polymorphism

We have already talked about the first two principles, and now it is time to dive deeper into the final two – inheritance and polymorphism.

Inheritance

Classes can be reused, thanks to the programming notion of inheritance. Different programming languages offer various inheritance implementations, but the underlying principle is always the same – the class relationship should answer the *is-a* question. For instance, Car is Vehicle; hence, we can inherit Car from Vehicle:

```
class Vehicle {
public:
    void move();
};
class Car : public Vehicle {
public:
    Car();
// ...
};
```

Car now has the move() member function derived from Vehicle. The relationship between generalization and specialization represented by inheritance is one in which the parent class (Vehicle) is the generalization, and the child class(Car)is the specialization.

> **Note**
>
> The child class can be referred to as the derived class or the subclass, whereas the parent class can be called the base class or the superclass.

Only in extreme cases should you consider using inheritance. Classes should satisfy the is-a relationship, as we noted previously, although this might occasionally be tricky. Consider the `Square` and `Rectangle` classes. The following code declares the `Rectangle` class in its simplest possible form:

```
class Rectangle {
public:
    // argument checks omitted for brevity
    void set_width(int w) { width_ = w; }
    void set_height(int h) { height_ = h; }
    int area() const { return width_ * height_; }
private:
    int width_;
    int height_;
};
```

The `Square` *is-a* `Rectangle`, so we could easily inherit it from `Rectangle`:

```
class Square : public Rectangle {
public:
    void set_side(int side) {
    set_width(side);
    set_height(side);
}
int area() {
    area_ = Rectangle::area();
    return area_;
}
private:
    int area_;
};
```

`Square` extends `Rectangle` by adding a new data member, `area_`, and overwriting the `area()` member function with its own implementation. In reality, `area_` and the method by which we calculate its value are redundant; we did this to highlight a poor class design and to make `Square` extend its parent to some extent. We'll soon conclude that choosing inheritance in this circumstance was a poor design decision. Since `Square` is a `Rectangle`, it should be used anywhere `Rectangle` is used, as demonstrated here:

```
void make_big_rectangle(Rectangle& ref) {
    ref->set_width(870);
    ref->set_height(940);
```

```
}
int main() {
    Rectangle rect;
    make_big_rectangle(rect);
    Square sq;
    // Square is a Rectangle
    make_big_rectangle(sq);
}
```

The make_big_rectangle() function takes a reference to Rectangle and Square inherits it, so it's totally fine to send a Square object to the make_big_rectangle() function; Square *is-a* a Rectangle. The Liskov Substitution Principle is an instance of a successful **type substitution** with its subtype. Decide whether it was a mistake to inherit the square from the rectangle after learning why this substitution works in practice.

Inheritance from the compiler perspective

We can picture the Rectangle class we declared earlier in the following way:

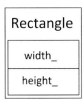

Figure 2.17 – The diagram of a Rectangle class

The stack space needed for the local objects of a function is allocated when the rect object is declared in the main() function. When the make_big_rectangle() method is used, the same logic is applied. It doesn't have local arguments; instead, it has an argument of the Rectangle& type, which behaves in a similar fashion to a pointer – it takes the memory space required to store a memory address (4 or 8 bytes in 32- and 64-bit systems respectively). The rect object is passed to make_big_rectangle() by reference, which means the ref argument refers to the local object in main():

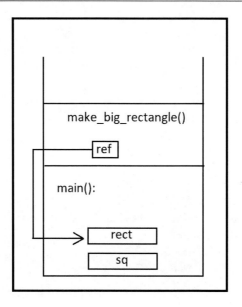

Figure 2.18 – The effect of passing by reference

Here is an illustration of the Square class:

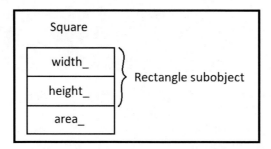

Figure 2.19 – The visual representation of a Square class that contains a Rectangle subobject

The Square object includes a subobject of Rectangle, as seen in the preceding diagram; it serves as a partial representation of Rectangle. In this instance, the Square class doesn't add any additional data members to the rectangle.

Although make_big_rectangle() accepts an argument of the Rectangle& type, the Square object is passed to it. We are aware that in order to access the underlying object, the type of the pointer (reference) is required. The type specifies how many bytes should be read from the pointer's starting location. In this case, ref stores a copy of the starting address of the local rect object declared in main(). When make_big_rectangle() accesses the member functions via ref, it actually calls global functions that take a `Rectangle` reference as their first parameter. The following is the function's translation (again, we have somewhat adjusted it for simplicity):

```
void make_big_rectangle(Rectangle * const ref) {
Rectangle_set_width(*ref, 870);
Rectangle_set_height(*ref, 940);
}
```

When `ref` is dereferenced, `sizeof(Rectangle)` bytes are read from the beginning of the memory address that `ref` points to. When we pass a `Square` object to `make_big_rectangle()`, we assign the starting address of `sq` (the `Square` object) to `ref`. Because the `Square` object really has a `Rectangle` subobject, this will work just fine. When the `make_big_rectangle()` function dereferences `ref`, it is only able to access the `sizeof(Rectangle)` bytes of the object and doesn't see the additional bytes of the actual `Square` object. The following diagram illustrates the part of the subobject that `ref` points to:

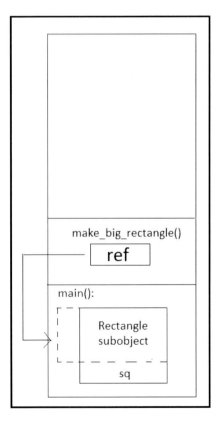

Figure 2.20 – The illustration of ref pointing to the Rectangle subobject

Inheriting `Square` from `Rectangle` is almost the same as declaring two structs, one of which (the child) contains the other (the parent):

```
struct Rectangle {
    int width_;
    int height_;
};

void Rectangle_set_width(Rectangle& this, int w) {
    this.width_ = w;
}

void Rectangle_set_height(Rectangle& this, int h) {
    this.height_ = h;
}

int Rectangle_area(const Rectangle& this) {
    return this.width_ * this.height_;
}

struct Square {
    Rectangle _parent_subobject_;
    int area_;
};

void Square_set_side(Square& this, int side) {
    // Rectangle_set_width(static_cast<Rectangle&>(this),
    // side);
    Rectangle_set_width(this._parent_subobject_, side);
    // Rectangle_set_height(static_cast<Rectangle&>(this),
    // side);
    Rectangle_set_height(this._parent_subobject_, side);
}

int Square_area(Square& this) {
    // this.area_ = Rectangle_area(
    // static_cast<Rectangle&>(this));
    this.area_ = Rectangle_area(this._parent_subobject_);
    return this.area_;
}
```

The preceding code shows how inheritance is supported by the compiler. Take a look at the commented lines of code for `Square_set_side` and `Square_area functions`. Although we don't really insist on this implementation, it perfectly captures how the compiler handles OOP code.

Composition versus inheritance

Although the compiler treats the inheritance relationship more like a composition than an inheritance, the C++ language gives us a straightforward and OOP-friendly syntax to describe it. Instead of using inheritance wherever possible, it is really far preferable to use composition. It was claimed that the link between the `Square` and `Rectangle` classes was a poor design decision. One of the reasons was the subtype substitution principle, which allowed us to use `Square` incorrectly by passing it to a function that transforms it into `Rectangle` instead of `Square`. This reveals that `Square` is not `Rectangle` after all, proving that the *is-a* connection is incorrect. It is an adaptation of `Rectangle` rather than `Rectangle` itself. Therefore, it doesn't exactly represent `Rectangle`; instead, it makes use of one to give class users certain restricted functionality.

Users shouldn't be aware that `Square` can be used as `Rectangle` because, if they did, they might at some time send incorrect or unsupported messages to `Square` instances. Calls to the `set_width` or `set_height` functions are examples of invalid messages. Since it declared that it had inherited from `Rectangle`, `Square` cannot truly allow two independent member methods to change each of its sides separately:

```
class Square : public Rectangle {
// code omitted for brevity
};
```

What if the modifier is private instead of public? Both public and private inheritance types are supported by C++. Additionally, protected inheritance is also supported. When inheriting privately from a class, the subclass intends to use the parent class and has access to its public interface. The client code, however, is unaware that it is inherited from a derived class. In addition, users of the child class no longer have access to the public interface that was inherited from the parent class. `Square` appears to convert inheritance into composition:

```
class Square : private Rectangle {
public:
    void set_side(int side) {
    // Rectangle's public interface is accessible to
    // the Square
    set_width(side);
    set_height(side);
    }
    int area() {
        area_ = Rectangle::area();
        return area_;
    }
private:
    int area_;
};
```

The client code cannot access members inherited from `Rectangle`:

```
Square sq;
sq.set_width(14); // compile error, the Square has no such
                  // public member
make_big_rectangle(sq); // compile error, can't cast Square
                        // to Rectangle
```

The same can be achieved by declaring a `Rectangle` member in the private section of `Square`:

```
class Square {
public:
    void set_side(int side) {
    rectangle_.set_width(side);
    rectangle_.set_height(side);
    }
    int area() {
        area_ = rectangle_.area();
        return area_;
    }
private:
    Rectangle rectangle_;
    int area_;
};
```

To use inheritance without a doubt, you should thoroughly examine use situations and provide a clear answer to the *is-a* question. When given the option between composition and inheritance, always pick composition.

We can omit the modifier when inheriting privately. The default access modifier for classes is private, so `class Square : private Rectangle {};` is the same as the `Square : Rectangle {};` class. Conversely, the default modifier for structs is public.

Protected inheritance

Finally, we have the protected access modifier. If class members are used in the class body, it describes the access level of those members. Users of the class can't access protected members, but derived classes can. If the modifier is used to specify the type of inheritance, it behaves similarly to the private inheritance for derived class users. Protected inheritance makes the public interface of the base class visible to descendants of the derived class, whereas private inheritance keeps it hidden from all users of the derived class.

Although it's difficult to see a situation where protected inheritance would be necessary, you should consider it as a tool that can be helpful in surprisingly obvious designs. Let's say we need to create an adapter for a stack data structure. Typically, a dequeue, a linked list, or a vector (a one-dimensional array) is used to implement the stack.

Here's a tip – the stack conforms to the LIFO rule, which states that the last element inserted into the stack will be accessed first. Similarly, the first element inserted into the stack will be accessed last.

The stack doesn't actually represent a data structure; rather, it sits on top of one and modifies, extends, or restricts how it is used. The following is a simple declaration of the Vector class representing a one-dimensional array of integers:

```
class Vector {
public:
    Vector();
    Vector(const Vector&);
    Vector(Vector&&) noexcept;
    Vector& operator=(const Vector&);
    Vector& operator=(Vector&&) noexcept;
    ~Vector();
public:
    void push_back(int value);
    void insert(int index, int value);
    void remove(int index);
    int operator[](int index);
    int size() const;
    int capacity() const;
private:
    int size_;
    int capacity_;
    int* array_;
};
```

The preceding Vector is not an STL-compatible container with random access iterator support; it contains the bare minimum for a dynamically increasing array. It can be declared and used in the following way:

```
Vector v;
v.push_back(4);
v.push_back(5);
v[1] = 2;
```

While the Vector class has operation[], which enables random access to any of its components, Stack forbids such access. Stack offers the push and pop operations so that we can, respectively, enter a value into its underlying data structure and get the value:

```
class Stack : private Vector {
public:
// constructors, assignment operators and the destructor
// are omitted for brevity
    void push(int value) {
```

```
    push_back(value);
    }
    int pop() {
        int value{this[size() - 1]};
        remove(size() - 1);
        return value;
    }
};
```

Stack can be used in the following way:

```
Stack s;
s.push(5);
s.push(6);
s.push(3);
std::cout << s.pop(); // outputs 3
std::cout << s.pop(); // outputs 6
s[2] = 42; // compile error, the Stack has no publicly
           // available operator[] defined
```

In order for us to access it, the stack adjusts Vector and offers two member functions. We can fully use Vector while hiding Stack to prevent users from knowing about the inheritance. What if we want to inherit Stack to create an advanced version of it? Let's imagine that the AdvancedStack class offers the min() function, which delivers the stack's lowest value in constant time.

The private inheritance prohibits AdvancedStack so that it uses the public interface of Vector, so we need a way to allow the Stack subclasses to use its base class but hide the base class's existence from class users. Protected inheritance serves that goal, as shown in the following code:

```
class Stack : protected Vector {
// code omitted for brevity
};
class AdvancedStack : public Stack {
// can use the Vector
};
```

By inheriting Stack from Vector, we allow the subclass of the Stack to use the Vector public interface. However, the users of both Stack and AdvancedStack won't be able to access them as Vector.

Polymorphism

Another crucial concept in OOP is polymorphism. It permits subclasses to implement the methods that are descended from the base class in their own unique ways. Consider the `Musician` class, which contains the `play()` member method:

```
class Musician {
public:
    void play() { std::cout << "Play an instrument"; }
};
```

Now, let's declare the `Guitarist` class, which has the `play_guitar()` function:

```
class Guitarist {
public:
    void play_guitar() { std::cout << "Play a guitar"; }
};
```

This is an obvious case of using inheritance because `Guitarist` just screams that it *is-a* `Musician`. It would make sense for `Guitarist` to provide its own version of the `play()` method, rather than extending `Musician` by adding a new function (such as `play_guitar()`). We can make use of virtual functions to do this:

```
class Musician {
public:
    virtual void play() { std::cout << "Play an instrument"; }
};

class Guitarist : public Musician {
public:
    void play() override { std::cout << "Play a guitar"; }
};
```

Now, it's obviousthat the `Guitarist` class provides its own implementation to the `play()` function, and that the client code can access it by just using the pointer to the base class:

```
Musician armstrong;
Guitarist steve;
Musician* m = &armstrong;
m->play();
m = &steve;
m->play();
```

The preceding code snippet demonstrates polymorphism in action. Although using virtual functions is natural, unless we implement it correctly, it doesn't really make much sense. First of all, the play() function of Musician should not have any implementation at all. The explanation is straightforward – since a musician cannot play more than one instrument at once, they should be able to play a certain instrument. By giving the function a value of 0, we make it a pure virtual function to get rid of the implementation:

```
class Musician {
public:
    virtual void play() = 0;
};
```

When the client code tries to declare an instance of Musician, a compile error occurs. Since you shouldn't be able to build an object with an *undefined* function, it must result in a compilation error. Musician has just one purpose, and additional classes are required to inherit it. An abstract class is a class that is designed to be inherited. Instead of being an abstract class, Musician is actually called an interface. An abstract class is a semi-interface semi-class that can have both types of functions – with and without implementation.

Getting back to our example, let's add the Pianist class, which also implements the Musician interface:

```
class Pianist : public Musician {
public:
    void play() override { std::cout << "Play a piano"; }
};
```

Let's assume we have a function declared somewhere that returns a collection of musicians, either guitarists or pianists, to demonstrate the full potential of polymorphism:

```
std::vector<Musician*> get_musicians();
```

It is challenging for the client code to evaluate the get_musicians() function's return value and determine the object's actual subtype. It may be Guitarist, Pianist, or just Musician in general. The point is that the client shouldn't really care about the actual type of objects, as it knows that the collection contains Musicians and a Musician object has the play() function. Since each object calls its implementation, the client only needs to loop through the collection to get each musician to play their appropriate instrument:

```
auto all_musicians = get_musicians();
for (const auto& m: all_musicians) {
m->play();
}
```

The whole potential of polymorphism is expressed in the preceding code. Let's now examine the language's low-level support for polymorphism.

Virtual functions under the hood

Although virtual functions are not the only instances of polymorphism, we will focus more on them because dynamic polymorphism is the most common type of polymorphism in C++. Once again, using a concept or technology on your own is the best way to understand it better. Whether we declare a virtual member function in a class or it has a base class with virtual functions, the compiler augments the class with an additional pointer. The pointer points to a table that's usually referred to as a virtual functions table, or simply a *virtual table*. We also refer to the pointer as the *virtual table pointer*.

Let's imagine we are developing a class subsystem to manage bank customers' accounts. Let's say the bank requests that we implement cashing out based on the kind of account. For example, a savings account allows you to cash out money once a year, while a checking account allows you to cash out money whenever a customer wants. Let's define the bare essentials to understand virtual member methods without going into any superfluous information regarding the Account class. We'll examine the definition of the Account class:

```
class Account
{
public:
    virtual void cash_out() {
    // the default implementation for cashing out
    }
    virtual ~Account() {}
private:
    double balance_;
};
```

The Account class is converted by a compiler into a structure, with a pointer to the virtual functions table. The pseudocode that follows demonstrates what occurs when we declare virtual functions in a class. As always, keep in mind that we offer an explanation, rather than an implementation that is unique to a particular compiler (the name mangling is also in a generic form – for example, we rename cash_out Account_cash_out):

```
struct Account
{
    VTable* __vptr;
    double balance_;
};
void Account_constructor(Account* this) {
    this->__vptr = &Account_VTable;
}
void Account_cash_out(Account* this) {
    // the default implementation for cashing out
}
void Account_destructor(Account* this) {}
```

Take a good look at the preceding pseudocode. The first member of the `Account` struct is named `__vptr`. Due to the two virtual functions that were previously defined for the `Account` class, we can think of the virtual table as an array containing two pointers to virtual member functions. See the following representation:

```
VTable Account_VTable[] = {
&Account_cash_out,
&Account_destructor
};
```

Let's figure out what code the compiler will produce when we call a virtual function on an object, using our prior assumptions as a guide:

```
// consider the get_account() function as already
//implemented and returning an Account*
Account* ptr = get_account();
ptr->cash_out();
```

Here's what we can imagine the compiler's generated code to be like for the preceding code:

```
Account* ptr = get_account();
ptr->__vptr[0]();
```

Virtual functions show their power when they're used in hierarchies. `SavingsAccount` inherits from the `Account` class, like so:

```
class SavingsAccount : public Account
{
public:
void cash_out() override {
// an implementation specific to SavingsAccount
}
virtual ~SavingsAccount() {}
};
```

When we call `cash_out()` via a pointer (or a reference), the virtual function is invoked based on the target object that the pointer points to. Let's say, for instance, that the `get savings_account()` function returns `SavingsAccount` as `Account*`. The following code will call the `SavingsAccount` implementation of `cash_out()`:

```
Account* p = get_savings_account();
p->cash_out(); // calls SavingsAccount version of the cash_out
```

Here's what the compiler generates for `SavingsClass`:

```
struct SavingsAccount
{
    Account _parent_subobject_;
    VTable* __vptr;
};
VTable* SavingsAccount_VTable[] = {
    &SavingsAccount_cash_out,
    &SavingsAccount_destructor,
};
void SavingsAccount_constructor(SavingsAccount* this) {
    this->__vptr = &SavingsAccount_VTable;
}
void SavingsAccount_cash_out(SavingsAccount* this) {
    // an implementation specific to SavingsAccount
}
void SavingsAccount_destructor(SavingsAccount* this) {}
```

Thus, we have two separate tables of virtual functions. The __vptr of an object of the Account type points to Account_VTable when it is created, whereas an object of the SavingsAccount type has its own __vptr that points to SavingsAccount_VTable. Let's take a look at the following code:

```
p->cash_out();
```

The preceding code translates into this:

```
p->__vptr[0]();
```

Now, it's obvious that __vptr[0] resolves to the correct function because it is read via the p pointer.

What if SavingsAccount doesn't override the cash_out() function? In that case, the compiler just places the address of the base class implementation in the same slot as SavingsAccount_ VTable, as shown here:

```
VTable* SavingsAccount_VTable[] = {
// the slot contains the base class version
// if the derived class doesn't have an implementation
&Account_cash_out,
&SavingsAccount_destructor
};
```

The representation and management of virtual functions are implemented differently by compilers. Some implementations use even different models, rather than the one we introduced earlier. For the purpose of simplicity, we introduced a well-liked strategy and presented it in a generalized manner.

Now that we have covered the technical part of OOP and understood how to use this paradigm in our programs, it is time to learn how to correctly use it based on the type of problem we deal with. There are accepted best practices on how to design your classes, based on the problem you are going to solve. Those designs are also known as *design patterns*.

Classical design patterns

Design patterns are powerful tools for programmers to use. They enable us to find beautiful and tried-and-true solutions to design problems. A well-known design pattern can help you when you are attempting to create the optimal layout for your classes and the relationships between them.

Reusing effective designs and architectures is made simpler by design patterns. It is easier for developers of new systems to use proven techniques when they are expressed as design patterns. Design patterns assist you in selecting design options that enhance reusability and avoiding those that do not. Even documentation and maintenance of current systems can be enhanced by design patterns. Design patterns, in other words, facilitate the creation of "correct" designs more quickly.

"Who created design patterns?" is a question you might ask, and the answer is both no one and everyone. It is no one because there is no specific person to whom we can ascribe the creation of design patterns, and it is everyone because many people had the idea of using a particular design that turned out to solve relatable problems. Then, a group known as the *Gang of Four* decided to gather those ideas, name them, and write a book, making them available to everyone.

It is also interesting to mention that the concept of patterns was first introduced by Christopher Alexander in his book *A Pattern Language: Towns, Buildings, Construction*, which had nothing to do with programming.

In the book by the Gang of Four, it is written that every design pattern has four essential elements:

- The pattern name
- The problem
- The solution
- The consequences

The **pattern name** serves as a handle that allows us to succinctly summarize a design problem, potential solutions, and outcomes. Naming a pattern instantly expands our understanding of design. It enables us to design at a more abstract level. We can discuss patterns with our coworkers, in our documentation, and even just among ourselves when we have a name for them. It makes it simpler to describe designs and their trade-offs to others and to conceptualize new ones.

The **problem** outlines when to use the pattern. It discusses the problem and its circumstances. It could go into detail about specific design problems, such as how to express algorithms as objects. It could refer to class or object structures that show signs of rigid design. There could be a list of prerequisites in the problem before it makes sense to use the pattern.

The **solution** outlines the components of the design, as well as their relationships, responsibilities, and cooperation. Because a pattern is like a template that can be used in several different scenarios, the solution does not specify a specific actual design or implementation. Instead, the pattern offers an abstract explanation of a design problem and how it is resolved by a standard arrangement of pieces (in our instance, classes and objects).

The outcomes and trade-offs of using a pattern are the **consequences**. Consequences for software sometimes include time and space trade-offs. They could also involve implementation and language issues.

Previously, we talked about the elements every design pattern has and in the first element which is a name we talked about the convenience of discussing this or that design pattern with a coworker. But if our coworker doesn't know the design pattern by name, how should we describe it?

To describe a design pattern, we can use the following aspects:

- **Intent**: A description of both the problem and the solution, which suggests the design pattern to solve the problem

- **Motivation**: An additional example of a design problem and a solution that design suggests, based on the class and object structure

- **Structure**: A class diagram illustrating the many components of the pattern and their relationships

- **Participants**: The classes that are used by the design pattern and their responsibilities

- **Code sample**: The implementation in one of the programming languages

A **singleton** is the most basic illustration of a design pattern. We can define and use just one instance of a class. Assume, for instance, that an e-commerce platform just has one `Warehouse`. The project may need us to include and use the `Warehouse` class in several source files in order to have access to it. Make `Warehouse` a singleton so that everything is in sync:

```cpp
class Warehouse {
public:
    static Warehouse* create_instance() {
        if (instance_ == nullptr) {
            instance_ = new Warehouse();
        }
        return instance_;
    }
    static void remove_instance() {
        delete instance_;
        instance_ = nullptr;
    }
private:
    Warehouse() = default;
    inline static Warehouse* instance_ = nullptr;
};
```

Two static methods to construct and delete the matching instance were declared along with a static `Warehouse` object. Every time a user attempts to define a `Warehouse` object using the private constructor, a compilation error occurs. The client code must use the `create_instance()` method in order to access `Warehouse`:

```
Warehouse* w = Warehouse::create_instance();
Product book;
w->add_product(book);
Warehouse::remove_instance();
```

The `Warehouse` object's singleton implementation is not complete and serves just as a demonstration of design patterns.

Design patterns overall can be classified into three categories:

- **Creational patterns**: These describe how to create more complex structures out of objects and classes while making these structures adaptable and effective

- **Structural patterns**: These provide a variety of object generation techniques, increasing code reuse and flexibility

- **Behavioral patterns**: These are focused on algorithms and the distribution of responsibilities among objects

Further, we are going to discuss two of the structural design patterns that are both similar and different – composite and decorator.

The composite pattern

When it's necessary to handle a collection of items similar to a single object, a composite pattern is used. To depict a section of a hierarchy as well as its entirety, a composite pattern combines elements in terms of a tree structure. This kind of design pattern falls under the category of a structural pattern, since it builds a tree structure out of a collection of elements.

According to the book by the **Gang of Four** (also known as the **GoF**), the composite design pattern has the following intent: *"Compose objects into tree structures to represent part-whole hierarchies. Composite lets clients treat individual objects and compositions of objects uniformly."*

The simplest example we can come up with is something that can contain itself and also other things that don't contain anything. Let us take, for example, a box. A box can contain anything that fits in it, such as books, phones, or a refrigerator. A box can also contain another box, both along with books and phones and also without them. The following figure shows this:

Figure 2.21 – A box that can contain another box and other items (a book in this example)

Now, let's continue with this scenario and consider that we have to count all the books that are inside the box. We know that the box can contain either a book or another box, and that logic applies to all boxes. We can open all the boxes, take out the books, and count them, which sounds easy in the real world. However, when that idea is used in programming, it becomes difficult because of the many nesting levels.

The composite pattern suggests a solution to this problem. The solution is to return the number of books in the box, and if the box contains another box, then the method should go through that box too, using the same logic. What composite really suggests here is not caring at all about what type of thing we are dealing with, as we treat them all the same way with the help of a common interface.

The common interface that the composite pattern provides is called a component, the object that can't contain itself (in our example, the books) is called a leaf, and the object that can contain itself is called a composite. The UML diagram for the composite design pattern is as follows:

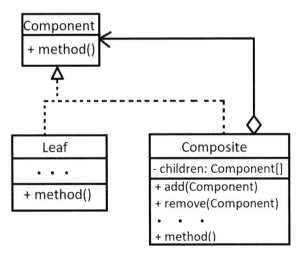

Figure 2.22 – A UML diagram of a composite design pattern

As we can see in the diagram, both `Leaf` and `Composite` implement `Component`. `Composite` can also add and remove components, which can turn out to be either `Leaf` or `Composite`.

As previously stated, the composite pattern combines elements in terms of a tree structure. Based on this statement, we can also draw the tree structure of a `Composite` object that can be formed from this design pattern.

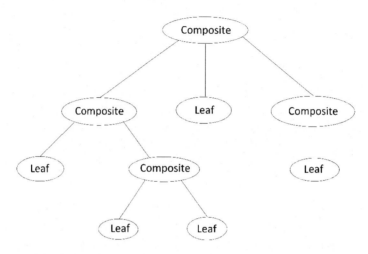

Figure 2.23 – The tree structure of a composite design pattern

The next aspect that describes a design pattern is the participants. The participants of the composite design pattern are obviously the component, the composite, and the leaf.

The **component** defines the composition's object's interface (when necessary), provides the default behavior for the interface shared by all classes, defines a management and access interface for its child components, and specifies (or, if necessary, implements) an interface to gain access to a component's parent in a recursive structure.

The **composite** describes how the components that have children should behave, stores components as its children, and implements operations relating to children in the component interface.

The **leaf** represents the composition's leaf objects; it cannot have children and describes how primitive objects should behave in the composition.

Clients communicate with objects in the composite structure using the `Component` class interface. Requests are processed directly if the receiver is a leaf. The receiver typically transmits requests to its child components if it is a composite, sometimes performing extra operations before or after forwarding.

Let us further discuss the composite design pattern with the help of an example. The example will be based on a task management system. Let's imagine that we have to write a program that allows a user to add tasks and also tasks with subtasks. The simple tasks we will call simply *tasks*, while other tasks that have subtasks we will call *projects*. The first and most basic UML diagram of our program will look like this:

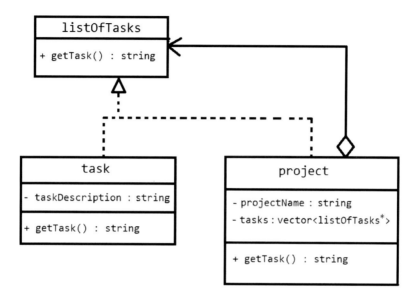

Figure 2.24 – A UML diagram of a program based on a composite design pattern

Note that the diagram is just an example and many methods are omitted for brevity.

The code representation of the preceding UML diagram is as follows:

```
class ListOfTasks {
public:
// code omitted for brevity
    virtual std::string getTask() = 0;
};

class Task : public ListOfTasks {
public:
    // code omitted for brevity
    std::string getTask();
private:
    std::string taskDescription;
};
```

```
class Project : public ListOfTasks {
public:
    // code omitted for brevity
    std::string getTask();
private:
    std::string projectName;
    std::vector<ListOfTasks*> tasks;
};
```

In our code, we only wrote the declaration of the classes and their data members, and also function prototypes. Many things are omitted in our code, including constructors, functions that add tasks or projects, and functions that help us set deadlines, mark completed tasks or projects, and so on. We will try to implement most of those functions but not all of them because it will become very long code, and we don't want to bore you. The code of the described program is as follows:

```
#include <vector>
#include <string>

class listOfTasks {
public:
    virtual void setTask(std::string) = 0;
    virtual std::string getTask() const = 0;
    virtual bool isDone() const = 0;
    virtual void setDeadline(std::string) = 0;
    virtual std::string getDeadline() const = 0;
};

class Task : public ListOfTasks {
public:
    Task() : m_task_description{}, m_done(false){}
    Task(std::string task) : m_task_description(task) {}
    Task(std::string task, std::string deadline) :
        m_task_description(task)
        {
            this->setDeadline(deadline);
        }
    void setTask(std::string task)
    {
        m_task_description = task;
    }
    std::string getTask() const {

        return (m_task_description + "\t---\t" +
```

```
            this->getDeadline() + '\n');
    }
    void setDeadline(std::string deadline)
    {
        m_deadline = deadline;
    }
    std::string getDeadline() const
    {
        return m_deadline;
    }
    void markDone()
    {
        m_done = true;
    }
    bool isDone() const
    {
        return (m_done == true);
    }
private:
    std::string m_task_description;
    std::string m_deadline;
    bool m_done;
};
```

The implementation of the `Project` class which inherits from `ListOfTasks` can be found on our GitHub account.

As you can see, we implemented the functionalities of our program following the concept of the composite design pattern. Our code is not complete; you can add different variations of parametrized constructors, destructors, and also a lot of functionality. The names of the functions can also be changed based on your preferences. In this coding example, we can see that there are pure virtual functions in our base class that have to be overridden in the children classes. The `getTask()` function perfectly depicts the concept of the composite design pattern. It treats everything as a task, also going inside the projects in order to find tasks there. It also bears the concept of tree traversals, which are discussed in further chapters.

Another key part of our program includes an array of the `listOfTasks*` type. It is the most logical thing to do. A composite can contain itself and also leaves, and in our case, our project can contain both tasks and also other projects, which is why we have chosen the `listOfTasks*` type so that we can create objects of both the `task` and `project` types. This is allowed because both inherit from the `listOfTasks` class.

By discussing the pattern, bringing examples, and drawing diagrams, we can introduce "rules" to implement the design pattern. They are as follows:

- Breaking down your project to understand what parts it consists of. If the project can be broken down into parts that can be structured into a tree, then you can use the composite design pattern. After breaking down the project into elements and arrays, you have to make sure that the array can hold types corresponding to both of those objects.

- Making a container class to hold complicated items. Provide an array to keep references to child components in this class. The array should be of the `component` type because it is going to store both the `leaves` and `composite` objects.

- Creating a component interface with functions that make sense for both the `leaves` and `composite` objects.

- Declaring and implementing `add` and `remove` functions in the `composite` class is better. The leaves shouldn't be able to add or remove anything, which is why it is better to declare those functions in the composite class and not in the component.

Summing up everything we have talked about, we can conclude that the composite design pattern is a great choice if you are going to work with complicated tree structures, as they make it easier to do by using recursion and polymorphism. Besides that, this design pattern adheres to one of the key design principles – the open-closed principle, which states that "*objects or entities should be open for extension but closed for modification.*"

The next design pattern we are going to discuss is a decorator pattern, which is kind of similar to the composite design pattern. We are not only going to discuss the properties of the decorator design pattern but also the differences between these two patterns that have similarities.

The decorator pattern

With the use of a structural design pattern called *decorator*, you can give existing objects new behaviors by enclosing them in special wrapper objects that also contain the new behaviors. Sometimes, we want to apply obligations to specific objects rather than a class as a whole.

Let us imagine that we have an application that allows us to edit photos. We import a photo and it is too long, so there is a need to add a scroll button. The scroll button is not always necessary because our picture can fit into the application size, and there would be no need to add one. Therefore, everything should be decided during runtime, and we shouldn't force our application to have a scroll button if it doesn't need it. Clients are not in charge of deciding how and when to add a scroller to our application, also called a component.

Enclosing the component in another object and adding the scroller provides a more adaptable strategy. Decorator is a term used to describe the enclosing object. The decorator might do something before or after sending requests to the component. You can recursively layer decorators thanks to transparency, which opens the door to an infinite number of extra responsibilities.

We should use the decorator design pattern in the following scenarios:

- If we want to dynamically and transparently assign responsibilities to specific objects – that is, without impacting other objects.

- If it is impossible to extend through subclassing. Sometimes, when we use the subclassing method, our program results in a class explosion, which looks like this:

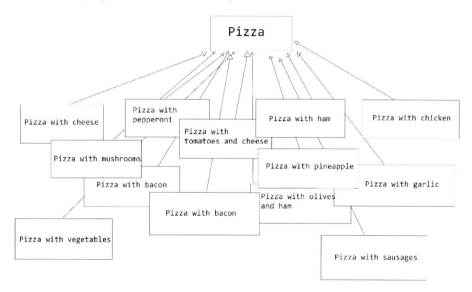

Figure 2.25 – An example of a class explosion

Based on our description, it is not that easy to guess the structure of the design pattern. We don't expect you to draw this structure yourself; instead, we will give you the real structure that this design pattern has. It consists of a component, a concrete component, a decorator, and a concrete decorator. A visual representation is as follows:

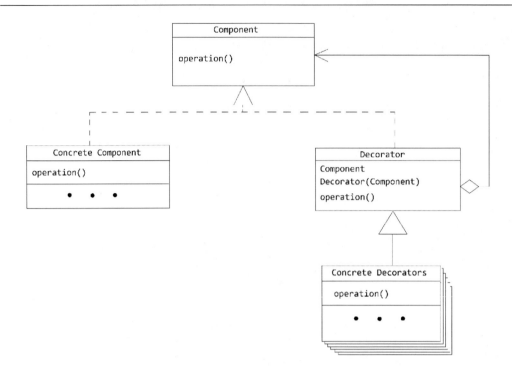

Figure 2.26 – A UML diagram of a decorator design pattern

If we ignore **Concrete Decorators** and the names in our structure, we can see that the structure of the decorator design pattern is similar to the structure of the composite design pattern. What is different is the part that said to ignore for comparing those two patterns.

The component specifies the interface for objects that may have dynamically assigned responsibilities, the concrete component specifies an object to which extra responsibilities can be assigned, the decorator keeps track of an instance of a **Component** object and creates an interface that complies with that of **Component**, and the concrete decorators add new responsibilities to the component.

The **Decorator** pattern should be used with a number of considerations in mind. For example, you shouldn't use this design pattern if you are going to add only one responsibility. As we have already said, we use the pattern to avoid class explosions, and if you think that your code is going to end up being one of the big explosions, then and only then you should consider using a decorator design pattern. As we have a common parent for both the decorator and the component, it is vital to keep the parent class as simple as possible. Subclasses should be given the responsibility to define the data representation; otherwise, the complexity of the Component class can make it difficult to apply decorators often. The likelihood of concrete subclasses paying for things they don't need arises when the component has a lot of functionality.

We have discussed class explosion, and the example was based on one of the most popular foods. We had pizza and pizza variations in our illustration. Let us imagine that there is a pizzeria that suggests buyers choose whatever topping they want, and a pizza without topping is a pizza with marinara sauce and one type of cheese. The customers can add whatever topping they want with different combinations. In this case, even if the pizzeria had only 10 ingredients, the number of variations will be a number that is equal to the factorial of 10, which is 3,628,800. With that many classes inheriting from a single class, it would be bigger than just an explosion (probably the end of the programming world). Decorator design patterns come in handy here to save our fast-growing programming world.

Let us consider a case where we have to write a program that can help a seller to get the price of the pizza, based on what topping the customer decided to add. In the following example, we demonstrate a definition of the classes that are connected over the logic of the decorator design pattern, as well as the implementation of the price function and the parametrized constructors. The code looks as follows:

```cpp
#include <iostream>
#include <vector>

class ItalianFood {
public:
    virtual ~ItalianFood() {}
    virtual int price() const = 0;
};

class Pizza : public ItalianFood {
public:
    int price() const override {
        return 8;
    }
};

class Topping : public ItalianFood {
protected:
    ItalianFood* m_component;
public:
    Topping(ItalianFood* component) :
      m_component(component) {
    }
    int price() const override {
        return this->m_component->price();
    }
};

class Pepperoni : public Topping {
public:
    Pepperoni(ItalianFood* component) :
      Topping(component) {}
```

```
    int price() const override {
        return 2 + Topping::price();
    }
};

class Ham : public Topping {
public:
    Ham(ItalianFood* component) : Topping(component) {}
    int price() const override {
        return 3 + Topping::price();
    }
};

//helper function to display the total price
void displayTotal(ItalianFood *component) {
    std::cout << "The total is " << component->price() << '$';
}
```

The preceding code looks somewhat similar to the code we demonstrated when we discussed the composite design pattern. We have the same inheritance hierarchy, but what is different in this code is the data member it holds, which is only one component. So, we can say that besides the structural difference, another difference is that in the decorator design pattern, the decorator has only one component, while in the composite design pattern, the composite contains multiple components. If we try to change the decorator and make it decorate multiple components, it will eventually become a composite design pattern, as it will form a tree-like structure. If we compare those structures as diagrams, they are different in the following way:

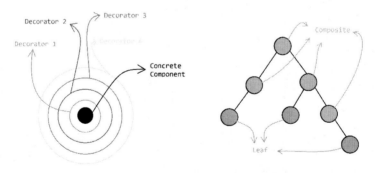

The form of the objects when applied the decorator pattern

The form of the objects when applied the composite pattern

Figure 2.27 – The formation of objects when decorator and composite design patterns are applied

So, anytime you design a program that is going to look like a tree, use the composite design pattern, and if you are going to wrap an object at some point, use the decorator design pattern.

We also mentioned that the composite design pattern adheres to the open-closed principle, while the decorator design pattern mostly adheres to the single responsibility principle, as a large class that implements all potential behavior variants can be broken down into multiple smaller classes. Meanwhile, if you decide to use the decorator design pattern, don't forget that it has some disadvantages, such as removing a certain wrapper from the stack of wrappers, or creating a decorator so that its behavior is independent of the position in the decorator's stack.

While design patterns help us design our projects in a specific way for a specific problem, design principles are universal for all types of projects.

Design principles

You can use a variety of principles and design techniques while creating your project. While keeping the design basic is usually preferable, there are certain fundamental rules that apply to practically all projects. For instance, SOLID is composed of five principles, all of which – or parts of them – can be beneficial to a design.

SOLID stands for the following principles:

- Single responsibility

- Open-closed

- Liskov substitution

- Interface segregation

- Dependency inversion

Let's discuss each principle with examples.

The single responsibility principle

The idea of one object and one job is what the single responsibility principle asserts. Try to simplify the functionality of your objects and the intricacy of their relationships. Even if breaking down a large object into smaller, simpler components isn't always simple, give each object a single task. Single responsibility is a context-bound concept. It's not about having just one method in a class; it's also about making the class or module responsible for one thing. For instance, the following User class just has one duty – saving user data:

```cpp
class User
{
public:
```

```
// constructors and assignment operators are omitted
// for code brevity
    void set_name(const std::string& name);
    std::string get_name() const;
    void set_email(const std::string&);
    std::string get_email() const;
// more setters and getters are omitted for code brevity
private:
    std::string name_;
    std::string email_;
    Address address_;
    int age;
};
```

However, we can compel the User class to include methods to add and delete payment options. Additionally, we can add a new type, PaymentOption. A user can have more than one payment option, so the relationship between User and PaymentOption is one-to-many, and the UML diagram looks like this:

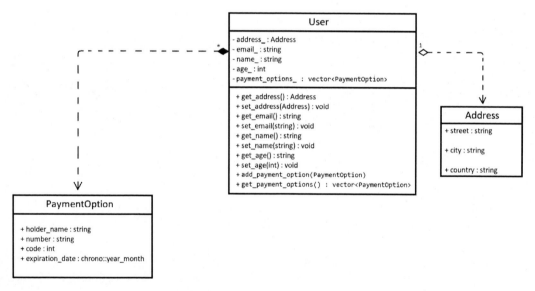

Figure 2.28 – The UML diagram

With this example, we can move in two directions. The first one suggests splitting the User class into two distinct classes. Each class will be in charge of just one thing. The concept is shown in the following class diagram:

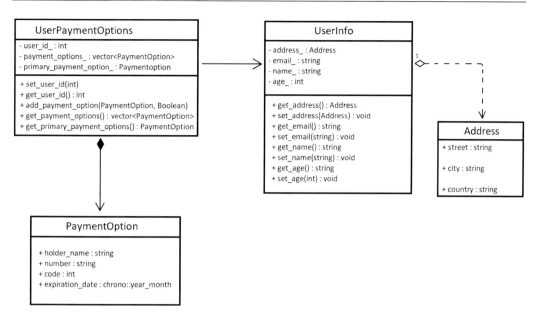

Figure 2.29 – A UML diagram of a program based on the decorator design pattern

Only the user's basic information will be stored in one of them, while the user's payment options will be stored in the other. Accordingly, we gave them the names `UserInfo` and `UserPaymentOptions`. Although some people might like the new design, we'll keep using the old one, and here's why. Though the `User` class contains both user information and payment options, the latter also represents a piece of information. We set and get payment options in the same way that we set and get a user's email. As a result, we don't change the `User` class, since it already adheres to the single responsibility principle. The peace will be broken when we provide users of the `User` class the ability to make payments. In that case, the `User` class would handle both storing user data and processing payments. We won't do that, since it violates the single responsibility principle.

The idea of single responsibility also applies to functions. There are two responsibilities for the `add_payment_option()` method. If the second (default) argument of the function is `true`, a new primary payment option is added. If not, the new payment option is added to the group of non-primary alternatives. It's preferable to create a primary payment option using a different method. Each of the methods will then be in charge of a particular task.

The open-closed principle

According to the open-closed principle, a class should be open for extension but closed for modification. This implies that it is always preferable to add additional features to the underlying functionality rather than changing it. Let's consider the `Product` class of the e-commerce application we designed. The following represents a simple diagram for the `Product` class:

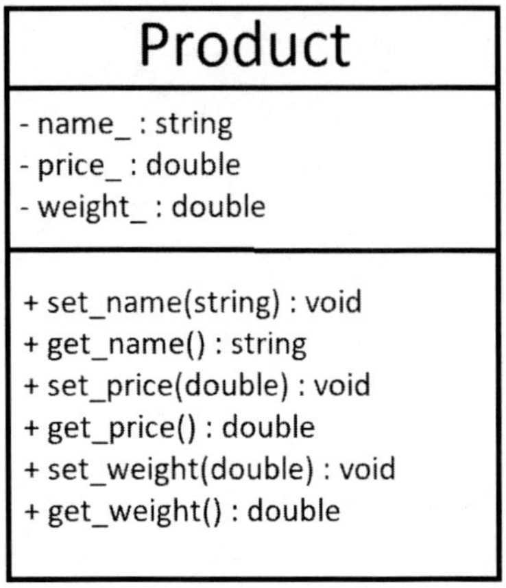

Figure 2.30 – A UML diagram of a Product class

The three properties of a `Product` object are **name**, **price**, and **weight**. Imagine that a client has a new request after you've designed the `Product` class and the entire e-commerce platform. They now want to purchase digital products, such as e-books, movies, and audio. Everything is fine except for the weight of the product. The product weight is the only item that needs improvement. We have to reconsider the logic behind `Product` usage now that there may be two different sorts of products – tangible and digital. We can add a new function to `Product`, as demonstrated in the following line of code:

```
class Product
{
public:
    // code omitted for brevity
    bool is_digital() const {
    return weight_ == 0.0;
    }
    // code omitted for brevity
};
```

We obviously changed the class, which is against the open-closed rule. According to the principle, the class should be closed to modifications. It should be open for extension. By rewriting the `Product` class and turning it into an abstract base class for all products, we can accomplish this. Next, we create two more classes that inherit the `Product` base class – `PhysicalProduct` and `DigitalProduct`. The new layout is shown in the following class diagram:

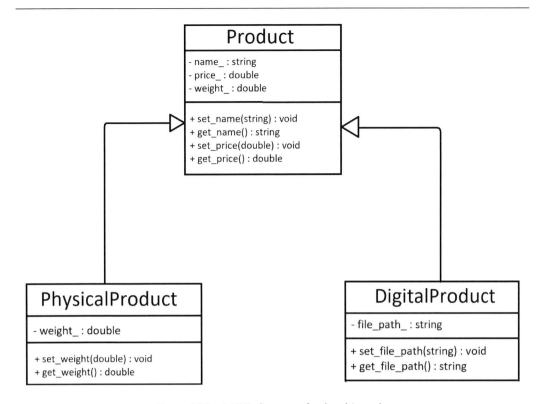

Figure 2.31 – A UML diagram of a class hierarchy

The `weight_` property was removed from the `Product` class, as shown in the preceding diagram. Now that there are two more classes, `DigitalProduct` lacks a `weight_` property, while `PhysicalProduct` has one. `DigitalProduct` contains a `file_path_` property instead. This approach satisfies the open-closed principle because now all the classes are open for extension. We use inheritance to extend classes, and the following principle is strongly related to that.

The Liskov substitution principle

The Liskov substitution principle is named after Barbara Liskov, a Turing Award winner and doctor of computer science. The Liskov substitution principle is associated with correctly deriving from a type. Simply put, this means that if a function accepts an argument of one type, it should also accept an argument of the derived type.

It's difficult to forget about inheritance and the Liskov substitution principle once you understand both. Let's continue developing the `Product` class and add a new method that returns the price of the product, based on the currency type. We can store the price in the same currency units and provide a function to convert the price into a specified currency. This is how the technique is easily applied:

```cpp
enum class Currency { USD, EUR, GBP };
// the list goes further
class Product
{
public:
    // code omitted for brevity
    double convert_price(Currency c) {
    // convert to proper value
    }
    // code omitted for brevity
    };
```

After some time passes, a business decides to provide lifelong discounts on all digital products. Every digital item will now be discounted by 12%. Soon, we'll add a separate function to the `DigitalProduct` class that returns a converted price by applying the discount. Here's how it looks in `DigitalProduct`:

```cpp
class DigitalProduct : public Product
{
public:
    // code omitted for brevity
    double convert_price_with_discount(Currency c) {
    // convert by applying a 12% discount
    }
};
```

The problem in the design is obvious. Calling `convert_price()` on the `DigitalProduct` instance will have no effect. Even worse, the client code must not call it. Instead, it should call `convert_price_with_discount()` because all digital products must sell with a 12% discount. The design contradicts the Liskov substitution principle.

We should keep in mind the elegance of polymorphism, rather than damage the class hierarchy. Here is how a better version might appear:

```cpp
class Product
{
    public:
    // code omitted for brevity
    virtual double convert_price(Currency c) {
    // default implementation
    }
    // code omitted for brevity
```

```
};
class DigitalProduct : public Product
{
public:
    // code omitted for brevity
    double convert_price(Currency c) override {
    // implementation applying a 12% discount
    }
    // code omitted for brevity
};
```

You can see that we are no longer in need of the `convert_price_with_discount()` method, but we need to go through the design problems once more. Let's improve the design by adding private virtual methods to the base class for discount calculation. The `Product` class now has a private virtual member method called `calculate_discount()` in the following modified version:

```
class Product
{
public:
    // code omitted for brevity
    virtual double convert_price(Currency c) {
    auto final_price = apply_discount();
    // convert the final_price based on the currency
    }
private:
    virtual double apply_discount() {
    return getPrice(); // no discount by default
    }
    // code omitted for brevity
};
```

The `convert_price()` function calls the private `apply_discount()` function, which returns the price as is. And here comes the trick – as shown in the following `DigitalProduct` implementation, we override the `apply_discount()` function in derived classes:

```
class DigitalProduct : public Product
{
public:
    // code omitted for brevity
private:
    double apply_discount() override {
    return getPrice() - (getPrice() * 0.12);
    }
    // code omitted for brevity
};
```

A private function cannot be called from outside the class, although it can be overridden in derived classes. The beauty of overriding private virtual functions is demonstrated by the previous code. We make changes to the implementation while leaving the interface unchanged. A derived class doesn't override the interface if it does not need to provide custom functionality for discount calculation. However, before converting the price, `DigitalProduct` must add a 12% discount. The base class's public interface doesn't need to be changed.

> **Tip**
>
> You should consider rethinking the design of the `Product` class. It's even better practice to call `apply_discount()` directly in `getPrice()`, hence always returning the latest effective price, although at some point you should force yourself to stop.

The design process is imaginative but occasionally unappreciative. It's not unusual to have to completely rebuild code due to new, unforeseen requirements. We employ strategies and concepts to reduce the number of disruptive changes that will occur with the addition of new features. The following SOLID principle is one of the greatest techniques to make your design flexible.

The interface segregation principle

According to the interface segregation principle, a complicated interface should be split up into smaller interfaces. Classes can avoid implementing an interface they don't use.

We need to include functionalities for product shipping, replacement, and expiration in our e-commerce application. The shipment of the product involves moving the product item to its buyer. At the moment, we don't care about the shipment details. Replacement of a product considers replacing a damaged or lost product after it has been shipped to the buyer. Finally, expiring a product means getting rid of products that did not sell by their expiry date.

We are free to implement all of the features in the aforementioned `Product` class, but eventually, we'll come across things that, for instance, can't be shipped (for example, selling a house rarely involves shipping it to the buyer). There may be certain products that cannot be replaced. An original painting, for instance, cannot be replaced, even if it is lost or destroyed. Finally, digital products won't expire ever – well, in most situations.

Client code shouldn't be forced to implement a functionality it doesn't need. The class that implements behaviors is referred to as the client. The example that follows is a bad practice that goes against the interface segregation principle:

```
class IShippableReplaceableExpirable
{
public:
    virtual void ship() = 0;
    virtual void replace() = 0;
```

```
    virtual void expire() = 0;
};
```

The Product class now implements the interface that was previously displayed. It has to provide an implementation for all of the methods. The following model is one suggested by the interface segregation principle:

```
class IShippable
{
public:
    virtual void ship() = 0;
    };
class IReplaceable
{
public:
    virtual void replace() = 0;
    };
class IExpirable
{
public:
    virtual void expire() = 0;
};
```

Now, none of the interfaces are implemented by the Product class. Its derived classes derive (implement) from specific types. The following example declares several types of product classes, each of which supports a limited number of the behaviors introduced earlier. Be aware that we exclude class bodies to keep the code concise:

```
class PhysicalProduct : public Product {};
// The book does not expire
class Book : public PhysicalProduct, public IShippable, public
IReplaceable
{
};
// A house is not shipped, not replaced, but it can expire
// if the landlord decided to put it on sell till
// a specified date
class House : public PhysicalProduct, public IExpirable
{
};
class DigitalProduct : public Product {};
// An audio book is not shippable and it cannot expire.
// But we implement IReplaceable in case we send a
// wrong file to the user.
class AudioBook : public DigitalProduct, public IReplaceable
{
};
```

Consider implementing IShippable for AudioBook if you want to wrap a file downloading as shipment.

The dependency inversion principle

Last but not least, objects shouldn't be strongly coupled, according to dependency inversion. It makes it simple to switch to a different dependency. For instance, when a user buys a product, we send a receipt for the user's purchase. Technically, there are various ways to send a receipt, including printing and mailing one or displaying it on the platform's user account page. For the latter, we notify the consumer that the receipt is available to view through email or the app. View the following user interface to print a receipt:

```cpp
class IReceiptSender
{
public:
    virtual void send_receipt() = 0;
};
```

Let's assume we've added the purchase() function to the Product class and sent the receipt once it completes. The mailing of the receipt is handled by the following portion of the code:

```cpp
class Product
{
public:
    // code omitted for brevity
    void purchase(IReceiptSender* receipt_sender) {
    // purchase logic omitted
    // we send the receipt passing purchase information
    receipt_sender->send _receipt(/*
      purchase-information */);
}
};
```

We can extend the application by adding as many receipt printing options as needed. The IReceiptSender interface is implemented by the class listed here:

```cpp
class MailReceiptSender : public IReceiptSender
{
public:
    // code omitted for brevity
    void send_receipt() override { /* ... */ }
};
```

Two more classes – EmailReceiptSender and InAppReceiptSender – both implement IReceiptSender. So, to use a specific receipt, we just inject the dependency to Product via the purchase() method, as shown here:

```
IReceiptSender* rs = new EmailReceiptSender();
// consider the get_purchasable_product() is
// implemented somewhere in the code
auto product = get_purchasable_product();
product.purchase(rs);
```

We can go further by implementing a method in the User class that returns the receipt-sending option, desirable for the concrete user. The classes will become much more uncoupled as a result.

The SOLID concepts covered here are all natural ways to construct classes. Although sticking to the principles is not required, your design will benefit if you do.

More UML in project design

Developers should agree upon and adhere to a shared set of standards and norms, some of which should be applicable to modeling when working on a software project. Models that use a standard notation and adhere to efficient style rules are simpler to comprehend and keep up with. These models will enhance communication both inside your team and with your partners and consumers, which will lessen the likelihood of expensive misunderstandings. By reducing the number of aesthetic options you must choose from, modeling guidelines help you save time so you can concentrate on what you do best – develop software. The first step in implementing modeling standards and rules within your company is to choose a common notation. The best one to choose is probably UML, as it depicts everything that the OOP paradigm suggests.

We have already shown the UML diagrams that depict the relationships between classes and objects, and in this part of the chapter, we will discuss the more advanced parts of the UML-like behavior diagrams.

UML provides the foundation necessary for you to precisely specify behavior, using its behavior diagrams. *Behavior* is the term used to describe the immediate results of at least one object's activity. It has an impact on how objects' states evolve over time. Behavior can be determined by an object's behaviors or can arise as a result of interactions between different objects. The different types of behavior diagrams are the use case diagram, the state machine diagram, the activity diagram, the sequence diagram, and so on.

The sequence diagram

We will continue talking about behavior diagrams with the help of a sequence diagram. The sequence diagram outlines how items interact to complete a certain task – for example, how a person gets money from an ATM. The chronological order of the communications sent and received by the interaction partners is what is highlighted. You can model complicated relationships using various components to regulate the messages' chronological sequence, as well as modularization techniques.

Generally, sequence diagrams are used to explore a design, since it gives you a visual method to follow the invocation of the operations that your classes describe, helping you to find any obstacles in the object-oriented design. You can easily determine where you need to alter your design to disperse a load throughout your system by looking at the messages that are delivered to an object, the approximate length of time it takes to perform a summoned function, which visually indicates which objects are going to end up complex, and so on.

Before going straight into creating a sequence diagram, let's list the general rules that should be followed to start the process of creating a sequence diagram. First of all, we should start from left to right, which means that the first message center is going to be in the top-left corner. If there are messages under the first message, it means that they are sent only after the first message is sent. Another rule is to layer your diagram to make it easier for others to read. The diagram should also have an actor, someone who starts the whole process. In the preceding example, the person who wants to get money from an ATM is supposed to be an actor. Having discussed the preceding rules, let's now create a sequence diagram. Our diagram will be based on the example we previously talked about. The actor of our program will be a person who tries to get money from an ATM, and the objects of our program will be an ATM, a bank server, and a bank account. Let's start by drawing what we discussed:

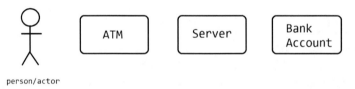

Figure 2.32 – The actor and objects illustrated with a sequence diagram

Our diagram is not complete, of course, and now that we have the main objects and the actor, we can continue drawing the messages and other details. Next, we will add the lifelines for both the actor and the objects. Lifelines show the existence of an object or an actor over time:

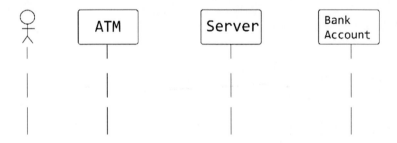

Figure 2.33 – The lifelines of the actor and objects

The lifelines are represented as dashed lines. Now, we can continue and start drawing the interactions between the actor and the objects. When people want to get money from an ATM, they should insert a card into it, which is the first interaction between an actor and an object.

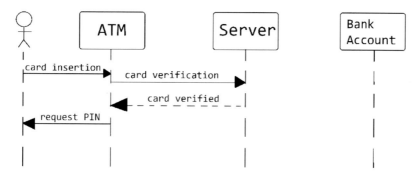

Figure 2.34 – The interaction between an actor and objects

Now, we see that four arrows are added to the diagram. The first one, named **card insertion**, is performed by the actor. The person inserts the card and sends a message to an ATM. The ATM itself should check whether the card is verified or not and send a message to the bank server to check it. The bank server checks it and responds with whether it is valid or not, and we can see that the return message is drawn with a dashed line and not a solid line, which is correct. The last arrow goes from an ATM to the actor, and the line of the arrow is not dashed, as it is not a reply message.

As you can see in the preceding diagram, only the case of a valid card is depicted. But what if the card is not valid? In that case, we should use an alternative frame. Let's try to depict that:

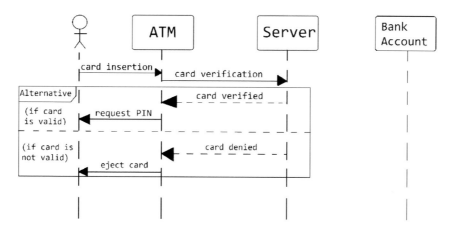

Figure 2.35 – The illustration of an alternative frame in a sequence diagram

Now, we can see the alternative frame we were talking about. It allows us to design a diagram that shows two different variations of the same process. If the card is valid, the process continues, and now the actor should enter the PIN.

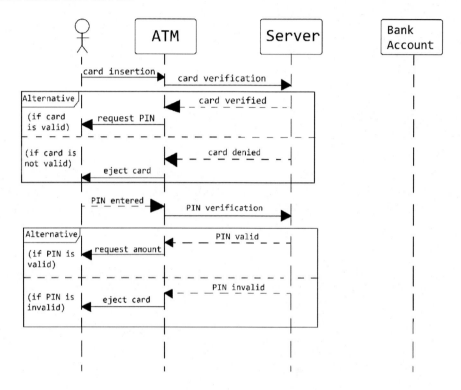

Figure 2.36 – The second alternative frame of our example, expressed with a sequence diagram

So, we can see that the process continues with the same logic. The message reaches the bank account when the amount is entered. In that case, the bank server should send a message to the bank account to see whether the person has enough money. Let's continue drawing the rest, and in the end, we will just add one more detail to our diagram and finish with it.

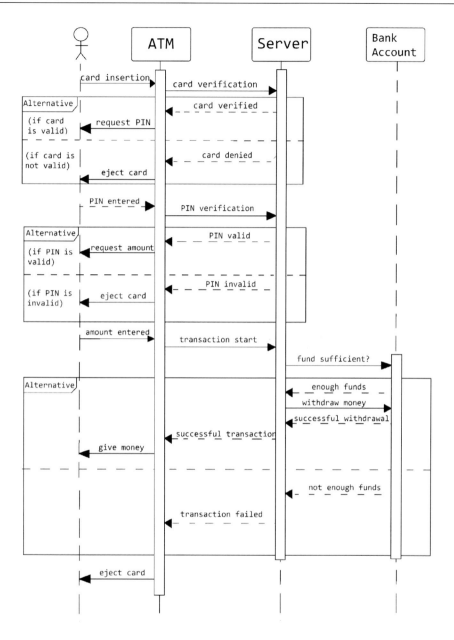

Figure 2.37 – The final sequence diagram of our example

We see in the final diagram that there is one more component. The shapes on the lines indicate the active time for each object.

Our diagram is based on a real-life example. When you start writing a program and want to use the sequence UML diagram to design it, your arrows represent the functions, and you can overwrite them with the names of your functions.

Following the rules and tips that we provided in the sequence diagram, you can now apply them to your projects if the logic of this diagram and the logic of your program match.

Summary

In this chapter, we discussed the fundamental concepts of OOP. We touched on the low-level details of classes and the compiler implementation of the C++ object model. Knowing how to design and implement classes without actually having classes helps a lot in using the classes the right way.

We also discussed the need for inheritance and tried to employ composition instead of inheritance, wherever it might be applicable. C++ supports three types of inheritance – public, private, and protected. All of these types have their applications in particular class designs. Finally, we understood the use and power of polymorphism by introducing an example that drastically increases the convenience of the client code.

We also talked about design patterns and the difference between two structural design patterns – composite and decorator.

And finally, we finished the chapter by diving into one of the advanced UML diagrams, providing a sequence diagram for our example and rules and tips on how you can use it in your programs.

The next chapter will introduce C++ templates, examples of template functions, template classes, template specialization, and template metaprogramming in general.

Questions

1. What are the three properties of objects?
2. What's the advantage of moving objects instead of copying them?
3. What's the difference between aggregation and composition relations?
4. What's the difference between private and protected inheritance?
5. List the differences between composite and decorator design patterns.
6. Draw a sequence diagram that will be based on some interaction between a student and a university.

Further reading

- Grady Booch – *Object-Oriented Analysis and Design*: `https://www.amazon.com/Object-Oriented-Analysis-Design-Applications-3rd/dp/020189551X`

- Stanley Lippman – *Inside the C++ Object Model*: `https://www.amazon.com/Inside-Object-Model-Stanley-Lippman/dp/0201834545/ref=sr_1_1?keywords=Inside+the+C%2B%2B+Object+Model&qid=1662479088&s=books&sr=1-1`

- Martina Seidl, Marion Scholz, and Christian Huemer – *UML @ Classroom: An Introduction to Object-Oriented Modeling*: `https://www.amazon.com/UML-Classroom-Introduction-Object-Oriented-Undergraduate/dp/3319127411`

3

Understanding and Designing Templates

Templates are a unique feature of C++ by which functions and classes have the ability to support generic data types—in other words, we can implement a function or class independent of a particular data type; for example, a client may request a max() function to handle different data types. Instead of implementing and maintaining many similar functions by using function overloading, we can just implement one max() function and pass the data type as a parameter. Moreover, templates can work together with multiple inheritance and operator overloading to create powerful generic data structures and algorithms in C++ such as the **Standard Template Library** (**STL**). Additionally, templates can also be applied to compile-time computation, compile-time and runtime code optimization, and more.

In this chapter, we will learn about the syntax of function and class templates, their instantiations, and their specializations. Then, we will introduce variadic templates and their applications. Next, we will discuss template parameters and the corresponding arguments that are used for instantiating them. After that, we'll learn how to implement a type trait and how to use this type of information to optimize algorithms. Finally, we will present techniques that we can use to speed up programs when they're executed, which include compile-time computation, compile-time code optimization, and static polymorphism.

This chapter will cover the following topics:

- Motivation for using templates
- Function templates
- Class templates
- Understanding variadic templates
- Exploring template parameters and arguments
- Traits
- **Template metaprogramming** (**TMP**) and its applications

Technical requirements

The code for this chapter can be found in this book's GitHub repository:

`https://github.com/PacktPublishing/Expert-CPP/tree/master/Chapter03`

Motivation for using templates

So far, when we have defined a function or a class, we have had to provide input, output, and intermediate parameters. For example, let's say we have a function to perform the addition of two `int`-type integers. How do we extend this so that it handles all the other basic data types, such as `float`, `double`, `char`, and so on? One way is to use function overloading by manually copying, pasting, and slightly modifying each function. Another way is to define a macro to do the addition operation. Both approaches have their side effects.

Moreover, what happens if we fix a bug or add a new feature for one type, and this update needs to be done for all the other overloading functions and classes later? Instead of using this silly copy-paste-and-replacement method, do we have a better way of handling this kind of situation?

In fact, this is a generic problem that any computer language can face. Pioneered by the general-purpose functional programming **Meta Language** (**ML**) in 1973, ML permits writing common functions or types that differ only in the set of types that they operate on when used, thus reducing duplication. Later inspired by the parameterized modules provided in the **chartered life underwriter** (**CLU**) and the generics provided by Ada, C++ adopted the template concept, which allows functions and classes to operate with generic types. In other words, it allows a function or class to work on different data types without them needing to be rewritten.

Actually, from an abstract point of view, C++ functions or class templates (such as cookie cutters) serve as a pattern for creating other similar functions or classes. The basic idea behind this is to create a function or class template without having to specify the exact type(s) of some or all variables. Instead, we define a function or class template using placeholder types, called **template type parameters**. Once we have a function or class template, we can automatically generate functions or classes by using an algorithm that has been implemented in other compilers.

There are three kinds of templates in C++: function templates, class templates, and variadic templates. We'll take a look at these in the next sections.

Function templates

A function template defines how a family of functions can be generated. A family here means a group of functions that behave similarly. As shown in *Figure 3.1* and outlined next, this includes two phases:

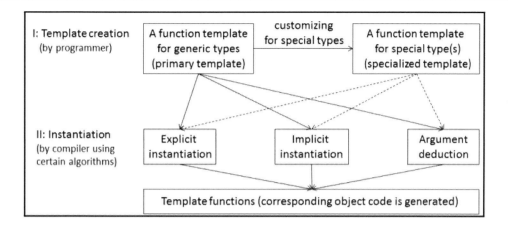

Figure 3.1 – Function template format

- Creating a function template, that is, the rules on how to write it

- Template instantiation, that is, the rules that are used to generate functions from their template

In *part I* of the preceding diagram, we discuss the format that will be used to create a function template for generic types, but with respect to the **specialized template**, which we also refer to as the **primary template**. Then, in *part II*, we introduce the three ways to generate functions from the template. Lastly, the *Specialization and overloading* subsection in this chapter tells us how to customize the primary template (by changing its behavior) for special types. In the following subsections, we will delve into various topics such as template creation syntax, template instantiation and its categories, as well as specialization and overloading of templates.

Syntax

There are two ways to define function templates, as shown in the following code snippet:

```
template <typename identifier_1, ..., typename identifier_n >
function_declaration;

template <class identifier_1,..., class identifier_n>
function_declaration;
```

Here, `identifier_i` (`i=1,...,n`) is the type or class parameter, and `function_declaration` declares the function body part. The only difference in the preceding two declarations is the keywords— one uses `class` while the other uses `typename`, but both have the same meaning and behavior. Since a type (such as the basic types—`int`, `float`, `double`, `enum`, `struct`, `union`, and so on) is not a class, the `typename` keyword method was introduced to avoid confusion.

For example, the classic find-maximum-value function template, `app_max()`, can be declared as follows:

```
template <class T>
T app_max (T a, T b) {
return (a>b?a:b);// note:we use ((a)>(b) ? (a):(b))
                   // in macros
}                 // it is safe to replace (a) by a, and (b)
                  // by b now
```

This function template can work for many data types or classes, as long as there's a copy constructible type where the a>b expression is valid. For user-defined classes, this means that the greater-than operator ((>)) must be defined.

Note that the function template and template function are different things. *Function template* refers to a kind of template that's used to generate functions by a compiler, so the compiler does not generate any object code for it. On the other hand, *template function* means an instance from a function template. Since it is a function, the corresponding object code is generated by the compiler. However, the latest C++ standard documents suggest avoiding using the imprecision term template function. Therefore, we will use function templates and member function templates in this book.

Instantiation

Since we may potentially have an infinite number of types and classes, the concept of function templates not only saves space in the source code file but also makes code easier to read and maintain. However, compared to writing separate functions or classes for the different data types that are used in our applications, it does not produce smaller object code. For instance, consider a program using a `float` and `int` version of `app_max()`:

```
cout << app_max(3,5) << endl;
cout << app_max(3.0f,5.0f) << endl;
```

The compiler will generate two new functions in the object file, as follows:

```
int app_max ( int a, int b) {
   return (a>b?a:b);
}
float app_max (float a, float b) {
   return (a>b?a:b);
}
```

This process of creating a new definition of a function from a function template declaration is called **template instantiation**. During this instantiation process, the compiler determines the template arguments and generates actual functional code on demand for your application. Typically, there are three forms: explicit instantiations, implicit instantiations, and template deductions. Let's discuss each form starting with template deductions and later looking at the other two forms.

Deduction

When you call a template function, the compiler needs to figure out the template arguments first, even if not every template argument is specified. Most of the time, it will deduce the missing template arguments from the function arguments. For example, in *part B* of the preceding function, when you call `app_max(5, 8)` in *line E*, the compiler deduces the template argument as an `int` type (`int app_max<int>(int,int)`) because the input parameters, 5 and 8, are integers. Similarly, *line F* will be deduced as a `float` type—that is, `float app_max<float>(float,float)`.

However, what happens if there is confusion during instantiation? For instance, in the commented-out *line G* of the previous program, depending on the compiler, it might call `app_max<double>(double, double)`, `app_max<int>(int, int)`, or just give a `compile error` message. The best way to help the compiler deduce the type is to call the function template by giving a template argument explicitly. In this case, if we call `app_max<double>(5, 8.0)`, any confusion will be resolved.

> **Note**
>
> From the compiler's point of view, there are several ways to do template argument deduction—deduction from a function call, deduction from a type, auto type deduction, and non-deduced contexts. However, from a programmer's point of view, you should never write fancy code to ill-use the concept of function template deduction to confuse other programmers, such as with *line G* in the previous example.

Specialization and overloading

Specialization allows us to customize the template code for a given set of template arguments. It allows us to define special behavior for specific template arguments. A specialization is still a template; you still need an instantiation to get the real code (automatically by the compiler).

In the sample code at `https://github.com/PacktPublishing/Expert-C-2nd-edition/tree/main/Chapter03/3_func_template_specialization.cpp`, the primary function template, `T app_max(T a, T b)`, will return a or b based on the return of operator a>b, but we can specialize it for `T = std::string` so that we only compare the *0-th* elements of a and b; that is, `a[0] >b[0]`.

The preceding code defines a primary template first, and then it explicitly specializes T as `std::string`; that is, instead of comparing the values of a and b, we only care about `a[0]` and `b[0]` (the behavior of `app_max()` is specialized). In the test function, *line A* calls `app_max(int,int)` and *line B* calls the specialized version because there is no ambiguity at the deduction time. If we uncomment lines C and D, the primary function template, `char* app_max (char*, char*)`, will be called, since `char*` and `std::string` are different data types.

Essentially, specialization somewhat conflicts with function overload resolution: the compiler needs an algorithm to resolve this conflict by finding the right match among the template and overloading functions. The algorithm for selecting the right function involves the following two steps:

1. Perform overload resolution among regular functions and non-specialized templates.

2. If a non-specialized template is selected, check whether a specialization exists that would be a better match for it.

For example, in the following code block, we're declaring the primary (*line 0*) and specialized function templates (*lines 1-4*), as well as the overload functions (*lines 5-6*) of f ( )):

```
template<tyename T1, typename T2> void f ( T1, T2 );//line 0
template<typename T> void f ( T ); // line 1
template<typename T> void f ( T, T ); // line 2
template<typename T> void f ( int, T* ); // line 3
template<> void f ( int ); // line 4
void f ( int, double ); // line 5
void f ( int ); // line 6
```

f () will be called several times in the following code block. Based on the preceding two-step rule, we can show which function is chosen in the comments. We'll explain the reason for doing this after:

```
int i=0;
double d=0;
float x=0;
complex c;
f(i);      //line A: choose f() defined in line 6
f(i,d);    //line B: choose f() defined in line 5
F<int>(i); //line C: choose f() defined in line 4
f(c);      //line D: choose f() defined in line 1
f(i,i);    //line E: choose f() defined in line 2
f(i,x);    //line F: choose f() defined in line 0
f(i, &d);  //line G: choose f() defined in line 3
```

For *lines A* and *B*, since f () defined in *lines 5* and *6* are regular functions, they have the highest priority to be chosen, so f (i) and f (i,d) will choose them, respectively. For *line C*, because the specialized template exists, the f () instance generated from *line 4* is a better match than what was created from *line 1*. For *line D*, since c is a complex type, only the primary function template defined in *line 1* matches it. *Line E* will choose the f () instance that was created by *line 2* because the two input variables are the same type. Finally, *line F* and *line G* will pick up the functions created from the templates in *lines 0* and *3*, respectively.

Having learned about functional templates, we will now move on to class templates.

Class templates

A class template defines a family of classes, and it is often used to implement a container. For example, the C++ Standard Library contains many class templates, such as `std::vector`, `std::map`, `std::deque`, and so on. In OpenCV, `cv::Mat` is a very powerful class template, and it can handle 1D, 2D, and 3D matrices or images with built-in data types such as `int8_t`, `uint8_t`, `int16_t`, `uint16_t`, `int32_t`, `uint32_t`, `float`, `double`, and so on.

Similar to function templates, as shown in *Figure 3.2*, the concept of class templates contains a template creation syntax, its specialization, and its implicit and explicit instantiations:

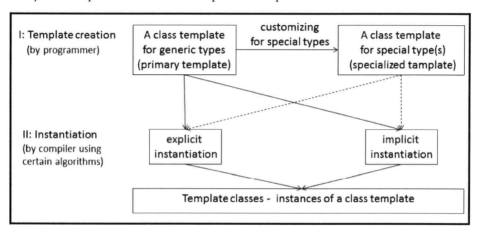

Figure 3.2 – Class template and its instantiation

In *part I* of the preceding diagram, with a certain syntax format, we can create a class template for generic types, also known as a **primary template**, and it can be customized for special types with different member functions and/or variables. Once we have a class template, in *part II*, the compiler will instantiate it to template classes either explicitly or implicitly based on the application's demand.

Now, let's look at the syntax for creating a class template.

Syntax

The syntax for creating a class template is as follows:

```
[export] template < template_parameter_list> class-declaration
```

Here, we have the following:

- `template_parameter-list` (see the link in the *Further reading* section) is a non-empty comma-separated list of the template parameters, each of which is either a non-type parameter, a type parameter, a template parameter, or a parameter pack of any of those.

- `class-declaration` is the part that's used to declare a class that contains a class name and its body in curly brackets. By doing so, the declared class name also becomes a template name.

For example, we can define a class template, `V`, so that it contains all kinds of 1D vector data types, as in `https://github.com/PacktPublishing/Expert-C-2nd-edition/tree/main/Chapter03/6_class_v.h`.

Once we have this class template, the compiler can generate classes during the instantiation process. For the reason we mentioned in the *Function templates* section, we will avoid using the imprecise term *template class* in this book. Instead, we will use *class template*.

Instantiation

Considering the class template, `V`, we defined in the previous section, we'll assume the following declarations appear later:

```
V<char> cV;
V<int> iV(10);
V<float> fV(5);
```

Then, the compiler will create three instances of the `V` class, as follows:

```
class V <char>{
    public:
        V(int n=0);
        // ...
    protected:
        int m_nEle;
        char *m_buf;
};
 class V<int>{
    public:
        V(int n=0);
        // ...
    protected:
        int m_nEle;
        int *m_buf;
};

class V<float>{
    public:
        V(int n = 0);
        // ...
    protected:
```

```
        int m_nEle;
        float *m_buf;
};
```

Similar to function template instantiation, there are two forms of class template instantiation—**explicit instantiation** and **implicit instantiation**. Let's take a look at them.

Explicit instantiation

The syntax for explicit instantiation is as follows:

```
template class template_name < argument_list >;
extern template class template_name < argument_list >;//(since C++11)
```

An explicit instantiation definition forces instantiation of the class, struct, or union it refers to. In the C++0x standard, the implicit instantiation of a template specialization or its members is suppressed. Similar to the explicit instantiation of function templates, the location of this explicit instantiation can be anywhere after its template definition, and it is only permitted to be defined once in the entire program in one file.

Moreover, since C++11, an implicit instantiation step will be bypassed by an explicit instantiation declaration (extern template). This can be used to reduce compilation times.

Going back to the template class, V, we can explicitly instantiate it as follows:

```
template class V<int>;
template class V<double>;
```

Alternatively, we can do the following (since C++11):

```
extern template class V<int>;
extern template class V<double>;
```

The compiler will present us with an error message if we explicitly instantiate a function or class template but there is no corresponding definition in the program, as shown at https://github.com/PacktPublishing/Expert-C-2nd-edition/blob/main/Chapter03/4_class_template_explicit.cpp.

In the preceding code block, we defined a class template between *lines A* and *B*, and then we implemented its member function, foo(), from *lines C* to *D*. Next, we explicitly instantiated it for the int type at *line E*. Since the code block between *lines F* and *G* is commented out (which means that there is no corresponding definition of foo() for this explicit int type instantiation), we have a linkage error. To fix this, we need to replace #if 0 with #if 1 at *line F*.

Finally, there are some additional restrictions for explicit instantiation declarations, as follows:

- **Static**: A static class member can be named, but a static function cannot be allowed in an explicit instantiation declaration

- **Inline**: There is no effect for inline functions in explicit instantiation declarations, and inline functions are implicitly instantiated

- **Class and its members**: There is no equivalent for explicitly instantiating a class and all its members

Implicit instantiation

When referring to a template class, the compiler will only generate code from its template on-demand if it has not been explicitly instantiated or explicitly specialized. This is called implicit instantiation, and its syntax is as follows:

```
class_name<argument list> object_name;      //for non-pointer object
class_name<argument list> *p_object_name; //for pointer object
```

For a non-pointer object, a template class is instantiated and its object is created, but only the member functions used by this object are generated. For a pointer object, unless a member is used in the program, it is not instantiated.

Consider the example at https://github.com/PacktPublishing/Expert-C-2nd-edition/tree/main/Chapter03/5_class_template_implicit_inst.h, where we define a class template, X, in the 5_class_template_implicit_inst.h file.

Then, it is included by the following four cpp files, which have main() in each (find the code at https://github.com/PacktPublishing/Expert-C-2nd-edition/tree/main/Chapter03/5_class_template_implicit_inst_A.cpp).

In 5_class_template_implicit_inst_A.cpp, the compiler will implicitly instantiate the X<int> and X<float> classes and then create xi and xf objects. But since X::f() and X::g() are not used, they are not instantiated.

Now, let's look at 5_class_template_implicit_inst_B.cpp at https://github.com/PacktPublishing/Expert-C-2nd-edition/tree/main/Chapter03/5_class_template_implicit_inst_B.cpp.

Here, the compiler will implicitly instantiate the X<int> class, create an xi object, and then generate the X<int>::f() function, but not X<int>::g(). Similarly, it will instantiate the X<float> class, create an xf object, and generate the X<float>::g() function, but not X<float>::f().

Then, we have 5_class_template_implicit_inst_C.cpp at https://github.com/PacktPublishing/Expert-C-2nd-edition/tree/main/Chapter03/5_class_template_implicit_inst_C.cpp.

Since p_xi and p_xf are pointer objects, there is no need to instantiate their corresponding template classes through the compiler.

Finally, we have 5_class_template_implicit_inst_D.cpp at https://github.com/ PacktPublishing/Expert-C-2nd-edition/tree/main/Chapter03/5_class_ template_implicit_inst_D.cpp.

This will implicitly instantiate X<int> and X<int>::f(), but not X<int>::g(); similarly, for X<float>, X<float>::f() and X<float>::g() will be instantiated.

Specialization

Similar to function specialization, the explicit specialization of a class template defines a different implementation for a primary template when a specific type is passed as a template parameter. However, it is still a class template and you need to get the real code by instantiation.

For example, let's suppose that we have a struct X template that can store one element of any data type, and it has just one member function named increase(). But for the char-type data, we want a different implementation of increase() and need to add a new member function called toUpperCase() to it. Therefore, we decide to declare a class template specialization for that type. We do this as follows:

1. Declare a primary class template, like so:

    ```
    template <typename T>
    struct X {
    X(T init) : m(init) {}
    T increase() { return ++m; }
    T m;
    };
    ```

    This step declares a primary class template in which its constructor initializes the m member variable and increase() adds one to m and returns its value.

2. Next, we need to perform specialization for the char-type data, as follows:

    ```
    template <> //No parameters inside <>, it tells
                //Compiler that this is a fully
                //specialized template.
    struct X<char> {  //<char> after X, tells compiler
                      //that this is specialized only for
                      //type char
        X( const char init) ; m(init) {}
        char increase() {
            return (m<127) ? ++m : (m=-128);
        }
    ```

```
      char toUpperCase() {
          if ((m >= 'a') && (m <= 'z')) m += 'A' - 'a';
      return m;
      }
      char m;
};
```

This step creates a specialized (with respect to the primary class template) class template with an additional member function, toUpperCase(), for the char-type data only.

3. Finally, we run a test:

```
int main() {
    X<int> x1(5);          //line A
    std::cout << x1.increase() << std::endl;
    X<char> x2('b');       //line B
    std::cout << x2.toUpperCase() << std::endl;
    return 0;
}
```

Finally, we have a main() function to test it. In *line A*, x1 is an object that has been implicitly instantiated from the primary template, X<T>. Since the initial value of x1.m is 5, 6 will be returned from x1.increase(). In *line B*, x2 is an object instantiated from the specialization template, X<char>, and the value of x2.m is b when it is executed. After calling x2.toUpperCase(), B will be the return value.

The complete code for this example can be found at 6_class_template_specialization.cpp.

In summary, the syntax that's used in the class template's explicit specialization is as follows:

```
template <> class[struct] class_name<template argument list> {
...
};
```

Here, the empty template parameter list, template <>, is used to explicitly declare it as a template specialization, and <template argument list> is the type parameter(s) to be specialized. For example, in ex3_6_class_template_specialization.cpp, we use the following:

```
template <> struct X<char> { ... };
```

Here, <char>, which is written after X, identifies the type for which we are going to declare a template class specialization.

Additionally, when we do specializations for a template class, all its members—even those that are identical in the primary template—must be defined because there is no inheritance concept for the primary template during template specializations.

Next, we'll take a look at partial specialization. This is a general statement of explicit specialization. Compared to the format of explicit specialization, which only has a template argument list, both the template parameter list and argument list are required for a partial specialization. For a template instantiation, the partial specialization template will be selected by the compiler if a user's template argument list matches a subset of the template arguments. Then, a new class definition from the partial specialization template will be generated by the compiler.

In the following example, for the primary class template A, we can partially specialize it for const T in the argument list. Note that both of them have the same parameter list, which is `<typename T>`:

```
//primary class template A
template <typename T> class A{
...
};

//partial specialization for const T
template <typename T> class A<const T>{
...
};
```

In the following example, the primary class template B has two parameters: `<typename T1>` and `<typename T2>`. We partially specialize it by using `T1=int`, keeping T2 unchanged:

```
//primary class template B
template <typename T1, typename T2> class B{
...
};

//partial specialization for T1 = int
template <typename T2> class B<int, T2>{
...
};
```

Finally, in the following example, we can see that the number of template parameters in a partial specialization does not have to match the parameter numbers that appeared in the original primary template. However, the number of template arguments (appearing after the class name in angle brackets) must match the number and type of the parameters in the primary template:

```
//primary class template C: template one parameter
template <typename T> struct C {
T type;
};

//specialization: two parameters in parameter list
//but still one argument (<T[N]>) in argument list
```

```
template <typename T, int N> struct C<T[N]>{
T type;
};
```

Again, a class template partial specialization is still a class template. You must provide definitions for its member functions and number variables separately.

To end this section, let's summarize what we've learned so far. In the following table, you can see a comparison between function and class templates, their instantiation, and their specialization:

	Function Templates	Class Templates	Comments
Declaration	`template <class T1, class T2> void f(T1 a, T2 b) { ... }`	`template <class T1, class T2> class X { ... };`	The declaration defines a function/class template, `<class T1, class T2>` call template parameters.
Explicit Instantiation	`template void f <int, int >( int, int);` or `extern template void f <int, int >( int, int);` (since c++11)	`template class X<int, float>;` or `extern template class X<int,float>;` (since c++11)	After instantiation there are now functions/classes, but they are called template functions/classes.
Implicit Instantiation	`{ ... f(3, 4.5); f<char, float>(120, 3.14); }`	`{ ... X<int,float> obj; X<char, char> *p; }`	When a function call or a class object/pointer is declared, if it has not been explicitly instantiated, the implicit instantiation approach used.
Specialization	`template <> void f<int,float>(int a, float b) { ... }`	`template <> class X <int, float>{ ... };`	A fully customized version (no parameter list) of the primary template still needs to be instantiated.
Partial Specialization	`template <class T> void f<T,T>(T a, T b) { ... }`	`template <class T> class X <T, T>{ ... };`	A partial customized version (has a parameter list) of the primary template still needs to be instantiated.

Table 3.1 – Differences between function and class templates

Five concepts need to be emphasized here, as follows:

- **Declaration**: We need to follow the syntax that's used to define a function or class template. At this point, a function or class template by itself is not a type, a function, or any other entity.

In other words, there are only template definitions in the source file, and no code, which can be compiled into an object file, is generated.

- **Implicit instantiation**: For any code to appear, a template must be instantiated. During this process, it becomes imperative to determine the template arguments so that the compiler can generate an actual function or class. In other words, they are compiled on-demand, which means that compiling the code of a template function or class does not happen until an instantiation with specific template arguments is given.

- **Explicit instantiation**: This tells the compiler to instantiate the template with the given types, regardless of whether they are used. Typically, it is used for providing libraries.

- **Full specialization**: This has no parameter list (fully customized); it only has an argument list. The most useful thing about template specialization is that you can create special templates for particular type arguments.

- **Partial specialization**: This is similar to full specialization, but is part parameter list (partially customized) and part argument list.

Understanding variadic templates

In the previous section, we learned how to write function or class templates with a fixed number of type parameters. But since C++11, standard generic functions and class templates can accept a variable number of type parameters. This is called **variadic templates**, which is an extension of C++ (see the link in the *Further reading* section, context *[6]*. We will learn about the syntax and usage of variadic templates by looking at examples.

Syntax

If a function or class template takes zero or more parameters, it can be defined as follows:

```
//a class template with zero or more type parameters
template <typename... Args>
class X {
...
};


//a function template with zero or more type parameters
template <typename... Args>
void foo( function param list) {
...
}
```

Here, `<typename ... Args>` declares a parameter pack. Note that here, `Args` is not a keyword; you can use any valid variable name. The preceding class/function template can take any number of `typename` instances as its arguments need to be instantiated, as shown here:

```
X<> x0;
//with 0 template type argument
X<int, std::vector<int>> x1;
//with 2 template type arguments
//with 4 template type arguments
X<int, std::vector<int>, std::map<std::string,
   std::vector<int>>> x2;
//with 2 template type arguments
foo<float, double>( function argument list );
//with 3 template type arguments
foo<float, double, std::vector<int>>(function argument list);
```

If a variadic template needs at least one type parameter, then the following definition is used:

```
template <typename A, typename... Rest>
class Y {
...
};

template <typename A, typename... Rest>
void goo( const int a, const float b) {
 ....
};
```

Similarly, we can instantiate them by using the following code:

```
Y<int > y1;
Y<int, std::vector<int>, std::map<std::string, std::vector<int>>> y2;
goo<int, float>( const int a, const float b );
goo<int,float, double, std::vector<int>>( const int a, const float b
);
```

In the preceding code, we created y1 and y2 objects from the instantiations of the variadic class template, Y, with one and three template arguments, respectively. For the variadic function goo template, we instantiate it as two template functions with two and three template arguments, respectively.

Examples

The following is probably the simplest example, showing a variadic template being used to find the minimum values of any input argument list: `https://github.com/PacktPublishing/`

Expert-C-2nd-edition/tree/main/Chapter03/7_variadic_my_min.cpp. This example uses the concept of recursion until it reaches my_min(double n) to exit.

The printf() variadic function is probably one of the most useful and powerful functions in C or C++; however, it's not type-safe. In the following code block, we're adopting the classic type-safe printf() example to demonstrate the usefulness of variadic templates. As always, first, we need to define a base function, void printf_vt(const char *s), which ends the recursion.

Then, in its variadic template function, printf_vt(), whenever % is hit, the value is printed, and the rest is passed to its recursion until the base function is reached.

Finally, we can test and compare it with the traditional printf() example. The code example can be found at https://github.com/PacktPublishing/Expert-C-2nd-edition/tree/main/Chapter03/8_variadic_printf.cpp.

The output of the preceding code is as follows:

```
p.]ï¿½U can accept 100 parameters (or more), x=10, y=3.600000
Variadic templates can accept 100 parameters (or more); x=10,y=3.6
```

At the beginning of the first line in the output, we can see some **American Standard Code for Information Exchange** (**ASCII**) characters from printf() because the corresponding variable type of %s should be a pointer to chars, but we give it a type of std::string. To fix this, we need to pass s.c_str(). However, with the variadic template version function, we do not have this issue. Moreover, we only need to provide %, which is even better—at least, it is for this implementation. Due to this and other benefits, variadic templates empower developers to write more versatile and efficient code while ensuring type safety and code reusability.

In summary, this section briefly introduced variadic templates and their applications. Variadic templates provide the following benefits (since C++11):

- They are a lightweight extension of the template family.
- They demonstrate the ability to implement numerous template libraries without the use of ugly templates and preprocessor macros. Thus, the implementation code is capable of being understood and debugged, and it saves compile time as well.
- They enable type-safe implementations of printf() variadic functions.

Next, we will explore template parameters and arguments.

Exploring template parameters and arguments

We learned about function and class templates and their instantiations in the previous three sections. We know that, when defining a template, its parameter list needs to be given. While we instantiate it, the corresponding argument list must be provided. In this section, we will further study the classifications and details of these two lists.

Template parameters

Recall the following syntax, which is used to define a class/function template. There is a < > symbol after the template keyword, in which one or more template parameters must be given:

```
//class template declaration
template <parameter-list> class-declaration

//function template declaration
template <parameter-list> function-declaration
```

A parameter inside the parameter list could be one of the following three types:

- **Non-type template parameter**: Refers to the compile-time constant values, such as integers and pointers, that reference static entities. These are often referred to as non-type parameters.

- **Type template parameter**: This refers to either built-in type names or user-defined classes.

- **Template template parameter**: This indicates the parameters are other templates.

We'll discuss these in more detail in the following subsections.

Non-type template parameter

The syntax of the non-type template parameter is as follows:

```
//for a non-type template parameter with an optional name
type name(optional)

//for a non-type template parameter with an optional name
//and a default value
type name(optional)=default

//For a non-type template parameter pack with an optional //name
type ... name(optional) (since C++11)
```

Here, type is one of the following types:

- Integral type

- Enumeration

- Pointer to an object or a function

- lvalue reference to an object or a function

- Pointer to a member object or a member function

- std::nullptr_t (since C++11)

Additionally, we may put arrays and/or function types in template declarations, but they are automatically replaced with data and/or function pointer(s).

The example at `https://github.com/PacktPublishing/Expert-C-2nd-edition/tree/main/Chapter03/9_none_type_template_param1.cpp` shows a class template that uses a non-type template parameter, `int N`. In `main()`, we instantiate and create an object, `x`, and thus `x.a` has five elements with initial values of `1`. After setting its fourth element value as `10`, we print the output.

The example at `https://github.com/PacktPublishing/Expert-C-2nd-edition/tree/main/Chapter03/10_none_type_template_param2.cpp` is an example of a function template that uses `const char*` as a non-type template parameter.

In `main()`, we successfully instantiate `foo()` with `str1` and `str2` since they are both compile-time constant values and have external linkages. Then, if we uncomment *lines 3-5*, the compiler will report error messages. The reasons for getting these compiler errors are as follows:

- *Line 3*: `str3` is not a `const` variable, so the value being pointed to by `str3` cannot be changed. However, the value of `str3` can be changed.

- *Line 4*: `str4` is not a valid template argument of the `const char*` type because it has no linkage.

- *Line 5*: `str5` is not a valid template argument of the `const char*` type because it has no linkage.

Another of the most common usages of non-type parameters is for specifying the size of an array. If you want to find out more, please go to `https://stackoverflow.com/questions/33234979`.

Type template parameter

The syntax of the type template parameter is as follows:

```
//A type Template Parameter (TP) with an optional name
typename |class name(optional)

//A type TP with an optional name and a default
typename[class] name(optional) = default

//A type TP pack with an optional name
typename[class] ... name(optional) (since C++11)
```

> **Note**
>
> Here, we use the `typename` and `class` keywords interchangeably. Inside the body of the template declaration, the name of a type parameter is a `typedef-name` instance. When the template is instantiated, it aliases the type supplied.

Now, let's look at some examples, as follows:

- Here's a type template parameter without the default:

```
Template<class T> //with name
class X { /* ... */ };
```

```
Template<class > //without name
class Y { /* ... */ };
```

- And here's a type template parameter with the default:

```
Template<class T = void> //with name
class X { /* ... */ };
```

```
Template<class = void > //without name
class Y { /* ... */ };
```

- Here's an example of a type template parameter pack:

```
template<typename... Ts> //with name
class X { /* ... */ };
```

```
template<typename... > //without name
class Y { /* ... */ };
```

This template parameter pack can accept zero or more template arguments, and it only works on C++11 onward.

Template template parameter

The syntax of the template template parameter is as follows:

```
//A template template parameter with an optional name
template <parameter-list> class name(optional)

//A template template parameter with an optional name and a //default
template <parameter-list> class name(optional) = default

//A template template parameter pack with an optional name
template <parameter-list> class ... name(optional) (since C++11)
```

> **Note**
>
> In template template parameter declaration, only the `class` keyword can be used; `typename` is not allowed. In the body of the template declaration, the name of a parameter is a `template-name` instance, and we need arguments to instantiate it.

Now, suppose you have a function that acts as a stream output operator for a list of objects, as follows:

```
template<typename T>
static inline std::ostream &operator << ( std::ostream &out,
        std::list<T> const& v)
{
/*...*/
}
```

From the preceding code, you can see that for sequence containers such as vectors, double-end queues, and a multitude of map types, they are the same. Hence, using the concept of the template template parameter, it would be possible to have a single operator, `<<`, to rule them all. An example of this can be found in `exch3_tp_c.cpp` at `https://github.com/PacktPublishing/Expert-C-2nd-edition/tree/main/Chapter03/11_template_template_param.cpp`.

The output of the preceding program is as follows:

```
class std::basic_ostream<char,struct std::char_traits<char> > &__cdecl
operator
<<<float,class std::vector,class std::allocator<float>>(class
std::basic_ostream
<char,struct std::char_traits<char> > &,const class
std::vector<float,class
std:
:allocator<float> > &):
3.14 4.2 7.9 8.08
```

```
class std::basic_ostream<char,struct std::char_traits<char> > & __cdecl
operator
<<<char,class std::list,class std::allocator<char>>(class
std::basic_ostream<cha
r,struct std::char_traits<char> > &,const class std::list<char,class
std::alloca
tor<char> > &):
E F G H I
class std::basic_ostream<char,struct std::char_traits<char> > & __cdecl
operator
<<<int,class std::deque,class std::allocator<int>>(class
std::basic_ostream<char
,struct std::char_traits<char> > &,const class std::deque<int,class
std::allocat
or<int> > &):
10 11 303 404
```

As expected, the first part of the output for each call is the template function name in a pretty format, while the second part outputs the element values of each container.

Template arguments

To instantiate a template, all the template parameters must be replaced with their corresponding template arguments. The arguments are either explicitly provided, deduced from the initializer (for class templates), deduced from the context (for function templates), or defaulted. Since there are three categories of template parameters, we will have three corresponding template arguments as well. These are template non-type arguments, template type arguments, and template template arguments. Besides these, we will also discuss the default template arguments.

Template non-type arguments

Recall that non-type template parameters refer to compile-time constant values such as integers, pointers, and references to static entities. A non-type template argument provided in the template argument list must match one of these values. Typically, non-type template arguments are used for class initialization or the class container's size specifications.

Although a discussion of the detailed rules for each type (integral and arithmetic types, pointers to objects/functions/members, lvalue reference parameters, and so on) of non-type argument is beyond the scope of this book, the overall general rule is that template non-type arguments should be converted into constant expressions of the corresponding template parameters.

Now, let's take a look at the following example:

```
//part 1: define template with non-type template parameters
```

```
/float pointer non-type parameter
template<const float* p> struct U {};

//L-value non-type parameter
template<const Y& b> struct V {};

//function pointer parameter
template<void (*pf)(int)> struct W {};

//part 2: define other related stuff
void g(int,float); //declare function g()
void g(int);       //declare an overload function of g()
struct Y {         //declare structure Y
float m1;
static float m2;
};
float a[10];
Y y; //line a: create a object of Y

//part 3: instantiation template with template non-type //arguments
U<a> u1;      //line b: ok: array to pointer conversion
U<&y> u2;     //line c: error: address of Y
U<&y.m1> u3; //line d: error: address of non-static member
U<&y.m2> u4; //line e: ok: address of static member
V<y> v;       //line f: ok: no conversion needed
W<&g> w;      //line g: ok: overload resolution selects g(int)
```

In the preceding code, in *part 1*, we defined three template structs with different non-type template parameters. Then, in *part 2*, we declared two overload functions and struct Y.

Finally, in *part 3*, we looked at the correct way to instantiate them by different non-type arguments.

Template type arguments

Compared to the template non-type arguments, the rule of a template type argument (for a type template parameter) is simple and requires that it must be a typeid instance. Here, typeid is a standard C++ operator that returns type identification information at runtime. It basically returns a type_info object that can be compared with other type_info objects.

Now, let's look at the example at https://github.com/PacktPublishing/Expert-C-2nd-edition/tree/main/Chapter03/12_template_type_argument.cpp.

In this example, in *part 1*, we defined three classes and function templates: the class template C with its type template parameter, two function templates with a type template parameter, and a non-type template parameter, respectively. In *part 2*, we have an incomplete struct A and an unnamed type, struct B. Finally, in *part 3*, we tested them. The outputs of the four `typeid()` instances in Ubuntu 18.04 are as follows:

```
Tid1=A; Tid2=P1A; Tid3=1B; Tid4=FivE
```

From x86 MSVC v19.24, we have the following:

```
Tid1=struct A; Tid2=struct A; Tid3=struct B; Tid4=int __cdecl(void)
```

Additionally, since A, A*, B, and int () have `typeid()` instances, the code segment from *lines A* to *D* is linked with the template type classes or functions. Only *line E* is instantiated from the non-type template parameter function template—that is, `f()`.

Template template arguments

For a template template parameter, its corresponding template argument is the name of a class template or a template alias. While finding a template to match the template template argument, only primary class templates are considered.

Here, a primary template refers to the template that is being specialized. Even though their parameter lists might match, the compiler will not consider any partial specialization with that of the template template parameter.

You can find an example of a template template argument at `https://github.com/PacktPublishing/Expert-C-2nd-edition/tree/main/Chapter03/13_template_template_argument.cpp`.

In this example, we're defining a primary class template, X, and its specialization, then a class template, Y, with a template template parameter. Next, we implicitly instantiate Y with template template argument X and create an object, c. Finally, `main()` outputs the names of the four `typeid()` instances; the results are int, char, char, and char, respectively.

Default template arguments

In C++, a function is called by passing arguments, and the arguments are used by the function. If, while invoking a function, the arguments are not passed, the default values are used. Similar to the function parameter default values, template parameters can have default arguments. When we define a template, we can set its default arguments, as at `https://github.com/PacktPublishing/Expert-C-2nd-edition/tree/main/Chapter03/14_default_template_arguments.cpp`.

Certain rules need to be followed when we set the default arguments for template parameters, as outlined here:

- The declaration order matters—the declaration of the default template arguments must be on top of the primary template declaration. For instance, in the preceding example, you cannot move the code at *lines 3* and *4* after *line 9*.

- If one parameter has a default argument, then all the parameters after it must also have default arguments. For example, the following code is incorrect:

```
template<class U = char, class V, class W = int> class X
{}; //Error
template<class V, class U = char, class W = int> class X
{}; //OK
```

- You cannot give the same parameter default arguments twice in the same scope. For example, you will get an error message if you use the following code:

```
template<class T = int> class Y;
//compiling error, to fix it, replace "<class T = int>"
by "<class T>"
template<class T = int> class Y {
public: T a;
};
```

Here, we have discussed two lists: `template_parameter_list` and `template_argument_list`. These are used in function or class template creation and instantiation, respectively.

We also learned about two other important rules, as follows:

- When we define a class or function template, we need to give its `parameter_list`, as follows:

```
template <template_parameter_list>
class X { ... }
template <template_parameter_list>
void foo( function_argument_list ) { ... } //assume
return
                                    //type is void
```

- When we instantiate them, we must provide the corresponding `argument_list`, as follows:

```
class X<template_argument_list> x
void foo<template_argument_list>( function_argument_list
)
```

The parameter or argument types in these two lists can be classified into three categories, as shown in the following table. Note that although the top row is for class templates, these properties also apply to function templates:

	When defining a template template <template_parameter_list> class X { ... }	When instantiating a template class X<template_argument_list> x
non-type	An entity in this parameter list can be one of the following: • Integral or enumeration • Pointer to object or pointer to function • `lvalue` reference to an object or `lvalue` reference to a function • Pointer to member • C++11 `std::nullptr_t` C++11 ends	• Non-type arguments in this list are expressions whose value can be determined at compile time. • Such arguments must be constant expressions, addresses of functions or objects with external linkage, or addresses of static class members. • Non-type arguments are normally used to initialize a class or to specify the sizes of class members.
type	An entity in this parameter list can be one of the following: • Must start with typename or class. • Inside the body of the template declaration, the name of a type parameter is a `typedef-name`. When the template is instantiated, it aliases the type supplied.	• The type of argument must have a `typeid`. • It cannot be a local type, a type with no linkage, an unnamed type, or a type compounded from any of these types.
template	An entity in this parameter list can be one of the following: • `template <parameter-list>` class name • `template <parameter-list>` class ... name (optional) (since C++11)	A template argument in this list is the name of a class template.

Table 3.2 – Categorization of parameter and argument types

Traits

Generic programming means writing code that works with any data type under certain requirements. It is the most efficient way of delivering reusable high-quality code in the software engineering industry. However, there are times in generic programming when being generic just isn't good enough. Whenever the differences between types are too complex, it is very hard for an efficient generic to optimize a common implementation. For example, while implementing a sort function template, if we know the argument type is a linked list but not an array, a different strategy will be implemented to optimize the performance.

Although template specialization is one approach to overcoming this problem, it doesn't provide type-related information in a broad way. A type trait is a technique that's used to collect information about the type. With its help, we can make more intelligent decisions to develop high-quality optimized algorithms in generic programming.

In this section, we will introduce how to implement a type trait, and then show you how to use type information to optimize algorithms.

Type trait implementation

To understand type traits, we'll look at the classic implementations of `boost::is_void` and `boost::is_pointer`.

boost::is_void

First, let's look at one of the simplest traits classes, the `is_void` trait, which was created by Boost. It defines a generic template that's used to implement the default behavior; that is, accept a `void` type, but not anything else. Hence, we have `is_void::value = false`:

```
//primary class template is_void
template< typename T >
struct is_void{
static const bool value = false; //default value=false
};
```

Then, we fully specialize it for the `void` type, like so:

```
//"<>" means a full specialization of template class is_void
template<>
struct is_void< void >{ //fully specialization for void
static const bool value = true; //only true for void type
};
```

Thus, we have a complete `traits` type that can be used to detect whether any given type, T, is void by checking the following expression:

```
is_void<T>::value
```

Next, let's learn how to use partial specialization in `boost::is_pointer` traits.

boost::is_pointer

Similar to `boost::is_void` traits, a primary class template is defined as follows:

```
//primary class template is_pointer
template< typename T >
struct is_pointer{
static const bool value = false;
};
```

Then, it is partially specialized for all pointer types, like so:

```
//"typename T" in "<>" means partial specialization
template< typename T >
struct is_pointer< T* >{ //<T*> means partial
                         // specialization only for type T*
static const bool value = true; //set value as true
};
```

Now, we have a complete `traits` type that can be used to detect whether any given type, T, is a pointer by checking the following expression:

```
is_pointer<T>::value
```

Since the boost type traits feature has already been formally introduced to the C++ 11 Standard Library, we can show the usage of `std::is_void` and `std::is_pointer` without including the preceding source code in the example at `https://github.com/PacktPublishing/Expert-C-2nd-edition/tree/main/Chapter03/15_traits_boost.cpp`.

The preceding code sets the `boolalpha` format flag for the string stream at the beginning. By doing so, all the Boolean values are extracted by their text representation, which is either `true` or `false`. Then, we use several `std::cout` instances to print the values of `is_void<T>::value` and `is_pointer<T>::value`. The output of each value is displayed at the end of the corresponding commented-out line.

Optimizing algorithms using traits

Instead of talking about this topic in a generic abstract way, we will use a classic optimized copy example to show the usage of type traits. Consider the standard library algorithm known as `copy`, shown here:

```
template<typename It1, typename It2>
It2 copy(It1 first, It1 last, It2 out);
```

Obviously, we can write a generic version of `copy()` for any iterator types—that is, `It1` and `It2` here. However, as explained by the authors of the Boost library, there are some circumstances where the copy operation can be performed by `memcpy()`. We can use `memcpy()` if all of the following conditions are satisfied:

- Both types of iterators, `It1` and `It2`, are pointers
- `It1` and `It2` must point to the same type, except for const and volatile qualifiers
- A trivial assignment operator must be provided by the type that `It1` points to

Here, the trivial assignment operator means that the type is either a scalar type or that one of the following applies:

- There is no user-defined assignment operator for the type
- There is no reference type of data members inside the type
- Trivial assignment operators must be defined in all the base classes and data member objects

Here, a scalar type includes an arithmetic type, an enumeration type, a pointer, a pointer to a member, or a const- or volatile-qualified version of one of these types.

Now, let's take a look at the original implementation. It includes two parts—the copier class template and the user interface function, that is, `copy()`:

```
namespace detail{
//1. Declare primary class template with a static function
// template
    template <bool b>
    struct copier {
        template<typename I1, typename I2>
        static I2 do_copy(I1 first, I1 last, I2 out);
    };
//2. Implementation of the static function template
    template <bool b>
    template<typename I1, typename I2>
    I2 copier<b>::do_copy(I1 first, I1 last, I2 out) {
        while(first != last) {
        *out = *first;
        ++out;
        ++first;
        }
    return out;
};
//3. a full specialization of the primary function template
template <>
struct copier<true> {
    template<typename I1, typename I2>
    static I2* do_copy(I1* first, I1* last, I2* out){
    memcpy(out, first, (last-first)*sizeof(I2));
    return out+(last-first);
    }
};
} //end namespace detail
```

As mentioned in the comment lines, the preceding copier class template has two static function templates—one is the primary and the other is fully specialized. The primary does an element-by-element hard copy, while the full specialization one copies all the elements at once via `memcpy()`, as follows:

```
//copy() user interface
template<typename I1, typename I2>
inline I2 copy(I1 first, I1 last, I2 out) {
    typedef typename boost::remove_cv
    <typename std::iterator_traits<I1>::value_type>::type v1_t;
    typedef typename boost::remove_cv
```

```
    <typename std::iterator_traits<I2>::value_type>::type v2_t;
    enum{ can_opt = boost::is_same<v1_t, v2_t>::value
       && boost::is_pointer<I1>::value
       && boost::is_pointer<I2>::value
       && boost::has_trivial_assign<v1_t>::value
};
//if can_opt= true, using memcpy() to copy whole block by
//one
//call(optimized); otherwise, using assignment operator to
//do item-by-item copy
return detail::copier<can_opt>::do_copy(first, last, out);
}
```

To optimize the copy operation, the preceding user interface function defines two remove_cv template objects, v1_t and v2_t, and then evaluates whether can_opt is true. After that, the do_copy() template function is called. By using the test code posted in the Boost utility library (algo_opt_ examples.cpp), we can see that there is a significant improvement in using the optimized implementation; that is, it could be eight or three times faster for copying char or int types of data.

Finally, let's conclude this section with the following highlights:

- A trait gives additional information other than just the type. It is implemented through template specializations.

- By convention, traits are always implemented as structs. The structs that are used to implement traits are known as trait classes.

- Bjarne Stroustrup said that we should think of a trait as a small object whose main purpose is to carry information that's used by another object or algorithm to determine policy or implementation details (see the *Further reading* section, context *[4]*).

- Scott Meyers also summarized that we should use traits classes to gather information about types (see the *Further reading* section, context *[5]*).

- Traits can help us implement generic algorithms in an efficient/optimized way.

Next, we will explore TMP in C++.

TMP and its applications

A programming technique in which computer programs have the ability to treat other programs as their data is known as **metaprogramming**. This means that a program can be designed to read, generate, analyze, or transform other programs, and even modify itself while running. One kind of metaprogramming is a compiler, which takes a text format program as an input language (C, Fortran, Java, and so on) and produces another binary machine code format program in an output language.

C++ TMP means producing metaprograms in C++ using templates. It has two components—a template must be defined, and a defined template must be instantiated. TMP is Turing-complete, which means it has the capability to compute anything computable, at least in principle. Also, because variables are all immutable (variables are constants) in TMP, recursion rather than iteration is used to process the elements of a set.

Why do we need TMP? Because it can speed up our programs during execution time! But since there is no free lunch in the optimization world, the prices we pay for TMP are longer compile time and/or larger binary code sizes. Additionally, not every problem can be solved with TMP; it only works when we're computing something constant during compile time—for example, finding out all the primary numbers that are smaller than a constant integer, finding the factorial of a constant integer, unrolling a constant number of loops or iterations, and so on.

From a practical point of view, TMP has the ability to solve problems in the following three categories: compile-time computation, compile-time optimization, and replacing dynamic polymorphism with static polymorphism by avoiding virtual table lookup during runtime.

The next chapter will provide comprehensive coverage of compile-time computation, compile-time optimization, and static polymorphism, offering a deeper exploration of these important concepts in C++.

Summary

In this chapter, we discussed generic programming-related topics in C++. Starting by reviewing C macros and function overloading, we introduced the development motivations of C++ templates. Then, we presented the syntax of class and function templates with a fixed number of parameters, as well as their specializations and instantiations. Since C++11, variadic templates are accepted by the standard generic function and class templates. Based on this, we further classified the template parameters and arguments into three categories: non-type template parameters/arguments, type template parameters/arguments, and template template parameters/arguments.

We also learned about traits and TMP. As a byproduct of template specialization, traits classes can provide us with more information about types. With the help of type information, eventually, the optimizations of implementing generic algorithms become possible. Another application of class and/or function templates is to compute some constant tasks during compile time via recursion, which is called TMP. It has the ability to perform compile-time computation and/or optimization, as well as avoid virtual table lookup during runtime.

You should now have a deep understanding of templates. You should be able to create your own function and class templates in applications, as well as practice using traits to optimize your algorithm and use TMP to do compile-time computation for additional optimization.

In the next chapter, we will explore how to implement traits in C++ and optimize algorithms using templates.

Questions

1. What are the negative side effects of macros and function overloading?

2. What is a class/function template? What is a template class/function?

3. What is a template parameter list? What is a template argument list? Once we have a class template, we can instantiate it either explicitly or implicitly. In what kind of scenario is explicit instantiation necessary?

4. What does polymorphism mean in C++? What is the difference between function overloading and function overriding?

5. What are type traits? How do we implement a type trait?

6. In the `5_class_template_implicit_inst_B.cpp` file, we said implicit instantiation generates the `X<int>` class, and then creates an `xi` object and generates the `X<int>::f()` function, but not `X<int>::g()`. How can you verify that `X<int>::g()` is not generated?

7. Using TMP, solve the problem of $f(x,n) = x^n$, where n is a const and x is a variable.

8. Extend `16_loop_unrolling_traditional.cpp` and `17_loop_unrolling_metaprogramming.cpp` to large $N=10,100,10^3,10^4,10^6, \ldots$, until you reach your system memory limits. Compare the compile time, object file size, and running CPU time.

Further reading

As referenced throughout this chapter, have a look at the following sources to find out more regarding what was covered in this chapter:

- *Milner, R., Morris, L., Newey, M. (1975). A Logic for Computable Functions with Reflexive and Polymorphic Types. Proceedings of the Conference on Proving and Improving Programs.* (`https://www.research.ed.ac.uk/portal/en/publications/a-logic-for-computable-functions-with-reflexive-and-polymorphic-types(9a69331e-b562-4061-8882-2a89a3c473bb).html`)

- *Curtis, Dorothy (2009-11-06). CLU home page. Programming Methodology Group, Computer Science and Artificial Intelligence Laboratory. Massachusetts Institute of Technology.* (`http://www.pmg.csail.mit.edu/CLU.html`)

- *Technical Corrigendum for Ada 2012, published by ISO. Ada Resource Association. 2016-01-29.* (`https://www.adaic.org/2016/01/technical-corrigendum-for-ada-2012-published-by-iso/`)

- *B. Stroustrup, C++.* (`https://dl.acm.org/doi/10.5555/1074100.1074189`)

- *S. Meyers. Effective C++ 55 Specific Ways to Improve Your Programs and Designs (3rd Edition), Chapter 7.* (`https://www.oreilly.com/library/view/effective-c-55/0321334876/`)

- *D. Gregor* and *J. Järvi (February 2008). Variadic Templates for C++0x. Journal of Object Technology. pp. 31-51.* (`http://www.jot.fm/issues/issue_2008_02/article2.pdf`)

- `https://www.boost.org/` for type traits, unit testing, and so on.

- `https://www.ibm.com/support/knowledgecenter/ssw_ibm_i_72/rzarg/templates.htm` for generic templates discussions.

- `https://stackoverflow.com/questions/546669/c-code-analysis-tool` for code analysis tools.

- *K. Czarnecki, U. W. Eisenecker. Generative Programming: Methods, Tools, and Applications, Chapter 10.*

- *N. Josuttis, D. Gregor,* and *D. Vandevoorde. C++ Templates: The Complete Guide (2nd Edition). Addison-Wesley Professional, 2017.*

4

Template Meta Programming

Template meta programming is a powerful technique in C++ that allows developers to write code that generates other code at compile time. This technique can be used to create highly efficient, generic, and reusable code, as well as to create domain-specific languages and other advanced features. In this book, you will learn the fundamentals of template metaprogramming and how to apply it to your own projects. You will also learn about the most important features of the C++ template system and the common pitfalls to avoid. Whether you are a beginner or an experienced C++ developer, this book will provide you with the knowledge and skills you need to master template metaprogramming and take your C++ programming to the next level.

In this chapter, we will discuss the following topics.

- Programming at compile time – the fundamentals (compile-time programming with templates)
- A `Constexpr`-based assessment of compile time
- **Substitution Failure Is Not an Error** (**SFINAE**) and the `enable_if` metafunction
- An introduction to `type_traits`
- Implementing trait functions

Technical requirements

To learn and understand template metaprogramming, you should have a solid understanding of the C++ programming language, including experience with templates, classes, and functions. Familiarity with the **Standard Template Library** (**STL**) and generic programming is also helpful. Additionally, you should have a development environment set up with a C++ compiler that supports at least C++11, the version of the standard that introduced many of the features used in template metaprogramming. You can find the source files used in this chapter at `https://github.com/PacktPublishing/ Expert-C-2nd-edition`.

Back to basics (compile-time programming with templates)

In the previous chapter, we discussed what templates are. In this chapter, we will go deeper into templates and will discuss why it is important to compute programs at compile time. In C++, there are some ways to compute values at compile time. New features have been added to language standards to carry out these functions.

The C++ template system is Turing-complete, meaning it has the ability to compute anything that can be computed, which was discovered during the process of standardizing the language. The first example of this was software that computed prime numbers, even though it did not complete compilation; the list of prime numbers was a component of the compiler's error message. In essence, code determines whether a given number is a prime number at compile time.

Let us see the following example:

```cpp
#include <iostream>
template <size_t n>
class Foo
{
public:
    Foo(void *);
    operator unsigned long();
};

template <size_t x, size_t y>
class DetectPrime
{
public:
    enum { prime = (x % y)
        && DetectPrime<(y > 2 ? x : 0),
        y>::prime };

};

template <size_t x>
class Print
{
public:
    Print<x - 1> obj;
    enum { prime = DetectPrime<x, x - 1>::prime };
```

```
        void f () { Foo<x> new_obj = prime; }
};


class DetectPrime<0, 0>
{
public:
    enum { prime = 1 };
};

class DetectPrime<0, 1>
{
public:
    enum { prime = 1 };
};

class Print<1>
{
public:
    enum { prime = 0 };
    void f () { Foo<1> new_obj = 0; }
};

int main()
{
    Print<18> obj;
}
```

Let's discuss the code.

In the main function, `Print<18>` is instantiated; it initiates a loop and creates `Print` with the values 18, 17, 16, and so on. Every instance of `Print<x>` creates `DetectPrime<x, x - 1>`. When the second argument of these `DetectPrime` templates is reduced one by one to 1, they begin to instantiate themselves. They check to see whether their first parameter is prime in these class templates. The class template Foo's constructor is used to transmit information about primeness to the member function in the `Print` class templates. Because the initialization of `new_obj` by `Display::f()` fails, the compiler will print errors. Because there is only one constructor for `void*` and only 0 is valid for `void*` when the initial value is 1, this is the case.

Let's look at error messages.

```
error: no viable conversion from 'const int' to 'D<17>'
error: no viable conversion from 'const int' to 'D<13>'
error: no viable conversion from 'const int' to 'D<11>'
error: no viable conversion from 'const int' to 'D<7>'
error: no viable conversion from 'const int' to 'D<5>'
error: no viable conversion from 'const int' to 'D<3>'
error: no viable conversion from 'const int' to 'D<2>'
```

Figure 4.1 – Depth error

When we talk about compile-time programming, the first thing that comes to mind is to calculate the factorial of a number. How can we implement it using templates?

```
1. template <unsigned long X>
2. class SimpleFactorial
3. {
4.  public:
5.      enum { val = X * SimpleFactorial<X-1>::val };
6. };
```

Let's examine our code now. We have a declaration for a non-type template argument in the first line. Note that the type is `size_t` because we must work with a positive value. In the second line, we have a declaration of the `SimpleFactorial` class; of course, we can declare a class, and in terms of visibility modifiers, a class is more convenient to use. In template metaprogramming terms, it is called a *metafunction*. Moving on, we will see a declaration of an anonymous enum, which has one value with the name `value`. You know that the name of the enumeration type is like a flag, but in this example, there is no need for one. A value is used to generate values of a metafunction. Let's use this code by instantiating the template and passing it the desired arguments:

```
int main()
{
    const auto x = SimpleFactorial<4>::val;
    static_assert(x == 24, "Factorial of 4");
}
```

What is the output of this code after compilation?

Yes, there is an ill-formed program. Now, let's go through the code and find out why. Templates are processed in two phases. In the first phase, everything that does not depend on template arguments is looked up and checked. The definition is checked for syntax errors such as missing semicolons or name lookup errors. Here's an example:

```
template <typename U>
class Deque
```

```
{
public:
    Deque() = default;
    Deque(const T &elem)
    : __container { new T(Elem) }
    // error : undefined identifier        Elem
{ }
private:
    U* __container // syntax error: missing semicolon
};
```

The second phase is argument-dependent lookup. A class template (or function template) is not a type; the source file does not contain templates, and a template must be instantiated. The compiler must generate an actual class (or function) using arguments. This is called the second phase of template processes. In our code after the first phase, the template class itself depends on *recursively* creating smaller instances of the same metafunction. The following code represents that form of generation:

```
#ifdef _SIMPLE_FACTORIAL_
template<>
class SimpleFactorial<4>
{
public:
    enum { val = static_cast<unsigned int>(4UL *
        static_cast<unsigned
        long>  (SimpleFactorial<3>::val)) };
};
#endif // To avoid code length, initializations with values, 3 and 2 are
// omitted
#ifdef _SIMPLE_FACTORIAL_
template<>
class SimpleFactorial<1>
{
public:
    enum { val = static_cast<unsigned int>(1UL *
        static_cast<unsigned long>
        (SimpleFactorial<0>::val)) };
};
```

And so on until it reaches the limit. Most compilers won't permit recursion depth to go past a certain point. This error is produced by the compiler:

```
enhance the depth of the recursive template instantiation:
enum { val = X * SimpleFactorial<X - 1>::val};
```

The solution is as follows – we have to declare a template specialization with argument 0. A specialization is a variation of a template designed for a certain template argument list:

```
template<>
class SimpleFactorial<0>
{
public:
    enum { val = 1 };
};
```

The `SimpleFactorial<0>` specialization represents the terminating condition. Now, our code will work smoothly. For this kind of computation, the `std::integral` constant might be used instead of an enum (wrapping a static constant of the specified type is a `std::integral` constant. It serves as the foundational class for C++ type characteristics):

```
template <unsigned long X>
class SimpleFactorial : std::integral_constant<unsigned long, X *
SimpleFactorial<X-1>::value>
{
};

template <>
class SimpleFactorial<0> : std::integral_constant<unsigned long, 1> {
};
```

Using `constexpr` is an alternate method:

```
constexpr unsigned long SimpleFactorial (unsigned long X)
{
    return (X == 0) ? 1 : X * SimpleFactorial(X - 1);
}



int main()
{
    int i = 4;
    constexpr auto x = SimpleFactorial(4);
    // auto y = SimpleFactorial(i);
}
```

The function is computed at compile time when we comment out the declaration of y.

The assembly code version is displayed in *Figure 4.2*. The first two instructions set EBP to point at that location on the stack while saving the previous base pointer (ebp – right below the return address). The third line is the declaration of the i variable, which is initialized with 4, and the next line shows that in the address rbp-16, moves a constant value, 24, which is called an immediate operand. Now, replace the comments from the *y* variable to *x*:

```
push    rbp
mov     rbp, rsp
mov     DWORD PTR [rbp-4], 4
mov     QWORD PTR [rbp-16], 24
mov     eax, 0
pop     rbp
ret
```

Figure 4.2 – A factorial representation in Assembly

```
int main ()
{
    int i = 4;
    //constexpr auto x = Factorial(4);
    auto y = Factorial(i);
}
```

Now, there is a function call in the fifth line in *Figure 4.3* that will compute the runtime.

```
mov     DWORD PTR [rbp-4], 4
mov     eax, DWORD PTR [rbp-4]
cdqe
mov     rdi, rax
call    factorial(long_long)
mov     QWORD PTR [rbp-16], rax
mov     eax, 0
leave
ret
```

Figure 4.3 – A factorial representation in Assembly

Note

The constexpr specifier was used in this example.

The second example computes the number's primeness; however, in this case, the code is modified so that it now compiles on standard conforming compilers:

```cpp
#include <iostream>

template<size_t x, size_t y>
class FindPrime
{
public:
    constexpr static  bool val = (x % y != 0)
        && FindPrime<x, y-1>::val;
};

template<size_t x>
class FindPrime<x, 2>
{
public:
    constexpr static bool val = (x % 2 != 0);
};

template <size_t x>
class Prime
{
public:
    constexpr static bool val = FindPrime<x, x/2>::val;
};

template<>
class Prime<0>
{
public:
    constexpr static bool val = false;
};

template<>
class Prime<1>
{
public:
    constexpr static bool val = false;
};

template<>
class Prime<2>
```

```
{
public:
    constexpr static bool val = true;
};

template<>
class Prime<3>
{
public:
    constexpr static bool val = true;
};

int main()
{
    constexpr auto x = Prime<7>::val;
    std::cout << std::boolalpha << x << std::endl;
}
```

Again, let's look at `constexpr` in this example – in the main function, there is a static assertion that performs static assertion at compile time. `Prime<7>::val` instantiates the `IsPrime` template expression. It doesn't match any specialization of `IsPrime`, so after instantiation, the template code of `Prime` is the following:

```
template<>
struct Prime<7>
{
inline static constexpr const bool value = Compute_Prime<7, 7 /
2>::value;
};
```

As you can see, another template expression, `FindPrime` (which has its own specialization), is called, and this must be instantiated too:

```
template<>
struct FindPrime<7, 3>
{
inline static constexpr const bool val = ((7U % 3U) != 0) &&
FindPrime<7,2>::val;
  };
```

This is called its **specialization**:

```
template <>
struct FindPrime<7, 2>
{
```

```
inline static constexpr const bool val = ((7U % 2) != 0);
};
```

The last expression evaluates to `true`, and after that, `FindPrime` has the following form:

```
template<>
struct FindPrime<7, 3>
{
inline static constexpr const bool val = ((7U % 3U) && true);
};
```

The value of `FindPrime` is `true` and it assigns the value of `Prime`. So, after that, we have a result that says that number 7 is a prime number.

Compile-time evaluation using constexpr

The `constexpr` function was added in C++11 and enhanced in C++14. Besides the fact that we can declare a variable as `constexpr`, it indicates that, where possible, the return value is computed at compile time and is constant. A `constexpr` function is one whose return value can be computed at compile time when the consuming code requires it, according to the definition. In our example, the body of the function is written as a single statement because only a very small subset of the language can be used by `constexpr` functions. Many `constexpr` constraints were removed in C++14, making it much easier to write them now. You have already seen its use in the examples, and now, we will go deeper.

Here's the syntax of `constexpr`:

* `constexpr literal identity = expression`
* `constexpr literal identity {expression};`
* `constexpr literal identity (parameters);`
* `constexpr constructor (parameters);`

As a `constexpr` variable, it must be immediately initialized. `const` variables can be initialized at runtime, whereas `constexpr` variables must be initialized at compile time. This is the difference between `const` and `constexpr` variables. `constexpr` variables are all fixed, as shown in the following code:

```
int main ()
{
int x = 24;
constexpr int result = x; // constexpr variable result
// needs to be initialized with a constant expression,
// causing a build problem
const int y = 24;
```

```
constexpr int result_2 = y; // Ok, y is constant expression

    constexpr int result_3; // compile error: not
                            // initialized!
}
```

The following guidelines apply to `constexpr` functions and constructors:

- As a `constexpr` function, its parameters type and return type must be a `LiteralType`.

- It can't be virtual.

- A `constexpr` function can be recursive.

- A `goto` statement and `try` blocks are not permitted in the body of a function.

- A description of a thread or static storage duration.

- Each constructor chosen to initialize base class members and non-static data members must be a `constexpr` constructor.

- A non-`constexpr` template may be explicitly specialized and declared as `constexpr`. It may also contain all looping statements, such as `for`, range-based `for`, `while`, and `do-while` (as of C++14). It may also contain the `if` and `switch` statements, as shown in the following code:

  ```
  template <typename U>
  constexpr auto large (U const& ob1, const U& obj2)
  {
  if ( obj1 < obj2 ) { return obj2; }
  else { return obj1; }
  }
  int main()
  {
  unsigned long x = large (34ul, 56ul);
  static_assert( x == 56ul, "56 is not greater");
  // The expression static assert is not an expression
  // for an integral constant.
  }
  ```

As you can see, the program is ill formed because static assertion requires a constant expression. The solution declares the *x* variable as `const` or `constexpr`. Variables of the `constexpr` type must be constant expressions, meaning their value can be determined at compile time. As a result, you cannot declare a function as `constexpr` because its value may change at runtime and cannot be determined at compile time, as shown in the following code:

```
short increase(short x, short y)
{
```

```
    if ( y == 0 ) { return 1; }
    return (x * increase(x, y - 1));
}
int main( )
{
constexpr short x = increase( 5, 2 ); // constexpr variable
// "x" must be initialized by a constant expression,
// causing a compilation problem}
```

Using constant expression in every function and assuming that it is better than templates would be the biggest mistake. This is because every time we write a constexpr function, it might not be executed at compile time. It says that the function has the potential to run at compile time. It's often a question of the compiler and the optimization level if a constexpr function runs at compile time or runtime. But since C++14, the restrictions that constexpr had in C++11 are gone (such as having new variables or loops in constexpr functions). The greatest common divisor of two numbers can be determined using the gcd function, as shown in the following code:

```
constexpr int gcd (short x, short y)
{
    while(y != 0)
    {
        int tmp = y;
        y = y % x;
        x = tmp;
    }
    return x;
}

int main( )
{
    constexpr short i = gcd (15, 25); // calculate the
                                      // result i at compile time
    int arr[ gcd(5, 4) ]; // calculate the size of array at
                          // compile time
    short a = 11;
    short b = 24;
    constexpr short res = gcd (a, b); // constexpr variable
// must be initialized with a constant expression, causing
// a compilation issue}
```

Constant expression-specified constructors (constexpr)

A constructor that is declared with a constexpr specifier is a constexpr constructor. With the constexpr constructor, objects of user-defined types can be included in valid constant expressions. constexpr constructor definitions must adhere to the following requirements:

- There cannot be any virtual base classes in the containing class.

- A literal type describes each of the parameter kinds.

- If its function body is not = delete or = default, then it must adhere to the following restrictions:

  - The function try block is not the issue

  - Only these statements may be included in the compound statement:

    - Declaring nothing (a null statement)

    - Statically defined assertions

    - Not defining classes or enumerations in typedef declarations

    - using

The constructor is implicitly specified as constexpr if a user-provided default constructor can fulfill the requirements of a constexpr constructor. Let's look at a code example:

```
#include <iostream>

class Base { };

struct B2
{
    int x;
};

struct NL
{
    virtual ~NL() { }
};

int x = 11;

struct Derived1 : Base
{
    constexpr Derived1() : Base(), _m{12} { }
    constexpr Derived1(const Derived1 &obj) : Base{obj},
```

```
        _m{12} { } constexpr Derived1(NL &n) : Base(),
        _m{12} { } private: int _m;
};
```

Here's a list of differences between template metaprogramming and `constexpr` functions:

- A template metaprogram executes at compile time, but `constexpr` functions can run at compile time or runtime.

- Arguments of templates can be types or values. Templates can take such arguments as containers, such as `std::vector<std::string>`.

- Instead of modifying a value, you return a new value every time in template metaprogramming.

- The function arguments of `constexpr` functions correspond to the template arguments of a metafunction.

- A `constexpr` function can have variables, and you can modify them. A metafunction generates a new value.

- A metafunction can use a loop (since C++ 14).

> **Note**
>
> You cannot have STL containers as `constexpr`. Container objects have a dynamic memory allocation, so they cannot be persistent at both compile and runtime. There was no support for them before C++20; however, since then, these objects are allowed to be in the same places as `constexpr` functions, so they are destroyed at the end of compile time.

The following code demonstrates the use of compile-time constants in C++, specifically the `constexpr` keyword, along with the `map` container from the C++ Standard Library:

```
/* include directives */
using namespace std;
int main ()
{
    constexpr map<string, int> cxpr_mp {{"one", 1}, {"two",
      2}}; // compile error,
            // because map is STL container
    const map<string, int> c_mp {{"one", 1}, {"two", 2}}; // Ok
}
```

constexpr if

C++17 added a new statement called `constexpr if`. The most important advantage is that `constexpr if` is evaluated at compile time, not at runtime. Based on a condition in a constant expression, the functionality enables you to eliminate `if` statement branches during compilation. The following shows the difference between ordinary `if` and `constexpr if` statements:

Ordinary `if`	`constexpr if`
Performs another statement subject to conditions. Used when runtime-based code execution is required.	Removes non-matching function overrides from the overload, set in place of the SFINAE approach.
Determines which of the two sub-statements to execute, skipping the other.	Determines which of the two sub-statements to compile, discarding the other.
Requires both sub-statements to be well formed, regardless of which one is actually selected at runtime.	A compile-time `if` allows us to enable or discard statements according to compile-time conditions (even outside templates).

Table 4.1 – Difference between ordinary if and constexpr if statements

You may now be asking the question, why a compile-time `if`? Where will I use it? Let's consider an example. How can we print out all the elements of the `variadic` template argument?

```
void print () {}

template <typename U, typename... T>
void print (U const& first, T const&... pack)
{
    cout << first << " ";
    print(pack...);
}
```

If this function receives one or more arguments, the template that represents the first argument independently will be used and prints it before *recursively* (I think *recursion* in templates is not a well-chosen word) calling for the remaining arguments. These remaining `pack` arguments are called a **function parameter pack**. For the base case, the `print` function is used; this is obviously invoked when emptying the function parameter pack and does not take an argument, as shown in the following code block:

```
print(3.14, "templates", 55);
```

C++11 introduced a brand-new `sizeof` operator with variadic templates. It expands depending on the number of elements. This unwittingly leads to the idea that we can use this in the `print` function to print out all the arguments of the variadic template:

```
template <typename U, typename... T>
void print (U const& first, T const&... pack)
{
    cout << first << " ";
    if(sizeof...(pack) > 0)
    {
        print(pack...);
    }
}
```

However, this approach cannot work because we know that if the `check` condition is a runtime operation – that is, all exemplars are generated during lookup – and if we call the function already with the last argument, then the same function is called without an argument, leading to a compile error. Here, the `constexpr if` statement can help us:

```
if constexpr(sizeof...(args) > 0)
```

If `print()` is called for one argument only, `args` becomes an empty parameter pack so that `sizeof...(args)` becomes 0. The call of `print()` becomes a *discarded statement*, for which the code is not instantiated. The fact that the code is not instantiated means that only the first translation phase is performed.

Let us now see another example:

```
template <typename U>
string foo(U const& val)
{
    if (is_convertible_v<U, string>)
    {
        return val;
    }
    return to_string(val);
}
int main()
{
    foo("example");
}
```

The `is_convertible` type trait yields `true` when we pass a string literal and just returns `val`, without any conversion. However, we get a compile error with the following output:

```
there isn't a matching function for the call to "to string"
return to_string(val);
  function template specialization "strchar [6]>" is requested here
during function invocation.
    cout << str("hello");
```

Both branches were compiled by the compiler, and the other case had an error. The `invalid` code for this specific template instantiation could not be rejected. In this code example, the `constexpr` `if` statement is required because of this:

```
if constexpr(std::is_convertible<T, std::string>)
```

Having discussed the limitations of traditional template instantiation in the previous example, it's time to move on to a more sophisticated solution for this issue. This is where SFINAE and `enable_if<>` come into play. These tools provide a way to modify the template instantiation process to handle specific cases differently, which is essential in solving complex template-related problems. By incorporating SFINAE and `enable_if<>` into your code, you can take your templates to the next level and unlock new possibilities. Let's dive into the details of SFINAE and `enable_if<>` in the next topic.

SFINAE AND enable_if<>

Before C++17, there were already ways to enable or disable templates as a whole – a compile-time `if`, partial specialization, SFINAE, and `enable_if<>`. Referring to our previous example, `is_prime<>`, where we determined the authenticity of a prime number, we can use partial specialization to choose at compile time between different type implementations. We can choose different implementations depending on the argument (we used a struct in the code because function templates do not support partial specialization):

```
template <std::size_t n, bool = IsPrime(n)>
class hash_table;

template <std::size_t n>
class hash_table<n, true>
{
public:
    std::array<int, n> bucket;
};

template <std::size_t n>
class hash_table<n, false>
{
```

```
public:
    array<int, next_prime<n>::value> bucket;
// next_prime<size_t n> is a meta function which compute
// the next prime number for the given integral.
};
```

Depending on whether *n* is a prime number, we use two different implementations of the hash_ table structure. So, we discovered that depending on the characteristics of the argument it is being invoked for, partial specialization can be used to choose between various implementations of a function template (we used class in the preceding code because function templates do not support partial specialization).

Argument substitution failure

As we already know, a type or value can be a parameter in the declaration of a class, a function, or a type alias in C++, thanks to the template mechanism. However, without instantiation at definition time, the template code itself is checked for correctness, ignoring the template parameters. At instantiation time, the template code is checked (again) to ensure that all code is valid. All these processes are called a two-phase translation of templates. Every template argument must be known, but not every argument needs to be provided when a function template is used. When possible, the compiler will infer the missing template arguments from the function arguments. Processing the template code, the compiler must at various times *substitute* arguments for the template parameters. However, this substitution can fail:

```
template <typename U>
typename U::value_type sub_phase
(U beg, U end)
{
// some code and return statement
}

void foo(list<short> &ls, short *p, short n)
{
    auto x = sub_phase(ls.begin( ), ls.end( ));
    auto y = sub_phase(p, p + n);
}
```

Because the arguments in this code match, and because vector<short>::iterator includes a member called value_type, instantiating x is successful. Although the arguments are identical, short* does not have a member called value_type; thus, we cannot conclude that y has been properly initialized:

```
short*::value_type sub_phase(short*, short*);
```

We must declare a new function, which will satisfy our requirements.

```
template <typename U>
typename U::value_type sub_phase
(U beg, U end)

template <typename U>
U sub_phase (U*, U*) {// some code and return statement}

void foo(list<short> &ls, short *p, short n)
{
    auto x = sub_phase(ls.begin( ), ls.end( ));
    auto y = sub_phase(p, p + n);
}
```

Both initializations are successful in this case, but why, when attempting to match sub_phase (p, p + n) with the initial template definition, did an error not occur? The argument is a perfect match; however, when the real template argument (short *) is substituted, the return value is unsuccessful. If the parameter can be utilized in the manner specified by the whole function template definition, the compiler takes that into account (including the return type). There is a grammar principle known as SFINAE. Function templates are simply ignored because they don't add a specialization to the overload set. The steps involved in function template argument deduction and overload resolution in C++ include name lookup, template argument deduction, the final variable function set, and selection of the best viable function. Understanding this process is important to writing correct and efficient C++ code that makes use of templates and function overloading.

In C++, it is pretty common to overload functions to account for various argument types. When a compiler sees a call to an overloaded function, it must therefore consider each candidate separately, evaluating the arguments of the call and picking the candidate that matches best. In cases where the set of candidates for a call includes function templates, before evaluating how well it matches, the compiler must first decide which arguments should be used for that candidate, and then substitute those arguments in the function parameter list with its return type (just like an ordinary function). However, the substitution process can run into problems – it can produce constructs that make no sense. Rather than deciding that such meaningless substitutions lead to errors, the language rules instead say that candidates with such substitution problems are simply ignored. This principle is called SFINAE, and it means that *a failed substitution is not an error* (David Vandevoorde).

The following are the types of SFINAE errors:

- Attempting to instantiate a pack expression with many packs of various lengths
- Attempting to build an array of size zero, a void, a reference, a function, or another type that doesn't have an integral size
- Using a type that is neither a class nor an enumeration that is on the left of a scope resolution operator
- Using a member of a type that the type does not have when trying to use that member
- Attempting to build a reference pointer
- Making an effort to establish a reference to void
- Trying to make a pointer to a T member when T is not a class type
- Attempting to assign a non-type template parameter to a type that is incorrect
- Attempting to define a function type that accepts void as an argument

Let's consider the following code:

```
#include <iostream>

enum numbers { one = 1, two, three, four };

template <long X>
void dismem (int(*)[I % 2 == 0] = 0)
{
    std::cout << "even" << std::endl;
}

template <long X>
void dismem (int(*)[I % 2 == 1] = 0)
{
    std::cout << "odd" << std::endl;
}

int main ()
{
    dismem<one> ();
    dismem<four> ();
}
```

There is an overload of non-type function templates (a non-type template argument is an expression that can have its value computed at compile time and is offered within a template argument list. Constant expressions, addresses of externally linked functions or objects, or addresses of static class members must be used as these parameters. In general, initializing a class or specifying the sizes of class members involves non-type template arguments). The parameter of the first version of div is a pointer to an array whose size is an expression and must be calculated at compile time. It's the same in the second function parameter, with one difference – the expression that checks the evenness in the first function; in this case, the check is performed for odd numbers. The main function, after instantiation of the function template, prints out odd and even numbers. However, this is not an error; this is SFINAE. Now, what if we comment on the second version of div? There will be a compilation error, which was previously mentioned in the SFINAE error types.

Disabling templates with enable_if<>

enable_if<> is a type trait that evaluates a given compile-time expression passed as its (first) template argument, which behaves as follows:

- If the expression yields true, its type member type yields type:

  - If the second template argument is not given, type is void

  - If not, the second template argument type is type

- If the expression yields false, the member type is not defined. Due to the template feature called SFINAE, this has the effect that the function template with the enable_if expression is ignored.

The implementation is almost trivial:

```
template <bool Condition, class U = void>
class enable_if { };

template <typename U>
class enable_if<true, U> { typedef U type; };
```

If Condition is true, the U type is enabled as a member type, enable if::type. If enable if::type is not defined, nothing happens. When a specific condition is not satisfied, this can be used to hide signatures during compilation because, in this case, the enable if::type member won't be specified, and attempting to build using it should fail:

```
/* include directives *
template <class U>
typename enable_if<(sizeof(U) > 4)>::type
custom_enable()
{
```

```
        std::cout << "enabled" << std::endl;
}

int main()
{
    map<string, short> mp {{"one", 1}, {"two", 2}};
    custom_enable<decltype(mp)>();
    // custom_enable<const char*>();
}
```

The function template demonstrates the usage of enable_if. The return type is void because the second argument does not exist. The point here is that the function will not be formed if the size of T is equal to or smaller than 4 bytes. After the first function call everything is OK, prints out enabled, because the size of the map is bigger than 4 bytes (depending on the system, it may vary from 24 to 32 bytes). However, when we comment on the first function call and remove the comments from the second one, it can be ill formed, depending on the size of the pointer (which is determined by different issues, such as the operating system and CPU architecture).

The next example shows an implementation of the std::advance algorithm, which is considered one of the standard library algorithms. It advances the iterator, it, by *n* element positions. What is of interest is that it has different implementations for different iterator categories:

```
#include <type_traits>
#include <iterator>
#include <set>
#include <deque>

namespace my_lib
{
// Implementation for random access iterators
template <typename X>
constexpr bool what_random_access_iterator =
  is_convertible<typename iterator_traits<X>::
  iterator_category, random_access_iterator_tag>::value;

template <typename X, typename Dist>
std::enable_if_t<what_random_access_iteraor<X>>
advance(X &x, Dist y) { x += y; }

// Implementation for bidirectional iterators
template <typename X>
constexpr bool what_bidirectional_iterator =
  is_convertible<typename std::iterator_traits<X>::
  iterator_category, std::bidirectional_iterator_tag>;
```

```cpp
template <typename X, typename Dist>
std::enable_if_t<what_bidirectional_iterator<X>
&& !what_random_access_iterator<X>>
advance(X &x, Dist y)
{
    if(y > 0)
    {
        for(; y> 0; ++x, --y) { }
    }
    else
    {
        for(; y < 0; --x, ++y) { }
    }
}


// Implementation for all other iterators

template <typename X, typename Dist>
std::enable_if_t<!what_bidirectional_iterator<X>
&& !what_random_access_iterator<X>>
advance(Iter &x, Dist y)
{
    if(y < 0)
    {
        throw "advance(): invalid category for negative y
    }
    while(y > 0)
    {
        ++x;
        --y;
    }
}
}

int main()
{
    std::set<int> st({1, 14, 5, 2});
    auto it = st.begin();
    my_lib::advance(it, 3);
    std::deque<std::string> dq({"hello", "some", "other"});
    auto it2 = dq.begin();
    my_lib::advance(it2, 2);
}
```

We have a global variable template declaration named `what_random_access_iterator`, which contains a Boolean value determining whether the passed iterator category is random-access or not. To find out, the `is_convertible` type trait is used; it checks whether the tag matches. The two template type parameters for the function are, respectively, `typename X` and `typename Dist` as distance. Because `enable if` returns `void` by default if the second argument is not sent, we already know that the function's return result is `void`.

The second example already declares the Boolean `what_bidirectional_iterator`, which checks whether the iterator is compatible with the bidirectional iterator. The function is slightly different from the previous one; here, the `enable_if` parameter checks whether it is bidirectional or not and, of course, denies the random-access case, as we know that the categories are in a hierarchical relationship with each other.

The body checks whether `y > 0` or not. The third example is intended for the other iterator categories as forward, or input. In the parameter of `enable_if`, the condition is checked by negating the bidirectional category. In the function, the body checks whether `y < 0`; if yes, an exception is thrown. We eventually want to check whether a type contains a specified member of the right type when using `enable if`. Be aware that using `enable if` will not make the built-in copy, move, or assignment operators inoperative. The reason is that member function templates never count as special member functions and are ignored when a copy constructor is needed:

```
class Person
{
public:
    template <typename T>
    Person(T const&) { }
...
};
```

The predefined copy constructor is still used. Deleting the predefined is not a solution because then `Person` results in an error if a copy operation is done. The solution is to declare the copy constructor `const` volatile and then mark it as deleted.

Now that we've covered the importance of copy constructors and the solution for their behavior, it's time to delve into another important aspect of C++ – type traits. Type traits are a mechanism for querying and manipulating the properties of types. By utilizing type traits, you can gain more control over your code and make it more efficient and readable. In the next chapter, we'll explore type traits in depth and see how they can help us better understand and use C++ templates.

Type traits

So far in this chapter, we can say that we have discussed only one technique of metaprogramming, which is called (as you already saw in its behavior) improved runtime performance. There is also a second approach, called improved type safety. If, with the first option, we could compute values at compile time, we can calculate the precise types required for algorithms or data structures in this section. Type features are a prime illustration of the second possibility. We can assess and alter types using a range of utilities called type traits, which are included in the Standard Library. This is also called the `metaprogramming` library. To use type traits, we must include the `<type_traits>` header:

Helper classes are the first category on the list:

- `integral_constant`(C++11)
- `bool_constant`(C++17)
- `true_type`
- `false_type`

As the `root` class for all C++ type traits is the `std::integral` constant, all standard type traits that produce values are descended from an instance of the integral constant. Let us see the following implementation:

```cpp
#include <iostream>
#include <type_traits>
namespace my_lib
{
    template <typename  U, U var>
    struct integral_constant
    {
    constexpr static U value = var;
    using value_type = U;
    using type = integral_constant;
    constexpr operator value_type() const noexcept
    {
        return value;
    }
    constexpr value_type operator()() const noexcept
    {
        return value;
    }
};
}

 enum numbers { one = 1, two, three };
```

```cpp
int main()
{
    using one_n = my_lib::integral_constant<numbers,
        numbers::one>;
    using three_n = my_lib::integral_constant<numbers,
        numbers::three>;
    static_assert(one_n() == numbers::one,
        "failed: val_1 != val_2 ");
}
```

Let's examine the integral constant's implementation. It has two parameters and is a class template. The type is described by the first parameter, while the non-type parameter with the U var is represented by the second. This U type is anticipated to be an integral type. The members are as follows:

- `static constexpr T value = v`, which means that we declare the T type value with a static `constexpr` specifier and assign it v, which is the second parameter of the class.

- `using value_type = T` – this declaration can be done with `typedef` too; it is the type alias for our T type.

- Using the injected class name and type = the integral constant.

- `value type()` – a conversion function for implicit type conversions that returns the wrapped value. It uses the `constexpr` operator.

- The `operator()() const noexcept constexpr value` type returns the wrapped value. With the help of this function, the integral constant can now be used in C++14 compilation-time function objects.

- Specializations of the integral constant named the `true` type and the `false` type have simple declarations, as shown in the following code:

    ```cpp
    typedef true_type my::lib::integral_constant<bool, true>
    typedef false_type my::lib::integral_constant<bool, false>
    ```

These two types are where almost all types of attributes come from. The alias `template bool` constant has been available since C++17:

```cpp
namespace my_lib
{
template <bool Argument>
using constant_bool = integral_constant<bool, Argument>;
using true_type = bool_constant<true>;
using false_type = bool_constant<false>;
}
```

Having distinct types for the resulting `true` and `false` values allows us to tag-dispatch, based on the result of the type traits:

```
#include <type_traits>
#include <iostream>

int main()
{
    using my_type = bool;
    const my_type x = 14;
    std::cout << std::boolaplha;
    std::cout << my_lib::bool_constant<x>::value; // true
}
```

Primary-type groups are the next feature. This category verifies whether or not a type is a main type:

- `isVoid`
- `isNull_pointer`
- `isIntegral`
- `isArray`
- `isEnum`
- `isClass`
- `isFunction`
- `isPointer`

If a type is `void`, `my_lib::isVoid` determines it. It contains the member constant value – if `U` is `void`, `const void`, `volatile void`, or `const volatile void`, the value is equal to `true`; otherwise, the value is `false`:

```
inherited from the trait of the same type:
namespace my_lib
{
template <typename U>
struct isVoid : my_lib::isSame<void, typename my_lib::remove_
cv<U>::type> { }
}

int main()
{
    cout << boolalpha;
    cout << my_lib::isVoid<void>::value << std::endl;
```

```
        cout << my_lib::isVoid<const void>::value;
        cout << my_lib::isVoid<int>::value << endl;
}
```

Since C++17, a trait has had a helper variable template (the _v suffix helps to get rid of the old syntax).

isNullpointer determines whether U is a null pointer. The member constant value is given. If U is nullptr t, const nullptr t, volatile nullptr t, or const volatile nullptr t, the value is true; otherwise, the value is false:

```
namespace my_lib
{
template <typename U>
struct isNullpointer
: my_lib::is_same<nullptr_t, my_lib::remove_cv_t<U>> { };
}

int main()
{
    cout << boolalpha;
    cout << my_lib::isNullpoitner<decltype(nullptr)>::value
      << endl;
    cout << my_lib::isNullpointer<char*>::value << endl;
}
```

The isIntegral type trait is a way to determine whether a T type is an integral type. It provides a member constant value that is equal to true if T is bool, char, short, int, long, or long long, and false otherwise. The value member is an integral constant, meaning that its value is determined at compile time. By utilizing the isIntegral type trait, you can gain more control over your code and make it more efficient and readable. Let's consider the following code:

```
{
template <typename U>
struct isIntegral : my_lib::false_type { };
template <> isIntegral<int> : true_type { };
template <> isIntegral<bool> : true_type { };
template <> isIntegral<char> : true_type { };
template <> isIntegral<short> : true_type { };
template <> isIntegral<long> : true_type { };
// and etc.
}
```

isArray determines whether T is a type of array. It gives the value of the member constant, which, if T is an array type, is equal to true; otherwise, it is equivalent to false:

```
namespace my_lib
{
    template <typename  U>
    struct isArray : false_type { };
    template <typename U>
    struct isArray<U[ ]> : true_type { };
    template <typename U, size_t N>
    struct isArray<U[N]> : true_type { };
}
int main()
{
    cout << std::boolalpha;
    cout << my_lib::isArray<int*>::value << endl;
    std::cout << my_lib::isArray<int[]>::value << endl;
}
```

The third category of traits is the composite type:

- isFundamental

- isArithmetic

- isScalar

- isReference

- isMemberPointer

Let us understand each in detail:

isFundamental

This determines whether U is a basic type, such as an arithmetic type, void, or nullptr t. It gives the value of the member constant, which is true if the T type is a fundamental type and false otherwise. IsFundamental inherits from integral_constant. It is already clear from the definition that the three aforementioned main types must be checked; if one of them evaluates as true, then the whole expression is true:

```
namespace my_lib
{
    template <typename U>
    struct isFundamental : my_lib::integral_constant<bool,
    my_lib::isArithmetic<U>::value ||
```

```
        my_lib::isVoid<U>::value ||
        my_lib::isNullpointer<U>::value> { };
// implementation of the is_arithmetic will be as follows
}

class Person { };
int main()
{
    cout << boolalpha;
    cout << my_lib::isFundamental<int>::value << " ";
    cout << my_lib::isFundamental<Person>::value;
    cout << endl;
}
```

In the preceding code, the first call of the `cout` operator prints `true` because `int` is a fundamental type. However, the second call evaluates `false`, as `Person` is not a fundamental data type in C++.

isArithmetic

Integral types and floating-point types are the two sub-types of the `isArithmetic` types. Arithmetic operators such as +, -, *, and / are defined for these sorts of data. They specify the value of the member constant – if T is an arithmetic type, it is `true`; otherwise, it is `false`. The `isArithmetic` type inherits from the integral constant:

```
namespace my_lib
{
template <typename U>
struct isArithmetic : my_lib::integral_constant<bool,
my_lib::isIntegral::value || my_lib::isFloating_point<U>::value> { };
}
class Person
{
public:
    Person(float x = 0.0) : _m{x} { }
    operator float() { return _m; }
private:
    float _m;
};

int main()
{
    cout << boolalpha;
```

```
    cout << my_lib::isArithmetic<Person>::value << " ";
    cout << my_lib::isArithmetic<float>::value << endl;
}
```

In the example, you can see that we created a `Person` class, which has a parametrized constructor and operator float, providing an implicit type conversion of the `Person` type to `float`. However, when we check for the `isArithmetic` type, we can see that it was not passed, and the result prints `false`.

isScalar

This determines whether U is a scalar type. Scalar data objects in C++ are those that have a single value and are not made up of other C++ objects, such as integers and pointers, while non-scalar data objects include arrays and classes. Although pointers to members seem to be simple scalars, implementations typically represent them using a variety of machine data. For instance, a function pointer and an offset value may both be included in a pointer to a member function. The member constant value is provided by the type trait; it is `true` if U is a scalar type and `false` otherwise. `IsScalar` inherits from the integral `constant`.`namespace my_lib`:

```
{
template <typename U>
struct isScalar : my_lib::integral_constant<bool,
my_lib::isArithmetic<U>::value ||
my_lib::isEnum<U>::value ||
my_lib::isPointer<U>::value ||
my_lib::isMember_pointer<U>::value ||
my_lib::isNullpointer<U>::value> { };
}

template <typename Arg1, typename... Args>
void are_scalars(Arg1&& first_arg, Args&&... args)
{
    using type = std::decay<decltype(first_arg)>::type;
    std::cout << typeid(type).name() << " is "
      << (my_lib::is_scalar<type>::value ? " " : "not ")
      << "a scalar" << std::endl;
    if constexpr(sizeof...(args) > 0)
    {
        are_scalars(std::forward<decltype(args)>(args)... );
    }
}
enum class E { one };
class M { int x; }obj;
```

```
int main()
{
    are_scalar(3.14, 4, E::e, obj, "string");
}
```

This example demonstrates the implementation of the `is_scalar` type trait and shows how to use it in different situations. We declared the `enum` class and the `ordinary` class, and in `function invocation`, we passed these types and also several scalar types as `int`, `double`, and `const char*`. The result in the console is the following.

```
double is a scalar
int is a scalar
E is a scalar
M is not a scalar
char const* is a scalar
```

`isReference` determines whether U is a reference type. Similar to a pointer, a reference keeps track of an object's address in another part of memory. A reference cannot be set to `null` or a different object after initialization, unlike a pointer. The member constant value equal to `true` is provided by the type trait. The value for any other type is `false`:

```
template <typename U>
struct isReference : my_lib::false_type { };
template <typename U>
struct isReference<U&> : my_lib::true_type { };
template <typename U>
struct isReference<U&&> : my_lib::true_type { };
```

With `isMember_pointer`, you can refer to non-static class members and non-static member functions using pointers for members. Because the address of a static member is not linked to any specific object, you cannot use a pointer for a member to point to a static class member. The member constant value equal to `true` is provided by the type trait. The value for any other type is `false`:

```
namespace my_lib
{
    template <typename U>
    struct isMember_pointer_helper : my_lib::false_type { };
    template <typename U, typename Y>
    struct isMember_pointer_helper<U Y::*> :
      my_lib::true_type { };
    template <typename U>
    struct isMember_pointer :
      isMember_pointer_helper<typename
      my_lib::remove_cv<U>::type> { };
}
```

The modifiers that can be applied to various variables are compared using type characteristics. These type features, as shown in the following list, are not usually immediately beneficial:

- `isConst`
- `isVolatile`
- `isPolymorphic`
- `isAbstract`
- `isFinal`
- `isSigned`
- `isUnsigned`

isConst

The `const` keyword in C++ instructs the compiler to prevent any modification of an object or variable by specifying that it cannot be changed. The `is_const` type trait provides a member constant `value` that equals `true` if U is a type that is qualified as `const` or `const volatile`, and `false` for any other type. The `value` member is an integral constant, meaning its value is determined at compile time and can be used in constant expressions. Here is a simple implementation of `is_const`:

```
namespace my_lib
{
template <typename U> struct isConst : my_lib::false_type { };
template <typename U> struct isConst<const T> :  my_lib::true_type {
};
}
int main()
{
    cout << boolalpha;
    cout << my_lib::isConst<int>::value << endl;
    cout << my_lib::isConst<const int*>::value << endl;
    std::cout << my_lib::isConst<int* const>::value
       << endl;
    std::cout << my_lib::
       is_const<typename my_lib::remove_reference<const
       int&>::type>::value << endl;
}
```

Here is an example where the constancy of `const int*` was tested, the potential result is `false` because `int` cannot be modified whereas a pointer can. Additionally, there is a restriction that states that `const<U>::value` is always `false` if U is a reference type. Removing the reference, as we did in the previous example, is the correct technique to determine whether a reference type is `const`.

isVolatile

The `isVolatile` qualifier is used to tell the compiler that the value may change at any time. There are some properties of `volatile`:

- It cannot cache the variables in the register

- The value cannot change in order of assignment

- The `volatile` keyword cannot remove the memory assignment

If `T` is a volatile-qualified type that is `volatile` or `const volatile`, then the provided member constant value is equal to `true`. For any other type, the value is `false`. Inherited from `std::integral_constant`. The implementation is the same as for the `is_const` type trait.

isPolymorphic

Polymorphism is the ability to treat objects of different types as if they are of the same type. In C++, polymorphism is divided into two categories – static and dynamic. Static polymorphism with overloaded functions, an overloaded operator, and templates happens at compile time. Dynamic polymorphism with runtime interface changes. If a non-union class inherits or declares at least one virtual function, then the polymorphic type trait determines whether `U` is a polymorphic class and gives the member constant a value of `true`. The value for any other type is `false`. The `isPolymorphic` type inherited from the integral constant:

```
namespace my_lib
{
namespace detail
{
template <typename U>
my_lib::true_type detect_isPolymorphic (decltype(dynamic_cast<const
volatile void*> (static_cast<U*>(nullptr))));
template <typename U>
my_lib::false_type detect_isPolymorphic(...);
}
template <typename U>
struct isPolymorphic : decltype(detail::detect_
isPolymorphic<U>(nullptr)) { };
}

struct Sirius { int i; };
struct Base { virtual void foo() { } };
struct Derived : Base { };
struct Aludra { virtual ~Aludra() = default; };
```

```
int main()
{
    cout << boolalpha;
    my_lib::isPolymorphic<Sirius>::value << endl;
    my_lib::isPolymorphic<Base>::value << endl;
    my_lib::isPolymorphic<Derived>::value << endl;
    my_lib::isPolymorphic<Aludra>::value << endl;
}
```

Now, let's dive into the implementation of type traits. We declare two namespaces – one is our library, named my_lib, and the second one is detail. In the detail namespace, there is declarations helper functions detect_is_polymorphic. The first overloaded version returns the true type and, as a parameter, first casts the T type statically and then dynamically. And the second overloaded version returns the false type and as a parameter takes ellipsis. The global is_polymorphic meta-function derives from the detect_is_polymorphic function.

isAbstract

The defining characteristic of an abstract class type is that you cannot get a value of that type; therefore, it is improper to define a function, for instance, whose parameter or return type is abstract. Creating an array type with an abstract element type is also improper. SFINAE will not be applicable to U if it is abstract. While defining an entity of a function type with an abstract return type is permitted, it is not well formed. Therefore, if U is an abstract class – a non-union class that declares or inherits at least one pure virtual function – it must have a member constant with the true value. The value for any other type is false:

```
namespace my_lib
{
template <typename U, typename>
struct detect_isAbstract : my_lib::true_type { };

template <typename U>
struct detect_isAbstract<U, std::void_t<U[ ]>> : false_type { };

template <typename U>
struct isAbstract : detect_isAbstract<my_lib::remove_cv_t<U>, void> {
};
}

class A
{
public:
    virtual void foo() = 0;
```

```
};

int main()
{
    cout << boolalpha;
    cout << my_lib::is_abstract<A>::value << endl;
}
```

is_signed

C++ has signed, unsigned, and `char` types. In practice, there are basically only two types, signed and unsigned, because different compilers treat `char` as either signed or unsigned char. In general, if `int` is 4 bytes, it can store a range of values from –2.147.483.648 to 2.147.483.647, whereas an unsigned `int` can store from 0 to 4.294.967.295. So, the `is_signed` type trait checks whether T is signed and provides the member constant value as equal to `true` if $T(-1) < T(0)$. For any other type, the value is `false`. It is inherited from `std::integral_constant`:

```
namespace my_lib
{
template <typename T, bool = my_lib::is_arithmetic<T>::value>
struct is_signed: my_lib::integral_constant<bool, T(-1) <T(0)>{};

template <typename T>
struct is_signed<T, false> : my_lib::false_type {};
} // namespace mylib
template <typename T>
struct is_signed : mylib::is_signed<T>::type {};
```

Summary

Templates in C++ enable computation to occur during the build process. This means that certain operations, such as computing the factorial of a number, can be performed at compile time instead of runtime. While most compile-time calculations can be replaced with "ordinary functions" using `constexpr` functions, templates are still useful in cases where they are necessary. In template metaprogramming, it is possible to examine and even change the attributes of a type using type traits. One important concept in this field is SFINAE, which states that the replacement of functional templated declarations should not produce bad code, and templates should only be used when necessary. Another important aspect of templates is the `constexpr if` statement, which serves as a compile-time `if` statement. It allows for the conditional execution of statements based on constant expressions, enabling even more complex computations to occur during the build process. In summary, templates provide a powerful tool to perform computations at compile time, making your code more efficient and readable. With the use of `constexpr` functions and `constexpr if` statements, as well as type traits to examine and change type attributes, the capabilities of templates in C++ are virtually limitless.

Questions

1. What does metaprogramming actually entail?

2. What was the first template metaprogramming program?

3. When should you use `constexpr`?

4. What is the difference between `const` and `constexpr`?

5. Can a recursive function be `constexpr`?

6. Implement a program that calculates the Fibonacci number at compile time.

5
Memory Management and Smart Pointers

Memory management can be defined as a process in which a computer's memory is managed – for example, assigning memory to programs, variables, and more – so that it doesn't affect the overall performance. Sometimes, the computer's data can range up to terabytes, so efficiently using memory is necessary to minimize memory wastage and boost performance.

Memory management and smart pointers come at a price in C++. Programmers often complain about C++ because of its manual memory management requirements. While languages such as C# and Java use automatic memory management, it makes the programs run slower than their C++ counterparts. Manual memory management is often error-prone and unsafe. As we already saw in the previous chapters, a program represents data and instructions. Almost every program uses computer memory to some extent. It's hard to imagine a useful program that doesn't require memory allocation.

Memory allocation and deallocation start with the simplest call of a function. Calling a function usually implies passing arguments to it. The function needs space to store those arguments. To make life easier, it's handled automatically. The same automatic allocation happens when we declare objects in the code. Their lifetime depends on the scope they have declared. Whenever they go out of scope, they are deallocated automatically.

Most programming languages provide similar automatic deallocation functionality for dynamic memory. Dynamically allocated memory – as opposed to automatic allocation – is a term used by programmers to identify code portions that request new memory upon requirements. For example, this would be used in a program that stores the list of customers' requests for new memory space upon the increase in the number of customers. To somehow differentiate between types of memory management, whether it's automatic or manual, programmers use memory segmentation. A program operates with several segments of memory, including the stack, the heap, the read-only segment, and others, although all of them have the same structure and are part of the same virtual memory.

Most languages provide simplified methods for accessing dynamic memory without being concerned with its deallocation strategies, leaving the hard work up to the runtime support environment. C++

programmers have to deal with the low-level details of memory management. Whether it's due to the philosophy, structure, or age of the language, C++ doesn't provide high-level memory management functionality. Therefore, a deep understanding of memory structure and its management is a must for every C++ programmer. Now, let's illuminate the mystery behind memory and proper memory management techniques. In this chapter, we will cover the following topics:

- What is memory and how do we access it in C++?
- Memory allocation in detail
- Memory management techniques and idioms
- Garbage collection basics

Technical requirements

Clang has support for some of the features of the C++ standard following C++20, informally referred to as C++2b. You can use Clang in C++2b mode with the -std=c++2b option, but you can use the g++ compiler with the -std=c++2a option to compile the examples throughout this chapter.

You can find the source files used in this chapter at https://github.com/PacktPublishing/Expert-C-2nd-edition.

Understanding computer memory

At the lowest level of representation, memory is a device that stores the state of a bit. Let's say we are inventing a device that can store a single bit of information. Nowadays, it seems both meaningless and magical at the same time. It's meaningless to invent something that was invented a long time ago. It's magical because programmers nowadays have the luxury of stable multifunctional environments providing tons of libraries, frameworks, and tools to create programs without them even understanding them under the hood. It has become ridiculously easy to declare a variable or allocate dynamic memory, as shown in the following code snippet:

```
int x;
double *pd = new double(3.14);
```

It's hard to describe how the device stores these variables. To somehow shed some light on that magical process, let's try to design a device that stores a bit of information.

Designing a memory storage device

We will use electrical circuits, relays, and logic gates to design a simple device that can store a bit. The purpose of this section is to understand the structure of memory at its lowest level.

Here's a simple illustration of an electric circuit, which should be familiar to you from physics classes:

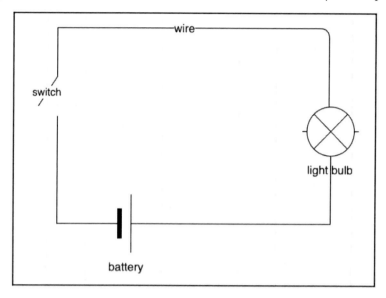

Figure 5.1: A memory storage device

It consists of a **wire** connecting a **battery** to a **light bulb**. The **wire** has a **switch** that controls the state of the light bulb. The light bulb is on when the switch is closed; otherwise, it's off. We will add two **Not OR** (**NOR**) logical elements to this circuit. A NOR is usually represented in the following way:

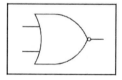

Figure 5.2: NOR logic gate

It has two inputs (the wires leading into the element), each of which represents an electrical signal. We say that the output (the wire coming out from the element) is 1 if both inputs are 0. That's why we call it *Not OR* – because the OR element outputs 1 if any of its inputs are 1. The preceding NOR element is simply constructed using two relays. A relay is a switch that uses an electromagnet to close and open the contacts. Look at the following diagram:

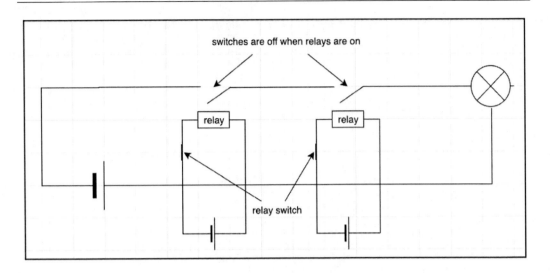

Figure 5.3: Open and close contacts

When both **switches** of **relays** are closed (meaning the relays are working and pulling down the switches of the circuit), the light bulb is *off*. When we move the switch to the open position of both relays, the light bulb turns *on*. The preceding diagram is one of the ways to depict a NOR gate. At this point, we can create a logic element using electric wires, light bulbs, batteries, and relays. Now, let's see a strange combination of two NOR elements leading to an interesting discovery:

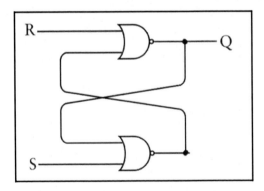

Figure 5.4: R-S flip-flop

The preceding diagram is a typical representation of an **R-S flip-flop**. **R** stands for *reset*, while **S** stands for *set*. The device built by the preceding scheme can store one bit. The output, **Q**, is the wire from which we can read the contents of the device. If we set the flip-flop to store the bit, the output will be 1. You should carefully examine the preceding diagram and imagine passing signals to its inputs one by one or both at the same time and see the output at **Q**. When the input, **S**, is 1, **Q** becomes 1.

When **R** is 1, **Q** becomes 0. This way, we *set* or *reset* the bit. It will store the bit so long as we supply current to the device.

Now, imagine we have a lot of devices, as designed earlier, interconnected so that we can store more than one bit of information. This way, we can construct complex memory devices that store bytes or even **kilobytes** (**KB**) of data.

The preceding device is similar to those used in computers before the invention of transistors. A transistor is a much smaller device capable of storing bits. Transistors differ in type. Modern devices don't use relays; instead, they incorporate millions of transistors for storing and manipulating data. A **central processing unit** (**CPU**) register is an example of a device that leverages transistors to store a specified number of bits. Usually, a general-purpose register stores up to 64 bits of data. However, you can't store all your programs and data using only registers. The organization of computer memory is much more sophisticated. Now, let's move on and examine the hierarchy of computer memory from a higher-level perspective.

Understanding computer memory from a higher-level perspective

Knowing the details of computer memory and data storage is crucial in writing professional programs. When programmers refer to the term *memory*, most of the time, they mean virtual memory. Virtual memory is an abstraction supported by the **operating system** (**OS**) that controls and provides memory space for processes. Each process has its address space represented as a collection of several segments. We discussed what memory segments there are and how a given program uses each in *Chapter 2, Low-Level Programming with C++*. From the programmer's perspective, accessing a memory space is mostly limited to object declaration and use. Whether we declare an object on the stack, heap, or static memory, we access the same memory abstraction – the virtual memory. Although complicated, virtual memory makes life a lot easier. Working directly with physical memory is harder, although it is a great advancement in a programmer's skills. You should at least know what memory storage units there are and how you can leverage that knowledge to write better code.

In this section, we discussed the physical memory hierarchy. We call it a *hierarchy* because each memory unit at a lower level provides faster access but a smaller space. Each consecutively higher level of memory provides more space in exchange for slower access.

We will discuss the physical memory hierarchy because it will help us design better code. Knowing how memory works at each level helps us improve as programmers and allows us to organize data manipulation better. The following diagram illustrates the memory hierarchy:

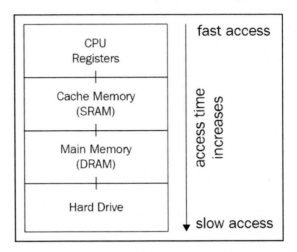

Figure 5.5: Memory hierarchy

Registers are the fastest accessible memory units placed in the CPU. The number of registers is limited, so we can't keep all the program data in them. On the other hand, **Dynamic RAM (DRAM)** can store a wide range of data for the program. It takes much longer to access data from the DRAM because of its physical structure and distance from the CPU. The CPU accesses DRAM via the data bus, which is a set of wires that transfers data between the CPU and DRAM. To signal to the DRAM controller whether it will read or write data, the CPU uses the control bus. We will refer to DRAM as the *main memory*. Let's look at the memory hierarchy in detail.

Registers

Registers hold a fixed amount of data. The CPU word size is usually defined by the maximum length of a register – for example, eight bytes or four bytes. We can't directly access a register from a C++ program.

C++ supports embedding assembly code using the **asm** declaration; for example, asm ("mov edx, 4 "). It's a platform-specific and artificial augmentation of the code, so we don't suggest using it.

> **Note**
> Visual C++ support for the standard C++ asm keyword is limited to the fact that the compiler will not generate an error on the keyword. However, an asm block will not generate any meaningful code. Use __asm instead of asm:

```
asm-block:
    __asm assembly-instruction; opt
    __asm {assembly-instruction-list}; opt
assembly-instruction-list:
    assembly-instruction; opt
```

```
    assembly-instruction; assembly-instruction-list; opt
```

Here's an example of this:

```
__asm {
  mov al,
  2 mov dx,
  0xD007 out dx, al
}
OR
  __asm mov al, 2
  __asm mov dx, 0xD007
  __asm out dx, al
```

In older versions of the language, we could use the `register` keyword when declaring a variable:

```
register int num = 14;
```

> **Note**
>
> The register storage class specifier was deprecated in C++11.

The keyword is unused and has been reserved since C++17.

The modifier specified that the compiler stores the variable in the register. This way, it gave programmers a fake sense of code optimization.

> **Tip**
>
> Compilers are sophisticated tools that translate higher-level C++ code into machine code. In the translation process, the code takes several transformations, including code optimizations. When programmers apply *tricks* to force the compiler to optimize a portion of the code, the compiler takes them as suggestions rather than commands.

For example, accessing a variable in a loop will be faster if that variable is placed in a register rather than in the DRAM. For example, the following loop accesses objects one million times:

```
int number{42};
for (int ix = 0; ix < 10000000; ++ix)
{
    int res{number + ix};
    // do something with res
}
```

As we know, the number has an automatic storage duration (it has nothing to do with the `auto` keyword) and is placed on the stack. The stack is a segment in the virtual memory, and the virtual memory is an abstraction over the physical DRAM. It's faster to access the object in a register than in DRAM. Let's suppose reading the value of a number from the DRAM is five times slower than from a register. It might seem obvious to optimize the preceding loop using the `register` keyword, as shown here:

```
auto number{42};
// the loop omitted for code brevity
```

However, compilers make better optimizations nowadays, so the need for a modifier has faded over time and it is now a deprecated language feature. A better optimization would be getting rid of the number object altogether. For example, the following code represents the compile-optimized version that uses the actual value rather than accessing it via the variable that resides in the DRAM:

```
for (int ix = 0; ix < 1000000; ++ix)
{
    int res{42 + ix};
    // do something with res
}
```

Although the preceding example is arguably simple, we should consider compiler optimizations that take place during compilation.

Discovering the registers improves our understanding of the program execution details. The point is that everything the CPU performs happens via the registers, including the instructions that the CPU should decode and execute, which are accessed using a specific register. These are commonly referred to as **instruction pointers**. When we run the program, the CPU accesses its instructions and decodes and executes them. Reading data from the main memory and writing data to memory is performed by copying it from and to the registers. Usually, general-purpose registers are used to temporarily hold data while the CPU performs operations on it. The following diagram depicts an abstract view of the **CPU** and its interaction with the main memory via buses:

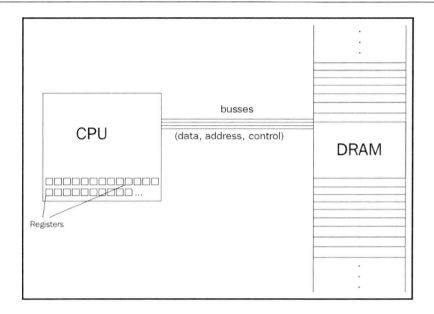

Figure 5.6: Connection between CPU and DRAM via buses

As you can see, the communication between the CPU and DRAM happens via various buses. In *Chapter 2, Low-Level Programming with C++*, we discussed the low-level representation of C++ programs – you should take a quick look at that to better understand the following example.

Now, let's see registers in action. The following C++ code declares two variables and stores their sum in a third variable:

```
int a{ 40 }, b{ 2 };
int c{ a + b };
```

To execute the sum instruction, the CPU moves the values of the a and b variables into its registers. After calculating the sum, it then moves the result into another register. An assembler pseudocode representation of the program looks similar to the following:

```
mov eax, a
mov ebx, b
add eax, ebx
```

The compiler doesn't need to generate code that maps each variable to one register – the number of registers is limited. You just need to remember that you should keep regularly accessed variables small enough that they fit into one of the registers. For larger objects, the cache memory comes to the rescue. Let's see how.

Cache memory

The idea of caching is common in programming and computer systems. Images loaded in the browser are cached to avoid further requests to the web server to download them in case the user visits the website again in the future. Caching makes programs run faster. This concept can be leveraged in many forms, including in single functions. For example, the following recursive function calculates the factorial of a number:

```
long long factorial(long long n)
{
    if (n <= 1) { return 1; }
        return n * factorial(n - 1);
}
```

The function doesn't remember its previously calculated values, so the following calls lead to five and six recursive calls, respectively:

```
factorial(5); // calls factorial(4), which calls factorial(3), and so
on
factorial(6); // calls factorial(5), which calls factorial(4), and so
on
```

We can cache already calculated values at each step by storing them in a globally accessible variable, as shown here:

```
std::unordered_map<long, long> cache;
long factorial(long n)
{
    if (n <= 1) return 1;
    if (cache.contains(n))
    {
        return cache[n];
    }
    cache[n] = n * factorial(n - 1);
    return cache[n];
}
```

These modifications optimize further calls to the function:

```
factorial(4);
```

Calling factorial(4) on its own on the previous line means that it's already been cached:

```
factorial(5);
factorial(6); // calls the factorial(5) which returns already
// calculated value in cache[5]
```

In the same way that the concept of caching makes the factorial function run faster, an actual memory device named the **cache** is placed inside the CPU. This device stores recently accessed data to make further access to that data faster. The following diagram depicts **registers** and **cache memory** inside the CPU:

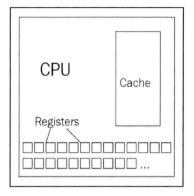

Figure 5.7: Registers and cache memory

The cache size usually ranges from 2 KB to 64 KB (and, rarely, 128 KB). While it doesn't seem big enough for applications such as Photoshop, where the image's data size can be way bigger than the cache size itself, it does help in many scenarios. For example, suppose we store more than 1,000 numbers in a vector:

```
std::vector<int> vec;
vec.push_back(1);
...
vec.push_back(9999);
```

The following code prints the vector items:

```
for (auto it: vec)
{
    std::cout << it;
}
    // 1
    // 2
    // 3
    // ...
    // 9999
```

Suppose that to print the item, the **CPU** copies it from memory to the rax register, then calls the << operator, which prints the value of the rax to the screen. On each iteration of the loop, the **CPU** copies the next item of the vector into the rax register and calls the function to print its value. Each copy operation requires the **CPU** to place the address of the item on the **address bus** and set the **control**

bus to read mode. The **DRAM** microcontroller accesses the data using the address received by the address bus and copies its value to the data bus, thereby sending the data to the **CPU**. The **CPU** directs the value to the rax register and then executes instructions to print its value. The following diagram shows this interaction between the **CPU** and **DRAM**:

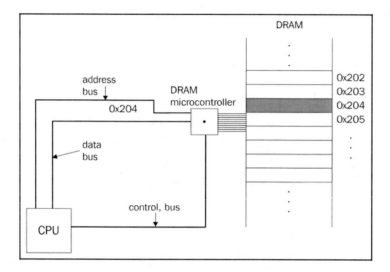

Figure 5.8: Intersection between the CPU and DRAM

To optimize the loop, the CPU maintains an idea of data locality – that is, it copies the whole vector into the cache and accesses vector items from the cache, omitting the unnecessary requests to DRAM. In the following diagram, you can see that the data received from DRAM via the data bus is then stored in the **cache memory**:

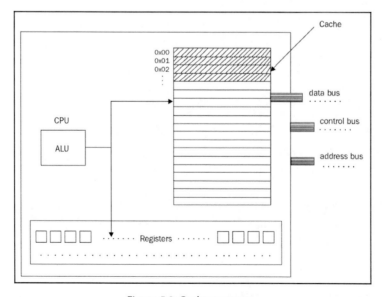

Figure 5.9: Cache memory

The cache residing in the CPU is known as a **level 1 (L1) cache**. This is the smallest in capacity and resides inside the CPU. Many architectures have a **level 2 (L2) cache**, which resides outside the CPU (though closer than the main memory) and is accessed the same way as DRAM. The difference between the L2 cache and DRAM is the physical structure and data access patterns. The L2 cache represents **Static RAM (SRAM)**, which is faster than DRAM but is also much more expensive.

> **Tip**
> Some runtime environments leverage the idea of caching when implementing garbage collection. They separate the objects into categories based on their lifetime with objects that have the smallest lifetime, such as the ones allocated to the local scope of the code, placed in the cache both to be accessed and deallocated faster.

New levels of cache memories serve as caches for the lower level. For example, the L2 cache serves as a cache memory for the L1 cache. When the CPU encounters a cache miss, it requests the L2 cache, and so on.

Main memory

The physical structure of DRAM forces it to refresh its charge to keep the data stable, while SRAM doesn't need to be refreshed like DRAM. We call DRAM the main memory mostly because programs are loaded into it; the OS maintains virtual memory and maps it to DRAM. All the actual work happens through the main memory first.

As we already discussed, the main memory represents a sequence of addressable bytes of data. Each byte has a unique address and is accessed using that address. We mentioned earlier how the CPU places the address of the data on the address bus, thereby letting the DRAM microcontroller fetch the requested data and send it via the data bus.

As we know, the OS introduces virtual memory as an abstraction over physical memory. It maps the contents of the virtual memory to the physical memory, which involves the CPU's **translation lookaside buffer (TLB)**. The TLB is another form of cache memory: it stores the recent translations of **virtual memory** into **physical memory**, thereby caching it for future requests. As shown in the following diagram, the **CPU** coordinates with the **TLB** to properly translate virtual addresses into physical addresses:

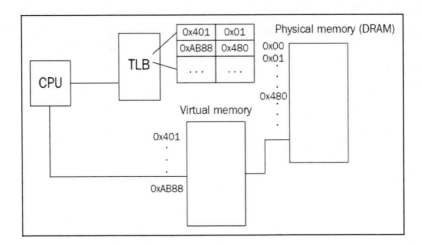

Figure 5.10: TLB

Though memory management is sophisticated, the OS provides us with a simple enough abstraction to manage the memory required for our programs. We can allocate it either automatically using the stack, or dynamically on the heap. Automatic memory allocation doesn't involve many concerns and difficulties; we just declare objects and they are placed on the stack and then automatically removed whenever the execution leaves the scope. In the case of dynamic memory (not to be confused with the hardware DRAM mentioned earlier), both allocation and deallocation should be done manually, which creates possibilities for making errors, which leads to memory leaks.

Permanent storage

When we turn off the computer, the contents of the main memory are erased (because the charge is not refreshed anymore). To store the data permanently, even when the power is off, computers are equipped with a **hard disk drive** (**HDD**) or a **solid-state drive** (**SSD**). From the perspective of programmers, permanent storage is used to store programs with their necessary data. We already know that to run a program, it should be loaded into the main memory – that is, copied from the HDD to DRAM. The OS handles this using a loader and creates a program image in memory, commonly referred to as a process. When the program is done or the user closes it, the OS marks the address range of the process as free to use.

Let's suppose we use a text editor to write notes while learning C++. The text that's typed into the editor resides in the main memory unless we save it on the HDD. This is important to note because most programs keep track of recent user activity and also allow the user to modify program settings. To keep these settings the way the user modified them, even after the program is relaunched, the program stores them as a separate *settings* file on the HDD. The next time the program runs, it first reads the corresponding settings file or files from the HDD and updates itself to apply the recent modifications of settings.

Usually, permanent storage has a much bigger capacity compared to the main memory, which makes it possible to use the HDD as a backup for virtual memory. The OS can maintain the virtual memory and fake its size, making it bigger than the physical DRAM. For example, the DRAM's 2-GB maximum capacity could be quickly exhausted by launching several heavyweight applications. However, the OS still can maintain a larger virtual memory by backing up its additional space with the HDD. When the user switches between applications, the OS copies the exceeding bytes of virtual memory to the HDD and maps the currently running application to the physical memory.

This makes programs and the OS run slower but allows us to keep them open without caring about the limited size of the main memory. Now, let's dive a little deeper into memory management in C++.

The basics of memory management

Most of the time, issues that arise during memory management happen when programmers forget about deallocating memory space. This results in memory leaks. A memory leak is a widespread issue in almost every program. When the program requests a new memory space for its data, the OS marks the provided space as **busy**. That is, no other instruction of the program or any other program can request that busy memory space. When the portion of the program is done with the memory space, ideally, it must notify the OS to remove the busy label to make the space available to others.

Some languages provide automatic control over dynamically allocated memory, leaving the programmer to worry about the logic of the application rather than constantly being concerned with deallocating memory resources. However, C++ assumes that the programmer is responsible and smart (which is not always the case). Dynamically allocated memory management is the programmer's responsibility. That's why the language provides both `new` and `delete` operators to deal with memory space, where the `new` operator allocates memory space and the `delete` operator deallocates it. In other words, the ideal code for dealing with dynamically allocated memory looks like this:

```
T* p = new T();
// allocate memory space p->do_something();
// use the space to do something useful delete p;
// deallocate memory space
```

Forgetting to call the `delete` operator makes the allocated memory space *busy forever*. By *forever*, we mean as long as the program is running. Now, imagine a web browser that is always open on the user's computer. Memory leaks here and there might lead to memory starvation over time, and sooner or later, the user has to restart the program or, even worse, the OS.

This issue applies to any resource that we work with, whether it's a file or a socket we forget to close (more about sockets in *Chapter 12*, *Networking and Security*). To solve this issue, C++ programmers use the **Resource Acquisition Is Initialization** (**RAII**) idiom, stating that a resource should be acquired on its initialization, which allows it to be properly released later. In the context of RAII, initialization specifically refers to the initialization of an object, tying the lifetime of the resource to the lifetime of the object. Let's see RAII in action.

An example of memory management

Consider the following function, which dynamically allocates an array of 420 shorts, reads their values from the user input, prints them in ascending order, and deallocates the array:

```
void print_sorted()
{
    short* arr{new short[420]};
    for (int ix = 0; ix < 420; ++ix)
    {
        std::cin >> arr[ix];
    }
    std::sort(arr, arr + 420);
    for (int ix = 0; ix < 420; ++ix)
    {
        std::cout << arr[ix];
    }
    delete arr; // very bad!
}
```

We already made a mistake in the preceding code by using the wrong `delete` operator to deallocate the memory. To deallocate an array, we must use the `delete[]` operator; otherwise, the code will lead to memory leaks. Here's how we illustrate the allocation of the array:

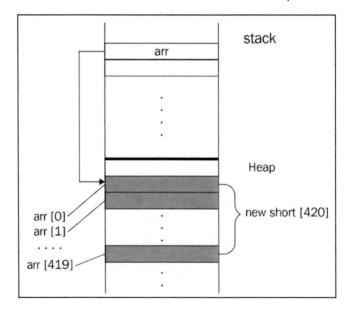

Figure 5.11: Dynamic array allocation

Let's say we release the space using `delete` instead of `delete[]`. It will treat `arr` as a short pointer, and therefore will remove the first 2 bytes starting at the address contained in the `arr` pointer, as shown in the following diagram:

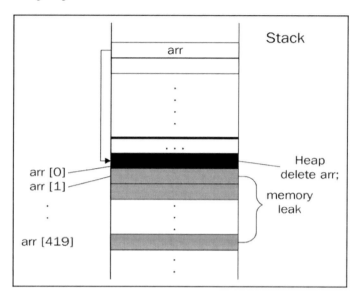

Figure 5.12: Dynamic array deletion

So, we've removed the first item out of 420 items and left the 419 shorts untouched on the heap. Whenever we need new space on the heap, that small section containing the 419 **untouchables** won't be reused again. Though the family of `new` and `delete` operators is implementation-defined, we shouldn't hope for the best implementation that avoids memory leaks.

Let's modify the preceding code to properly release the allocated memory for the array and make sure we eliminate the possibility of inputting negative numbers:

```
void print_sorted()
{
    short* arr{new short[420]};
for (int ix = 0; ix < 420; ++ix)
        {
            std::cin >> arr[ix];
            if (arr[ix] < 0) return;
        }
std::sort(arr, arr + 420);
//print the sorted array, code omitted for brevity
delete[] arr;
}
```

The preceding modifications are another example of a possible memory leak, though we clearly wrote ugly code for the sake of simplicity. The point is that whenever the user inputs a negative number, the function returns. This leaves us with 420 orphan shorts that should be released somehow. However, the only access to the allocated memory was the `arr` pointer, which is declared on the stack, so it will be automatically deleted (the pointer variable, not the memory space pointed to it) when the function returns. To eliminate the possibility of a memory leak, we should simply call the `delete[]` operator before the function exits:

```
void print_sorted()
{
    short* arr{ new short[420] };
    for(int ix = 0; ix < 420; ++ix)
    {
        std::cin >> arr[ix];
        if (arr[ix] < 0)
        {
        delete[] arr;
        return;
        }
    }
}
// sort and print the sorted array, code omitted for
// brevity
    delete[] arr;
}
```

The code gets somewhat ugly, but it fixes the memory leak. What if we modify the function further and use a third-party library function to sort the array?

```
include <strange_sort.h>
void print_sorted()
{
short* arr{new short[420]};
for (...) { /* code omitted for brevity */ }
        strange_sort::sort(arr, arr + 420);
// print the sorted array, code omitted for brevity
        delete[] arr;
}
```

It turns out that `strange_sort::sort` throws an exception when the value of the array item exceeds 420 (that's why it's a strange sort, after all). If the exception is left uncaught, it will bubble up to the caller function unless it is caught somewhere or the program crashes. The uncaught exception leads to stack unwinding, which leads to the automatic destruction of the `arr` variable (the pointer), so we face another possibility of a memory leak. To fix it, we could wrap `strange_sort::sort` in a try-catch block:

```
try
{
strange_sort::sort(arr, arr + 420);
}
catch (ex) { delete[] arr; }
```

C++ programmers constantly seek ways to deal with memory leaks, such as the RAII idiom and smart pointers, which we will discuss in the next sections.

Using smart pointers

Many languages support automated garbage collection. For example, memory acquired for an object is tracked by the runtime environment. It will deallocate the memory space after the object with a reference to it goes out of scope. Consider the following, for example:

```
// a code sample of the language (not-C++) supporting
// automated garbage collection
void foo(int age) {
Person p = new Person("John", 35);
        if (age <= 0) { return; }
        if (age > 18) {
                p.setAge(18);
}
    // do something useful with the "p"
}
// no need to deallocate memory manually
```

In the preceding code block, the p reference (usually, references in garbage-collected languages are similar to pointers in C++) refers to the memory location returned by the new operator. The automatic garbage collector manages the lifetime of the object created by the new operator. It also tracks references to that object. Whenever the object has no references, the garbage collector deallocates its space. Something similar to that might be achieved by using the RAII idiom in C++. Let's see it in action.

Leveraging the RAII idiom

As already mentioned, the RAII idiom suggests acquiring the resource on its initialization. Look at the following class:

```
template <typename T>
class ArrayManager
{
public:
    ArrayManager(T* arr) : arr_{arr} {}
    virtual ~ArrayManager() { delete[] arr_; }
```

```
    T& operator[](int ix) { return arr_[ix]; }
    T* raw() { return arr_; }
};
```

The `print_sorted` function can now use `ArrayManager` to properly release the allocated array:

```
void print_sorted()
{
ArrayManager<short> arr{ new short[420] };
for (int ix = 0; ix < 420; ++ix)
{
    std::cin >> arr[ix];
}
strange_sort::sort(arr.raw(), arr.raw() + 420);
  for (int ix = 0; ix < 420; ++ix)
  {
    std::cout << arr[ix];
  }
}
```

We suggest using standard containers such as `std::vector` rather than `ArrayManager`, though it's a good example of the RAII application: acquiring the resource on initialization. We created an instance of `ArrayManager` and initialized it with the memory resource. From that point, we can forget about its release because the actual release happens in the destructor of `ArrayManager`. And, as we declared the `ArrayManager` instance on the stack, it will be automatically destroyed when the function returns or an uncaught exception occurs, and the destructor will be called.

Using a standard container is preferred in this scenario, so let's implement the RAII idiom for single pointers. The following code dynamically allocates memory to a `Product` instance:

```
Product* apple{new Product};
apple->set_name("Red apple");
apple->set_price(0.42);
apple->set_available(true);
// use the apple
// don't forget to release the resource
delete apple;
```

If we apply the RAII idiom to the preceding code, it will release the resource at the proper point of code execution:

```
ResourceManager<Product> res{new Product};
res->set_name("Red apple");
res->set_price(0.42);
```

```
res->set_available(true);
// use the res the way we use a Product
// no need to delete the res, it will automatically delete
// when gets out of the scope
```

The `ResourceManager` class should also overload the `*` and `->` operators because it has to behave like a pointer to properly acquire and manage a pointer:

```
template <typename T>
class ResourceManager
{
public:
ResourceManager(T* ptr) : ptr_{ptr} {}
        ~ResourceManager() { delete ptr_; }
        T& operator*() { return *ptr_; }
        T* operator->() { return ptr_; }
public:
    void set_name(const std::string& name) {
        name_ = name;
    }
}
    void set_price(double price) {
        price_ = price;
    }
private:
    T *ptr_;
    std::string name_;
    double price_;
};
```

The `ResourceManager` class cares about the idea of the smart pointer in C++. C++11 introduced several types of smart pointers. We call them smart because they wrap around the resource and manage its automatic deallocation. This happens solely because the destructor of an object will be called when the object is set to destroy. That said, we operate with the dynamically allocated space through the object with an automatic storage duration. When the handler object goes out of scope, its destructor executes the necessary actions to deallocate the underlying resource.

However, smart pointers might bring additional issues. The simple smart pointer discussed in the preceding paragraph has several issues that will arise eventually. For example, we didn't take care of `ResourceManager` copying the following:

```
void print_name(ResourceManager<Product> apple)
{
std::cout << apple->name();
}
```

```
ResourceManager<Product> res{ new Product };
res->set_name("Red apple");
print_name(res);
res->set_price(0.42);
//...
```

The preceding code leads to undefined behavior. The following diagram shows the disguised problem:

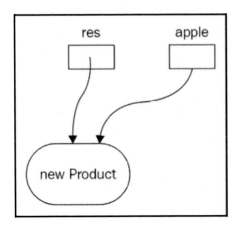

Figure 5.13: Resource acquisition

Both **res** and **apple** acquire the same resource. Whenever one of them goes out of scope (**apple**), the underlying resource is released, which leaves the other ResourceManager instance with a dangling pointer. When the other ResourceManager instance goes out of scope, it will try to delete the pointer twice. Usually, programmers are aware of the *kind* of smart pointer they need in a specific case. That's why C++ provides several types of smart pointers that we will discuss further. To use them in your programs, you should import the <memory> header.

std::unique_ptr

Similar to the ResourceManager instance we implemented earlier, std::unique_ptr represents a basic smart pointer. For example, to manage the Product object using this smart pointer, we can do the following:

```
std::unique_ptr<Product> res{ new Product };
res->set_name("Red apple");
// res will delete its acquired resource when goes out of
// scope
```

Note how we access the Product member function, set_name. We treat the res object as something that is of the Pointer* type.

unique_ptr is unique because it provides the semantics of strict ownership – it is obligated to destroy the acquired object. More interestingly, unique_ptr can't be copied. It doesn't have a copy constructor or assignment operator. That's why its **ownership** is *strict*. Of course, that doesn't mean that we can't move a unique_ptr class. In that case, we completely pass ownership to the other instance of the unique pointer.

One of the main requirements for smart pointers is keeping them lightweight. We can surely agree on that. While unique_ptr is a full class with several member functions, it doesn't *pollute* with additional data members. It's just a wrapper around the raw pointer to the allocated object. We can access that raw pointer by calling the release() member function of unique_ptr, as shown here:

```
Product* p = res.release();
// now we should delete p manually to deallocate memory
```

Note that the release() function doesn't call the delete operator. It only gives back ownership. After calling the release() function, unique_ptr no longer owns the resource. To reuse a unique_ptr that already owns a resource, you should use the reset() member function. It calls the delete operator for the underlying pointer and *resets* the unique pointer for further use. On the other hand, if you want to get the underlying object without releasing the ownership, you should call the get() member function:

```
std::unique_ptr<Product> up{ new Product() };
Product* p = res.get();
// now p also points to the object managed by up
```

We can't use a unique_ptr class in the following scenario because it can't be copied:

```
// Don't do this
void print_name(std::unique_ptr<Product> apple)
{
std::cout << apple->name();
}
std::unique_ptr<Product> res{ new Product };
res->set_name("Red apple");
print_name(res); // bad code res->set_price(0.42);
// ...
```

However, it's not what we're looking for in the preceding code. You can consider the preceding code a bad design because it confuses the ownership details. Let's move on to the next smart pointer in C++, which solves the issue of passing unique_ptr to functions.

std::shared_ptr and std::weak_ptr

We need a smart pointer that provides *shared ownership*. What we needed was introduced back in C++11 as std::shared_ptr. It's harder to implement a smart pointer with shared ownership because you should take care of correctly deallocating the resource. For example, when the print_name() function in the preceding code block finishes its work, its arguments and local objects will be destroyed. Destroying a smart pointer leads to the proper deallocation of the resource it owns. How would the smart pointer know if that resource was still owned by another smart pointer? One of the popular solutions is keeping a count of references to the resource. The shared_ptr class does the same: it keeps the number of pointers pointing to the underlying object and deletes it when the use count becomes 0. Therefore, several shared pointers can own the same object.

Now, the example we just discussed should be rewritten like this:

```cpp
void print_name(std::shared_ptr<Product> apple)
{
std::cout << apple->name();
}
std::shared_ptr<Product> res{ new Product };
res->set_name("Red apple");
print_name(res);
res->set_price(0.42);
// ...
```

After calling the print_name() function, the use count of the shared pointer increases by 1. It will decrease by 1 when the function finishes its work but the managed object won't be deallocated. That's because the res object is not out of scope yet. Let's slightly modify the example to print the count of references to the shared object:

```cpp
void print_name(std::shared_ptr<Product> apple)
{
std::cout << apple.use_count() << " eyes on the " << apple->name();
}
std::shared_ptr<Product> res{ new Product };
res->set_name("Red apple");
std::cout << res.use_count() << std::endl;
print_name(res);
std::cout << res.use_count() << std::endl;
res->set_price(0.42);
// ...
```

The preceding code will print the following to the screen:

```
1
2 eyes on the Red apple
1
```

When the last `shared_ptr` goes out of scope, it also destroys the underlying object. However, you should be careful when sharing an object between shared pointers. The following code shows an obvious issue with shared ownership:

```cpp
std::shared_ptr<Product> ptr1{ new Product() };
Product* temp = ptr1.get();
if (true)
{
std::shared_ptr<Product> ptr2{temp};
    ptr2->set_name("Apple of truth");
}
ptr1->set_name("Peach"); // danger!
```

Both `ptr1` and `ptr2` point to the same object, but they are not aware of each other. So, when we modify the `Product` object via `ptr2`, it will affect `ptr1`. When `ptr2` goes out of scope (after the `if` statement), it will destroy the underlying object, which is still owned by `ptr1`. This happens because we make `ptr2` own the object by passing the raw `temp` pointer to it. `ptr1` can't track that.

Ownership can only be shared using the copy constructor or the assignment operator of `std::shared_ptr`. This way, we avoid deleting the object if it's in use by another `shared_ptr` instance. Shared pointers implement shared ownership using control blocks. Each shared pointer holds two pointers – one for the object it manages and another for the control block. The control block represents a dynamically allocated space containing the use count of the resource. It also contains several other things crucial to `shared_ptr`, such as the resource's `allocator` and `deleter`. We will introduce allocators in the next section. `deleter` is usually the regular `delete` operator.

The control block also contains several weak references. This is because the owned resource might be pointed to a weak pointer, too. `std::weak_ptr` is the smaller brother of `std::shared_ptr`. It refers to an object managed by a `shared_ptr` instance but doesn't own it. `weak_ptr` is a way to access and use the resource owned by `shared_ptr` without owning it. However, there is a way to convert a `weak_ptr` instance into `shared_ptr` using the `lock()` member function.

Both `unique_ptr` and `shared_ptr` can be used to manage dynamically allocated arrays. The template parameter must be specified correctly:

```cpp
std::shared_ptr<int[]> sh_arr{ new int[42] };
sh_arr[11] = 44;
```

To access an element of the underlying array, we can use the `[ ]` operator of the shared pointer. Also, note that using a smart pointer won't have drawbacks when used in dynamic polymorphism. For example, let's suppose we have the following class hierarchy:

```cpp
struct Base
{
virtual void test()
```

```
{
std::cout << "Base::test()" << std::endl;
}
};

struct Derived : Base
{
void test() override
{
std::cout << "Derived::test()" << std::endl;
}
};
```

The following code works as expected and outputs `Derived::test()` to the screen:

```
std::unique_ptr<Base> ptr =      std::make_unique_default_init<Derived>
();
ptr->test();
```

Although the use of smart pointers might seem to spoil the beauty of pointers, it is suggested that you use smart pointers intensively to avoid memory leaks. However, it's worth noting that replacing all pointers with smart pointers, whether it's a `unique_ptr` or a `shared_ptr` pointer, will not solve all the memory leak problems. They have their disadvantages, too. Consider a balanced approach, or better, thoroughly understand both the problem and the smart pointers themselves in detail before applying them to the problem.

Managing memory in C++ programs comes at a price. The most important thing that we've discussed is the proper deallocation of memory space. The language doesn't support automatic memory deallocation, but it's worth mentioning garbage collectors. However, to have a complete garbage collector, we need language-level support. C++ doesn't provide any of that. Let's try to imitate a garbage collector in C++.

Garbage collection

A garbage collector is a separate module that's usually incorporated in the runtime environments of interpretable languages. For example, C# and Java both have garbage collectors, which makes programmers' lives a lot easier. The garbage collector tracks all the object allocations in the code and deallocates them once they are not in use anymore. It's called a **garbage collector** because it deletes the memory resource after it's been used: it collects the garbage left by programmers.

It's said that C++ programmers don't leave garbage after them; that's why the language doesn't have support for a garbage collector. Though programmers tend to defend the language by stating that it doesn't have a garbage collector because it's a fast language, the truth is that it can survive without one.

Languages such as C# compile the program into an intermediate byte-code representation, which is then interpreted and executed by the runtime environment. The garbage collector is a part of the environment and actively tracks all object allocations. It is a sophisticated beast that tries its best to manage memory in a reasonable time. The following diagram depicts a typical runtime environment that allocates memory supervised by the garbage collector:

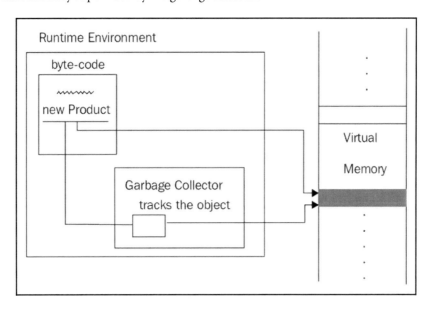

Figure 5.14: Garbage collector

We manually call the `delete` operator to release the memory space in C++, even when using smart pointers. Smart pointers just acquire the object and delete the object when it goes out of scope. The key point is that even though smart pointers introduce some semi-automatic behavior, they still act as if the programmer didn't forget to release the resource at a specified point of the code. The garbage collector does that automatically and usually uses separate execution threads. It tries its best not to slow down the program's execution speed.

Some garbage collection implementation techniques involve classifying objects by their lifetime duration. Classification makes the garbage collector visit the objects and release the memory space if objects aren't in use anymore. To make this process faster, objects with short lifetimes should be visited more often than objects with longer lifetimes. Take, for example, the following code:

```
class Garbage
{
    public:
        char ch;
        int i;
};

void foo()
```

```
{
    Garbage* g1 = new Garbage();
    if (true)
    {
        Garbage* g2 = new Garbage();
    }
}

int main()
{
    Garbage* g3 = new Garbage();
}
```

If C++ had a garbage collector, then the g1, g2, and g3 objects would be deleted in different time slots of the program's execution. If the garbage collector classifies them by their lifetime duration, then g2 would have the shortest lifetime and should be visited first to release it.

To implement a garbage collector in C++, we should make it a part of the program. The garbage collector should first take care of allocating memory to track and remove it:

```
class GarbageCollector
{
public:
template <typename T>
        static T* allocate()
        {
            T* ptr{new T()};
            objects_[ptr] = true;
            return ptr;
        }

        static void deallocate(T* p)
        {
            if (objects_[p])
            {
                objects_[p] = false;
                delete p;
            }
        }
    private:
std::unordered_map<T*, bool> objects_;
};
```

The preceding class keeps track of objects allocated through the static `allocate()` function. If the object is in use, it deletes it through the `deallocate()` function. Here's how `GarbageCollector` can be used:

```
int* ptr = GarbageCollector::allocate<int>();
*ptr = 42;
GarbageCollector::deallocate(ptr);
```

This class makes memory management a little bit harder than smart pointers. There is no need to implement a garbage collector in C++ because smart pointers can handle almost any scenario regarding automatic memory deallocation.

However, let's see one of the tricks that will allow the garbage collector to properly deallocate the space pointed to by some pointer. In our simplest possible implementation, shown previously, we kept track of all the pointers that we provided to users. Each pointer points to some space on the heap that should be freed at some point in the program's execution. In `GarbageCollector`, we would use the standard `delete` operator. The question is, how does it know how many bytes should be freed? Take a look at the following example:

```
Student* ptr = new Student; int* ip = new int{42};
// do something with ptr and ip delete ptr;
delete ip;
```

Let's suppose that a `Student` instance takes 40 bytes of memory and an integer takes 4 bytes. We should somehow pass that information to the `delete` operator. In the preceding code, we deleted both `ptr` and `ip`, each of which points to memory spaces of different sizes. So, how does it know that 40 bytes should be marked as free in the case of `ptr` and 4 bytes should be marked as free in the case of `ip`? There is more than one solution to this problem, so let's look at one of them.

Whenever we allocate memory, the `new` operator puts the size of the allocated space just before the actual memory space, as shown in the following diagram:

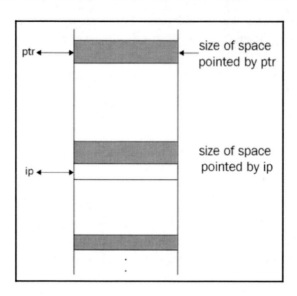

Figure 5.15: Space size of allocated memory

This information is then used by the `delete` operator, which reads the size of the memory space by reading the corresponding bytes placed before the memory space. One of the top concerns of C++ is managing memory for collections of data. STL containers, such as `std::vector` and `std::list`, as described in *Chapter 6, Digging into Data Structures and Algorithms in STL*, have different models for working with memory. By default, a container has a specified memory allocator that handles the memory allocation and deallocation of container elements. Let's look at allocators in more detail.

Using allocators

The idea behind an allocator is to provide control to container memory management. In simpler words, an allocator is an advanced garbage collector for C++ containers. Although we discuss allocators in the scope of container memory management, you can expand the idea to a generic garbage collector. At the beginning of this section, we implemented a badly designed garbage collector. When examining allocators, you will find a lot of similarities between the poorly designed `GarbageCollector` class and the default allocator in C++. Defined in `<memory>`, the default allocator has two basic functions – `allocate()` and `deallocate()`. The `allocate()` function is defined as follows:

```
[[nodiscard]] constexpr T* allocate(std::size_t num);
```

The `allocate()` function acquires space for num objects of the T type. Pay attention to the `[[nodiscard]]` attribute – it means that the return value should not be discarded by the caller. The compiler will print a warning message otherwise.

Let's use the allocator to acquire space for five integers:

```
import <memory>;
  int main()
{
std::allocator<int> IntAlloc;
int* ptr = IntAlloc.allocate(5);
/* construct an integer at the second position
*/                      std::allocator_traits<IntAlloc>::
construct(IntAlloc, ptr + 1, 42);
IntAlloc.deallocate(ptr, 5); // deallocate all
}
```

Note how we used `std::allocator_traits` to construct objects in the allocated space.

The `deallocate()` function is defined as follows:

```
constexpr void deallocate(T* p, std::size_t n)
```

In the previous code snippet, we used the `deallocate()` function by passing the pointer returned by the `allocate()` function.

Types of allocators

Allocators are divided into three categories:

- Linear allocators
- Pool allocators
- Stack allocators

Linear allocators are the simplest. The idea is to keep a pointer at the beginning of the memory block next to the allocated allocator, and also use a different pointer or numeric representation that needs to be moved every time you allocate space:

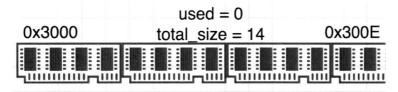

Figure 5.16: Linear allocator

Let's imagine that the allocator gets a request to allocate 4 bytes of memory. The allocator's actions to execute the request will be as follows:

1. Check whether there is enough memory to allocate.

2. Add the specified size to the used variable (4 bytes).

3. Return the memory pointer as the memory that's been used:

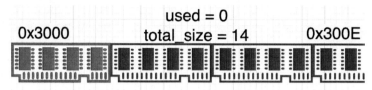

Figure 5.17: 4 bytes in the linear allocator

Then, there is a request to allocate 8 bytes, and, accordingly, the allocator actions will be the same. This will keep happening until the memory runs out:

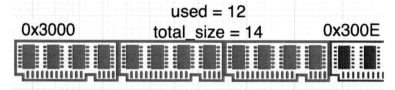

Figure 5.18: 8 bytes in the linear allocator

Now, it's time to talk about freeing up memory. This type of allocator does not support selectively freeing certain memory blocks – that is, with `delete`/`free` and with the `0x3000` pointer, we can free this memory, but the linear allocator cannot afford it.

All we need to do is free all the allocator's occupied memory and continue working with it until we get empty memory:

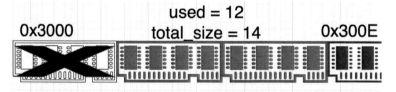

Figure 5.19: Freeing up the memory

The following code shows the declaration of the `LinearAlloc` class:

```
class LinearAlloc
{
public:
    LinearAlloc(const std::size_t size);
```

```
    ~LinearAlloc();
public:
    void state()
    {
        std::cout << used << std::endl;
        std::cout << total_size << std::endl;
    }
    template <typename T>
    T* allocate(const std::size_t size = 1);
    void reset(const std::size_t size);
private:
    void *memory;
    std::size_t used;
    std::size_t total_size;
};
```

Let's look at the constructors and methods of the `LinearAlloc` class:

- `LinearAlloc(const std::size_t size)`: This is a parameterized constructor that gets the total size of the memory that needs to be allocated.

- `~LienarAlloc()`: This is a destructor that erases the entire memory space.

- `Allocate(std::const std::size_t size = 1)`: This is a function template (method) that returns a pointer of the specified type if there is enough space in memory. The `size` variable shows how many objects of the same type to create. By default, this is set to `1`.

- The `reset` method frees the memory and creates a new one with the passed argument.

- Three data members describe the pointer for the memory, the total size for the allocator, and the size used, respectively.

The next allocator type is the pool allocator, which is also called a *memory pool*. The idea of the pool allocator is that it divides most of the memory into pieces of the same size. It is also a simple allocator because when allocation is required, it simply returns one of the free fragments of fixed-size memory, and when any fragment needs to be freed, it saves this fragment of memory for use later.

I suggest we look at an example to understand how it works. So, let's take a block of memory equal to 14 bytes and pass it to the allocator.

As shown in the following figure, we store the beginning and the end of the memory managed by the allocator, as well as a list (`forward_list`) of addresses of free blocks and a fixed small size for each block. Let's assume this is 2:

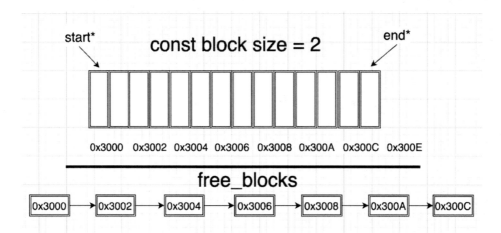

Figure 5.20: Pool allocator

If a request arrives to allocate one block of memory, the allocator's actions are very primitive. First, it checks whether there are links to the list of free blocks; if there are none, it is not difficult to guess that the allocator's memory has already expired. If there is at least one link, it simply deletes from the beginning or end of the list (in this implementation, from the beginning) and gives its address to the user:

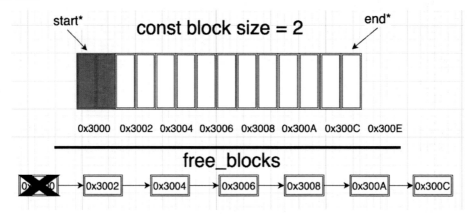

Figure 5.21: Allocated two bytes

As you can see, the first 2 bytes are already being used and the first block of free_blocks is deleted. If there are several blocks to allocate memory, then the allocator, in turn, performs the same actions that it did previously:

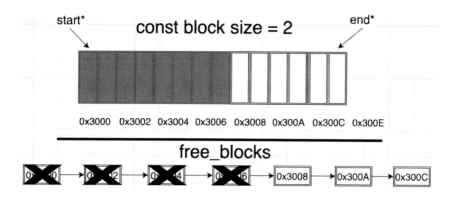

Figure 5.22: 6 bytes allocated

In this example, you can see that there has already been a request to allocate 6 bytes of memory, which has been successfully provided. As for releasing a block, if a command is used to release a block, the allocator simply adds this address to one of the ends of the linked list (free_blocks). If an address does not match the memory address of the allocator – for example, 0x3010 – we will give the user a memory that does not belong to us (of course, this will lead to undefined behavior or, if you are *lucky*, just close the application). To avoid this possible problem, initial and final indicators are used, which allow you to check whether the user made a mistake when requesting a release action with the address. There is another possible problem: the user can give the command to release absolutely any address located in the allocator memory area (that is, in the area from the beginning to the end), but not the ending address of any of the equal blocks; for example, a block with the 0x3005 address. This action will lead to undefined behavior (this is a description of behavior that can lead to completely unpredictable consequences – for example, a request outside the array or redirecting a pointer in place of the freed space. The worst thing is that the program will not terminate immediately or will give some kind of error):

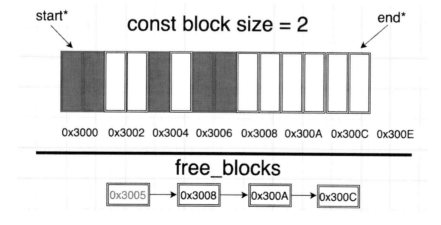

Figure 5.23: Deallocation

The following code shows the declaration of the `PoolAlloc` class:

```
class PoolAlloc
{
public:
    PoolAlloc(std::size_t all_size, std::size_t b_size);
    ~PoolAlloc();
public:
    int8_t* allocate(const std::size_t size = 1);
    void deallocate(int8_t *p, const std::size_t size = 1);
    void free();
private:
    int8_t *start;
    int8_t *end;
    std::size_t block_size;
    std::size_t block_count;
    std::forward_list<int8_t*> free_blocks;
};
```

Let's look at the constructors and methods of the `PoolAllocator` class:

- `PoolAllocator(std::size_t all_size, std::size_t block_size)`: As in `LinearAlloc`, there is also a parameterized constructor that gets the size of the memory. The second argument is the fixed size of the block.

- `~PoolAllocator()`: This is a destructor that frees all memory.

- `Allocate(std::size_t size)`: This is a method that returns a free pointer. If its size is greater than 1, then the program should look for addresses that are next to each other. If there are no such addresses, it returns `nullptr`.

- `Deallocate`: The method frees the specified address from the size.

- `Free`: This method clears the memory.

The last allocator type is `StackAlloc`, which is a powerful linear allocator that allows you to manage memory as a *stack*. Everything is the same as before in that we store the pointer at the beginning of our memory, but, unlike a linear allocator, we can also move it back – that is, we can perform a redistribution operation, which is not supported by linear allocators:

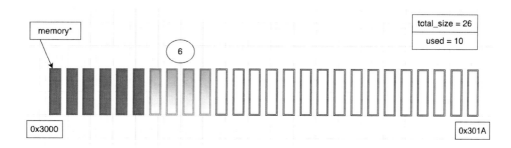

Figure 5.24: Stack allocator – 6 bytes allocated

When the allocation command comes to allocate 6 bytes, in addition to the part of the memory provided by the user, we assign a header (the user will not interact with it in any way), in which we store information about how many bytes were allocated (in this example, the header size is 4 bytes).

This situation will occur when allocating 10 bytes:

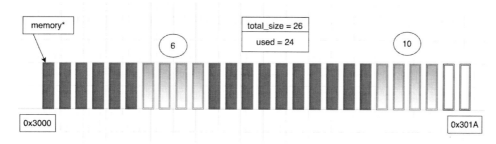

Figure 5.25: 24 bytes allocated

It's time to release the blocks. Everything is already a little more interesting (as discussed earlier, you can only allocate and free the memory using the LIFO technique). First, you have to subtract the header size, then subtract this header value, and only after that substruction can you subtract the number from the header plus the header size from used.

The following code shows the declaration of the `StackAlloc` class:

```
struct Header
{
    int bytes;
    Header(int size)  : bytes(size) { }
};

class StackAllocator
{
public:
```

```
        StackAllocator(std::size_t);
        ~StackAllocator();

public:
        template <typename T>
        T* allocate(const std::size_t t = 1);
        void deallocate(std::size_t t = 1);
        void Free();
private:
        int8_t *memory;
        int total_size;
        int used;
        int header_count;
};
```

Let's look at the constructors and methods of the `StackAllocator` class:

- `Header`: This is a structure that stores the size of each block.

- `StackAllocator(std::size_t)`: This is a parameterized constructor that gets the whole size of memory.

- `~StackAllocator()`: This is a destructor that frees all memory.

- `allocate(std::size_t t)`: This is a function template that returns a pointer of a given type if there is enough space in memory. The `size` variable shows how many objects of the same type to create. By default, it is set to `1`.

- `deallocate(std::size_t t)`: This is a method that deallocates the memory from the end-sized elements. By default, the size is `1`.

- `Free()`: This method clears the memory.

- Now, let's summarize this chapter.

Summary

Garbage collectors in languages such as C# are provided by the environment. They work in parallel with the user program and try to clean up after the program whenever it seems efficient. We cannot do the same in C++; all we can do is implement a garbage collector directly in the program, providing a semi-automatic way of freeing the used memory resource. This mechanism is properly covered by the smart pointers that have been part of the language since C++11.

Memory management is one of the key components of every computer program. A program should be able to request memory dynamically during its execution. Good programmers understand the inner details of memory management. That helps them design and implement more performant applications.

While manual memory management is considered an advantage, it tends to become painful in larger applications. In this chapter, we learned how we can avoid errors and handle memory deallocation using smart pointers. Having this basic understanding, you should be confident in designing programs that avoid memory leaks. In the next chapter, we will learn about STL, focusing on data structures and algorithms, and will dive into their STL implementation. Besides comparing data structures and algorithms, we will introduce one of the notable new features in C++20: concepts.

Questions

1. From a high-level perspective, explain memory hierarchy.
2. What is garbage collection and how does it work?
3. Explain the different types of allocators.

Part 2: Designing Robust and Efficient Applications

This part will concentrate on the efficiency of data processing using data structures and algorithms, concurrency tools. You will also get introduced to essential design patterns and best practices.

This part has the following chapters:

- Chapter 6, Digging into Data Structures and Algorithms in STL
- Chapter 7, Advanced Data Structures
- Chapter 8, Functional Programming
- Chapter 9, Concurrency and Multithreading
- Chapter 10, Designing Concurrent Data
- Chapter 11, Designing World-Ready Applications
- Chapter 12, Incorporating Design Patterns in C++ Applications
- Chapter 13, Networking and Security
- Chapter 14, Debugging and Testing
- Chapter 15, Large-Scale Application Design

6

Digging into Data Structures and Algorithms in STL

For programmers, understanding data structures is crucial. The majority of the time, the way you store your data determines the application's overall efficiency. Take, for example, an email client. You may create an email client that displays the 10 most recent emails and it will have the best user interface available; showing the 10 most recent emails will operate on nearly every device. After 2 years of using your email application, the user will have received hundreds of thousands of emails. When the user needs to find an email, your data structure expertise will come in handy. The way you store the hundreds of thousands of emails and the methods (algorithms) you employ to sort and search them will set your application apart from the others.

While working on different projects, programmers face many problems and try to find the best solutions to those problems – by saying best, I mean the most efficient ones. Using tried-and-true data structures and methods may vastly increase a programmer's productivity. One of the most significant characteristics of a successful program is its speed, which we may achieve by creating new algorithms and using or modifying old ones.

The question arises of how to use data structures and algorithms using a programming language, which is, in our case, C++. **C++20** introduces concepts for defining meta types – types describing other types. The data design is complete thanks to this powerful feature of the language.

The **C++ Standard Template Library** (**STL**) covers a wide range of **data structures and algorithms**. We will look at how to use STL containers to arrange data effectively using data structures. Then, we will look at some of the STL's algorithm implementations. It is crucial to understand and use concepts in STL containers because C++20 introduces big improvements into iterators by introducing iterator concepts.

In this chapter, we are going to discuss the following topics:

- Sequential data structures (with an introduction to STL and iterators)
- Node-based data structures

- Graphs and trees
- Hash tables
- Algorithms

Technical requirements

The g++ compiler with the `-std=c++20` option was used to compile the examples throughout this chapter. You can find the source files that have been used in this chapter in the GitHub repository for this book at `https://github.com/PacktPublishing/Expert-C-2nd-edition`.

Sequential data structures

Even if you are a programmer who has never heard of a single data structure and you do not even know what they are, you may be surprised to learn that you have probably used one in your projects. Let's take, for example, an array, which every experienced programmer must have used at least once. We can use an array to store and order a collection of data.

Programmers frequently use data structures other than arrays in their projects. Knowing about and using the right data structures might make a big difference in the way your software runs. You must have a deeper understanding of data structures before you can select the most appropriate one.

The obvious question is whether we need to learn about the variety of data structures, such as vectors, linked lists, hash tables, graphs, and trees. Let's imagine a hypothetical situation in which the need for a better data structure emerges.

In the introductory part of this chapter, we briefly discussed an example that we will use to extend our discussions. We mentioned designing an email client. The basics for designing an application are decisions, and among the most important decisions is choosing a data structure. This is because, eventually, everything is going to revolve around it. Let's have a look at the basic tasks that will be performed during the design and implementation of the email client.

Imagine an email client being a program that keeps track of emails from numerous senders. We may install it on our computers or smartphones, or we can use the web version. Sending and receiving emails are the primary functions of an email client program. Let's pretend we are working on an email client, which is easy enough to use, and that, as is customary in programming books, we use a library that encapsulates the task of sending and receiving emails.

Instead, we want to focus on developing methods for storing and retrieving emails. The user of an email client should be able to see a list of emails in the app's inbox area. We also have to consider that the user is not only going to receive and send emails but also the fact that they may wish to perform other operations (for example, deleting).

The deletion itself can be performed in two ways:

- The user can delete just one message at a time

- The user can delete the messages in bulk

Other operations that are applied to emails can include choosing an email by randomly selecting and replying to its sender or forwarding the email to someone else.

Let's start by drawing a basic struct that describes an `Email` object:

```cpp
#include <chrono>
#include <string>

struct Email
{
    std::string subject;
    std::string body;
    std::string from;
    std::chrono::time_point<std::chrono::system_clock>
        datetime;
};
```

The first concern should be organizing a collection of emails into a structure that is easily accessible. In this case, what could be a better idea other than an array? The elements of an array appear to be very easy to access, and if we talk about time complexity, it is good to mention that the access time complexity of an array element is $O(1)$, which is the best possible time out there. Let's look at a code example that shows that all the incoming emails are kept in an array:

```cpp
// let's suppose a million emails is the max for anyone
const int MAX_EMAILS = 1'000'000;
Email inbox[MAX_EMAILS];
```

When it comes to an array of 10 elements or 20 elements, it is okay to work with and manipulate arrays, but when we are talking about hundreds of thousands of emails, different problems can arise. For each newly received email, we push an `Email` object with the corresponding fields into the `inbox` array. The last pushed element is the most recent message. To display a list of 10 recent emails, we must read and return the array's last 10 entries.

Issues may and definitely will arise when we are working with hundreds of thousands of emails that are simply stored in an `inbox` array. What should we do and how should we use an array if we want to search for a single word in all those emails? We must scan all the emails in the array and collect those that include the word in a new array.

Look at the following pseudocode:

```
std::vector<Email> search(const std::string& word) {
    std::vector<Email> search_results;
    for (all-million-emails) {
        if (inbox[i].subject.contains(word)) {
            search_results.push_back(inbox[i]);
        }
    }
    return search_results;
}
```

For small collections, using an array to hold all the data is more than sufficient. In the case of real-world applications that deal with larger sets of data, the situation changes dramatically. The point of using an appropriate data structure is a big part of the solutions to those problems as it improves the performance of the application. The preceding example illustrates a trivial problem: finding a value in a collection of emails. It takes a decent amount of time to find that value in a single email.

If we assume that we are looking for a word in an email's subject field, which contains up to 10 words, searching for a specific word in an email's subject means comparing the word to all of the other words in the subject. In the worst-case scenario, there is no match at all.

The worst-case scenario has been highlighted since it is the only one in which the lookup will require verifying each word in the subject field. If you do this for hundreds of thousands of emails, the user will have to wait for an unreasonable amount of time.

Choosing the right data structure for the specific problem is crucial in terms of application efficiency. Let's say we want to map words to email objects using a hash table. Each word will be associated with a list of email objects that include it. As illustrated in the following figure, this strategy will improve the efficiency of the search operation:

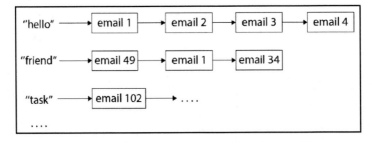

Figure 6.1: Association of a word with a list of email objects

The search() function will just return the list referred to by the hash table key:

```
std::vector<Email> search(const std::string& word) {
    return table[word];
```

}

This method only requires splitting each incoming email into words and updating the hash table.

We use Email objects as values rather than references for simplicity. It is worth noting that storing references to Email in the vector would be preferable.

There are different approaches to categorizing data structures into types. People mainly talk about two categories but their names differ for different people. Some say, for example, that data structures can be classified into linear and non-linear structures; some call those types sequential and node-based structures, and so on. So long as you understand what those classifications mean, you can call them whatever you want. In this book, we are going to address them as sequential and node-based data structures.

Let's have a look at some different data structures and how they might be used.

The dynamically growing one-dimensional array, sometimes called a vector, is one of the most common data structures used by programmers. In the STL library, this dynamically growing array is called std::vector. The main principle of a vector is that it comprises objects of the same kind, which are stored in memory in sequential order. A vector of 4-byte integers, for example, would have the memory arrangement shown next. A 4-byte space is represented by each box.

On the right-hand side of *Figure 6.2*, we can see the vector's indexes:

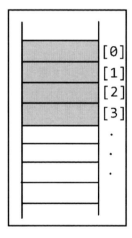

Figure 6.2: Vector representation in RAM

Any of the vector's elements may be accessed in real time because of their physical structure.

To apply containers correctly to certain problems, we must separate containers based on the functions they perform. To do so, we commonly measure the complexity of their operations in terms of the number of elements in the container. The vector's element access, for example, is specified as a constant-time operation, which implies that fetching a vector item requires the same number of instructions, regardless of the vector's length.

Because accessing the first and 100th elements of a vector requires the same amount of work, we refer to it as a constant-time operation, commonly known as an O(1) operation.

But can we consider that every operation that we perform on a vector takes O(1) time? For some operations, the answer to the previous questions is a strict *no* and for other operations, it is sometimes *yes* and sometimes *no*.

How is that possible? To understand the case of *sometimes yes and sometimes no*, we are going to discuss the operation that adds new elements. When adding a new item to the end of a vector, it's important to keep the vector's capacity in mind. When there is no more space available for the vector, it should dynamically expand in size.

Consider the following Vector class and its push_back() method at https://github.com/PacktPublishing/Expert-C-2nd-edition/tree/main/Chapter%2006/1_vector.h.

To fully understand how the push_back() function works and before putting the explanation into words, let's take a look at the following diagram, where the capacity of the vector is 6 and the size of the vector is 4 at first:

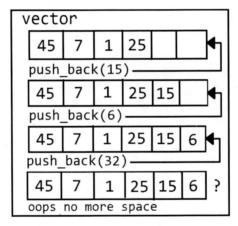

Figure 6.3: Representation of the push_back function

Every time we push back an element, the size of the vector increases. We can see that when there is space (enough capacity) in our vector, adding an element to the end of the vector takes O(1) time, but what happens when there is no more capacity? In that case, we should allocate a brand-new array, copy all the elements of the old one into the new array, and then add the newly inserted element at the next free slot at the end of the new array. The code at https://github.com/PacktPublishing/Expert-C-2nd-edition/blob/main/Chapter%2006/2_vector_push_back.h demonstrates this.

> **Note**
>
> Although the preceding code is correct and works fine, we should also consider the fact that the newly allocated space might be adjacent to our array, and in that case, the compilers are so smart nowadays that they don't copy elements. Instead, they just add the new space to our already existing array.

The decision of choosing a resizing factor depends on the person who implements the vector – we set it to 2, which causes the vector to expand so that it's twice as big when it's full. As a result, we may claim that inserting a new item at the end of the vector takes a consistent amount of time the vast majority of the time. It just inserts the item into the empty slot and raises the private value of the `size_` variable. Adding a new element will occasionally involve creating a new, larger vector and copying the old one into the new one. For cases like this, the operation is said to take amortized constant time to complete.

After discussing the *sometimes yes and sometimes no* case, I think there is a need to also bring an example of a *no* case. Again, the example will be based on adding elements to a vector, but this time, it adds them from the front, not from the back. For the push front function, all the other elements should be moved by one slot to the right to free up a slot for the new element, as shown in the following diagram:

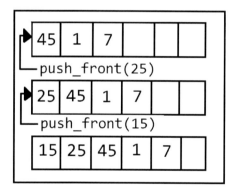

Figure 6.4: Representation of the push_front function

You can see how we would implement the `push_front()` function in our `Vector` class at `https://github.com/PacktPublishing/Expert-C-2nd-edition/tree/main/Chapter%2006/2_vector_push_back.h`.

Choosing a vector is not a suitable solution when you simply need to put new items at the front of the container. Other containers should be explored in situations like these.

STL containers

To take advantage of the data structures and different algorithms provided, C++ decided to combine most of those advantages into one library and called it **STL**. STL combines all those privileges into different containers and algorithms. Although understanding and constructing data structures is a valuable programming skill, you do not have to do it every time you require one in your project. We entrust the implementation of stable and tested data structures and algorithms to the people who contributed to creating that library. Understanding the underlying details of data structures and algorithms allows us to make better STL container and algorithm choices when facing challenges in our projects.

The vectors and linked lists discussed previously are implemented in STL as `std::vector<T>` and `std::list<T>`, where `T` is the type of each element of the collection. Besides the type, containers also take a second default `template` parameter as an allocator. `std::vector`, for example, is declared as follows:

```
template <typename T, typename Allocator = std::allocator<T> >
class vector;
```

An allocator handles the efficient allocation/deallocation of container elements. `std::allocator` is the default allocator for all standard containers in STL. A more sophisticated allocator that behaves differently based on the memory resource is `std::pmr::polymorphic_allocator`. STL provides `std::pmr::vector` as an alias template that uses a polymorphic allocator. It is defined as follows:

```
namespace pmr {
template <typename T>
using vector = std::vector<T,std::pmr::polymorphic_allocator<T>>;
}
```

Now, let's take a closer look at `std::vector` and `std::list`.

Using std::vector and std::list

`std::vector` is defined in the `<vector>` header. You can find a simple usage example at `https://github.com/PacktPublishing/Expert-C-2nd-edition/tree/main/Chapter%2006/3_vector.cpp`.

`std::vector` grows dynamically. We should consider the growth factor. When declaring a vector, it has some default capacity, which will then grow upon element insertion. Every time the number of elements exceeds the capacity of the vector, it increases its capacity by a given factor (usually, it doubles its capacity). If we know the approximate number of elements that we will need in the vector, we can optimize its use by initially allocating that capacity for the vector using the `reserve()` method. For example, the following code reserves a capacity for 10,000 elements:

```
std::vector<int> vec;
vec.reserve(10000);
```

It forces the compiler and hence the vector to allocate space for 10,000 elements, thereby avoiding resizing during element insertion (unless we reach the 10,000-element threshold).

On the other hand, if we encounter a scenario where the capacity is much bigger than the actual number of elements in the vector, we can shrink the vector to free the unused memory. We need to call the `shrink_to_fit()` function, as shown in the following example:

```
vec.shrink_to_fit();
```

This reduces the capacity so that it fits the size of the vector.

`operator[]` is used to access vector elements in the same way that it is used to access a regular array. If you have a closer look at the functions that `std::vector` provides, you'll come across a function named `at()`. If you read what it does, you might be surprised that it does the same thing as `operator[]`. So, the question arises: why do we need two ways of accessing elements of a vector? The answer is simple: there are differences between those two functions (operator overloading is also considered a function). The `at()` function returns a reference to the element at the specified location, with bounds checking.

Let's take a look at the following example:

```
std::cout << vec.at(2);
// is the same as
std::cout << vec[2];
// which is the same as
std::cout << vec.data()[2];
```

The difference between `at()` and `operator[]` is that `at()` accesses the specified element with bounds checking; that is, the following line throws a `std::out_of_range` exception:

```
try {
vec.at(999999);
} catch (std::out_of_range& e) { }
```

`std::list` is used similarly. We will talk about iterators later in this chapter, which allow us to abstract from specific containers so that we may easily substitute a list with a vector. First, though, let's look at the differences between the public interfaces of a list and a vector.

Although there are a set of functions that both `std::list` and `std::vector` support, such as `size()`, `resize()`, `empty()`, `clear()`, `erase()`, and others, some functions are supported by one of those containers. The list has the `push_front()` function, which inserts an element at the front of the list. This is done efficiently because `std::list` represents a doubly linked list. As shown in the following code, `std::list` supports `push_back()` as well:

```
std::list<double> lst;
lst.push_back(4.2);
lst.push_front(3.14);
// the list contains: "3.14 -> 4.2"
```

The list supports additional operations that come in handy in many situations. The merge() function, for example, can be used to combine two sorted lists. It accepts another list as input and combines all of its nodes with the current list's nodes. After this operation, the list that was supplied as input to the merge() function becomes empty.

> **Note**
>
> When we talked about the list and its corresponding container std::list, we meant a doubly linked list. We know that there is also another type of list: a singly linked list, which is slightly different from a doubly linked list. The STL library takes care of a singly linked list as well by providing a container called std::forward_list, which is defined in the <forward_list> header file.

The splice() method is somewhat similar to merge(), except that it moves a portion of the list provided as an argument. By moving, we mean re-pointing internal pointers to proper list nodes. This is true for both merge() and splice().

Both merge() and splice() have multiple overloads. The merge() function has four overloads, whereas splice() has six overloads. The prototypes of the merge() function's overloads are as follows:

```
void merge(list& rhs);

void merge(list&& rhs);

template <typename Cmp>
void merge(list& rhs, Cmp compare);

template <typename Cmp>
void merge(list&& rhs, Cmp compare);
```

The prototypes of the splice() function's overloads are as follows:

```
void splice(const_iterator position, list& rhs);
void splice(const_iterator position, list&& rhs);
void splice(const_iterator position, list& rhs, const_iterator it);
void splice(const_iterator position, list&& rhs, const_iterator it);
void splice(const_iterator position, list& rhs, const_iterator start,
const_iterator end);
void splice(const_iterator position, list&& rhs, const_iterator start,
const_iterator end);
```

Let's look at a simple example of how these functions work when they're applied to two different lists: https://github.com/PacktPublishing/Expert-C-2nd-edition/tree/main/Chapter%2006/4_list_example.cpp.

When we use containers to store and manipulate complex objects, the price of copying elements plays a big role in the program's performance. Consider the following `struct`, which represents a three-dimensional point:

```
struct Point
{
float x;
float y;
float z;
Point(float px, float py, float pz) : x(px), y(py), z(pz){}
Point(Point&& p): x(p.x), y(p.y), z(p.z){}
};
```

Now, look at the following code, which inserts a `Point` object into a vector:

```
std::vector<Point> points;
points.push_back(Point(1.1, 2.2, 3.3));
```

A temporary object is constructed and then moved to the vector's corresponding slot. We can represent this visually as follows:

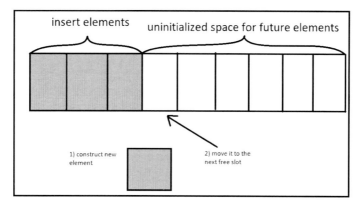

Figure 6.5: Inserting an object of the Point type into the vector with the push_back function

To postpone resizing operations for as long as possible, the vector takes up more space before being used. When we insert a new element, the vector transfers it to the next available slot (and, if that slot is filled, reallocates extra space). We can use that uninitialized space to create a new element in place. For this, the vector provides the `emplace_back()` method. Here is how we can put it to use:

```
points.emplace_back(1.1, 2.2, 3.3);
```

Pay attention to the arguments we passed directly to the function. The following illustration depicts the use of `emplace_back()`:

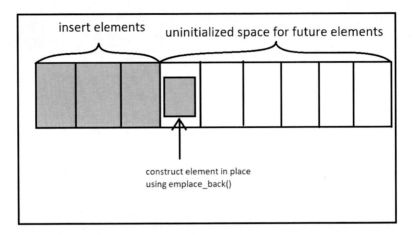

Figure 6.6: Inserting an object of the Point type into the vector with the emplace_back function

emplace_back() constructs the element through std::allocator_traits::construct().
The latter typically uses the placement of the new operator to construct the element at the already
allocated uninitialized space.

std::list, in turn, provides an emplace_front() method. Both functions return a reference to
the inserted element. The only requirement is for the type of element to be EmplaceConstructible.
For vectors, the type should also be MoveInsertable.

Using container adapters

You may have come across depictions of the stack and queue as data structures (or containers in
the C++ language). Technically, they are data structure adapters rather than data structures. In STL,
std::stack and std::queue adopt containers by providing a special interface to access them.
"Stack" is a phrase that is universally used. We have only used it to represent a memory segment for
items that have an automated storage period. Because of its allocation/deallocation mechanism, the
segment is given the name stack.

When we define objects, they are pushed to the stack and pulled out when they are destroyed. The
objects are popped in the opposite order to that they were pushed in. That is why the memory section
is referred to as the stack. The stack adapter uses the same **last in, first out** (**LIFO**) mechanism. The
following are the most important functions that std::stack provides:

```
void push(const value_type& value);
void push(value_type&& value);
```

The push() function invokes the underlying container's push_back() method. Typically, a vector
is used to implement the stack. The container is one of the two template arguments that std::stack
takes. It doesn't matter what you select, but it must have a member method called push_back().
std::stack and std::queue have a default container called std::deque.

`std::deque` allows fast insertion at its beginning and its end. It is an indexed sequential container similar to `std::vector`. **Deque** stands for **double-ended queue**.

Let's see `stack` in action:

```
#include <stack>
int main()
{
    std::stack<int> st;
    st.push(1); // stack contains: 1
    st.push(2); // stack contains: 2 1
    st.push(3); // stack contains: 3 2 1
}
```

A better alternative to the `push()` function is `emplace()`. It calls `emplace_back()` of the underlying container, so it constructs elements in place.

The `pop()` method is used to remove the element. It takes no parameters and returns nothing; all it does is remove the top element from the stack. The `top()` method is used to get the stack's top member. Let's change the preceding example so that all of the stack members are printed before they are popped out (the code for this can be found at `https://github.com/PacktPublishing/Expert-C-2nd-edition/tree/main/Chapter%206/5_stack_example.cpp`).

The `top()` function returns a reference to the top element. It calls the `back()` function of the underlying container. Pay attention to the last `top()` function that we called on the empty stack. We suggest that you check the size of the stack using `size()` before calling `top()` on the empty one.

`queue` is another adapter with slightly different behavior from the stack. The logic behind the queue is that it returns the first inserted element first: it maintains the **first in, first out** (**FIFO**) principle. Look at the following diagram:

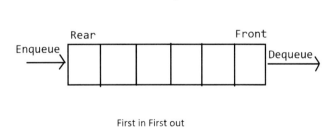

Figure 6.7: Illustration of the FIFO principle

The formal names for inserting and retrieving operations in a queue are enqueue and dequeue. `std::queue` keeps a consistent approach and provides the `push()` and `pop()` functions. To access the first and last elements of the queue, you should use `front()` and `back()`. Both return references to elements. Here is a simple usage example:

```cpp
#include <iostream>
#include <queue>
int main()
{
    std::queue<char> q;
    q.push('a');
    q.push('b');
    q.push('c');
    std::cout << q.front(); // prints 'a'
    std::cout << q.back(); // prints 'c'
    q.pop(); // removes the top element
    std::cout << q.front(); // prints 'b'
}
```

Knowing how to use various containers and adapters is beneficial when they are used appropriately. There is not a one-size-fits-all solution for all types of problems when it comes to selecting the correct container. The stack is used by several compilers to parse code expressions. The stack, for example, makes validating the parentheses in the following equation simple:

```cpp
int r = (a + b) + (((x * y) - (a / b)) / 4);
```

To practice, write a small program that validates the preceding expression using a stack.

`std::priority_queue` is another container adapter. A balanced, node-based data structure, such as `max-heap` or `min-heap`, is frequently used by a priority queue. Let's take a look at a simple usage scenario for `std::priority_queue`: `https://github.com/PacktPublishing/Expert-C-2nd-edition/tree/main/Chapter%2006/6_priority_queue_example.cpp`.

At the end of this chapter, we will look at trees and graphs to learn how the priority queue works under the hood.

Now that we have talked about some of the sequence containers and container adapters that are available, it is time to learn about the techniques that will allow us to iterate over the elements of those containers or adapters.

Iterating containers

A container that is not iterable is analogous to a car that cannot be driven. A container, after all, is a collection of items. The `for` loop is one of the most frequent techniques we can use to iterate over container elements:

```cpp
std::vector<int> vec{1, 2, 3, 4, 5};
```

```
for (int ix = 0; ix < vec.size(); ++ix) {
std::cout << vec[ix] << ", ";
}
```

For element access, containers offer a distinct set of actions. `operator[]`, for example, is provided by the vector but not by the list. `std::list` has the `front()` and `back()` methods, which return the first and last elements, respectively. `std::vector`, as already discussed, additionally provides `at()` and `operator[]`.

This means that we cannot use the preceding loop to iterate list elements. However, we can loop over a list (and vector) with a range-based `for` loop, as follows:

```
std::list<double> lst{1.1, 2.2, 3.3, 4.2};
for (auto& elem : lst) {
std::cout << elem << ", ";
}
```

The secret is buried in the range-based `for` loop's implementation, which may appear confusing. It uses the `std::begin()` method to get an iterator that points to the container's first element.

Based on the physical structure of the container, an iterator is an object that points to the container element and may be advanced to the next element. Declare a `vector` iterator and initialize it with an iterator pointing to the beginning of the `vector` iterator with the following code:

```
std::vector<int> vec{1, 2, 3, 4};
std::vector<int>::iterator it{vec.begin()};
```

Almost all containers provide four member functions (not taking into consideration the functions that return constant iterators) – `begin()`, `end()`, `rbegin()`, and `rend()`. They return iterators to either the beginning or end of the container. The functions and their descriptions are as follows:

- `begin()`: Returns an iterator to the first element.

- `end()`: Returns an iterator to the element following the last element.

- `rbegin()`: Returns a reverse iterator to the first element of the reversed container. It corresponds to the last element of the container.

- `rend()`: Returns a reverse iterator to the element following the last element of the reversed container. It corresponds to the element preceding the first element of the container.

The following diagram shows how we treat the beginning and the end of the container:

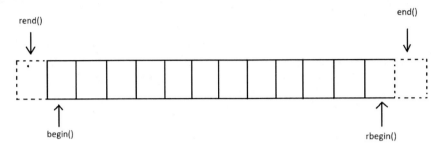

Figure 6.8: Illustration of where iterators returned from the functions point to

The preceding code, which iterated over the list elements using a range-based `for` loop, may look something like this:

```
auto it_begin = std::begin(lst);
auto it_end = std::end(lst);
for ( ; it_begin != it_end; ++it_begin) {
std::cout << *it_begin << ", ";
}
```

Pay attention to the * operator that we used in the previous code to access the underlying element of the iterator. We consider an iterator a *clever* pointer to the container element.

The `std::begin()` and `std::end()` functions typically call the containers' `begin()` and `end()` methods, respectively. However, they are also applicable to regular arrays.

As we mentioned previously, not all containers have those four functions. The container that stands out from the rest is `std::forward_list`. It only has `begin()` and `end()` functions, as well as `before_begin()` functions, which return an iterator to the element before the first element of the container. This element acts as a placeholder, attempting to access it results in undefined behavior. The only use cases can be found in the `insert_after()`, `emplace_after()`, `erase_after()`, and `splice_after()` functions and the increment operator.

The container iterator knows exactly how to work with the container elements. As seen in the code at `https://github.com/PacktPublishing/Expert-C-2nd-edition/tree/main/Chapter%2006/7_iterating_containers.cpp`, advancing a vector iterator moves it to the next slot in the array, while advancing a list iterator moves it to the next node using the associated pointer.

Because each container implements its own iterator, list and vector iterators have the same interface but function differently. The iterator's behavior is determined by its category. The iterator of a vector, for example, is a random-access iterator, which means we may use it to read any element at random. The following code gets the vector's fourth member through its iterator by adding three to it:

```
std::vector<int> vec { 2, 4, 6, 8, 10 };
auto it = vec.begin();
std::cout << *(it + 3);
```

There are six iterator categories in STL. Let's look at each in detail:

- The **input iterator** allows read access (through the * operator) as well as forwarding the position of the iterator using the prefix and postfix increment operators. We can only iterate through the container once while using an input iterator because it does not support multiple passes. On the other hand, the forward iterator allows numerous passes. We can read the value of the element through the iterator many times using multiple-pass capability.

- The **output iterator** does not provide access to the element, but it allows us to assign new values to it.

- A combination of an input iterator and output iterator with the multiple passes feature comprises the **forward iterator**.

- The forward iterator, on the other hand, can only increment, but **bidirectional iterators** can move the iterator to any position. They support decrementing operations. For example, std::list supports bidirectional iterators.

- Finally, the **random access iterator** allows you to *jump* through elements by adding/subtracting a number to/from the iterator. The iterator will jump to the position specified by the arithmetic operation. std::vector provides random access iterators.

  The set of operations that may be applied to the iterator is defined by each of the categories. For example, the input iterator may be used to read the value of one element and then increment the iterator to proceed to the next element. The random access iterator, on the other hand, allows you to increment and decrement the iterator with arbitrary values, read and write the element's value, and so on.

- The **contiguous iterator** category has all of the qualities stated thus far in this section, and in addition, it expects the container to be contiguous. This means that container elements are guaranteed to reside right next to each other. std::array is an example of a contiguous container.

The information about the iterator is used by functions such as distance() to get the quickest result in execution. The distance() function between two bidirectional iterators, for example, takes a linear amount of time to execute, but the same function takes a constant amount of time for random access iterators.

An example implementation is shown in the pseudocode at https://github.com/PacktPublishing/Expert-C-2nd-edition/tree/main/Chapter%2006/8_distance.cpp.

Although the preceding pseudocode works, we should keep in mind that testing an iterator's category at runtime is not an option. It is defined at compile time, so we need to use template specialization to generate the `distance()` function for random access iterators. A better solution would be using the `std::is_same` type trait, defined in `<type_traits>` (the code can be found at `https://github.com/PacktPublishing/Expert-C-2nd-edition/tree/main/Chapter%2006/9_distance_2.cpp`).

`std::is_same_v` is a helper template for `std::is_same` and is defined as follows:

```
template <class T, class U>
inline constexpr bool is_same_v = is_same<T, U>::value;
```

An iterator's most essential feature is that it allows containers and algorithms to be loosely coupled.

The struct iterator described in this section has been deprecated and is now considered a legacy feature. C++20 introduced a new system of iterators based on concepts.

Concepts and iterators

C++20 introduced concepts as one of its major features. Along with concepts, C++20 has new iterators based on concepts. Even though the iterators we've explained up to this point are now considered legacy features, they have already been used in many lines of code. That is why we introduced them first before continuing with the new iterator concepts. Now, let's find out what concepts are and how to use them.

Understanding concepts

Abstraction is essential in computer programming. In the previous chapters, we discussed that OOP is a way to represent data and operations as abstract entities. We also covered template metaprogramming by diving into templates and making our classes even more flexible by reusing them for various aggregate types. Templates allow not just abstraction from specific types but also loose coupling between entity and aggregate types. Consider the `std::vector` class. It offers a general interface for storing and manipulating object collections. We can easily define three separate vectors, each of which will contain three different types of objects:

```
std::vector<int> ivec;
std::vector<Person> persons;
std::vector<std::vector<double>> float_matrix;
```

We would have to perform something like this for the previous code if we did not have templates:

```
int_vector ivec;
custom_vector persons; // supposing the custom_vector
                       // stores void*
double_vector_vector float_matrix;
```

Even though the preceding code is completely inappropriate, we should all agree that templates are the foundation of generic programming. Concepts introduce even more flexibility into generic programming. Now, it is possible to set restrictions on template parameters, check for constraints, and discover inconsistent behavior at compile time. A template class declaration looks like this:

```
template <typename T>
class Wallet
{
// the body of the class using the T type
};
```

In the preceding code block, pay close attention to the typename keyword. Concepts take this a step further by allowing it to be replaced with a type description that explains the template parameter. Let's say we want the Wallet class to work with types that can be added together – that is, they should be addable. Here is how employing an idea in the code can help us do that:

```
template <addable T>
class Wallet
{
// the body of the class using addable T's
};
```

As a result, we can now build Wallet instances by providing addable types. The compiler will produce an error if the type does not fulfill the requirement. It appears to be supernatural. Two Wallet objects are declared in the following snippet:

```
class Book
{
// doesn't have an operator+
// the body is omitted for brevity
};
constexpr bool operator+(const Money& a, const Money& b) {
return Money{a.value_ + b.value_};
}
class Money
{
friend constexpr bool operator+(const Money&, const Money&);
// code omitted for brevity
private:
double value_;
};
Wallet<Money> w; // works fine
Wallet<Book> g; // compile error
```

The `Book` class has no `+operator`, so the construction of `g` will fail because of the `template` parameter type restriction.

We can declare a concept using the `concept` keyword, which has the following form:

```
template <parameter-list>
concept name-of-the-concept = constraint-expression;
```

As you can see, a concept is also declared using templates. We can refer to them as types that describe other types. Concepts rely heavily on constraints. A constraint is a way to specify requirements for template arguments, and, as follows, a concept is a set of constraints. Here is how we can implement the preceding `addable` concept:

```
template <typename T>
concept addable = requires (T obj) {obj + obj;}
```

Standard concepts are defined in the `<concepts>` header.

We can also combine several concepts by requiring the new concept to support the others. To achieve that, we can use `&& operator`. Let's see how iterators leverage concepts and bring an example of an `incrementable` iterator concept that combines other concepts.

Using iterators in C++20

Iterators were the first to fully use concepts after they were introduced. Iterators and their categories are now considered legacy because, starting from C++20, we use iterator concepts such as `readable` (which specifies that the type is `readable` by applying the `*` operator) and `writable` (which specifies that a value can be written to an object referenced by the iterator). Let's look at how `incrementable` is defined in the `<iterator>` header, as promised:

```
template <typename T>
concept incrementable = std::regular<T> && std::weakly_
incrementable<T> && requires (T t) { {t++} -> std::same_as<T>; };
```

Therefore, the `incrementable` concept requires the type to be `std::regular`. This means it should be constructible by default and have a copy constructor and `operator==()`. Besides that, the `incrementable` concept requires the type to be `weakly_incrementable`, which means the type supports pre- and post-increment operators, except that the type is not required to be equality-comparable. That is why `incrementable` joins `std::regular` to require the type to be equality-comparable. Finally, the addition requires constraint points since the type should not change after an increment – that is, it should be the same type as before. Although `std::same_as` is represented as a concept (defined in `<concepts>` in previous versions), we used to use `std::is_same`, which is defined in `<type_traits>`. They do the same thing, but the C++17 version, `std::is_same_v`, was verbose, with additional suffixes.

As a result, instead of iterator categories, we now refer to iterator concepts. In addition to the ones we have already discussed, the following concepts should be considered:

- `input_iterator`: This specifies that the type allows its referenced values to be read and is both pre- and post-incrementable

- `output_iterator`: This specifies that values of the type can be written to and that the type is both pre- and post-incrementable

- `input_or_output_iterator`: The unnecessarily long name aside, this specifies that the type is incrementable and can also be dereferenced.

- `forward_iterator`: This specifies that the type is `input_iterator` and that it also supports equality comparison and multi-pass

- `bidirectional_iterator`: This specifies that the type supports `forward_iterator` and that it also supports backward movement

- `random_access_iterator`: This specifies that the type is `bidirectional_iterator` and supports advancement in constant time and subscripting

- `contiguous_iterator`: This specifies that the type is `random_access_iterator` and refers to elements that are contiguous in memory

Let's look at an example where we implemented the `distance` function using iterator concepts instead of categories: `https://github.com/PacktPublishing/Expert-C-2nd-edition/blob/main/Chapter%2006/10_distance_3.cpp`.

They almost repeat the legacy iterators that we discussed earlier, but now, they can be used when declaring template parameters so that the compiler will take care of the rest.

So far, we have discussed sequence data structures and their corresponding containers, container adapters, and iterators, but since sequence data structures are not almighty and can't solve all the problems in the world, we will continue to learn about other types of data structures. First, we'll cover node-based data structures.

Node-based data structures

Node-based data structures do not necessarily take contiguous blocks of memory. They mainly allocate nodes in memory that are connected. In this case, logically, there is no need to allocate a block of memory when nodes can occupy node-size spaces and be connected in some way. This means that nodes might be spread randomly in memory.

The **linked list** is the most often used and most basic node-based data structure. A visual representation of a doubly linked list is shown in the following diagram:

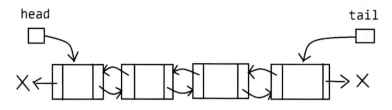

Figure 6.9: Illustration of a doubly linked list

Apart from the structural differences, the way that operations run on node-based data structures also differs from that of sequential data structures. Some of the operations are faster, while some are slower. For example, if we compare an array and a list, the time complexity of reading an element will be O(1) for an array and O(n) for a list. Here, the insertion will be O(n) for an array because it has to copy elements, while for a list, it will be O(1) if we consider that it just changes pointers that point to nodes, and so on. To keep it short, let's implement the element insertion at the front of the list. We will keep each node as a struct:

```
template <typename T>
struct Node
{
node(const T& it) : item{it}, next{nullptr}, prev{nullptr} {}
T item;
Node<T>* next;
Node<T>* prev;
};
```

Take a look at the data members that the node contains. To explain this more figuratively, let's imagine students who are going to cross a street. They are told to hold hands so that they can all cross the street together. Each hand of a child that holds the hand of the child in front can be considered a next pointer, which provides a connection between nodes, while the hand of a child who stands in front and holds the hand of the child behind them can be considered as a prev pointer. Nodes are chained similarly.

To implement a linked list, all we need is to keep a pointer to its first node, usually called the head of the list. Now, let's look at the way operations run on a linked list. Inserting an element at the front of the list is simple (the code for this can be found at https://github.com/PacktPublishing/Expert-C-2nd-edition/blob/main/Chapter%2006/12_linked_list.h).

There are three cases that we should consider when performing an insertion on a list:

- Inserting at the front
- Inserting at the end
- Inserting in the middle

Let's illustrate these operations and the steps that are needed to make insertions at different positions.

Inserting an element at the front of the list, as discussed earlier, involves the steps shown in the following diagram:

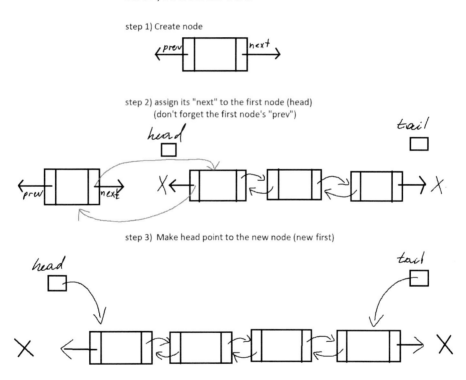

Figure 6.10: Inserting an element at the front of a list

Inserting an element in the middle of the list is shown in the following diagram:

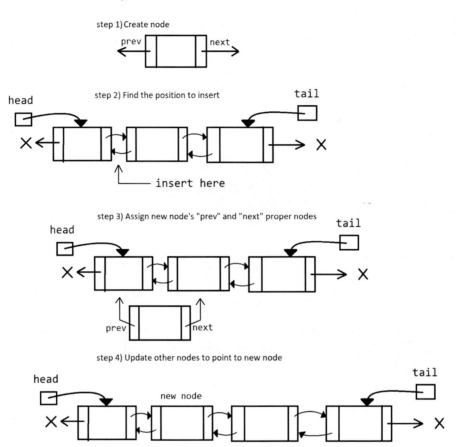

Figure 6.11: Inserting an element in the middle of a list

Finally, inserting an element at the end of the list is done as follows:

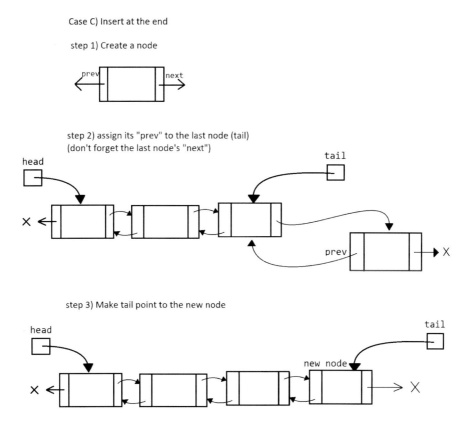

Figure 6.12: Inserting an element at the end of a list

In the preceding diagrams, inserting an element into a vector is different from inserting an element into a list. How would you choose between a vector and a list? You should concentrate on the operations and their speed. For example, reading any element from the vector takes constant time. We can store one million emails in a vector, and retrieve the one at position 834,000 without any additional effort. For linked lists, the operation is linear. Therefore, if you need to store a collection of data that will be mostly read, but not written, then using a vector is a reasonable choice.

Inserting an element at any position in the list takes a constant-time operation, while the vector will strive to insert an element at a random position. Therefore, when you need a collection of objects to/ from which data can be intensively added/removed, the better choice would be a linked list.

We should also take into account the cache memory. Vectors have good data locality. Reading the first element of a vector involves copying the first N elements into the cache. Further reads of vector elements will be even faster. We cannot say the same for linked lists. To find out the reason, let's compare the memory layouts of a vector and a linked list.

Graphs and trees

Graphs and trees are considered non-linear data structures, which come in handy in solving various kinds of problems. Though they are both non-linear data structures, they have differences, which help us distinguish them from each other. For example, the tree should have a root node, while the graph doesn't have one; the tree forms a tree-like structure when dealing with data while the graph organizes the data into a network-like structure; there can be loops in a graph, while a tree doesn't allow this; and so on.

Trees

Thinking about a combination of a binary search algorithm and sorting algorithms can lead to the idea of having a container that maintains objects so that they're sorted by default. `std::set`, which is built on a balanced tree, is one such container. Before discussing balanced trees, let's look at the binary search tree, which is a great option for quick lookups.

The binary search tree's concept is that the values of a node's left-hand subtree are smaller than the node's value. The right-hand subtree of a node, on the other hand, has values that are greater than the node's value. A binary search tree looks like this:

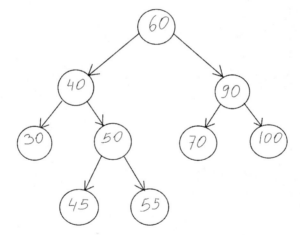

Figure 6.13: Example of a binary search tree

The element with a value of 40 is located in the left-hand subtree, as shown in the preceding diagram, because it is less than 60 (the root element). On the other hand, the element with a value of 90 resides in the right-hand subtree because it is greater than the root element. The same logic applies to the rest of the tree elements.

A binary tree node is represented as a struct containing the item and two pointers to each child. Here is a sample code representation of a tree node:

```
template <typename T>
struct TreeNode
{
    T item;
    TreeNode<T>* left;
    TreeNode<T>* right;
};
```

In a completely balanced binary search tree, searching, inserting, and deleting elements takes O(log n). STL does not have a specific container for trees, but it does have some that are comparable and are based on a tree implementation. For example, the std::set container is based on a balanced tree that uniquely stores elements in sorted order:

```
#include <set>
...
std::set<int> s{1, 5, 2, 4, 4, 4, 3};
// s has {1, 2, 3, 4, 5}
```

std::map is also based on a balanced tree, but this one provides a container that maps a key to some value, as follows:

```
#include <map>
...
std::map<int, std::string> numbers;
numbers[3] = "three";
numbers[4] = "four";
...
```

As shown in the preceding code, we mapped integers to strings. In our case, when we wrote numbers[3], 3 became a key for a map named numbers, and when we assigned "three" to it, "three" became a value for the 3 key. So, when we tell the map to store the value of 3 as a key and three as a value, it adds a new node to its inner tree with the key equal to 3 and the value equal to three.

The set and map operations are logarithmic, which makes it a very efficient data structure in most cases. However, there is a more efficient data structure, which we will discuss later.

Graphs

The binary search tree's balancing nature is based on a variety of search index implementations. For example, database systems use a balanced tree called a B-tree for table indexing. Although the B-tree is not a *binary* tree, it follows the same balancing logic as a binary tree, as shown here:

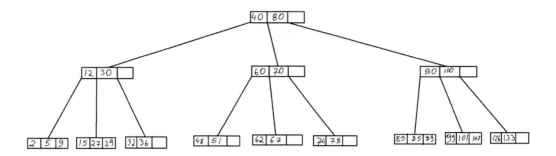

Figure 6.14: Example of a B-tree

Graphs, on the other hand, represent connected nodes with no proper order:

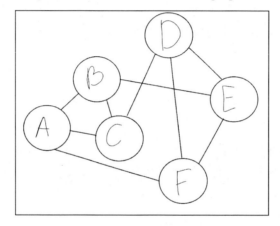

Figure 6.15: Example of a graph

Let's suppose we are building a social network that will eventually beat Facebook or TikTok within the market. The users in the social network can follow each other, which can be represented as a graph. For example, if A follows B, B follows C, and C follows both B and A at the same time, then we can represent the relationships like so:

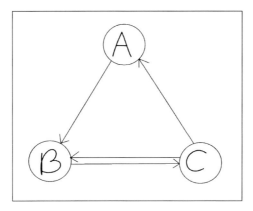

Figure 6.16: Representation of user connections with graphs

A node is called a vertex in a graph. The link between two nodes is called an edge. There is no fixed graph representation, so we should choose from several. Let's think about our social network – how would we represent that user A follows user B?

One of the best options here is using a hash table. We can map each user to all of the users they follow:

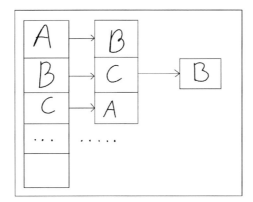

Figure 6.17: Representation of user connections with hash tables

The graph implementation becomes a hybrid container, as shown at `https://github.com/ PacktPublishing/Expert-C-2nd-edition/tree/main/Chapter%2006/13_graph.h`.

To make an STL-compatible container, we must add an iterator to the graph. Although iterating a graph is not a good idea, adding an iterator is not a bad idea.

Though graphs are really powerful data structures, we are not going to stop at this point – the next data structure we are going to talk about does not yield a graph.

Hash tables

The hash table is the most efficient data structure currently available. It is based on the concept of vector indexing, which is a rather simple concept. Consider the following example of a large vector with list pointers:

```
std::vector<std::list<T> > hash_table;
```

Accessing the elements of a vector takes constant time – that is the primary superpower of a vector. The hash table enables us to use any type as the container's key. The basic idea of the hash table is to use a well-curated hash function that will generate a unique index for the input key. For example, when we use a string as a hash table key, the hash table uses a hash function to generate the hash as the index value for the underlying vector (the code for this can be found at https://github.com/PacktPublishing/Expert-C-2nd-edition/tree/main/Chapter%2006/14_insert_hashtable.cpp).

Here is how we can illustrate a hash table:

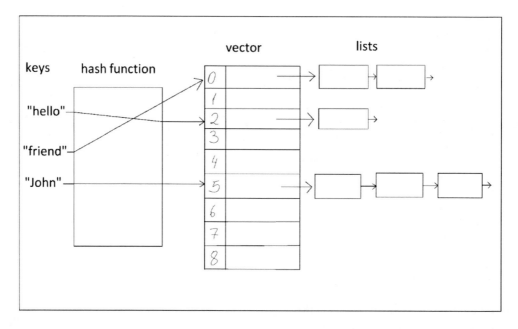

Figure 6.18: Illustration of a hash table

Because it is based on a vector, accessing a hash table takes constant time every time. Although various keys may provide the same hash values, causing collisions, those collisions can be avoided by using a list of values as the vector element (as shown in the preceding diagram).

STL supports the concept of a hash table through a container named `std::unordered_map`:

```
#include <unordered_map>
...
std::unordered_map<std::string, std::string> hashtable;
hashtable["key1"] = "value 1";
hashtable["key2"] = "value 2";
...
```

The `std::unordered_map` function uses the `std::hash()` function defined in the `<functional>` header to generate the hash value for the provided keys. You can define a custom implementation for the hash function. The third template parameter of `std::unordered_map` is the hash function, which defaults to `std::hash`.

Algorithms

Algorithms, as mentioned previously, are functions that take an input, process it, and provide an output. In most cases, in STL, an algorithm refers to a function that processes a set of data. Containers, such as `std::vector`, `std::list`, and others, are used to store data collections.

One of the common tasks in a programmer's routine is to select an efficient algorithm. For example, using the binary search technique to search a sorted vector will be significantly faster than using sequential searching. An asymptotic analysis, which considers the speed of the algorithm concerning the size of the input data, is used to compare the efficiency of algorithms. This means that we should not compare two algorithms by applying them to a container with 10 or 100 elements.

The true difference between methods becomes apparent when they're applied to a large enough container – one with one million or even one billion elements. Verifying an algorithm's complexity is the process of determining its efficiency. You may have come across **O(n)** or **O(log n)** algorithms. The `O()` function (pronounced big-oh) determines an algorithm's complexity.

Let's have a look at the different types of search algorithms and see how they differ in terms of complexity.

Search algorithms

Search algorithms are an essential part of a programmer's toolkit. They allow us to find specific elements within a collection of data efficiently. Two commonly used search algorithms are sequential search and binary search.

Sequential search, also known as linear search, is a simple algorithm that goes through each element of a collection until it finds the desired element or reaches the end. It has a linear time complexity, denoted as `O(n)`, where n is the size of the input. Sequential search is straightforward to implement but may become inefficient for large datasets.

Binary search, on the other hand, is a more efficient algorithm that requires the collection to be sorted beforehand. It works by repeatedly dividing the search space in half, eliminating the half where the desired element cannot be located. This process continues until the element is found or it is determined that it does not exist in the collection. Binary search has a logarithmic time complexity, denoted as $O(\log n)$, where n is the size of the input. This algorithm is particularly useful for large datasets as it reduces the number of comparisons needed to find the element significantly.

When selecting an algorithm, it is important to consider its time complexity and how it scales with the size of the input data. The asymptotic analysis, represented by the big O notation, provides a way to compare and evaluate the efficiency of different algorithms. By analyzing the number of operations performed relative to the input size, we can determine how the algorithm's performance will be affected as the dataset grows.

STL provides various algorithms, including search algorithms, to operate on collections of data. These algorithms are designed to work with iterators, which allow us to access and traverse different types of containers generically. By using iterators, the STL algorithms offer flexibility and abstraction, allowing them to be used with a wide range of containers that supports the required iterator operations.

In summary, search algorithms play a vital role in finding elements within data collections. Sequential search is a simple but less efficient algorithm, while binary search offers a significant improvement in efficiency but requires a sorted collection. Understanding the time complexity and choosing the appropriate algorithm based on the size of the input data are crucial considerations. STL provides a set of powerful algorithms that operate on containers through iterators, making them versatile and widely applicable in various programming scenarios.

Sorting

Sorting is a fundamental task in computer programming, and it involves arranging a collection of elements in a specific order. Sorted containers are particularly useful when utilizing search algorithms such as binary search. While programmers rarely implement their own sorting algorithms these days, they have access to built-in sorting functions such as `std::sort()` in STL.

Quicksort is one of the most popular and fastest sorting algorithms available. The core idea behind any sorting algorithm is to identify smaller or larger elements and swap them until the entire collection is sorted. For example, selection sort divides the collection into two parts: a sorted subarray and an unsorted subarray. It continuously searches for the smallest element in the unsorted subarray and swaps it with the first element of the unsorted subarray. This process repeats until the unsorted subarray becomes empty.

STL provides the `std::sort()` function, which takes two random-access iterators and sorts the elements between them. It is a versatile function that can be used with various container types, such as `std::vector`. However, for containers that do not support random access iterators, such as `std::list`, the sort function cannot be directly used. Instead, such containers provide their own `sort()` member function for efficient sorting.

The `std::sort()` function also allows a third parameter, a comparing function, which is used to determine the order of elements in the container. For custom types, the elements must support the less than operator (<) for proper sorting. Alternatively, a separate comparison function can be defined, or a lambda function can be used as an elegant and anonymous way to define the comparison logic.

Efficient software development involves understanding and utilizing appropriate data structures and algorithms. By harnessing the power of C++20 and familiarizing yourself with the data structures and algorithms covered in this chapter, you can optimize your programs for improved performance. A strong grasp of the fundamental algorithms and data structures is crucial for developing effective problem-solving skills, and it enables the creation of efficient software that saves time and enhances the user experience, making it a superior choice among alternatives.

Summary

In this chapter, we went over the basics of data structures and the differences between them. We learned how to use them based on problem analysis. For example, because of the difficulty of linked-list element access operations, using a linked list in applications requiring random lookups is deemed time-consuming. Due to its constant-time element access, a dynamically increasing vector is more suited to such cases. In contrast to, for example, a list, using a vector in problems that require quick insertions at the front of the container is more costly.

This chapter also covered algorithms and how to measure their effectiveness. We compared several problems to develop better methods for solving them more quickly.

In the next chapter, we are going to continue the topic of data structures by diving deeper into it and discussing advanced data structures, their properties, and their implementation details.

Further reading

For more information, refer to the following resources:

- *Programming Pearls*, by Jon Bentley, available at `https://www.amazon.com/Programming-Pearls-2nd-Jon-Bentley/dp/0201657880/`

- *Data Abstraction and Problem Solving Using C++: Walls and Mirrors*, by Frank Carrano and Timothy Henry, available at `https://www.amazon.com/Data-Abstraction-Problem-Solving-Mirrors/dp/0134463978/`

- *Introduction to Algorithms*, by Cormen, Leiserson, Rivest, and Stein, available at `https://www.amazon.com/Introduction-Algorithms-3rd-MIT-Press/dp/0262033844/`

- *C++ Data Structures and Algorithms by Wisnu Anggoro*, available at `https://www.packtpub.com/product/c-data-structures-and-algorithms/9781788835213`

Questions

Answer the following questions to test your knowledge of this chapter:

1. Describe how an element is added to a vector that is expanding dynamically.

2. What distinguishes inserting an element at the front of a linked list from inserting it at the front of a vector?

3. Implement a hybrid data structure that stores its elements as a vector and a list, respectively. Pick the underlying data structure that implements the operation in each case as quickly as possible.

4. How would a binary search tree look if 100 elements were added in increasing order?

7
Advanced Data Structures

In the previous chapter, we discussed the importance of knowing what data structures and algorithms are and how to use them in everyday problems. In this chapter, we are going to dive even deeper into what data structures there are, some of which you may have never heard about before.

Knowing about basic data structures is one thing but knowing and understanding how some of the advanced data structures work is a goal every programmer should strive to achieve. But what are advanced data structures and how are they considered to be advanced? We talked briefly about trees and graphs in the previous chapter. Even looking back at their names brings thoughts about those data structures being of an advanced type. They sound so serious; they even look like something solid. And to answer the question you may now have: yes, they are considered to be advanced data structures. Should we just say that, for example, trees are advanced data structures and stop at that point? Definitely not, as there are different types of trees, some of which are more advanced than others. Among the different types of trees, we can find a general tree, a binary tree, a binary search tree, an AVL tree, a red-black tree, a B-tree, and so on.

Let us consider a simple case where one type of tree is more advanced than the other. The difference will be discussed between a binary search tree and an AVL tree. Both of those trees keep the elements in such a way that small elements are on the left side of the root while the large elements are on the right side of the root. Let us take, for example, the following sequence of numbers: {1, 2, 3, 4, 5, 6, 7}. They will form both a binary search tree and an AVL tree and we will compare their structures with the diagrams shown here:

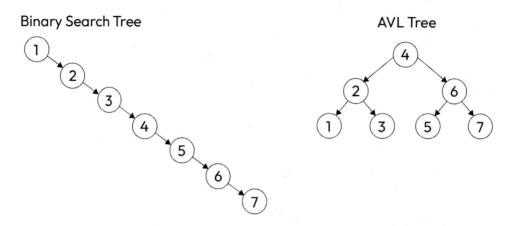

Figure 7.1 – Binary search tree versus AVL tree

The difference is impossible not to notice. We formed two types of trees with the same elements and got different tree structures. Let us consider we want to search for an element and it is number seven. In the case of a binary search tree, we have to go through every node to get to the last element because it is not a balanced tree and it looks more like a linked list than a binary search tree. Meanwhile, in the case of an AVL tree, we need half the steps to reach the element we want as it is balanced. Therefore, which one of these trees is more advanced? It is definitely an AVL tree as it is more complicated. Complicated not in a visual way but based on the self-balancing functionality: every time an insertion takes place, it checks whether the tree is balanced or not and self-balances itself if necessary.

Trees and graphs are not the only advanced data structures: there are also advanced lists, hash tables, tries, and so on. You don't have to learn them by heart because having even a general idea of what they are adds another precious tool to your knowledge base.

In this chapter, we are obviously not going to cover all the advanced data structures, only the ones we find interesting and worth mentioning. We will touch upon the following topics:

- B-trees
- Heaps and their applications
- Advanced lists
- Implementation details of `std::unordered_map`

The last topic is not an advanced data structure, as you can see; it is an STL container, which we talked about briefly in the previous chapter. Since it is based on one of the advanced data structures, which is the hash table, we decided to include it in this chapter as well.

Technical requirements

The g++ compiler with the `-std=c++20` option is used to compile the examples throughout the chapter. You can find the source files used in this chapter in the GitHub repository for this book at `https://github.com/PacktPublishing/Expert-C-2nd-edition`.

B-trees

A B-tree is a self-balancing tree data structure through which you can organize search, insertion, deletion, and sequential access in logarithmic time. For some operations, the time is not always logarithmic. In the previous chapter, we learned about the time complexity of the `std::vector` container's `push_back()` function. When calculating it, we mentioned that it was amortized, `O(1)`. The same happens for B-trees. Performing deletion and insertion on a B-tree takes amortized `O(log n)` time. The B-tree is a generalization of the binary search tree that allows nodes to have multiple children. The number of children and keys that a node of a B-tree can hold depends on what order it is in. According to Knuth's definition, a B-tree of order m is a tree that satisfies the following properties:

- Every node has at most m children

- Every internal node has at least $\{m/2\}$ children

- Every non-leaf node has at least two children

- All leaves appear on the same level and carry no information

- A non-leaf node with k children contains $k-1$ keys

The following diagram shows a B-tree of order 5 formed of elements $\{4,24,67,234,12,11,160,2,6,43,54,5,3,301\}$:

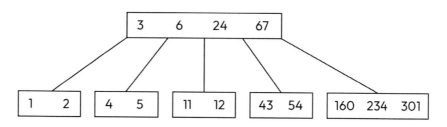

Figure 7.2 – B-tree of order 5

Why use B-trees is a question that most programmers ask. There is a binary search tree that also works in `O(log n)` time and also keeps the elements in a structure that a B-tree supports: smaller elements are on the left side of the root and larger elements are on the right side of the root. What is the use of a tree that can hold multiple keys and multiple children? To answer the question, we have to dig deep to understand why, in fact, B-trees were created.

Bayer and McCreight first introduced the idea of a B-tree in 1972. It was first created with the intention of being used as an external memory data structure but became useful in many different ways.

Let us remember the memory hierarchy of a computer by looking at the following diagram:

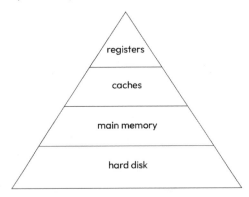

Figure 7.3 – Memory hierarchy of a computer

In this case, the memory device, which is higher in the hierarchy, is the closest to the CPU; hence, the process of reading data from that device is much faster. This means that things start to go a little bit slower when the CPU has to read or write data from a hard disk. To understand how we can organize the reading and writing process so that it is faster and how all of this is connected to a B-tree, we have to look at the hard disk structure and how it stores data:

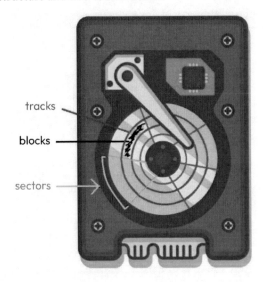

Figure 7.4 – Hard disk structure

The physical block size is usually 512 bytes, which is the size of the smallest block that the disk controller can read or write. So, the information inside those blocks should be structured in a way that takes less time to work with the data. When we read from a hard disk or write to it, the block of information is put inside the RAM and is then read or written. No change actually takes place on the hard disk itself.

Let us say we have a list of students, where the student IDs, names, ages, and their marks in each subject are kept. The list will look like this:

ID	Name Surname	Age	Algebra	Computer Science	Physics	...
1	Kurt Carey	18	90	78	86	...
2	Kezia Holloway	22	99	65	76	...
3	Camilla Bolton	21	65	98	87	...
4	Connah Weber	19	46	88	63	...
5	Emyr Dillon	20	89	68	54	...
6	Joshua Pierce	22	78	56	45	...
...	...	...	...	...	...	...

Let us imagine that the full list occupies 20 blocks of hard disk, which is, of course, a lot, and if the data is searched inside those blocks, we have to go inside 20 blocks at worst in order to find the data we need. We can reorganize this by adding another list that holds only the IDs of students and a pointer that points to the row associated with the student. In that case, the size of the list will reduce, and if we imagine that it takes 2 blocks instead of 20 blocks of memory, we can look for the data by only going through those 2 blocks. Another thing that can happen is that the information takes 200 blocks and the list we created takes 20 blocks, which is again more, and we will need a new list, which will take up only 2 blocks, and so on and so forth.

The following diagram shows the structure we will get at the end:

id	name surname	age	physics	...
1	Kurt Carey	age	physics	...
2				
3				
⋮				
⋮				
24				
25				
⋮				
46				
⋮				
67				
⋮				
99				
100				
⋮				

id	pointer
1	
2	
3	
⋮	
⋮	
9	
10	
11	
⋮	
⋮	
19	
20	
⋮	

id	pointer
1	
2	
. . . .	. . . .

The diagram even looks like a tree when we rotate it. This principle and the principle of a B-tree coincide in the following way: the children of a root grow as the number of keys also grows and, eventually, new children are created. We can now say that for reading blocks of data from a hard disk, B-trees are used. The usage of a B-tree in these kinds of problems is crucial if not mandatory.

When talking about trees, we cannot just skip the part of operations that trees allow us to perform on the data. The most important operations that are performed on trees are searching, insertion, and deletion. We are going to discuss those three operations for a B-tree but, as we have to specify the order of a B-tree before moving on to those discussions, we decided to take a specification of a B-tree, which is a 2-3 tree, and show how insertion, deletion, and searching work on a 2-3 tree.

A 2-3 tree is a B-tree of order 3 and follows the general properties and rules of a B-tree. Its specific properties are as follows:

- Nodes that have 2 children are called "2-nodes"
- "2-nodes" nodes must have 1 data value
- Nodes that have 3 children are called "3-nodes"
- "3-nodes" nodes must have 2 data values

Let us look at how our node structure will look from the code perspective:

```
template <class valueType>
struct node{
```

```
    valueType _small_value;
    valueType _large_value;
    node <valueType>* _left_node;
    node <valueType>* _mid_node;
    node <valueType>* _right_node;
    node <valueType>* _parent_node;
};
```

We can also provide helper functions such as parametrized constructors and Boolean functions that tell whether the node is a leaf, 2-node, or 3-node. Those functions can be included in the `struct node` itself.

If we try to construct a 2-3 tree, it will probably look like the code at `https://github.com/PacktPublishing/Expert-C-2nd-edition/blob/main/Chapter07/ch7_two_to_three_tree.h`.

Searching

Let us start with the `find` function. The idea behind the strategy of finding an element lies in looking at a root node and then, based on the results, going to the left subtree or the right subtree. As you can see in the preceding code, we also have Boolean functions, which will help us implement the `find` function based on the type of node we are dealing with. A node of a 2-3 tree can be a leaf, a 2-node, or a 3-node and as those nodes have a different number of keys, the implementations of a search function should slightly differ for each type of node.

Before the implementation of the `find` function, let us first look at a simple illustrative example of looking for an element with a value of `554` in a 2-3 tree:

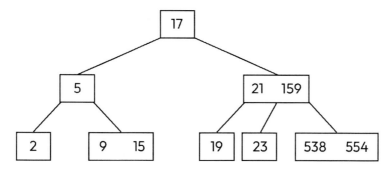

Figure 7.5 – A 2-3 tree example

First, we look at the root node. We see that its value is `17` and it is not equal to `554`. So, we continue looking for the number:

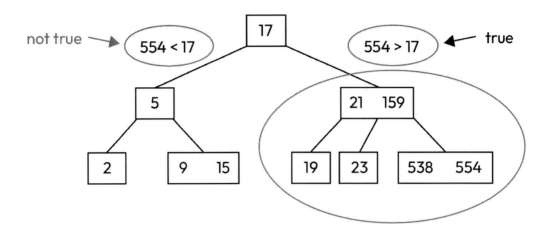

Figure 7.6 – First step to find a value inside a 2-3 tree

As the number is bigger than the root node's value, we continue with the right subtree of the tree:

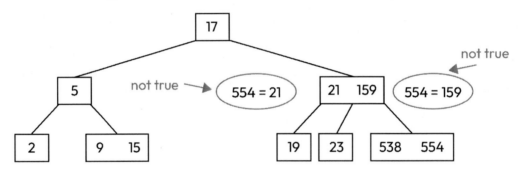

Figure 7.7 – Second step to find a value inside a 2-3 tree

Trying to find out the value in the right subtree's node failed so we have to make more comparisons in order to move to the next subtree if there is one. In our case, we have more subtrees, so we continue comparing our elements:

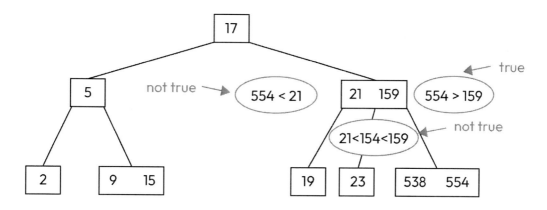

Figure 7.8 – Third step to find a value inside a 2-3 tree

As we can see, we continue with the right subtree:

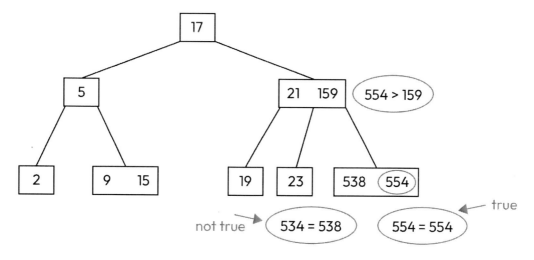

Figure 7.9 – Last step to find a value inside a 2-3 tree

Therefore, as you can see, we have found our element. However, what would happen if we did not find it in that node either? In that case, as our node is a leaf node, there would be no need to compare to find out whether it is greater or smaller than the node's values because leaf nodes do not have children.

Now, let us implement the `find` function by inserting the logic described previously into our code. We are going to have two functions: one will be public to the user and the other will be a private function. This is done because of the way we implement the logic. Our function will be a recursive function and for that, we have to pass a node to our function. And as we don't want to make the user pass a node instead of the tree object, we cover it with a function that only takes the target value. In the code at `https://github.com/PacktPublishing/Expert-C-2nd-edition/blob/main/Chapter07/ch7_two_to_three_tree_2.h`, we also implemented `isLeaf()`, `isTwoNode()`, and `isThreeNode()` functions considering that our tree is constructed in the right way.

As you can see, we have two functions for performing the `find` operation. One of them is public and the other is private for our own use. We have two functions because we don't want to bother the user by making them pass any other argument other than the value that should be searched. As we are going to use recursion for this operation, we declared a private function, which we will call from the public function and our user will never know about that. The implementation of the public `find` function can be found at `https://github.com/PacktPublishing/Expert-C-2nd-edition/blob/main/Chapter07/ch7_two_to_three_tree.cpp`.

In the preceding code, you can see that we have one node structure and we treat it as both a 2-node and a 3-node. The confusion arises when we treat a node as a 2-node because, in this case, we have additional elements such as `_mid_node`, `_small_value`, and `_large_value`. If our node is a two-node, we don't need `_mid_node` (a pointer to a `middle` node); hence, we can assign `nullptr` to it when constructing our node (two-node), and when it comes to `_small_value` and `_large_value`, our two-node doesn't need it either as a two-node node has only one data member and, in that case, we can take either `_small_value` or `_large_value` as our one element and we can assign zero to it or we can take both elements and assign the same value to both of them. We can also use a flag that will point out our node being a two-node or a three-node.

Insertion

As with the `find` function, in the case of the `insert` function, we are going to first look at the illustrations of how inserting elements into a 2-3 tree works. We will perform insertion with the following elements:

{19, 7, 11, 21, 14, 13, 12}

1. Insert 19 into a node:

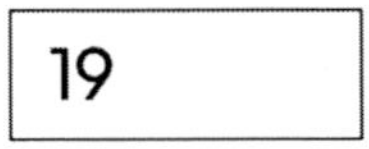

Figure 7.10 – Inserting 19 into a node

2. Check whether a node is a two-node or a three-node. If it is a two-node, compare the element with the element of the two-node and insert it, making necessary changes.

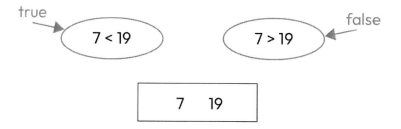

7 is placed on the left side as it is less than 19

Figure 7.11 – Inserting 7 into a node that already has 1 element

Now we have a three-node node and we want to make another insertion but there is no place, as the maximum number of keys is two, so we have to make structural changes:

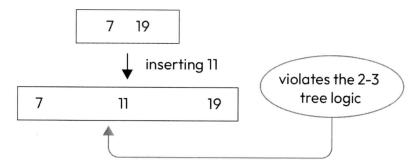

Figure 7.12 – Inserting the third value when the node has the maximum number of elements

In this case, we have to split the node and promote the median of the three values by creating a new node, which will become a parent.

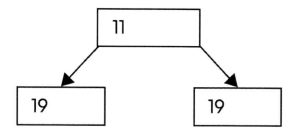

Figure 7.13 – Splitting of a node

But there is also a case when the node we split has a parent and the median is promoted to the parent node. Two cases also arise from it: when the parent has one element, the promoted element is inserted into the parent node, but if the parent node has two elements, we have to continue splitting and promoting the median. We will discuss this case in a few illustrations; now, let us continue with the rest of the elements:

inserting 21

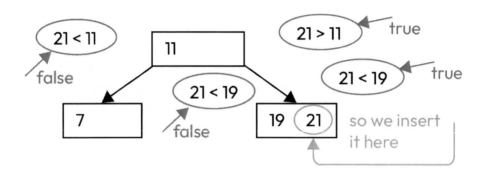

Figure 7.14 – Inserting 21 into a node that has only 1 element

Now that we have to insert 14 into our 2-3 tree, we come across one of the cases described previously, where we have to split a node in order to insert an element and not ruin the structure of a 2-3 tree:

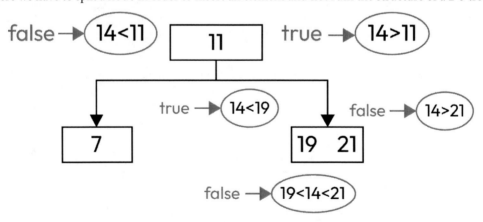

Figure 7.15 – Inserting 14 into a node that already has 2 elements

After inserting 14 into the leaf node, we get the following diagram:

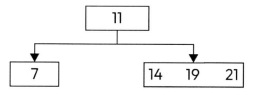

Figure 7.16 – Ruined structure after inserting 14

Now that the 2-3 tree structure is ruined, we have to split the leaf node and promote the median (19) element to the parent node:

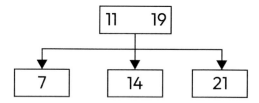

Figure 7.17 – Splitting of a node

Next, we insert 13:

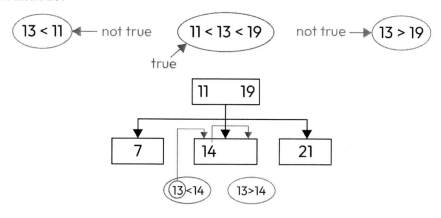

after inserting 13

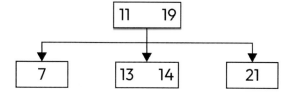

Figure 7.18 – Inserting 13 into a node that has only 1 element

The next insertion follows the previously described logic, but it is a little bit more complicated as we have to split two nodes. We will now try to insert 12:

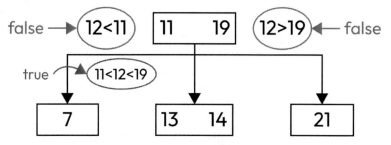

Figure 7.19 – Inserting 12 into a node that already has 2 elements

We should insert 12 into the middle node and, after doing so, we get the following diagram:

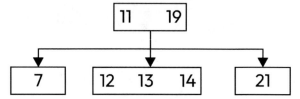

Figure 7.20 – Ruined structure after inserting 12

As the 2-3 tree structure is again ruined, we have to repeat the process of splitting and promoting the median (13) element. After doing it, we get the following diagram:

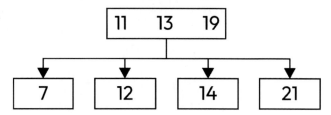

Figure 7.21 – Structure is still ruined after the first split

After promoting 13, our 2-3 tree structure is not restored so we have to continue splitting and promoting the median (13) element:

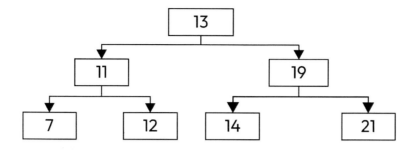

Figure 7.22 – Structure after the last split

Now, we can see that the 2-3 tree structure is correct.

Deletion

After discussing how the insertion is done, we can pass on to the last and probably the most complex of the operations on a 2-3 tree: deletion. The strategy of a deletion process is the opposite of the strategy used in insertion. In the case of insertion, for example, we split a node, while in the case of deletion, we have to merge the elements, but it only sounds that easy. When we perform deletion on a 2-3 tree, we have to remember the following points:

- To delete a value, we have to replace it with its in-order successor and then remove

- If a node is left with less than one data value, then two nodes must be merged together

- If a node becomes empty after deleting a value, it is then merged with another node

Let us first look at the visual representation of a deletion process performed on a 2-3 tree. The examples will be shown using the following tree:

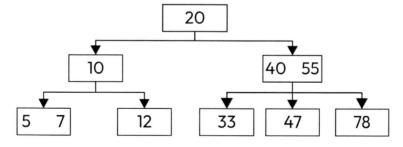

Figure 7.23 – A 2-3 tree example

So, let us assume we want to delete 40. We find the node where 40 is located and try to remove it. If 40 is not located in the leaf node, it makes it hard to just remove it. That is why, firstly, we have to move it inside a leaf node by performing swapping, and then perform the deletion. Following the first point just discussed, we swap 40 with its in-order successor, which is 47. The tree will look like this:

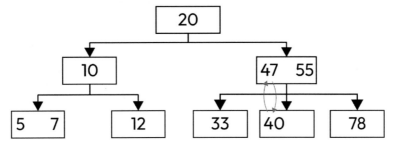

Figure 7.24 – Swapping with a leaf node

We can see that after swapping the elements, 40 is ruining the logic of a 2-3 tree as it is not greater than 47, though it has to be, while 47 is in a legal position as it is larger than its left subtree and smaller than its right subtree. We don't have to worry about 40 being in an illegal position, as the next step is to delete it:

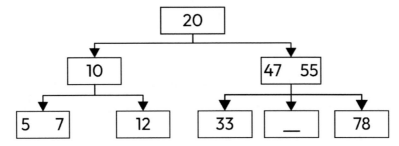

Figure 7.25 – Ruined structure after removing 40 from a leaf node

Before removing a value from a leaf node, there are two cases:

- The leaf node has two values, one of which has to be removed
- The leaf node has only one value, which has to be removed

This means that if we remove a value from a leaf node and it still has a value in it, then our job is done because the logic of a 2-3 tree remains. In our example, we remove 40 and there is no value in the node, which means we have an empty node, which is not acceptable. In the preceding figure, the node without a value is pictured. So now we have to delete a node itself. After deleting a node, we have a structure where the parent node contains 2 values and has 2 children, which again ruins the structure of a 2-3 tree. To delete a node without harming the structure of a 2-3 tree, we have to perform merging. We are going to move down the smaller value of the parent node, which is 47, and merge it with the leaf's left sibling:

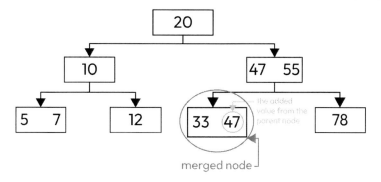

Figure 7.26 – Merging 47 with the leaf's left sibling

Let us now remove 78 from the tree. As 78 is already in the leaf node, we will not swap the values, and at the first step, we will just remove the value:

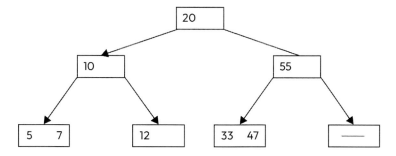

Figure 7.27 – Ruined structure after removing 78

Now, we again face the problem where we have a node without a value, and we have to do something about it. If we try the technique described previously, which is deleting a node without a value and merging the parent's value with its left sibling, we will have the following diagram:

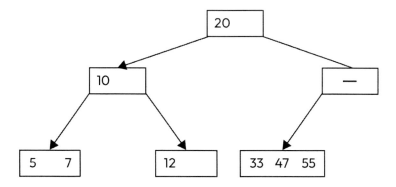

Figure 7.28 – Structure is still ruined when 55 is merged with the leaf's left sibling

The preceding structure is a disaster in all the dimensions and timelines of a tree world. We want to avoid the disaster and are not going to do what we just did. We see that our left node has two values, and it can spare one of the values. If it spares 4 7 and makes it a right node of a node with a value of 5 5, we will have a ruined structure, as shown here:

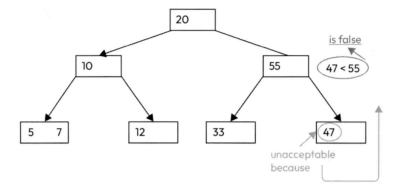

Figure 7.29 – Structure is still ruined after sparing 47

So, what we are going to do here is take the greater value of the left leaf node, which is 4 7, and we are going to promote it to the parent node and the value of a parent node is going down to the left leaf node:

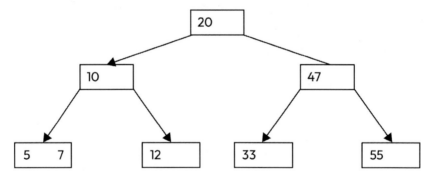

Figure 7.30 – Restored structure of a 2-3 tree

The preceding 2-3 tree is perfectly structured, which means that deletion was performed correctly. Now, let us try to remove the value 4 7. As we can see, 4 7 is in an internal node of the tree so we have to swap it with its in-order successor, 5 5, as shown in the following illustration:

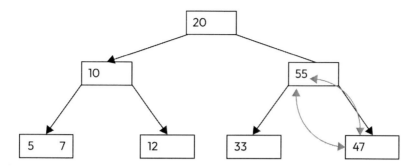

Figure 7.31 – The 2-3 tree after swapping 47 with 55

Now when 47 is in the leaf node, we can remove it from the node, leaving the leaf node empty and facing the same problem of having a leaf node without any value. Since the left leaf node doesn't have two values, we can't spare it in this case, so we have to perform the other operation: merging. The merging operation has to be performed on a parent node and a left leaf node by bringing down the value of a parent node and also deleting the right leaf node:

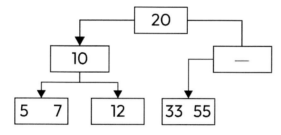

Figure 7.32 – Ruined structure after removing 47

However, we are not done with the removal as we have a parent node that contains no value and only one child with two values. We must apply the recursive removal strategy to the parent node that contains no value. The first thing we should do is check whether the parent node's sibling can spare a value. Because the sibling has only one value, 10, we can't spare a value, so we have to perform merging. Merging two internal nodes is similar to merging two leaf nodes, with one exception – in the case of merging internal nodes, the children of an empty node must be adopted:

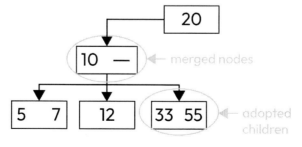

Figure 7.33 – Structure is still ruined after merging

The structure we got after performing the operations listed previously is not a 2-3 tree and we are one step away from making it. We have to merge the root node with its child to make a 2-3 tree by bringing the root node's value down and removing the root node:

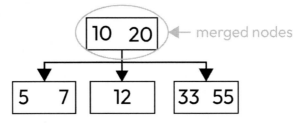

Figure 7.34 – Restored structure of a 2-3 tree

To perform deletion on a 2-3 tree, we have to locate the correct node and start the process of deletion. The process is different for leaf nodes and internal nodes. During the process, it is decided whether merging or distributing is going to be performed.

In this section, we discussed B-trees and dived deeper into one of their specializations: 2-3 trees. We also went through the most important functions performed on a 2-3 tree, showing the illustrations and describing the steps that are performed during each operation.

In the next section, we are going to discuss one of the most powerful containers that the C++ STL library provides to its users: `std::unordered_map`.

Implementation details of std::unordered_map

In the previous chapter, we discussed `std::unordered_map` very briefly, saying only that it is the representation of the hash table data structure in C++. At first, along with other hash containers, `std::unordered_map` wasn't in the original STL. It was introduced to C++ users only with the TR1 library extension.

`std::unordered_map` is an associative container that is part of the STL library. It holds key-value pairs with distinctive keys. The time complexity of search, insertion, and removal of items is amortized `O(1)`. This means that all the operations listed are performed in a constant time almost always. In an unordered map, the key value often serves as a means of uniquely identifying each element, and the mapped value is an object connected to that key. Key-value and mapped value types may vary.

Internally, the components are arranged into buckets rather than being sorted in any specific sequence. The hash of an element's key determines which bucket it will be put into. Similar hash codes for keys cause them to be put in the same bucket. As soon as the hash is calculated, it links to the exact bucket the element was put into, allowing for quick access to particular elements.

There is also another variation of `std::unordered_map` called `std::unordered_multimap`. The latter may contain multiple copies of each key value. In this part of the book, we are not going to go any further and discuss `std::unordered_multimap`. Instead, we will dive deeper into the concept and implementation details of `std::unordered_map`.

The implementation details that we will discuss are as follows:

- How `std::unordered_map` organizes element storing
- How elements are inserted into or searched in `std::unordered_map`
- The hash functions and strategies that are used to implement them
- Collisions and how they are handled

Let's begin with discussing the first two points.

How std::unordered_map organizes element storing and how elements are inserted into or searched in std::unordered_map

`std::unordered_map` is organized into buckets. Imagine having an array where every cell is a bucket that contains elements. A question might arise from these words: "that contains elements." Are we talking about giving an array as the second parameter in the following code?

```
#include <unordered_map>
#include <vector>
#include <string>

int main() {
  std::unordered_map<std::string, std::vector<int>> table;
  table["Word"] = { 45,6,2,6 };
}
```

In this case, we see clearly that there is more than one value that has to be stored. Although this example might seem reasonable and a logical motivation to have buckets, it is not the case. The bucket an element is placed into depends entirely on the hash of its key. Two different keys with different values could generate the same hash (bucket). The bucket interface implementation can differ from compiler to compiler as there is no fixed rule, only best practices.

The first practice is to use lists. This means that each bucket contains lists that hold pairs: a pair of a key type and a value type. And every time different keys result in the same hash value, the bucket under that index adds a node and holds the new values inside it. If we illustrate this, it will look like this:

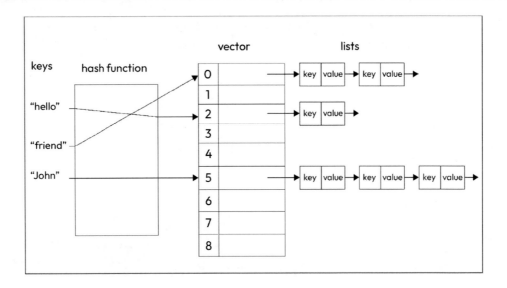

Figure 7.35 – Bucket that contains lists that hold pairs

This method of using a linked list to deal with collisions is called separate chaining. The worst thing that could happen is that the hash function always returns the same hash value for all the keys passed to it. In that case, the time complexity of operations such as insert, find, and delete will be O(n). To avoid such complications, which hardly ever occur, there is also another way to organize the bucket interface of std::unordered_map.

The second way to do this is to use another data structure that is better than a linked list. We have already discussed a data structure that performs operations faster than a linked list in the previous part of this chapter, and that is a self-balancing binary search tree. This technique is better for looking up an element as its time complexity is O(log n), but the self-balancing operations during insertion, for example, make it harder to insert an element than it is with linked lists where no comparison is needed.

std::unordered_map provides functions that work with the bucket interface. Those functions are as follows:

- begin(size_type), cbegin(size_type): Returns an iterator or a constant iterator to the beginning of the specified bucket

- end(size_type), cend(size_type): Returns an iterator or a constant iterator to the end of the specified bucket

- bucket_count(): Returns the number of buckets

- max_bucket_count(): Returns the maximum number of buckets

- bucket_size (size_type): Returns the number of elements in a specific bucket

- bucket(const Key& key): Returns the bucket for a specific key

Knowing how storing is organized, we already know what happens when we insert an element into `std::unordered_map`. First of all, the key that was passed to the container is passed to a hashing function, which returns a value that becomes an index of an array. Then, under that index, both the key and the value are stored.

The search for an element, when we have separate chaining and use linked lists, can differ in effectiveness. The basic approach is to locate the bucket that corresponds to the key and then carry out a linear search within that bucket when looking for an item in a hash table using a key. The hash function is used in the first phase; a different method must be used in the second.

Utilizing `std::find()` or its equivalent to discover an object whose key equals our key is the most straightforward method. Naturally, it would be incorrect to hard-wire `operator==`; instead, the user should be able to supply a function object with equality semantics.

Consider the case where the user is storing C-style strings. In this case, it is better to check them by using the `strcmp()` function.

Two function objects—a hash function and an equality function—are used as parameters for hashed associative containers. Each has its own default ones.

We can do the lookup of an element in an alternative way. Let us take, for example, the case where we decided to sort the bucket elements in ascending order. In this case, instead of comparing the keys for an equality case, we will compare them using `operator<`. What this will give us is that the average number of comparisons, for example, for a failed search when we use the equality operator will be n, while using *less than* operator results in $n/2$.

Hash functions and strategies that are used to implement them

The hash function is used to convert keys into indexes of an array. The hash function should, in theory, map every potential key to a distinct slot index, but in reality, this is challenging to do.

A hash function that takes a set of items as input and maps each one to a distinct slot is called a perfect hash function. It is feasible to create a perfect hash function if we know the items and the collection won't change. Unfortunately, there is no methodical way to build a perfect hash function given a random set of elements. Thankfully, we can still gain performance efficiency, even if the hash algorithm is not perfect.

The size of the hash table can be increased in order to include all possible values for the element range, which is one technique to ensure that the hash function is always perfect. This ensures that every component will have a unique slot. Although this is doable for small numbers of items, it is impractical for huge numbers of elements.

It is sufficient to take into account hash functions that accept any integer as an input. Why? Even if a key is not an integer, it may be easily converted into one so that it can be hashed. Hash functions that take an argument of the integer type can also differ in their implementation. Here are a few simple hashing operations that work with positive numbers:

- Digit selection
- Folding
- Using modulo

Digit selection

The digit selection method can be applied if the user knows exactly how many digits there are in the numbers that are passed to the hash function as keys. In this case, the user can choose two or three digits depending on how much space the hash table occupies. Let us take, for example, numbers that have eight digits and we also know that the first two digits are zeros. Skipping the first two digits, we can take the third and the last digit and make a number out of them. For example, we have an integer, 00637981. We take the digits 6 and 1 and make an index where the key should be stored. The key will be stored under index 61. The digits you select in a given scenario do require some caution because if, for example, you choose the first two digits, the index where all the keys will be stored is going to be index 0.

Although this method is simple and quick, it doesn't typically distribute the elements fairly.

Folding

Adding the digits is one technique to enhance the prior method of choosing digits. Folding is the process that results from this. You may, for instance, sum up all the numbers in 00637981, which gives us the following:

$$0 + 0 + 6 + 3 + 7 + 9 + 8 + 1 = 34$$

The key will be kept under index 34. The indexes can vary from 0 to 54 considering that the biggest number obtained is the one where the first 2 digits are 0 (as always) and all other digits are 9 (00999999). You may group the numbers in the search key and then add the groups to adjust this or expand the size of the hash table. For example, if we group the numbers by two, we will have the following result:

$$00 + 63 + 79 + 81 = 223$$

In this case, the index will range from 0 to 297. We can also group the number by four digits, as in this example:

$$0063 + 7981 = 8044$$

And in this case, the index will range from 0 to 10098.

Using modulo

This method's logic is to take the number that is passed to the hash function and module it with the size of the hash table. So, for example, if we have 1,000 elements, then our number can be stored under the index ranging from 0 to 999. The number in the previous example in this method will be stored under index 981 for the following reason:

$$637981 \% 1000 = 981$$

The one problem with this method is that if you choose the size of the hash table in a way that it is not a prime number, then the collision will be much more common than if you had chosen a prime number. The number 1000 can be replaced by 1009 because it is a prime number and 1000 is not. In the examples we have used, the numbers are too small to be useful as the size of a hash table.

In the beginning, we also talked about passing only an integer to a hash function. In this case, we also have to take care of converting other data types, for example, a string into an integer. Let us take, for example, the word "ant." We can convert this into an integer by just assigning each letter its ASCII number:

$$a - 97$$

$$n - 110$$

$$t - 116$$

We then sum them up:

$$97 + 110 + 116 = 323$$

Or we can just concatenate them together:

$$97110116$$

After that, the number will be passed to a hash function that will work with it. Another way of converting the string into a number can be just replacing each letter with its position in the alphabet:

$$a - 1$$

$$n - 14$$

$$t - 20$$

We can then apply the same tactics used previously:

$$1+14+20 = 35$$

or

$$11420$$

The problem of summing up the numbers will result in a collision when other words are formed with the same letter – for example, the word "tan" will result in the same number if we apply the first tactic. In this case, it is better to use the version that concatenates the numbers. We can also use another concatenation tactic, which says that we can take the positions of the letters in the alphabet, turn them into their binary representations, and then concatenate them.

There is also the suggestion of making a function that calls different hash functions and randomly decides what function is going to be called. This practice is called universal hashing.

We introduced and discussed simple hashing tactics because the hashing function should itself be simple and compute the result very quickly. Of the methods discussed, the modulo method is most widely used.

Collisions and how they are handled

When talking about organizing elements for implementing `std::unordered_map` by using a hash function, we couldn't miss the part where the collisions happen, as it is one of the basic problems that results in different organization types. Earlier, we talked about solutions such as separate chaining and perfect hashing, which could solve the problem of handling collisions. Another concept that solves this problem is called linear probing. It is one of the forms of open addressing, along with quadratic probing and double hashing.

When the hash function creates a collision by mapping a new key to a hash table cell that is currently filled by another key, linear probing looks for the next available space in the table and inserts the new key there. The same procedure is used for lookups: systematically scanning the table from the hash function's location until a cell with the right key or an empty cell is found.

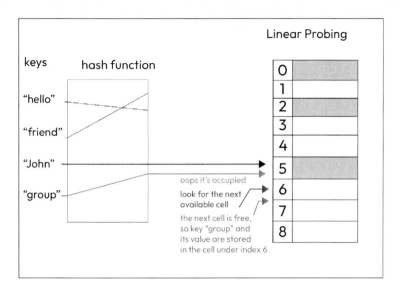

Figure 7.36 – Example of linear probing

Nevertheless, there is a drawback to linear probing. The problem with this particular method is that putting an element in the "next open space" merely by going to the next accessible hash bucket causes clustering. By clustering, we mean that our data eventually ends up clustered in one area of our container; in other words, it is just grouped in one place.

The clustering effect is bad for hash tables and containers that are implemented using that logic. In fact, if a table is clustered, it is by definition badly constructed. This often indicates that there is an issue with our hash algorithm inside. Clustering is typically caused by one of two problems with hash functions: either they don't use the whole container range, or they don't distribute the data uniformly across the hash buckets. It turns out that employing linear probing as a collision resolution approach can occasionally cause both of these two things to happen, which results in a clustered container.

Naturally, again, this relies on our dataset. If we use linear probing to solve the collision problem and we have a lot of items that end up in one hash bucket, the container will start to get occupied, fairly rapidly, and we'll have a clustered container in the end.

To avoid such problems, our container can hold a load factor. The entire table may be replaced by a new table, bigger by a constant factor if the insertion would increase the load factor of the table (its proportion of occupied cells) over a certain threshold. As opposed to threshold values near 1 and low growth rates, setting this threshold close to 0 and employing a high growth rate for the container size results in quicker container operations but higher memory usage. When the load factor exceeds 1/2, doubling the container's size is a frequent solution that keeps the load factor between 1/4 and 1/2.

`std::unordered_map` provides two functions related to the load factor; `max_load_factor()` has an overload to get or set the max load factor:

- `load_factor()`: Returns the average number of elements per bucket
- `max_load_factor()`: Returns the current maximum load factor
- `max_load_factor(float)`: Sets the maximum load factor to the passed argument

Everything we have discussed before is details that are used to implement `std::unordered_map`. We cannot exactly say which of the details described are used to implement the container because, as we have already said, every compiler has its own implementation and the programmers are the ones who decide what tactics to use to implement the container. Later, those implementations are put in the compiler for the usage of the users.

Heaps and their applications

The term *heap* is definitely familiar to you but, most probably, the heap we are going to talk about has nothing to do with the heap you know. When studying computer systems, it is unavoidable not to touch on topics connected with memory, especially RAM. And when talking about RAM and virtual memory, we can't skip the part where we separate the memory into stack and heap. Is this heap, which is used for dynamic memory allocation, connected to the heap we are going to discuss? The answer can be guessed from the first sentence of this subchapter and it is no.

A heap is an abstract tree-based data structure. What does that mean? Well, it is structured as a tree and has some properties of trees, specifically a binary tree. Let us not dive deep into what types of trees are there, and just talk about what kind of binary trees do exist and to what category our heap belongs. There are full, complete, and other types of binary trees, but we are going to talk about the two categories mentioned. A full binary tree is considered to be a tree in which every node except for leaves should have two children. You can see an example illustration of a full binary tree here:

Full Binary tree

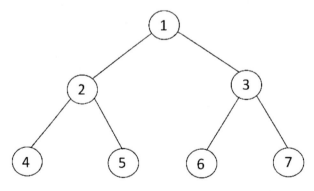

Figure 7.37 – Full binary tree

Some people think that a full binary tree is a tree where all the nodes have two children except for the leaf nodes, but also that all the nodes are at the same level. In the preceding example, we have a full binary tree, and all the nodes are at the same level. But you should bear in mind that the example that follows is also a full binary tree, as it corresponds to the preconditions of a full binary tree that we mentioned at first:

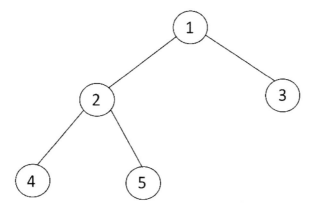

Figure 7.38 – Also a full binary tree

The following tree meets all the pre-conditions for a full binary tree; therefore, it is also a full binary tree:

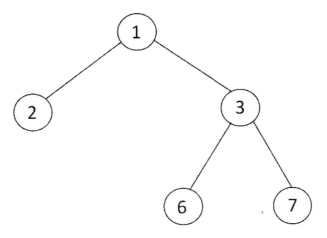

Figure 7.39 – Also a full binary tree

A complete binary tree seems like a full binary tree, but not all full binary trees can be a complete binary tree, and also, not all complete binary trees are full binary trees. A binary tree is said to be complete if all the levels of a tree are filled except for the last one, which can only be half-filled from left to right. The first and second full binary trees are also considered to be complete binary trees, as they both fall under the conditions that form a complete binary tree. The third example is a full binary tree, but not a complete binary tree because it lacks the left nodes and it is half-filled from right to left, not from left to right. The following illustration is a perfect example of that:

must be right to left (handwritten annotation)

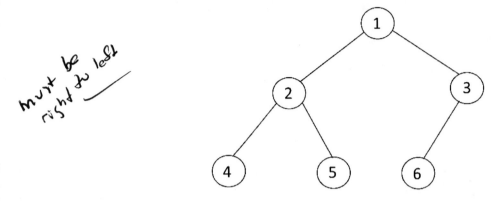

Figure 7.40 – Full but not complete binary tree

Here we see that the tree is half-filled from left to right and this is okay for a complete binary tree, but when it comes to fulfilling the conditions of a full binary tree, we see that we have a node that has only one child, which is against the concept of a full binary tree.

Heap data structure follows the concept of a complete binary tree. Let us consider we are given an array and we have to make a heap from it. This means that we have to form a complete binary tree. The heap is formed by making the values line up from left to right; for example, let's imagine we are given an array with values {1,3,7,11,51,9,4,8}. The formed heap/complete binary tree will look like this:

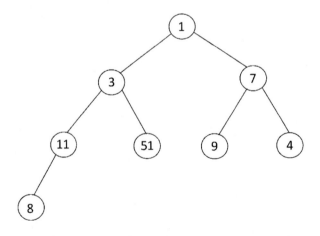

Figure 7.41 – Heap/complete binary tree

The indexing works in the following way:

- If a node is at index `i`
- Its left child is at `2*i`
- Its right child is at `2*i + 1`
- Its parent is at `i/2`

If we look at the indexes in the array and the structure of the tree, we can clearly see that all these points are true.

The heap we formed is just a general heap and, in this case, has nothing special. So, if it is not special and it is just a complete binary tree, why make a big deal out of it? The thing is that we don't use general heaps, we use its specifications: min heap and max heap.

The idea behind max heap is that the root of the tree has the largest value among all the nodes of a tree, and this property is applied to all the subtrees that the tree has:

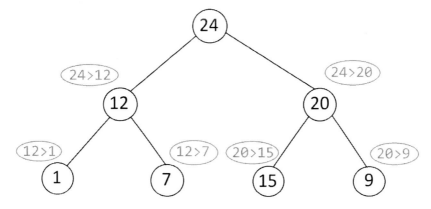

Figure 7.42 – Example of a max heap

Intuitively, the opposite should be true for a min heap – the root of the tree has the smallest value among all the nodes of a tree, and this property is applied to all the subtrees that the tree has:

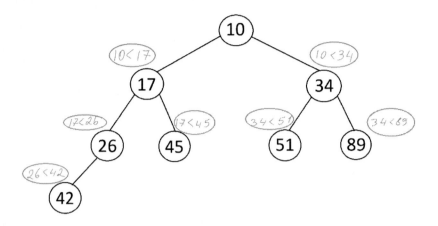

Figure 7.43 – Example of a min heap

The operations supported by max heap or min heap are the following, among others:

- Finding the maximum/minimum element

- Inserting an element

- Deleting the maximum/minimum element

- Max-heapify/min-heapify

The first operation from the list is the easiest one. We are going to work with either a max heap or a min heap, and as we know that the maximum element in a max heap is the root value and the minimum element in a min heap is also a root value, in these functions, we have nothing to do but to return the root value.

The insertion is either performed on a min heap or a max heap and, by that, we mean that when inserting an element, we know exactly that the structure we are making an insertion into follows all the rules provided by a mean heap or a max heap. The process of inserting an element is always performed at the end of the heap and then the necessary operations are performed to keep the min heap or max heap structure. Let us try to implement the `insert` function considering that our heap class has a vector named `values` that holds all the values. The implementation of an `insert` function for a max heap will look like this:

```
template <typename itemType>
void myHeap<itemType>::insert(itemType newItem)
{

    values.push_back(newItem);
    int newItemIndex = values.size() - 1;
    bool isPlaced = false;
```

```
while ((newItemIndex > 0) && !isPlaced)
{
   int parentIndex = (newItemIndex - 1) / 2;
   if (values[newItemIndex] < values[parentIndex])
   {
      isPlaced = true;
   }
   else
   {
      std::swap(values[newItemIndex], values[parentIndex]);
      newItemIndex = parentIndex;
   }
}
}
```

The complexity of an insert function is O(log n) as the worst that can happen is swapping the values from a leaf to the root, which doesn't exceed the height of a tree; hence, the complexity is not more than O(log n).

The deletion is performed on the root of a heap. Its logic is to swap the root with the last element and get a partial heap and then turn the semiheap into a heap by making the necessary comparisons and swapping. Let us look at a simple illustration that shows how the deletion of a max heap root is done step by step.

Swap the root node's value with the value of the last node.

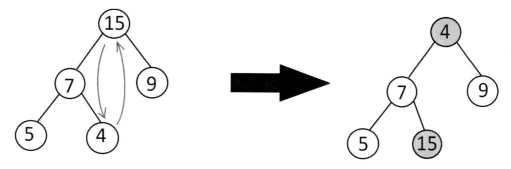

Figure 7.44 – First step of deleting the root of a max heap

Delete the last node.

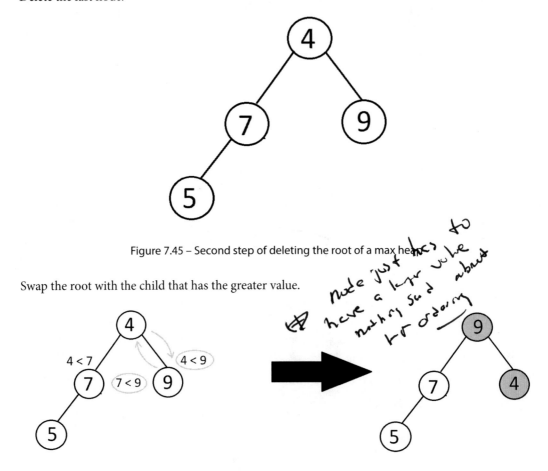

Figure 7.45 – Second step of deleting the root of a max heap

Swap the root with the child that has the greater value.

[handwritten notes: node just goes to have a later value nothing said about ↳ ordering]

Figure 7.46 – Last step of deleting the root of a max heap

And finally, the last function on our list is the `heapify` function. Imagine that we have an array and we form a heap based on its indexes without following any rules. Let us imagine that we have the following array: $\{4,7,34,23,1,0,21\}$.

And when we form a heap with these values, we get the following diagram:

[handwritten notes: basically heap says nothing about order. Its about layout of tree. min/max only implies m/max at top. Except maybe root that parent of tree ?]

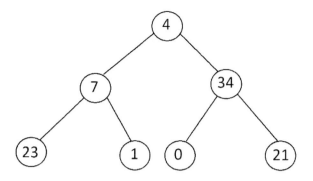

Figure 7.47 – Example of a heap formed from array elements

We see that the heap we got is neither a min heap nor a max heap. We need a function that can make a min heap or a max heap from such a structure, and here is where the heapify function comes in handy. The logic that is put inside the heapify function is also very easy to understand. The function starts from the bottom of the tree and looks at the leaves. As the leaves are heaps themselves, the function then goes up to the parents of those leaves and compares the values of the parents to the values of their children and makes necessary changes by swapping. The function goes up until it reaches the root of the tree. By the time it reaches the root of the tree and makes the necessary changes by swapping, the tree becomes a min heap or a max heap. Let us min heapify the previous structure step by step (as leaves are already heaps themselves, they need no change or swapping at that level):

1. Move on to the leaves' parents and compare their values to the values of their children.

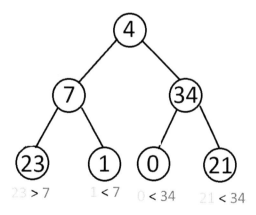

Figure 7.48 – First step of the min heapify function

2. Swap the parent with a child if the value of the parent is bigger than any of the values of its children. If both children have smaller values than the value of their parent, swap the parent's value with the smallest value of its children.

Figure 7.49 – Second step of the min heapify function

3. Compare the values of the swapped (if they were swapped) nodes' values with the value of their parent.

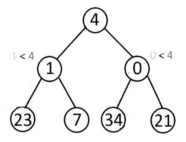

Figure 7.50 – Third step of the min heapify function

4. Swap the parent with a child if the value of the parent is bigger than any of the values of its children. If both children have smaller values than the value of their parent, swap the parent's value with the smallest value of its children. Stop when you reach the root.

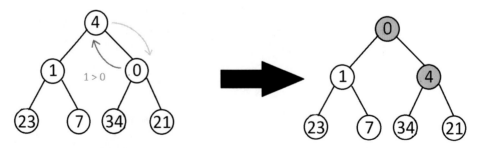

Figure 7.51 – Last step of the min heapify function

After talking about the most important function and features the heap abstract data structure has, it is also important to talk about the applications of a heap ADT. We should understand how, when, or where to use such a data structure.

The heap data structure has many applications, including the following:

- Priority queue
- Heap sort
- Selection and graph algorithms
- Order statistics

We are not going to dive deep into every heap application mentioned. We will discuss using heaps in priority queues and in the implementation of the heap sort. Before moving on to those two points, we will give a short description in a sentence or two to help you understand how the heap is used in selection and graph algorithms and also order statistics, leaving it to your curiosity to dive deeper into those topics yourself.

A heap makes it possible to retrieve the minimum or maximum element in constant time and make additional selections (such as the median or kth element) in data stored in a heap in sub-linear time, which is a great reason to use heaps in selection algorithms.

A heap is used in graph algorithms based on its ability to traverse the data structure in polynomial order.

The heap data structure may be used to rapidly and accurately determine the kth lowest/biggest member in an array, something which will be useful for order statistics.

As you can guess from its name, the priority queue is a queue that holds elements in priority order. This means that, for example, the largest value has the highest priority or the lowest value has the highest priority. This logic is similar to the logic of a heap ADT. If you managed to implement a heap, it should be no problem to implement a priority queue as the operations of a priority queue are comparable with the operations of a heap. Consequently, we can use a max heap, for example, to implement a priority queue. Is it better to make a max heap a data member of a priority queue class or is it better to use inheritance? To answer the question, we have to try to understand what type of relationship they can be. The inheritance corresponds to the "is-a relationship." Can we say that a priority queue is a max heap? We definitely can't. That is why we can either keep an object inside the priority queue class or we can inherit it privately, which doesn't belong to the concept of an "is-a relationship." The operations that are used in the implementation of the priority queue will call the functions of a max heap. For example, if the priority queue has a `top()` function, it will call the function that returns the maximum element. The `delete()` function of a priority queue will call the `delete_max()` function of a max heap, and so on.

We talked about implementing a priority queue with the help of a heap, but why do we do that? Isn't there a better data structure for doing so? For example, a binary search tree can also provide the same functionality, as its leftmost child will contain the smallest element and the rightmost child will contain the biggest. The thing about binary search trees is that they are not always balanced, while heaps are. And sometimes, in the worst case, finding an element will take O(n) time rather than O(log n). This brings us back to the idea that implementing a priority queue with a heap is the right decision.

The heap sort method, as its name suggests, uses a heap to sort an array of elements that is not in any particular order. Let us assume that we have an array out of which we formed a heap, or to be more specific, a max heap. Then, we can remember from this subsection that we talked about deleting a root of the heap. Its logic was to swap the value of the root with the value of the last element of a heap, delete the last element, and perform max_heapify() on the new root. By applying the same tactics (without deleting the last element), we can implement a heap sort algorithm, which is one of the fastest sorting algorithms. Let us write the implementation of the heap sort algorithm considering that we already have a max_heapify() function:

```
template <typename itemType>
void heapSort(itemType array[], int size)
{
  for (int index = (size / 2) - 1; index >= 0; --index)
  {
    max_heapify(array, size, index);
  }
  for (int index = size - 1; index >= 0; --index) {
    std::swap(array[0], array[index]);
    max_heapify(array, index, 0);
  }
}
```

The implementation is very simple. First, we call the max_heapify() function to make a heap out of the array elements, and then perform sorting by applying logic similar to the delete() function.

Heap sort's efficiency is comparable to that of merge sort. They both take O(n logn) time for the worst and average cases. Heap sort has an advantage over merge sort as it doesn't require additional space for performing sorting. Quick sort can also be compared to heap sort as it also takes O(n logn) time to sort an array in the average case, but in the worst case, it takes O(n²) time, which makes it different from heap sort. Despite having a worst-case efficiency of O(n²), quick sort is typically chosen more than other sorting algorithms as it hardly ever faces its worst-case scenario.

Advanced lists

We have already talked about lists in the previous chapter as node-based data structures. Knowing how lists work, it may be interesting for us to dive deeper into the data structure to understand what other variations it has. In this part of the chapter, we are going to find out whether lists can be any better or not and what other variations of lists there are.

Among the list variations are skip lists, XOR lists, unrolled lists, self-organizing lists, and so on. We are not going to talk about every advanced list type there is, but only one or two to make the idea of an advanced data structure, specifically an advanced list data structure, clearer.

Skip lists

The name "skip list" hints that the data structure should be connected with skipping something. The only thing it can skip is a node, as it is composed of nodes. This means that in some operations that are performed on lists, we can skip the accepted steps. Let us take for example the search algorithm. In order to find an element inside a list, we spend $O(n)$ time even if it is sorted. To mention the elements in a list being sorted is important in this case because the logic that the skip list applies can work only with sorted elements. Carrying on the thought of skipping steps, what if we could shorten the amount of time spent on that operation such as search? "Skip list" is a data structure that allows us to do that. To make a "skip list" to bypass some nodes, we build several layers. Let us imagine we have the following list, which contains 13 elements:

Figure 7.52 – List with 13 elements

The elements are in a sorted order, as you can see. To make a skip list out of this, we should just add another layer to it that skips some of its elements. The following illustration shows this idea:

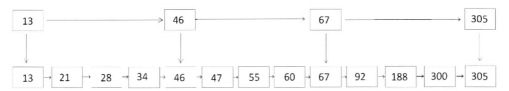

Figure 7.53 – Adding a layer to form a skip list

Now let us imagine that we want to search for the number 188. We will check the elements of the layer we have created until we find the node whose next node's element is greater than 188. After finding the node, we go down to the initial lane and search for an element linearly. Let us show the illustration of how that works:

1) 188 is bigger than the value of the first node's next node

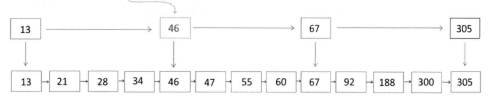

2) move on to the next node and compare 188 with the value of its next node

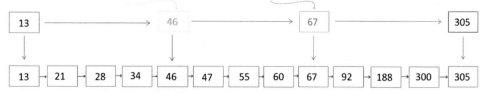

3) 188 is bigger than 67 so we move on to the node containing value 67 and compare 188 with the value of the next node

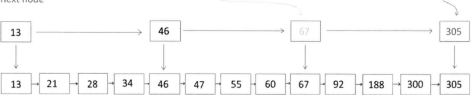

4) 188 is less than 305 so we move down from the node we are on and start to search for 188 linearly

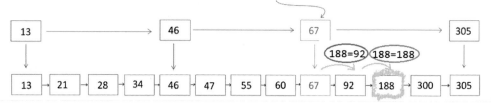

Figure 7.54 – The searching process in a skip list

Based on the example, we see that we skipped some nodes by adding a layer to our list. What will be the time complexity of this example? When we use only two layers for a "skip list," we create a new space to keep some of the elements in a new layer, and if we divide the whole list equally, we get $O(\sqrt{n})$, (square root of n), extra space. And by having an $O(\sqrt{n})$ extra space, we can achieve time complexity that is equal to $O(\sqrt{n})$ in this particular example.

We talked about having only two layers, but can there be more? The answer is yes! There can be as many layers as you want (unless there are no nodes left to add a layer); it will increase the space complexity meanwhile decreasing the time complexity reaching $O(\log\ n)$. Deciding the maximum level of nodes is also one of the important problems, and the accepted limit is $\log(p-1)N$, where N is the maximum number of elements in the list.

A "skip list," like any other type of list, can grow. By saying *grow*, we mean that the elements can be added to it and also can be deleted. Thinking about inserting an element into a skip list seems easy because all we have to do is find the position as it is a sorted list and add a node by changing some pointers. The real problem arises when we add an element and our structure of having evenly distributed nodes in other layers is crashed. What do we have to do now? Should we destroy all the layers and start from scratch, or should we leave it as it is? Should we promote the newly added node to the layer above or not? If we promote it to a higher level, should it be only at that level, or be promoted to even higher levels? The answer is both yes and no to those questions, except for destroying the layers and starting from scratch. That is something we don't really want to do.

Inserting a node into a skip list starts at the lowest level because it is the level where we can find all the nodes. Then, promoting the node to a higher level or not depends on coincidence. Let us imagine that randomly returns either `true` or `false`. A function that decides whether a node will be promoted or not will return `true` if the node is not at the maximum level and it needs to be promoted. In this case, the process will be repeated until the maximum level is reached or the function returns `false`. Let's look at the following example where we try to insert 68 into the skip list with the following steps:

1. Find the right position at the lowest level:

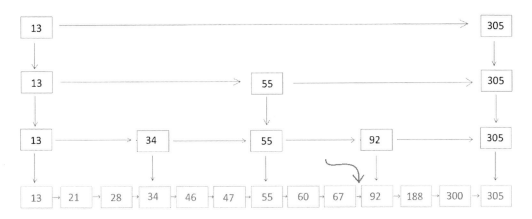

Figure 7.55 – Locating the right position at the lowest level

2. Insert the new node at the right position and call the function that either promotes it or not:

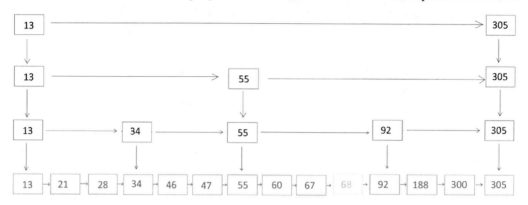

Figure 7.56 – Inserting the new node at the right position

3. If the function returns `true` and we are not at the maximum level, we promote it and call the function for a higher level again. If the function returns `false`, we keep the node only at the lowest level:

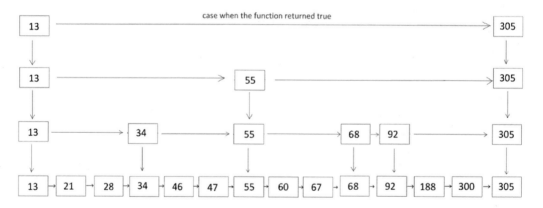

Figure 7.57 – Promoting the node to a higher level

4. Call the promoting function for the higher level:

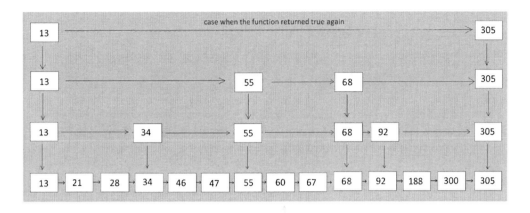

5) the function returns false and we leave the skip list like this

Figure 7.58 – Function for promoting the node returns false

The simple code representation will look something like this:

```
//consider all as member functions of a class SkipList
bool true_or_false() //function that randomly decides
                     //whether the node will be promoted
{                    //or not
    srand(time(0));
    return rand() % 2;
}

void promote(Node<T>* node, int level) //function that
                                        //promotes the
{                                       //node
    if (true_or_false() && level != MAX_LEVEL) {
        insert(node, level);
        promote(node, level + 1);
    }
    return;
}

void insert(Node<T>* node, int level)
{
    find_pos(node, level); // finds the position and
                           // inserts there
// implementation omitted for brevity
    promote(node, level + 1);
}
```

The deletion of a node is very simple and depends on no coincidence. We should just delete the node from every level it is in.

Having understood how skip lists are structured and how they work, as a conclusion, we want to quote the author who described skip lists first:

"Skip lists are a probabilistic data structure that seem likely to supplant balanced trees as the implementation method of choice for many applications. Skip list algorithms have the same asymptotic expected time bounds as balanced trees and are simpler, faster, and use less space."

- William Pugh

XOR lists

We have already talked about an advanced list data structure that is more time-efficient than the normal list data structure. Now it's time to talk about an advanced list data structure whose distinguishing feature is its space efficiency. The list, as you can guess from the title, is called an XOR list. **XOR** is short for **exclusive or**.

If you are not familiar with logical operations and logic gates, it is time to read about them as XOR belongs to the list of logical operations. XOR can return two values only: 1 (true) and 0 (false). If we picture the truth table of the XOR operation, it will look like this:

A	B	A XOR B
1	0	1
1	1	0
0	0	0
0	1	1

Figure 7.59 – Table of the XOR operation

What would happen if we performed XOR on the two numbers that are the same? Well, the result will always be 0. This logic that is inserted into the operation is very useful in the construction and use of our XOR linked list.

This advanced data structure uses a bitwise XOR operation to reduce the amount of storage needed for doubly linked lists. A single node in a typical doubly linked list needs two address fields to point to the node before it and the node after it. As a result, memory use increases. Instead of storing the next and previous nodes' real memory locations in the XOR linked list, storing two addresses, one for the previous node and one for the next node, only one address is stored, and this is the result of XORing two addresses. So, if we visually illustrate the structure of an XOR list, it would look like this:

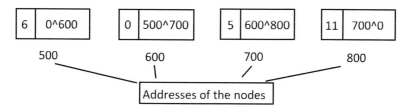

Figure 7.60 – Example of an XOR list

We can see that each node stores the XOR of the previous and next nodes' addresses and since the first and the last nodes don't have a previous and next node, respectively, we consider them to be NULL. So, we might ask what this gives us. As we have already said, when the number is XORed with itself, it gives us a zero. And now, for example, if we want to move forward from the second node, we just can XOR the address of the previous node with the address that holds the second node, which is 500^700. And for moving backward, we do the opposite, which is XORing the address of the next node (700) with the address that holds the second node (500^700).

If we try to implement an XOR list, the first thing that we are going to do is declare a Node structure. It can be part of the XOR_list class. First of all, let us take a look at what our Node structure should contain:

```
template <typename T>
  struct Node {
        T m_data;
        Node<T>* npx; // traditionally called npx meaning next,
                      // previous, XOR
  };
```

As we can see, our node has only two data members, which are m_data and npx, and nothing more. From this structure, the whole concept can be built, and if we put it in a XOR_list class, it will help us construct the memory-efficient doubly linked list as can be seen at https://github.com/PacktPublishing/Expert-C-2nd-edition/blob/main/Chapter07/ch7_xor_list.h.

We are not going to implement all the functionality of the XOR list; that is why we will omit the parametrized constructors, but we will try to implement the insert function. To make the insert function work, we need to have a method that calculates and returns the XORed value of the necessary addresses. The function will look like this:

```
Node<T>* Xor(Node<T>* addr1, Node<T>* addr2)
{
        return reinterpret_cast<Node<T>*> (reinterpret_cast<uintptr_
  t>(addr1) ^ reinterpret_cast<uintptr_t>(addr2));
}
```

The odd thing about this function is the casts that are performed. We see that `addr1` and `addr2` are both of the `Node<T>*` type and to perform the operation, we cast them to `uintptr_t` and then recast them back to `Node<T>*`. At first, it seems like a dumb thing to do, but if you have experience with pointers and addresses, you should probably guess that you can't XOR the addresses unless they are cast to some other type that can be XORed. In our case, that type is `uintptr_t`, which is an unsigned integer big enough to contain a `void*`.

Now we can implement the `insert` function, which is as simple as the following code:

```
    template <typename T>
  void insert(T data)
{
      std::shared_ptr<Node<T>> new_node =
        std::make_shared <Node<T>>();
      new_node->m_data = data;
      new_node->npx = head;
      if (head != nullptr)
{
          head->npx = Xor(new_node, head->npx);
}

      head = new_node;
}
```

After completing the insertion, our head points to the last node, but we can iterate over it and come back to the last node or the other node we want. The combined look of all the functions and the preceding class looks like the code at `https://github.com/PacktPublishing/Expert-C-2nd-edition/blob/main/Chapter07/ch7_xor_list.cpp` (we also added a `print` function so that you can test whether this works or not).

We remind you that the preceding code is not the whole implementation of the XOR list and we would be happy if you tried to implement it using the knowledge and the strategy that this chapter imparted.

Summary

In this chapter, we discussed advanced data structures such as B-trees, heaps, and advanced lists. We also talked about one of the best containers STL has to hand and also about the strategies that are used to implement the container.

First, we went for the B-tree by understanding the importance of using B-trees and also where they are mostly used. We dived deeper into one of many specializations of B-trees – a 2-3 tree. After giving the structural implementation of the 2-3 tree, we also implemented the search function for the tree and discussed insertion and deletion in the most detailed way possible.

The implementation strategies of `std::unordered_map` were also put into light within this chapter. The most important operations that make up `std::unordered_map` are hashing, collision handling, and storing strategies.

We also discussed the heap data structure by talking about its structure and the operations that it performs. The heap data structure has many applications, which include the following:

- Priority queue
- Heap-sort
- Selection and graph algorithms
- Order statistics

In the last part of the chapter, we talked about two advanced lists: the skip list and the XOR list. By implementing some of the skip list's functionality and the XOR list, we understood the logic that is applied in both of those data structures.

Questions

1. List the properties that a B-tree of order *m* should satisfy.
2. What strategies can be used to handle collisions in implementing `unordered_map` by yourself?
3. What types of heaps are there and how do they differ?
4. Implement an `insert` function for the min heap.
5. Why is a heap used to implement a priority queue?
6. On what logic do the skip list and XOR list rely?

Further reading

For more information regarding what was covered in this chapter, please take a look at the following links:

- *Data Abstraction & Problem Solving with C++: Walls and Mirrors* by Frank M. Carrano – `https://www.amazon.com/Data-Abstraction-Problem-Solving-Mirrors/dp/0132923726`
- *Advanced Data Structures* by Peter Brass – `https://www.amazon.com/Advanced-Data-Structures-Peter-Brass/dp/1108735517/ref=sr_1_1?crid=2VE0ZP2ZHHISR&keywords=peter+brass&qid=1660662754&s=books&sprefix=peter+bras%2Cstripbooks%2C327&sr=1-1`
- *Data Structures and Algorithms Made Easy* by Narasimha Karumanchi – `https://www.amazon.com/Data-Structures-Algorithms-Made-Easy/dp/819324527X/ref=sr_1_1?crid=3B1D4IZHTSW7E&keywords=data+structures+and+algorithms+made+easy+narasimha&qid=1660662838&s=books&sprefix=data+structures+and+algorithms+made+easy+narasimha%2Cstripbooks%2C253&sr=1-1`

8
Functional Programming

One of the most famous programming paradigms, which is **object-oriented programming** (**OOP**), provides us with a way of thinking about objects, thus expressing the real world in terms of classes and their relationships. Functional programming is an entirely distinct programming paradigm that allows us to focus on the functional structure rather than the physical structure of code. Functional programming has two benefits that make it worthwhile to learn and use. Firstly, it is a new paradigm, which encourages you to think differently. Flexible thinking is necessary for solving problems. People who adhere to a single paradigm tend to offer similar solutions to every problem, but the most elegant solutions require a broader perspective. Developers may solve problems even more effectively by using the new skills they get from mastering functional programming. Secondly, functional programming helps to cut down on software errors. Functional programming's distinctive methodology is largely due to the fact that it breaks programs down into functions, none of which alter the state of the data.

In this chapter, we will talk about the fundamental blocks of functional programming, as well as ranges. Ranges, which were first introduced in C++20, give us a fantastic approach to constructing algorithms that operate on collections of data. The core of functional programming is creating algorithms that can be applied sequentially to a set of data. That is why this chapter will also include ranges.

The topics discussed in this chapter will be as follows:

- Introduction to functional programming
- Introduction to the ranges library
- First-class and higher-order functions
- Pure functions
- Delving more deeply into recursion
- Metaprogramming in functional C++

Technical requirements

The g++ compiler, along with the -std=c++20 option (which requires gcc10 or later), will be used to compile the examples in this chapter. You can find the source files used in this chapter at https://github.com/PacktPublishing/Expert-C-2nd-edition.

Functional programming revealed

As we mentioned earlier, functional programming is a programming paradigm. When building programs, you might think of a paradigm as a way of thinking. C++ is a multiparadigm language. It can be used to create programs using a procedural paradigm, which means executing statements one at a time. We have already spoken about the object-oriented approach, which divides a complicated system into objects that interact with each other. Contrarily, functional programming encourages us to break the system down into functions rather than objects. It operates with expressions rather than statements. In essence, you send an input to a function, which then returns an output. This can then be used as input for another function. Although it may appear straightforward at first, functional programming contains a number of rules and techniques that are challenging to understand at first. Nevertheless, if you succeed in doing so, a new way of thinking—the functional way—will be unlocked by your brain.

Let us begin with an example that will explain the concept of functional programming to make this a little clearer. Consider a scenario in which we are required to determine the number of even numbers in a given vector of integers. The sole drawback is that there are several vectors of this kind. To output a result as a new vector including the results of the computation for each input vector, we must count the even integers in each vector individually.

The input is given in the form of a matrix: a vector of vectors. The simplest way to express this in C++ is by using the following type:

```
std::vector<std::vector<int>>
```

We can further reduce the complexity of the preceding code by using type aliases as follows:

```
using IntMatrix = std::vector<std::vector<int>>;
```

An illustration of this problem is provided next. We have a bunch of vectors containing integers, and as a result, we should get a vector containing a count of even numbers:

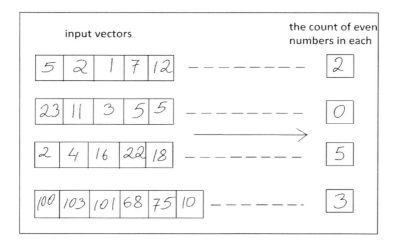

Figure 8.1 – Counting the even numbers in multiple vectors

Take a look at the following function. It accepts a matrix, commonly known as a vector of int-type vectors, as a parameter. The function determines how many even numbers there are:

```
std::vector<int> count_all_evens(const IntMatrix& numbers)
{
    std::vector<int> even_numbers_count;
    for (const auto& number_line: numbers) {
        int even{0};
        for (const auto& number: number_line) {
            if (number % 2 == 0) {
            ++even;
            }
        }
    even_numbers_count.push_back(even);
    }
    return even_numbers_count;
}
```

The preceding function keeps a separate vector to store the count of even numbers for each vector. Due to the fact that the input is a vector of vectors, the method loops over the first vector to extract the inner vectors. It goes over each retrieved vector once and advances a counter if it comes across an even value in the vector. After completing the loop for each vector, the final result is pushed to the vector containing the list of numbers. Although you might want to return to the previous example and improve the code, we will go on for now and break it down into smaller functions. The first thing we do is to make a separate function, which only counts the even numbers.

Let us name it `count_evens`, as follows:

```cpp
int64_t count_evens(const std::vector<int>& number_line) {
    return std::count_if(number_line.begin(),
    number_line.end(), [](int num){return num % 2 == 0;});
}
```

Note how we applied the `count_if()` algorithm. It takes two iterators: the first iterator indicates the beginning of a range and the second indicates the end of a range. As we can see, it also takes a third parameter, a unary predicate, which is called for each element of a collection. In our case, a lambda expression was passed as a third parameter. Any other callable entity, such as a function pointer, an `std::` function, and so on, may also be used.

Now that we have a separate counting function, we can call it in the original `count_all_evens()` function. The following implementation of `count_all_evens()` expresses functional programming in C++:

```cpp
auto count_all_evens(const std::vector<std::vector<int>>&
numbers) {
    return numbers |
        std::ranges::views::transform(count_evens);
}
```

Before delving into the preceding code, let us agree that the first thing that strikes our attention in this code is not the strange use of the | operator but rather its clarity. Take a look at it in comparison to the code version we presented at the start of this section. While both of them accomplish the same task, the second one—the functional one—does it more succinctly. Keep in mind that the function neither keeps nor modifies any state. It has no negative consequences. This is essential in functional programming since a function needs to be a pure function. It accepts an argument, processes it without altering it, and then returns a new value (usually based on the input). The first difficulty in functional programming is breaking a task down into smaller, more manageable independent functions.

Although we came to the functional solution from an imperative one, this is not the right way to use it when leveraging the functional programming paradigm. You need to alter your method and style of thinking rather than creating the imperative code first and then rewriting it to achieve the functional version. You should tame the process of thinking functionally. We can solve the problem by first trying to count all the even integers for a single vector. If we can figure out how to solve the problem for a single vector, we can solve it for all of the vectors. The following screenshot illustrates how the `count_evens()` method takes a vector to generate a single value:

Figure 8.2 – Workflow of the count_evens() function

Once the problem with one vector has been solved, we should proceed to the original problem by applying the solution to all the vectors. The `std::transform()` function essentially does what we need: it takes a function that can be applied to a single value and transforms it in order to process a collection. The following figure illustrates how we use it to implement a function (`count_all_evens`) that can process a collection of items from functions (`count_evens`) that process only one item at a time:

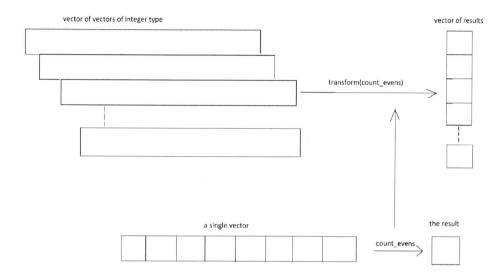

Figure 8.3 – The usage of the count_evens() function by the std::transform() function

The core concept of functional programming is the division of a larger problem into smaller, independent tasks. Each function is specialized to do a single, manageable task, without comprehending the root of the problem. A collection of transformed items is then produced from the initial raw input by composing several functions together.

Now, the final version of the `count_all_evens()` function leverages ranges. Let us find out what they are and how to use them because we will need them in further examples.

Using ranges

Ranges represent a collection of objects or anything iterable abstractly. The simplest definition merely requires `begin()` and `end()` to exist on the range. Ranges may be categorized in a variety of ways, but the most crucial one is according to the abilities of its iterators.

Ranges are connected to views. In this chapter, we will look at them both. They give us a general approach to creating and managing groupings of items. We often use iterators to loop through containers and work with their elements, as you have already seen. Thanks to iterators, we can have a loose connection between algorithms and containers.

For example, earlier, we applied `count_if()` to the vector, but `count_if()` is not aware of what container it was applied to. Take a look at the following declaration of `count_if()`:

```
template <typename InputIterator, typename UnaryPredicate>
constexpr typename iterator_traits<InputIterator>::difference_type
count_if(InputIterator first, InputIterator last, UnaryPredicate p);
```

As you can see, besides its verbose declaration, which is specific to C++, `count_if()` does not take a container as an argument. Instead, it operates with iterators – specifically, input iterators.

An input iterator supports iterating forward using the ++ operator and accessing each element using the * operator. We also can compare input iterators using the == and != relationships.

Algorithms repeatedly iterate over containers, without truly understanding what kind of container they are iterating over. Any entity with a beginning and an end is capable of being used with the `count_if()` function. By this, we mean an entity that has `begin()` and `end()` functions, the first of which returns an iterator (pointer) to the first element of the container while the second one returns an iterator one past the last element of the container. Let us look at the following syntax:

```
#include <array>
#include <iostream>
#include <algorithm>
int main()
{
    std::array<int, 4> arr{1, 2, 3, 4};
    auto res = std::count_if(arr.cbegin(), arr.cend(),
      [](int x){ return x == 3; });
    std::cout << "There are " << res << " number of
      elements equal to 3";
}
```

In addition to being general, algorithms are difficult to assemble. In most cases, we apply an algorithm to a collection and then save the outcome in another collection, which we can then use to apply further algorithms in the same way in the future. In order to put the outcomes into another container, we utilize `std::transform()`. For example, the following code defines a vector of `Product`:

```
// consider the Product is already declared and has a
// "name", "price", and "weight"
// also consider the get_products() is defined
// and returns a vector of Product instances
using ProductList = std::vector<std::shared_ptr<Product>>;
ProductList vec{get_products()};
```

Imagine that a separate group of programmers worked on the project and decided to keep the product names as numbers, such as 1 for an apple, 2 for a peach, and so on. This means that `vec` will contain

Product instances, each of which will have a number character in its name field (whereas the name's type is std::string – this is why we keep the number as a character instead of its integer value). Now, our task is to transform the names of products from numbers into full strings (apple, peach, and so on). Create a list of products and add two apples, one peach, and three bananas and transform the names using std::transform:

```
ProductList full_named_products; // type alias has been
                                 // defined above
using ProductPtr = std::shared_ptr<Product>;
std::transform(vec.cbegin(), vec.cend(),
  std::back_inserter(full_named_products), [](ProductPtr
  p){ /* modify the name and return */ });
```

After executing the preceding code, the full_named_products vector will contain products with full product names. Now, to filter out all the apples and copy them to a vector of apples, we need to use std::copy_if:

```
ProductList apples;
std::copy_if(full_named_products.cbegin(),
  full_named_products.cend(),
  std::back_inserter(apples),
  [](ProductPtr p){ return p->name() == "apple"; });
```

Prior to the introduction of ranges, the lack of nice composition was one of the greatest drawbacks of the preceding code samples. We can interact with container items and construct algorithms in an elegant way thanks to ranges.

A range, like the containers we have worked with so far, has a begin() and an end() – thus, to put it simply, a range is a traversable entity. Every STL container may be thought of as a range in this context. Ranges are now accepted as direct arguments for STL algorithms. They do this so that we can send a result from one algorithm to another without having to store intermediary results in local variables. For instance, when applied to a range, std::transform, which we previously used with begin() and end(), has the following form (the following code is pseudocode). We can rebuild the preceding example using ranges. Note that we simplified these code examples by omitting std::ranges::views from in front of the filter and transform functions. Use them as std::ranges::views::filter and std::ranges::views::transform, accordingly:

```
auto apples = filter(
transform(vec, [](ProductPtr p){/* normalize the name */}),
[](ProductPtr p){return p->name() == "apple";}
);
```

Do not forget to import the <ranges> header. The transform function will return a range containing Product pointers whose names are normalized; that is, the numerical value is replaced with a string value. The `filter` function will then take the result and return the range of products that have `apple` as their name.

Finally, we can pipe ranges together using the overloaded operator, |, which we used in the example at the beginning of this chapter. In this manner, we can combine algorithms to generate a result, as follows:

```
auto apples = vec | transform([](ProductPtr p)
  {/* normalize the name */})
    | filter([](ProductPtr p){return p->name() ==
            "apple";});
for (auto fruit : apples)
    std::cout << fruit->name_ << std::endl;
```

Instead of nested function calls, we used piping. Due to the fact that we previously used the | operator as a bitwise OR, this may at first seem strange. Whenever you see it applied to a collection, it refers to piping ranges.

The | operator is inspired by the Unix shell pipe operator. In Unix, we can pipe the results of several processes together; for example, `ls -l | grep cpp | less` will find `cpp` in the result of the `ls` command and show the final result one screen at a time using the `less` program.

A range is an abstraction over a collection, as we just said. This is not necessarily a collection. The preceding example only transfers a range from function to function, where the range merely specifies the start and finish of a collection, therefore it does not carry any cost. In addition, it allows us to access the underlying collection elements. The following diagram illuminates this idea:

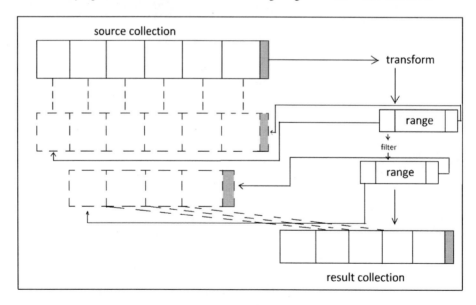

Figure 8.4 – The process of transforming a source collection into a result collection

Instead of returning a collection, the function (`transform()` or `filter()`) returns a range structure. The `begin()` iterator of the range will point to the element in the source collection that satisfies the predicate. The iterator for the range is a proxy object; in contrast to a typical iterator, it leads to an element that fulfills the provided criteria. They are frequently referred to as "clever iterators" since they always find the next element in the collection that meets the criterion when we advance them (by incrementing, for instance). What's more intriguing is that the type of function we use to organize the collection affects how "smart" the iterator is. For instance, the range returned by the `filter()` method contains smart iterators for its increment operator. The main reason for this is that `filter` may produce fewer items than the initial collection. On the other hand, `transform` just transforms the elements, not returning a result with fewer elements. This means that a range produced by `transform` will have different element access but the same capability for increment/decrement operations. For each access, the smart iterator of the range will return the transformed element from the original collection. In other words, it simply implements the `*()` operator for the iterator, similar to what can be seen in the following code snippet:

```
auto operator*()
{
    return predicate(*current_position);
}
```

This way, we are creating a new *view* of the collection rather than a new collection of transformed elements. The same applies to `filter` and other functions. More interestingly, range views leverage *lazy evaluation*. For our preceding example, even if we have two range transformations, the result is produced by evaluating them in a single pass.

In the example with `transform` and `filter`, each of the functions defines a view, but they do not modify or evaluate anything. When we assign the result to the result collection, the vector is constructed from the view by accessing each element. That is where the evaluation happens.

It is as simple as that – ranges provide us with function composition with lazy evaluation.

First-class and higher-order functions

In functional programming, functions are regarded as first-class objects (but you may also come across as first-class citizens). This implies that we should handle them as objects as opposed to a set of instructions. What difference does this make to us? The only criterion for a function to be considered an object at this point is its ability to be passed to other functions. Higher-order functions are defined as functions that accept other functions as arguments.

Programmers in C++ frequently pass one function to another. Here's how to do it the old-school way:

```
typedef void (*PF)(int);
void foo(int arg)
{
```

```
        // do something with arg
    }
    int bar(int arg, PF f)
    {
        f(arg);
        return arg;
    }
    bar(42, foo);
```

We declared a pointer to a function in the code that was written here. With one integer parameter and no value returned, PF denotes a type definition for the function. This illustration shows a common method for passing function pointers as parameters to other functions. We treat the function as if it were an object. However, this depends on what we understand by an object.

An object is something that has a state, according to our definition from earlier chapters. As a result, if we treat a function as an object, we should be able to alter its state in some way. This isn't true for function pointers, though. A better method for passing a function to another function is as follows:

```
    class Function
    {
        public:
        void modify_state(int a) {
        state_ = a;
    }
    int get_state() {
        return state_;
    }
    void operator()() {
        // do something that a function would do
    }
    private:
    int state_;
    };
    void foo(Function f)
    {
        f();
        // some other useful code
    }
```

Look closely at the preceding code. It declares a class that has an overloaded operator(). We make an operator callable whenever we overload one for a class. As simple as it may seem, anything that can be called is considered to be a function. Therefore, an object of a class with an overloaded operator() might be considered a function (also referred to as a functor). This seems like a trick, as we made an object callable rather than making a function an object. However, this allowed us to achieve what we were looking for: a function that has a state. The client code shown here shows that a `Function` object has a state:

```
void foo(Function f)
{
    f();
    f.modify_state(11);
    cout << f.get_state(); // get the state
    f(); // call the "function"
}
```

This, for instance, allows us to keep track of how many times the function has been invoked. Here is a straightforward example that counts calls:

```
class Function
{
    public:
    void operator()() {
    // some useful stuff
    ++called_;
}
private:
    int called_ = 0;
};
```

Finally, `std::function`, which is defined in the `<functional>` header in the following code, demonstrates another way of defining a higher-order function:

```
#include <functional>
void print_it(int a) {
    cout << a;
}
std::function<void(int)> function_object = print_it;
```

When `function_object` is called (using `operator()`), it delegates the call to the `print_it` function. `std::function` encapsulates any function and allows it to work with it as an object (and pass it to other functions as well).

Higher-order functions may be seen in all of the aforementioned examples of functions that accepted other functions as arguments. A higher-order function is also another name for a function that returns a function. In conclusion, a higher-order function is a function that accepts or returns a different function or set of functions. Take a look at the following example:

```
#include <functional>
#include <iostream>
```

```
std::function<int (int, int)> get_multiplier()
{
    return [](int a, int b) { return a * b; };
}
int main()
{
    auto multiply = get_multiplier();
    std::cout << multiply(3, 5) << std::endl;
    // outputs 15
}
```

get_multiplier() returns a lambda wrapped in std::function. Then, we call the result, just like we would call a regular function. The get_multiplier() function is a higher-order function. Similar to what we did in the previous example, we can implement currying using a higher-order function. Currying is the process of splitting up functions that take many arguments into smaller functions that each take a single parameter in functional programming. For instance, multiply(3, 5) would become multiply(3) (5). This is how we can do it:

```
std::function<int (int)> multiply(int a)
{
    return [a](int b) { return a * b; };
}
int main()
{
    std::cout << multiply(3)(5) << std::endl;
}
```

multiply() takes one argument and returns a function that also takes a single argument. Pay attention to the lambda capture: it captures the value of a so that it can multiply it by b in its body.

Currying is a reference to the logician Haskell Curry. The Haskell, Brook, and Curry programming languages are also named after him.

Having abstract functions that we can combine is one of currying's most advantageous features. multiply() can be customized, and then we can use it where applicable or pass these customized versions to other methods. The following code illustrates this:

```
auto multiplyBy22 = multiply(22);
auto fiveTimes = multiply(5);
std::cout << multiplyBy22(10); // outputs 220
std::cout << fiveTimes(4); // outputs 20
```

You must've used a higher-order function when working with the STL. Predicates are used by several STL algorithms to filter out or handle collections of objects. For example, the `std::find_if` function finds the element that satisfies the passed predicate object, as shown in the following example:

```
std::vector<int> elems{1, 2, 3, 4, 5, 6};
std::find_if(elems.begin(), elems.end(), [](int el) {return el % 3 ==
0;});
```

`std::find_if` takes a lambda as its predicate and calls it for all the elements in the vector. Whichever element satisfies the condition is returned as the requested one.

Another example of a higher-order function would be `std::transform`, which we introduced at the beginning of this chapter (not to be confused with `ranges::view::transform`). Let's use it to transform a string into uppercase letters:

```
std::string str = "lowercase";
std::transform(str.begin(), str.end(), str.begin(),
[](unsigned char c) { return std::toupper(c); });
std::cout << str; // "LOWERCASE"
```

The third parameter is the beginning of the container and is where the `std::transform` function inserts its current results.

Why use functional programming?

First of all, functional programming brings forth conciseness. Compared to its imperative counterparts, the code is substantially shorter. It offers straightforward yet very expressive tools. Less code means less chance of errors appearing.

Functions don't cause any mutations, which makes parallelizing them considerably easier. This is one of the main concerns in concurrent programs because concurrent tasks need to share mutable data between them. The majority of the time, primitives such as mutexes must be used to deliberately synchronize threads. Explicit synchronization is eliminated when using functional programming, and the code can be executed on several threads without modification.

According to the functional paradigm, those functions that do not alter the state of the program are considered to be *pure*. They only accept an input, alter it in a way that is determined by the user, and provide an output. No matter how many times it is called, a pure function always produces the same output for the same input. Whenever we speak about functional programming, we should take all pure functions into account by default.

The following function takes `double` as its input and returns its square:

```
double square(double num) { return num * num; }
```

Only writing pure functions could seem like a deliberate slowdown of the program.

> **Tip**
>
> Some compilers, such as GCC, provide attributes that help the compiler optimize the code. For example, the `[[gnu::pure]]` attribute tells the compiler that the function can be considered a pure function. This will reassure the compiler that the function doesn't access any global variables and that the function's result depends solely on its input.

There are many situations in which a regular function might provide a quicker solution. However, you must push yourself to think practically in order to adjust to the paradigm. The following program, for instance, defines a vector and determines the square roots of each of its components:

```cpp
void calc_square_roots(std::vector<double>& vec)
{
    for (auto& elem : vec) {
      elem = std::sqrt(elem);
    }
}
int main()
{
    std::vector<double> vec{1.1, 2.2, 4.3, 5.6, 2.4};
    calc_square_roots(vec);
}
```

In this case, the vector is passed by reference. This implies that altering it in the function also alters the initial collection. Given that the input vector is altered, it is evident that this is not a pure function. A practical substitute would preserve the input and return the changed items in a new vector:

```cpp
std::vector<double> pure_calc_square_roots(const std::vector<double>&
vec)
{
    std::vector<double> new_vector;
    for (const auto& elem : vec) {
    new_vector.push_back(std::sqrt(elem));
    }
    return new_vector;
}
```

An even better example of functional thinking is to solve a smaller problem and apply it to the collection. The smaller problem, in this case, is calculating the square root of a single number, which is already implemented as `std::sqrt`. Applying it to the collection is done with `std::ranges::views::transform`, as follows:

```cpp
#include <ranges>
#include <vector>
#include <cmath>
```

```
int main()
{
    std::vector<double> vec{1.1, 2.2, 4.3, 5.6, 2.4};
    auto wrapper = [] (double x) {return std::sqrt(x);};
    auto result = vec |
        std::ranges::views::transform(wrapper);
}
```

As we already know, storing intermediary objects can be avoided by employing ranges. In the preceding example, we directly applied `transform` to the vector. `transform` only returns a view of the source vector's altered items, not the entire collection. The actual transformed copies of elements are made when we construct the result vector. Also, keep in mind that `std::sqrt` is considered a pure function.

The chapter's first example, which we solved, provided us with the required context for functional programming. We should familiarize ourselves with this paradigm's guiding principles in order to comprehend it better. We will explore the fundamentals of functional programming in the next part to provide you with a deeper understanding of how and when to use the paradigm.

Principles of functional programming

Despite its age (it was created in the 1950s), the functional paradigm didn't completely revolutionize programming. Most of the dominant paradigms these days include imperative and object-oriented languages. C++ is a multi-paradigm language, as we have repeatedly said in this book and as is said in many other books. The benefit of learning C++ is that we can modify it to match practically any environment. The paradigm is difficult to comprehend. Before you can begin to conceive in terms of the paradigm, you must first feel it and put it into practice. After that, you will instantly see answers to common problems.

You may be able to recall the concepts that you first struggled with before realizing the full potential of object-oriented programming. Functional programming follows the same rules. The fundamental ideas of functional programming that will serve as the foundation for subsequent advancement are covered in this part. Some of these ideas are applicable beyond or have already been used outside the functional paradigm. Nevertheless, make an attempt to comprehend and use each of the following principles.

Pure functions

As we previously stated, a function is considered pure if it does not mutate the state. Pure functions may be thought of as less efficient than their non-pure counterparts, but they are wonderful since they prevent the majority of errors that develop in code as a result of state changes. Bugs are related to the program state in some way. Obviously, programs work with data, so they set up the functionality to modify the state and this leads to the expected results for the end user.

In OOP, we decompose the program into objects, each of which has a list of special features. In OOP, the state of an object is one of its core characteristics. OOP relies heavily on the ability to change an object's state by interacting with it (in other words, calling its methods). Invoking a member function typically causes the object's state to change. In functional programming, we organize code into a collection of pure functions, each of which has its own purpose and is independent of the others.

Let us take a look at a simple example, just to make this concept clear. Let's say we're dealing with User objects in a program and each user object contains the age associated with the user. The User type is described as a struct in the following code block:

```
struct User
{
    int age;
    string name;
    string phone_number;
    string email;
};
```

There is a need to update users' ages on a yearly basis. Let's suppose we have a function that is invoked for each User object once a year. The following function takes a User object as input and increases its age property by 1:

```
void update_age(User& u)
{
    u.age = u.age + 1;
}
```

The update_age() function takes the input by reference and updates the original object. This is not the case in functional programming. Instead of taking the original object by reference and mutating its value, the following pure function returns a totally different User object with the same properties, except for the updated age property:

```
User pure_update_age(const User& u) // cannot modify the
                                    // input argument
{
    User tmp{u};
    tmp.age = tmp.age + 1;
    return tmp;
}
```

Although it seems inefficient compared to update_age(), one of the pros of this approach is that it makes operations crystal clear (this is really useful when we're debugging code). Now, it's guaranteed that pure_update_age() won't modify the original object. We can modify the preceding code so that it will take the object by value. This way, we skip creating the tmp object, as the argument itself represents a copy:

```
User pure_update_age(User u) // u is the copy of the
```

```
                              // passed object
{
    u.age = u.age + 1;
    return u;
}
```

If a pure function is called multiple times with the same arguments, it must return the same result every time. The following code demonstrates that our pure_update_age() function returns the same value when it's given the same input:

```
User john{.age{21}, .name{"John"}};
auto updated{pure_update_age(john)};
std::cout << updated.age; // prints 22
updated = pure_update_age(john);
std::cout << updated.age; // prints 22
```

When a function is called repeatedly with the same input data, it is very advantageous for it to react consistently. This implies that we can create the application's logic by breaking it down into smaller functions, each of which has a specific and obvious purpose. The additional temporary object is an overhead for the pure function, though. In a typical approach, the program state is kept in a centralized store and is indirectly updated by pure functions. Every time a pure function is called, the changed object is returned as a new object that can be saved if required. You may think of it as modifying the code so that the entire object is not passed.

Folding

Combining a set of values in order to get a smaller reduced number of outcomes is known as folding (or reduction). Most of the time, we are discussing a single outcome. The operation of iterating across recursive structures is abstracted via folding. For instance, recursive access to elements is common in structures such as linked lists and vectors. Although the vector's recursiveness is debatable, we will treat it as such because it enables us to access its members by continually incrementing the index. In order to deal with these structures, we typically keep track of the outcome at each stage and process the next item so that the outcome from the prior step can be integrated with it later. Folding is called left or right folding based on the direction in which we process the collection elements.

For example, the std::accumulate function (another example of a higher-order function) is a perfect example of folding functionality because it combines values in the collection. Take a look at the following simple example:

```
std::vector<double> elems{1.1, 2.2, 3.3, 4.4, 5.5};
auto sum = std::accumulate(elems.begin(), elems.end(), 0.0);
```

The last argument passed to the function is the accumulator. This is the starting value that ought to be used as the prior value for the collection's first item. The preceding code calculates the sum of the vector elements. It's the default behavior of the `std::accumulate` function. As we mentioned previously, it is a higher-order function, which implies that a function could be passed as its argument. This will then be called for each element to produce the desired result. For example, let's find the product of the `elems` vector we declared previously:

```
auto product = std::accumulate(elems.begin(), elems.end(), 1.0,
[](int prev, int cur) { return prev * cur; });
```

It requires a binary operation; that is, a function with two arguments. The first argument of the operation is the previous value that's been calculated so far, while the second argument is the current value. The result of the binary operation will be the previous value for the next step. Using one of the STL's existing operations, the preceding code may be rewritten succinctly:

```
auto product = std::accumulate(elems.begin(), elems.end(), 1.0,
std::multiplies<double>());
```

A better alternative to the `std::accumulate` function is the `std::reduce` function. `reduce()` is similar to `accumulate()`, except it doesn't keep the order of the operation; that is, it doesn't necessarily process the collection elements sequentially. You can pass an execution policy to the `std::reduce` function and change its behavior, say, to processing elements in parallel. Here's how the `reduce` function can be applied to the `elems` vector from the previous example using the parallel execution policy:

```
//include header <execution> to compile
std::reduce(std::execution::par, elems.begin(), elems.end(),
1, std::multiplies<double>());
```

Although `std::reduce` seems faster compared to `std::accumulate`, you should be careful when using it with non-commutative binary operations.

Recursion and folding go hand in hand. Breaking a difficult task into smaller ones and completing them separately can be accomplished using recursion.

Delving more deeply into recursion

The primary characteristics of a recursive function have previously been covered. Almost all the problems that can be solved with an iterative solution can also be solved with a recursive solution. Let us take a look at the simple recursive solution of one of the most famous problems: the calculation of the nth Fibonacci number:

```
int fibonacci(int n)
{
    if (n <= 1) return n;
    return fibonacci(n-1) + fibonacci(n - 2);
}
```

Let us illustrate the process that happens when the preceding function is called. In our example, we will consider that the argument passed to the function is 6, which means that n is equal to 6. The process starts like this:

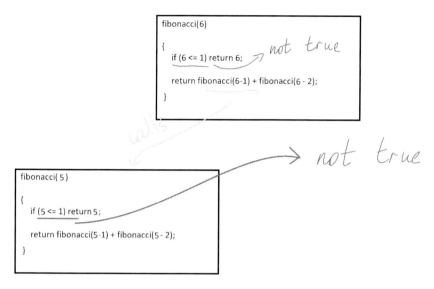

Figure 8.5 – First call of the recursive fibonacci() function

The function calls itself until n is equal to or smaller than 1, but what happens when it becomes equal to 1?

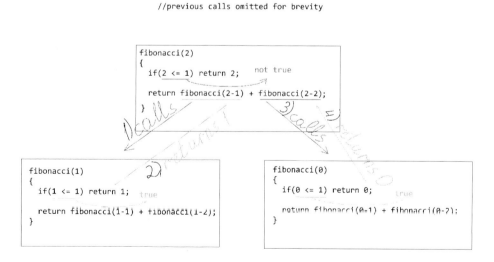

Figure 8.6 – When the function reaches the base case

As we can see in the diagram, the function where n is equal to 1 returns it to the function, which is fibonacci(2), from where the next function call happens as fibonacci(2-2) and is the next function call our compiler sees. That function also meets our condition and returns 0. This means that now we have two resolved values, which are 1 and 0, that can be added together. When they are added together, they return to the fibonacci(3) function, as shown in the following diagram:

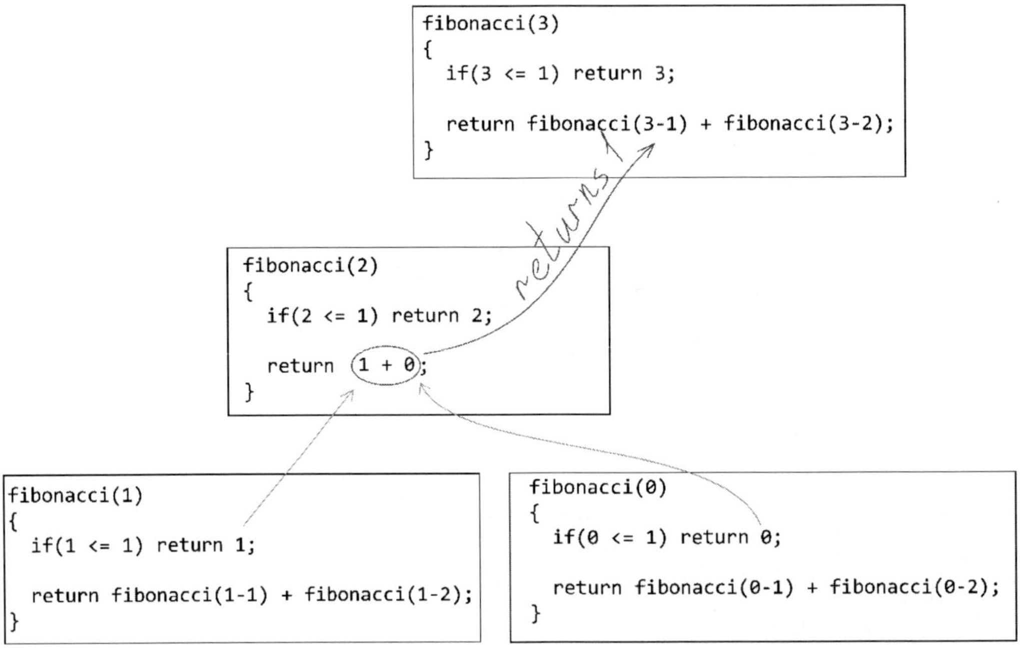

Figure 8.7 – Return to the function that resulted in the addition of two base case results

Other calls follow the same logic. Looking at these diagrams, we notice that they are somewhat similar to tree structures and, in fact, they form a tree structure. The following diagrams show the whole tree structure we get when calling a fibonnaci function for a number, 6 here:

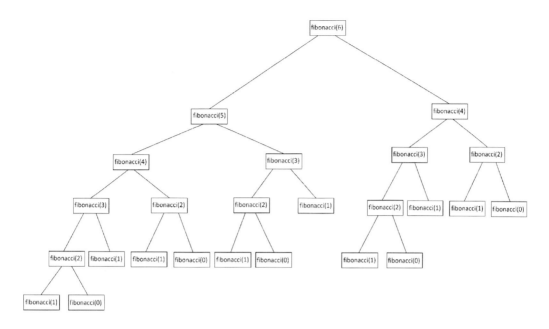

Figure 8.8 – The tree structure of a recursive fibonacci() function

Compared to iterative functions, recursive functions offer beautiful solutions. However, choosing to employ recursion should be done with caution. Stack overflows are one of the most often encountered problems with recursive functions.

Head recursion

Head recursion is the regular type of recursion that we are already familiar with. For example, a factorial counting function is implemented recursively, as follows:

```
int factorial(int n)
{
    if (n <= 1) return 1;
    return n * factorial(n - 1);
}
```

It behaves as a head recursive function, meaning that it makes the recursive call before processing the result at the current step. Take a look at the following line from the factorial function:

```
...
return n * factorial(n - 1);
...
```

To find and return the result of the product, the function factorial is called with a reduced argument, that is, (n - 1). This means that the product (the * operator) is kind of on hold and is waiting for its second argument to be returned by factorial(n - 1). The stack grows in line with the number of recursive calls to the function. Let's try to compare the recursive factorial implementation with the following iterative approach:

```
int factorial(int n)
{
    int result = 1;
    for (int ix = n; ix > 1; --ix) {
        result *= ix;
    }
    return result;
}
```

We keep the outcome of the product at each stage in the same variable (the named result), which is one of the key distinctions in this case. With this in mind, let's try to decompose the recursive implementation of the factorial function.

It is evident that each function call occupies a specific amount of stack space. Every result from each stage should be kept on the stack in a different location. The recursive function allocates space to its variables even though we are aware that they should—and even must—be the same variable. The counter-intuitiveness of regular recursive functions prompts us to find a solution that somehow knows that the result of each recursive call should be stored in the same place.

Tail recursion

The issue of dealing with several unnecessary variables in recursive functions is solved by tail recursion. The fundamental concept behind tail-recursive functions is to do the real processing prior to the recursive call. To convert the factorial function into a tail-recursive one, follow these steps:

```
int tail_factorial(int n, int result)
{
    if (n <= 1) return result;
    return tail_factorial(n - 1, n * result);
}
```

Pay attention to the new argument of the function. Carefully reading the preceding code gives us a basic idea of the tail recursion that's occurring: the processing is done before the recursive call. Before tail_factorial is called again in its body, the current result is calculated (n * result) and passed to it.

While this idea might not seem fascinating, it would be really efficient if **Tail Call Optimization** (**TCO**) was supported by the compiler. TCO basically involves knowing that the second argument of the factorial function (the tail) can be stored at the same location for every recursive call. This allows for the stack to stay the same size, independent of the number of recursive calls.

We can't forget template metaprogramming while we're talking about compiler optimizations. We're mentioning it here alongside compiler optimizations because we can treat metaprogramming as the biggest optimization that can be done to the program.

Metaprogramming in functional C++

One more paradigm of programming is metaprogramming. Due to the fact that we are not working with the regular process of programming, this method of coding is completely different. A program's three stages of coding, compiling, and executing are referred to as a "regular process" in this context. It's obvious that a program does what it's supposed to do when it is executed. The compiler uses linking and compilation to generate an executable. Metaprogramming, on the other hand, is where the code is executed during the compilation of the code. This might sound magical if you are dealing with it for the first time. How can we execute code if the program doesn't even exist yet? Recalling what we learned about templates in the previous chapters, we know that the compiler processes them with more than one pass. In the first pass, the compiler defines the necessary types and parameters that are used in the template class or function. With the next pass, the compiler starts to compile them in the way we're familiar with; that is, it generates some code, which will be linked by the linker to produce the final executable file.

Here's a classic mind-blowing example of metaprogramming in C++:

```cpp
template <int N>
struct MetaFactorial
{
    enum {
        value = N * MetaFactorial<N - 1>::value
    };
};

template <>
struct MetaFactorial<0>
{
    enum {
        value = 1
    };
};
int main() {
    std::cout << MetaFactorial<5>::value; // outputs 120
    std::cout << MetaFactorial<6>::value; // outputs 720
}
```

Why would we bother writing so much code for a factorial when we could have done it as in the previous section with only a few lines of code? Its efficiency is the cause. Although compiling the code will take a little longer, it is much more efficient than the normal factorial function (implemented either recursively or iteratively). And the reason behind this efficiency is the fact that the actual calculation of the factorial is happening at compile time. In other words, the results are already usable when the executable is run. No calculations are performed at runtime; we just use the computed result. If you're encountering this code for the first time, the explanation that follows will make you fall in love with metaprogramming.

Let's decompose and analyze the preceding code in detail. First of all, the MetaFactorial template is declared with a single enum with a value property. This enum is chosen solely because its properties are calculated at compile time. So, whenever we access the value property of MetaFactorial, it is already being calculated (evaluated) at compile time. Take a look at the actual value of the enumeration. It makes a recursive dependency from the same MetaFactorial class:

```
template <int N>
struct MetaFactorial
{
    enum {
        value = N * MetaFactorial<N - 1>::value
    };
};
```

Some of you may have already noticed the trick here. MetaFactorial<N - 1> is not the same struct as MetaFactorial<N>. Although it has the same name, each template with a different type or value is generated as a separate new type. So, let's say we call something like the following:

```
std::cout << MetaFactorial<5>::value;
```

Here, the hard-working compiler generates three different structs for each value (the following is some pseudocode representing how we should picture the compiler working):

```
struct MetaFactorial<5>
{
    enum {
        value = 5 * MetaFactorial<4>::value
    };
};
struct MetaFactorial<4>
{
    enum {
        value = 4 * MetaFactorial<3>::value
    };
};
struct MetaFactorial<3>
```

```
{
    enum {
        value = 3 * MetaFactorial<2>::value
    };
};
struct MetaFactorial<2>
{
    enum {
        value = 2 * MetaFactorial<1>::value;
    };
};
struct MetaFactorial<1>
{
    enum {
        value = 1 * MetaFactorial<0>::value;
    };
};
```

In the next pass, the compiler replaces each of the generated struct's values with their respective numeric values, as shown in the following pseudocode:

```
struct MetaFactorial<5>
{
enum {
    value = 5 * 4
    };
};
struct MetaFactorial<4>
{
    enum {
        value = 4 * 3
    };
};
struct MetaFactorial<3>
{
    enum {
        value = 3 * 2
    };
};
struct MetaFactorial<2>
{
    enum {
        value = 2 * 1
    };
```

```
};
struct MetaFactorial<1>
{
    enum {
        value = 1 * 1
    };
};
```

Then, the compiler removes the unused generated structs, leaving only `MetaFactorial<3>`, which is, again, only used as `MetaFactorial<3>::value`. This can also be optimized. By doing this, we get the following result:

```
std::cout << 720;
```

Compare this with the previous line we had:

```
std::cout << MetaFactorial<5>::value;
```

That's the beauty of metaprogramming – it's done at compile time and leaves no trace, like a ninja. The compilation takes longer but the execution of the program is the fastest it can possibly be compared to regular solutions. We advise you to attempt constructing meta-versions of cost-expensive calculations, such as calculating the nth Fibonacci number. Although it's not quite as simple as writing code for runtime rather than compile time, you can immediately see its power.

Summary

In this chapter, we learned a new viewpoint on making use of C++. It may be used as a functional programming language since it is a multi-paradigm language.

We studied the fundamentals of functional programming, including folding, higher-order functions, and pure functions. Pure functions are those that don't alter the state of the system. One advantage of pure functions is that they don't create as many bugs as state modifications do.

Higher-order functions are functions that take or return other functions. Other than in functional programming, C++ programmers use higher-order functions when dealing with the STL.

Pure functions, along with higher-order functions, allow us to decompose the whole application into a big assembly line of functions. Each function in this assembly line is responsible for receiving data and returning a new, modified version of the original data (without mutating the original state). When combined, these functions provide a well-coordinated line of tasks.

In the next chapter, we will dive into multithreaded programming and discuss the thread support library components that were introduced in C++.

Questions

1. List the advantages of ranges.

2. What functions are known to be pure?

3. What's the difference between a pure virtual function and a pure function in terms of functional programming?

4. What is folding?

5. What is the advantage of tail recursion overhead recursion?

Further reading

For more information regarding what was covered in this chapter, please take a look at the following links:

- *Learning C++ Functional Programming* by Wisnu Anggoro: `https://www.packtpub.com/application-development/learning-c-functional-programming`

- *Functional Programming in C++: How to Improve Your C++ Programs Using Functional Techniques* by Ivan Cukic: `https://www.amazon.com/Functional-Programming-programs-functional-techniques/dp/1617293814/`

9

Concurrency and Multithreading

Concurrent programming allows us to create more efficient programs. C++ didn't have built-in support for concurrency or multithreading for a long time. Now, it has full support for concurrent programming, threads, thread synchronization objects, and other functionality that we will discuss in this chapter.

Before the language was updated for thread support, programmers had to use third-party libraries. One of the most popular multithreading solutions was **Portable Operating System Interface** (**POSIX**) threads. C++ introduced thread support with C++11. It makes the language even more robust and applicable to wider areas of software development. Understanding threads is somewhat crucial for C++ programmers as they tend to squeeze every bit of the program to make it run even faster. Threads introduce us to a completely different way of making programs faster by running functions concurrently. Learning about multithreading at a fundamental level is a must for every C++ programmer. There are lots of programs where you can't avoid using multithreading, such as network applications, games, and GUI applications. This chapter will introduce you to concurrency and multithreading fundamentals in C++ and the best practices for concurrent code design.

The following topics will be covered in this chapter:

- Understanding concurrency and multithreading
- Working with threads
- Managing threads and sharing data
- Designing concurrent code
- Using thread pools to avoid thread creation overheads
- Getting familiar with coroutines in C++20

Technical requirements

The g++ compiler with the `-std=c++2a` option was used to compile the examples in this chapter. You can find the source files that were used in this chapter at `https://github.com/PacktPublishing/Expert-CPP`.

Understanding concurrency and multithreading

The simplest form of running a program involves its instructions being executed one by one by the **central processing unit** (**CPU**). As you already know from previous chapters, a program consists of several sections, one of them containing the instructions of the program. Each instruction is loaded into a CPU register for the CPU to decode and execute it. It doesn't matter what programming paradigm you use to produce an application as the result is always the same – the executable file contains machine code.

We mentioned that programming languages such as Java and C# use support environments. However, if you cut down the support environment in the middle (usually, the virtual machine), the final instructions being executed should have a form and format familiar to that particular CPU. It's obvious to programmers that the order of statements run by the CPU is not mixed in any circumstance. For example, we are sure and can continue to be so that the following program will output 4, `"hello"`, and 5, respectively:

```
int a{4};
std::cout << a << std::endl;
int b{a};
++b;
std::cout << "hello" << std::endl; b--;
std::cout << (b + 1) << std::endl;
```

We can guarantee that the value of a variable will be initialized before we print it on the screen, in the same way, we can guarantee that the `"hello"` string will be printed before we decrement the value of b and that the `(b + 1)` sum will be calculated before printing the result to the screen. The execution of each instruction might involve reading data from or writing to memory.

As introduced in *Chapter 5*, *Memory Management and Smart Pointers*, the memory hierarchy is sophisticated enough to make our understanding of program execution a little bit harder. For example, the `int b{a};` line from the previous example assumes that the value of a is loaded from memory into a register in the CPU, which will then be used to write into the memory location of b. The keyword here is *location* because it carries a little bit of special interpretation for us. More specifically, we are speaking about memory location. Concurrency support depends on the memory model of the language – that is, a set of guarantees for concurrent memory access. Although the byte is the smallest addressable memory unit, the CPU works with words in data. That said, words are the smallest units the CPU reads from or writes to memory. For example, we consider the following two declarations as separate variables:

```
char one;
char two;
```

If those variables are allocated to the same word (considering the word size is bigger than the size of a char), reading and writing any of the variables involves reading the word containing both of them. Concurrent access to the variables might lead to unexpected behavior. That's the issue that requires memory model guarantees. The C++ memory model guarantees that two threads can access and update separate memory locations without interfering with each other. A memory location is a scalar type. A **scalar type** is an arithmetic type, pointer, enumeration, or `nullptr_t`. The largest sequence of adjacent bit-fields of non-zero length is considered a memory location too. A classic example would be the following structure:

```
struct S {
   char a;
   int b: 5;
   unsigned c: 11;
   unsigned :0;
   unsigned d: 8;
   struct {
        int ee: 8;
   } e;
};
```

As shown in the preceding example, two threads accessing the same separate `struct` memory locations won't interfere with each other. So, what should we consider when speaking about concurrency or multithreading?

Concurrency is usually confused with multithreading. They are similar but are different concepts in detail. To make things easy, just imagine concurrency as two operations whose running times interleave together. Operation A runs concurrently with operation B if their start and end times are interleaved at any point, as shown in the following diagram:

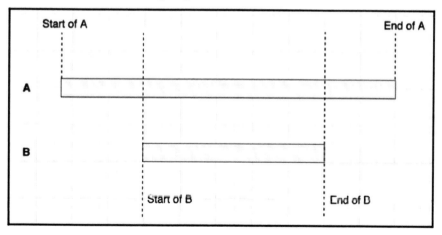

Figure 9.1 – Operations A and B running concurrently

When two tasks run concurrently, they don't have to run in parallel. Imagine the following situation: you are watching TV while surfing the internet. Although multitasking in this way is not a good practice, let's imagine for a moment that you have a favorite TV show that you can't miss and at the same time, your friend asks you to do some research on bees. You would find it difficult to concentrate on both tasks; at any fixed moment, your attention is grabbed by either the show you are watching or the interesting facts about bees that you are reading in an article found on the web. So, your attention would go from the show to the bees from time to time.

In concurrency, however, you can do two tasks concurrently. To make this happen, your brain allots a specific time slot to the show during which you can watch the show and enjoy it. After this, your brain allows you to switch to the article, read a couple of sentences, and then switch back to the show. This is a simple example of concurrently running tasks. Just because their start and end times interleave doesn't mean they run at the same time. On the other hand, you breathe while doing any of the tasks mentioned earlier. Breathing happens in the background; your brain doesn't switch your attention from the show or the article to your lungs to inhale or exhale. Breathing while watching the show is an example of running tasks in parallel. Hence, both examples show us the essence of concurrency.

So, what is going on when you run more than one application on your computer? Are they running in parallel? We can be certain that they run concurrently; however, the actual parallelism depends on your computer's hardware. As we know from previous chapters, the main job of the CPU is to run an application's instructions, one by one. How would a single CPU handle running two applications at the same time? To understand this, we should learn about processes.

Processes

A process is an image of a program running in memory. When we start a program, the OS reads the content of the program from the hard disk, copies it to memory, and points the CPU to the starting instruction of the program. The process has a private virtual address space, stack, and heap. Two processes don't interfere with each other in any way. That's a guarantee provided by the OS. That also makes a programmer's job very difficult if they aim for **interprocess communication** (**IPC**). We won't discuss low-level hardware features in this book but you should have a general understanding of what is going on when we run a program. It depends on the underlying hardware – more specifically, the kind and structure of the CPU. The number of CPUs, number of CPU cores, levels of cache memory, and shared cache memory between CPUs or their cores – all of these affect the way the OS runs and executes programs.

The number of CPU cores in a computer system determines the number of processes running in parallel.

When we speak about multiprocessing, we consider an environment that allows several processes to run concurrently. And here comes the tricky part: if the processes run at the same time, then we say that they run in parallel. So, concurrency is not parallelism, but parallelism implies concurrency.

If the system has just one CPU, processes run concurrently but not in parallel. The OS manages this with a mechanism called **context switching**. Context switching implies freezing the work of the process for a moment, copying all the register values that the process was using at the current time, and storing all of the active resources and values of the process. When a process is stopped, another process takes on the right to run. After the specified amount of time provided for this second process, the OS starts context switching. Again, it copies all of the resources used by the process. Then, the previous process is started. Before starting it, the OS copies the resources and values to the corresponding slots that were used by the first process and then resumes the execution of this process.

The interesting thing is that the processes are not even aware of such a thing. The described process happens so fast that the user cannot notice that the programs running in the OS are not running at the same time. The following diagram depicts two processes run by a single CPU. When one of the processes is active, the CPU executes its instructions sequentially, storing any intermediary data in its registers (you should consider cache memory as in any game, too). The other process is waiting for the OS to provide its portion of time to run. See the following figure:

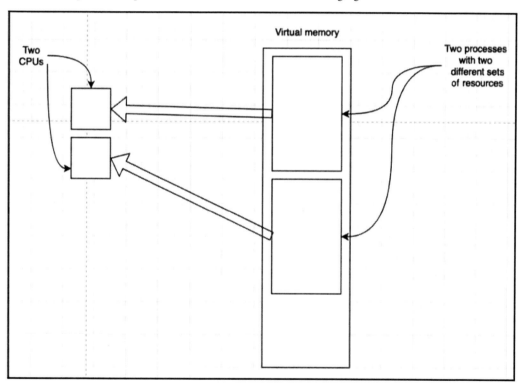

Figure 9.2 – IPC

Running more than one process is a sophisticated job for the OS. It manages the states of processes, defines which process should take more CPU time than others, and so on. Each process gets a fixed time to run before the OS switches to another process. This time can be longer for one process and shorter for another. The process of scheduling takes place through the use of priority tables. The OS provides more time for processes with a higher priority – for example, a system process has a higher priority than user processes. Another example could be that a background task monitoring network health has a higher priority than a calculator application. When the provided time slice is up, the OS initiates a context switch – that is, it stores the state of **Process A** to resume its execution later. See the following diagram:

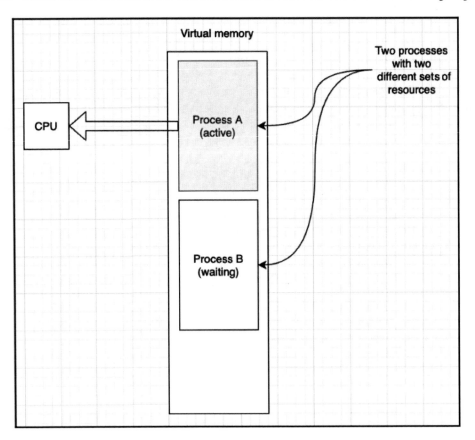

Figure 9.3 – Context switch

After storing the state, as shown in the following diagram, it switches to the next process to execute it:

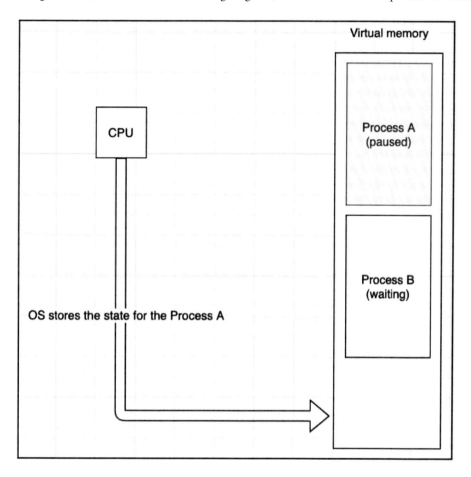

Figure 9.4 – Process switch A

And here's switch B:

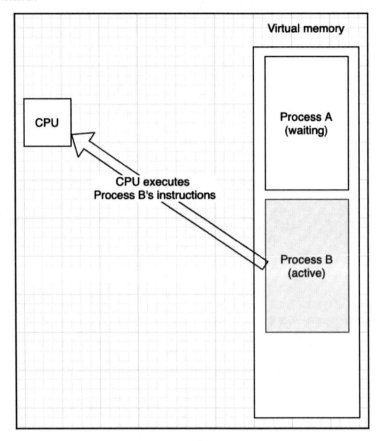

Figure 9.5 – Process switch B

If **Process B** was running before, its state should be loaded back to the CPU. In the same way, when the time slice (or time quantum) is up for **Process B**, the OS stores its state and loads the state of **Process A** back to the CPU (the state it had before being paused by the OS). See the following diagram to understand this better:

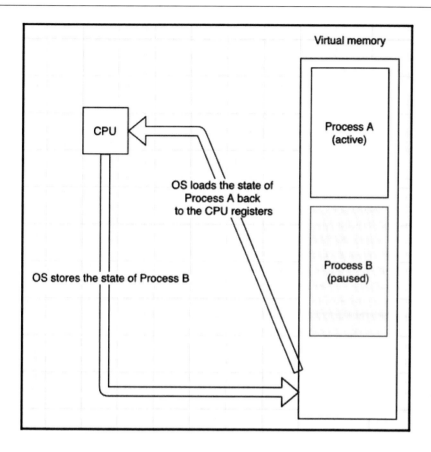

Figure 9.6 – Image caption

Processes do not share anything in common – or at least they think so. Each running process behaves as if it's alone in the system. It has all of the resources the OS can provide. In reality, the OS manages to keep processes unaware of each other, hence simulating freedom for each one. Finally, as shown in *Figure 9.7*, after loading the state of **Process A** back, the CPU continues executing its instructions like nothing happened:

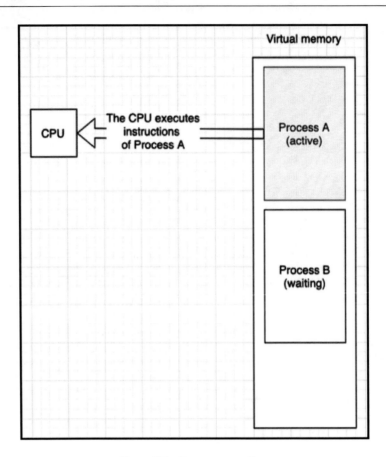

Figure 9.7 – Process execution

Process B is frozen until a new time slice is available for it to run.

A single CPU running more than one process is similar to a teacher checking the examination papers of students. The teacher can check only one exam paper at a time, though they can introduce some concurrency by checking answers one by one for each exam test. First, they check the answer to the first question for one student, then switch to the first answer of the test of the second student, and then may switch back to the first student's second answer, and so on. Whenever the teacher switches from one exam paper to the other, they note down the number of the question where they left off. This way, they will know where exactly to start when they go back to the same paper.

In the same way, the OS notes down the point of execution of a process before pausing it to resume another process. The second process can (and most probably will) use the same register set used by the paused process. This forces the OS to store register values for the first process somewhere so that they can be recovered later. When the OS pauses the second process to resume the first one, it loads already saved register values back into corresponding registers. The resumed process won't notice any difference and will continue its work like it was never paused.

At this juncture, we should be mindful of the fact that everything discussed in the previous chapters relates to single-CPU systems. In the case of multi-CPU systems, each CPU in the system consists of multiple cores, and each core has its own set of registers. Also, each core can execute program instructions independently of the other cores, which allows you to run processes in parallel without pausing and resuming them. In this example, a teacher with a couple of assistants is similar to a system with multiple CPU cores. Each core can check one exam paper; all of them are checking different exam papers simultaneously.

Challenges with processes

Difficulties arise when processes need to contact each other in some way. Let's say a process should calculate something and pass the value to a completely different process. There are several methods to achieve IPC – one of them is using a memory segment shared between processes. The following diagram depicts two processes accessing the shared memory segment:

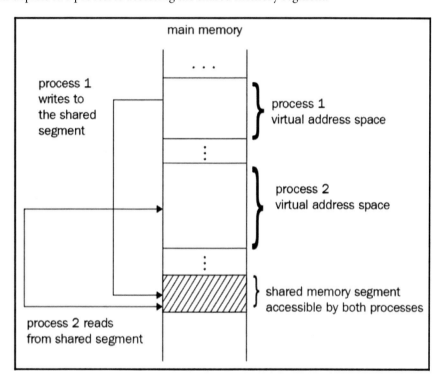

Figure 9.8 – Shared memory

As shown in *Figure 9.8*, **process 1** stores the results of the calculation to shared memory, and **process 2** reads it from the segment. In the context of our previous example, the teacher and their assistants share their checking results in a shared paper. Threads, on the other hand, share the address space of the process because they run in the context of the process. While a process is a program, a thread is a function rather than a program. That said, a process must have at least one thread, which we call the thread of execution.

> **Note**
>
> A thread is the container of instructions of a program that is run in the system, while the process encapsulates the thread and provides resources for it.

Most of our interest lies in threads and their orchestration mechanisms. Let's take a closer look at them.

Threads

A **thread** is a section of code in the scope of a process that can be scheduled by the OS scheduler. While a process is the image of the running program, managing multi-process projects along with IPC is much harder and sometimes useless compared to projects leveraging **multithreading**. Programs deal with data and, usually, collections of data. Accessing, processing, and updating data is done by functions that are either the methods of objects or free functions composed together to achieve a result. In most projects, we deal with tens of thousands of functions and objects. Each function represents a bunch of instructions wrapped under a sensible name; these are created so that they can be invoked by other functions. Multithreading aims to run functions concurrently to achieve better performance.

For example, a program that calculates the sum of three different vectors and prints them calls the function calculating the sum for the first vector, then for the second vector, and finally, for the last one. It all happens sequentially. If the processing of a single vector takes A amount of time, then the program will run in 3A time. The following code demonstrates this example:

```
void process_vector(const std::vector<int> &vec)
{
// calculate the sum and print it
}
int main()
{
    std::vector<int> vec1{1, 2, 3, 4, 5};
    std::vector<int> vec2{6, 7, 8, 9, 10};
    std::vector<int> vec3{11, 12, 13, 14, 15};
    process_vector(vec1);
// takes A amount of time, process_vector(vec2); // takes A amount
of time, process_vector(vec3), and // takes A amount of time.
```

If there was a way to run the same function for three different vectors simultaneously, it would take just A amount of time for the whole program in the preceding example. Threads of execution, or just threads, are exact ways of running tasks concurrently. By tasks, we usually mean a function, although you should remember `std::packaged_task` as well. Again, concurrency shouldn't be confused with parallelism. When we speak about threads running concurrently, you should consider context switching for the process, as discussed previously. A similar principle applies to threads.

`std::packaged_task` is similar to `std::function`. It wraps a callable object – a function, lambda, function object, or bind expression. The difference with `std::packaged_task` is that it can be invoked asynchronously. More on this will be covered later in this chapter.

Each process has a single thread of execution, sometimes called the **main thread**. A process can have more than one thread, and that's when we call it multithreading. Threads run in almost the same way as processes. They also have context switching.

Threads run separately from each other, but they share most of the resources of a process because all of the threads belong to the process. The process occupies hardware and software resources such as CPU registers and memory segments, including its stack and heap. While a process doesn't share its stack or heap with other processes, its threads have to use the same resources that are occupied by the process. *Everything that happens in a thread's life happens within the process.*

However, threads don't share the stack. Each thread has its portion of the stack. The reason behind this segregation relies on the fact that a thread is just a function and the function itself should have access to the stack to manage the life cycle of its arguments and local variables. When we run the same function as two (or more) separately running threads, the runtime should somehow handle their boundaries. Although it's error-prone, you can pass a variable from one thread to another (either by value or by reference). Let's suppose that we started three threads by running the `process_vector()` function for the three vectors in the preceding example. Note that starting a thread means *copying* the underlying function somehow (its variables but not the instructions) and running it separately from any other thread. In this scenario, the same function will be copied as three different images, and each will run independently of the others. Hence, each should have its own stack. On the other hand, the heap is shared between threads. So, we arrive at the following:

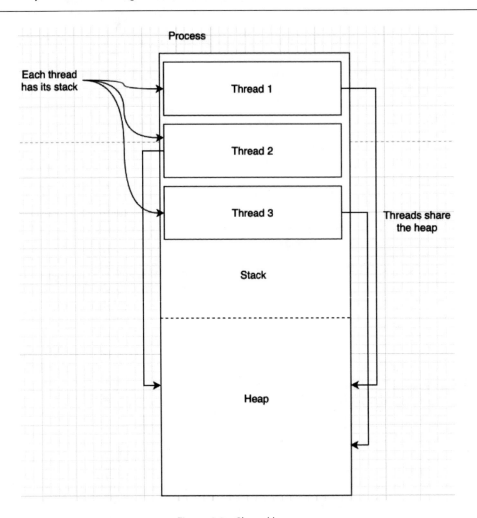

Figure 9.9 – Shared heap

As in the case of processes, threads running concurrently are not necessarily running in parallel. As shown in *Figure 9.9*, each thread gets a small portion of CPU time to be run and, again, there is an overhead regarding the switching from one thread to another. Each paused thread's state should be stored somewhere to be recovered later when resuming it. The internal structure of the CPU defines whether threads could truly run in parallel. The number of CPU cores defines the number of threads that can truly run in parallel.

> **Tip**
>
> The C++ thread library provides the `hardware_concurrency()` function to find out the number of threads that can truly run concurrently. You can refer to this number when designing concurrent code.

The following diagram depicts two CPUs with four cores each. Each core can run a thread independently of the other:

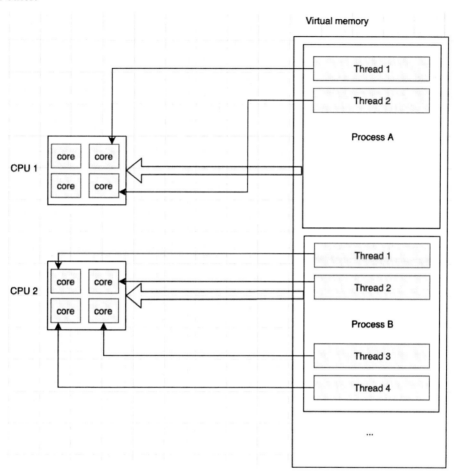

Figure 9.10 – Threads in multiple CPUs

Not only do two processes run in parallel but also their threads are run in parallel using the CPU cores. Now, how will the situation change if we have several threads but one single-core CPU? The result would be the same as what was illustrated earlier for processes. Look at the preceding diagram – it depicts how the CPU executes **Thread 1** for some time slice:

The currently active **Process A** has two threads that run concurrently. At each specified point in time, only one of the threads is executed. When the time slice is up for **Thread 1**, **Thread 2** is executed. The difference from the model we discussed for processes is that threads share the resources of the process, which leads to unnatural behavior if we aren't concerned with concurrent code design issues. Now, let's dive into C++ threading support and find out what issues arise when using multithreading.

Working with threads

When the C++ program starts – that is, the `main()` function starts its execution – you can create and launch new threads that will run concurrently with the main thread. To start a thread in C++, you should declare a thread object and pass it the function that you want to run concurrently to the main thread. The following code demonstrates declaring and starting a thread using `std::thread`, which is defined as follows:

```cpp
#include<thread>
#include <iostream>
void foo()
{
    std::cout << "Testing a thread in C++" << std::endl;
}
int main()
{
    std::thread test_thread{foo};
}
```

That's it. We can create a better example to show how two threads work concurrently. Let's say we print numbers in a loop concurrently to see which thread prints what:

```cpp
#include <thread>
#include <iostream>
void print_numbers_in_background()
{
    auto ix{0};
    // Attention: an infinite loop!
    while (true)
    {
        std::cout << "Background: " << ix++ << std::endl;
    }
}
int main()
{
    std::thread background{print_numbers_in_background};
    auto jx{0};
    while (jx < 1000000)
    {
        std::cout << "Main: " << jx++ << std::endl;
    }
}
```

The preceding example will print both outputs with the `Main:` and `Background:` prefixes mixed. An excerpt from the output might look like this:

```
. . .
Main: 90
Main: 91
Background: 149
Background: 150
Background: 151
Background: 152
Background: 153
Background:
Main: 92
Main: 93
. . .
```

Whenever the main thread finishes its work (printing to the screen one million times), the program wants to finish without waiting for the background thread to complete. This leads to program termination. Let's see how we should modify the previous example.

Waiting for threads

The thread class provides the `join()` function if you want to wait for it to finish. Here is a modified version of the previous example that waits for the background thread:

```
#include <thread>
#include <iostream>
void print_numbers_in_background()
{
    // code omitted for brevity
}
int main()
{
    std::thread background{print_numbers_in_background};
// the while loop omitted for brevity background.join();
}
```

As we discussed previously, the `thread` function is run as a separate entity independently from other threads – even the one that started it. It won't wait for the thread it has just started, and that's why you should explicitly tell the caller function to wait for it to finish. It is necessary to signal that the calling thread (the main thread) is waiting for the thread to finish before itself.

Although detaching a thread might seem natural, there are plenty of scenarios when we need to wait for the thread to finish. For example, we might pass `loc` to the caller variables for the running thread. In this case, we can't let the caller detach the thread as the caller might finish its work earlier than the thread started it. Let's illustrate this for the sake of clarity. *Thread 1* declares the `loc` variable and passes it to *Thread 2*, which has been started from *Thread 1*:

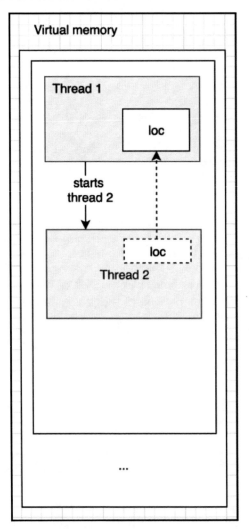

Figure 9.11 – Threads relationship

Passing the address of `loc` to *Thread 2* is error-prone if *Thread 1* doesn't join it. If *Thread 1* finishes its execution before *Thread 2*, then accessing `loc` by its address leads to an undefined behavior:

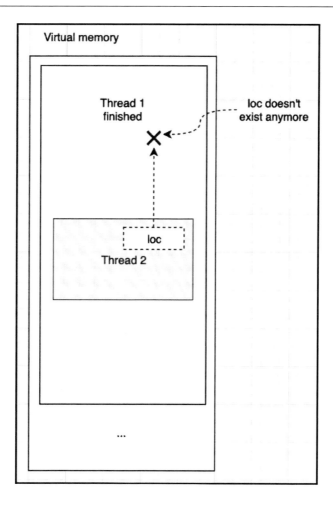

Figure 9.12 – Threads crush

There is no such object anymore, so the best that we can hope for is the program crashing. This will lead to unexpected behavior because the running thread won't have access to the caller's local variables anymore. You should either join or detach a thread.

We can pass any callable object to `std::thread`. The following example shows passing a lambda expression to the thread:

```
#include <iostream>
#include <thread>

int main()
{
```

```
    std::thread tl{[]
    {
        std::cout << "A lambda passed to the thread"; }};
    tl.join();
}
```

Furthermore, we can use callable objects as thread arguments. Take a look at the following code, which declare the `TestTask` class with the overridden `operator()` function:

```cpp
#include <thread>
class TestTask
{
public:
    TestTask() = default;
    void operator()()
    {
        state_++;
    }
private:
    int state_ = 0;
};
int main()
{
    std::thread t{TestTask()};
    t.join();
}
```

One of the advantages of a functor (the `TestTask` class with the overridden `operator()` function) is its ability to store state information. Functors are a beautiful implementation of the command design pattern; we will discuss them in *Chapter 11, Designing a Strategy Game Using Design Patterns*. Getting back to threads, let's move on to a new addition in the language that allows for better ways to join threads.

Using std::jthread

C++20 introduced a joinable thread, `std::jthread`. It provides the same interface as `std::thread`. This means we can replace all threads with `jthreads` in the code. It wraps `std::thread`, so it delegates down to the wrapped thread.

If the version of your compiler doesn't support `std::jthread`, you are free to go with the **Resource Acquisition Is Initialization** (**RAII**) idiom, which is perfectly applicable to threads. Take a look at the following code:

```cpp
class thread_raii
{
```

```
public:
    explicit thread_raii(std::thread &t)
        : thread_(std::move(t))
    {
    }
    ~thread_raii()
    {
        thread_.join();
    }
private:
    std::thread thread_;
};
void foo()
{
    std::cout << "Testing thread join";
}
int main()
{
    std::thread t{foo};
    thread_raii r{t};
    // will automatically join the thread
}
```

However, the preceding code lacks an additional check because a thread passed to the RAII class might have already been detached. To see whether the thread could be joined, we can use the joinable() function. This is how we should overwrite the thread_raii class:

```
class thread_raii
{
public:
    explicit thread_raii(std::thread &t)
    : thread_(std::move(t))
    {
    }
    ~thread_raii()
    {
        if (thread_.joinable())
        {
            thread_.join();
        }
    }
private:
    std::thread thread_;
};
```

First, the destructor tests whether the thread is joinable before calling the `join()` function. However, instead of dealing with idioms and being concerned about whether the thread has been joined already before joining it, we prefer using `std::jthread`. Here's how we can do that using the `TestTask` function we declared previously:

```
std::jthread jt{TestTask()};
```

That's it – there's no need to call `jt.join()` and a new cooperative interruptible feature out of the box that we use by incorporating `jthread`. We say that `jthread` is a cooperative interruptible because it provides the `request_stop()` function, which allows us to request the thread to stop. When this function is called, the thread is informed of the request, and it's up to the thread to respond appropriately. In the case of the `print_numbers_in_background` function, we could modify it to periodically check for the stop request using a loop and gracefully exit the thread's execution if the request has been made. Recall the example with the thread printing numbers in an infinite loop. We modified the main thread to wait for it, which leads to us waiting for it forever. Here's how we can modify the thread using `std::jthread` to leverage the `request_stop()` function:

```
int main()
{
    std::jthread background{print_numbers_in_background};
    auto jx{0};
    while (jx < 1000000)
    {
        std::cout << "Main: " << jx << std::endl;
    }
// The main thread is about to finish, so we request the
// background thread to stop
background.request_stop();
}
```

The `print_numbers_in_background()` function now receives a request and can behave accordingly. Now, let's learn how to pass arguments to the thread function.

Passing arguments to the thread function

The `std::thread` constructor takes arguments and forwards them to the underlying `thread` function. For example, to pass the 4 and 2 arguments to the `foo()` function, we will pass the arguments to the `std::thread` constructor:

```
void foo(int one, int two)
{ // do something
}
std::thread t{foo, 4, 2};
```

4 and 2 will be passed as the first and second arguments to the `foo()` function, respectively.

The following example illustrates passing an argument by reference:

```
class big_object
{
};
void make_changes(big_object &);
void error_prone()
{
    big_object b;
    std::jthread t{make_changes, b};
    // do something else
}
```

To understand why we named the function `error_prone`, we should know that the thread constructor copies the values passed to it and then passes them to the thread function with `rvalue` references. This is done so that it works with move-only types. So, it will try to call the `make_changes()` function with `rvalue`, which will fail to compile (you can't pass `rvalue` to a function that expects a non-constant reference). We need to wrap the arguments that need to be a reference in `std::ref`:

```
std::thread t{make_changes, std::ref(b)};
```

The preceding code emphasizes that the argument should be passed by reference. Working with threads requires being a little more attentive because there are many ways to get unexpected results or undefined behavior in the program. Let's see how we can manage threads to produce safer multithreaded applications.

Managing threads and sharing data

As discussed previously, executing threads involves pausing and resuming some of them if the number of threads exceeds the number of parallel running threads supported by the hardware. Besides that, creating a thread also has an overhead. One of the suggested practices to deal with having many threads in a project is using thread pools.

The idea of a thread pool lies in the concept of caching. We create and keep threads in a container to be used later. This container is called a pool. For example, the following vector represents a simple thread pool:

```
#include <thread>
#include <vector>
std::vector<std::thread> pool;
```

Whenever we need a new thread, instead of declaring the corresponding `std::thread` object, we use one already created in the pool. When we are done with the thread, we can push it back to the vector to use it later if necessary. This saves us some time when we're working with 10 or more threads. A proper example would be a web server.

A web server is a program that waits for incoming client connections and creates a separate connection for each client to be processed independently from others. A typical web server usually deals with thousands of clients at the same time. Each time a new connection is initiated with some client, the web server creates a new thread and handles the client requests. The following pseudocode demonstrates a simple implementation of a web server's incoming connection management:

```
void process_incoming_connections()
{
    if (new connection from client)
    {
        t = create_thread(); // potential overhead
        t.handle_requests(client);
    }
}
while (true)
{
    process_incoming_connections();
}
```

When using a thread pool, the preceding code will avoid creating a thread every time it needs to process a client request. Creating a new thread requires additional and rather expensive work from the OS. To save that time, we use a mechanism that omits creating new threads on each request. To make the pool even better, let's replace its container with a queue. Whenever we ask for a thread, the pool will return a free thread, and whenever we are done with a thread, we push it back to the pool. A simple design for a thread pool would look like this:

```
#include <queue>
#include <thread>
#include <mutex>
class ThreadPool
{
public:
    ThreadPool(int number_of_threads = 1000)
    {
        for (int ix = 0; ix < number_of_threads; ++ix)
        {
            pool_.push(std::thread());
        }
    }
    std::thread get_free_thread()
    {
```

```
    std::unique_lock<std::mutex> lock(mutex_)
    if (pool_.empty())
    {
        throw std::exception("no available thread");
    }
    auto t = std::move(pool_.front());
    pool_.pop();
    return t;
}
void push_thread(std::thread t)
{
    std::unique_lock<std::mutex> lock(mutex_)
    pool_.push(std::move(t));
}
private:
    std::queue<std::thread> pool_;
    std::mutex mutex_;
};
```

The constructor creates and pushes threads to the queue. In the following pseudocode, we replace the direct creation of a thread for client request processing with `ThreadPool`, which we looked at previously:

```
ThreadPool pool;
void process_incoming_connections()
{
    if (new connection from client)
    {
        auto t = pool.get_free_thread();
        t.handle_request(client);
    }
}
while (true)
{
    process_incoming_connections();
}
```

Supposing that the `handle_request()` function pushes the thread back to the pool when it's done, the pool behaves as a centralized store for connection threads. Though what's shown in the preceding snippet is far from being ready for production, it conveys the basic idea of using thread pools in intensive applications.

Sharing data

A race condition is something that programmers using multithreading are scared of and try to avoid as much as possible. Imagine two functions that work concurrently with the same data, as shown here:

```
int global = 0;
void inc()
{
global = global + 1;
}
...
std::thread t1{inc};
std::thread t2{inc};
```

To address the potential race condition arising from non-atomic operations on a shared variable, one effective approach is to protect the data using a mutex, which ensures exclusive access and prevents concurrent modifications by multiple threads.

A potential race condition is happening because t1 and t2 are modifying the same variable with more than one step. Any operation that is performed in a single thread-safe step is called an **atomic operation**. An atomic operation refers to an operation that is performed indivisibly, without interference from other concurrent operations. It guarantees that the operation is completed as a single thread-safe step, ensuring consistency and avoiding race conditions. In this case, incrementing the value of the variable is not an atomic operation, even if we use the increment operator. Atomic operations are essential in multithreaded programming to ensure data integrity when multiple threads access and modify shared data concurrently. Instead of using a mutex or other synchronization mechanisms to protect critical sections, atomic operations provide an alternative approach. They allow you to directly manipulate shared data without the need for explicit locking and unlocking, resulting in potentially higher performance and reduced contention between threads.

Protecting shared data using a mutex

To protect shared data, objects called **mutexes** are widely used. A mutex is an object that controls the running of a thread. Imagine threads in the same context as humans trying to find a way to work with data, one by one. When a thread locks a mutex, the other thread waits until it is done with the data and unlocks the mutex. The other thread then locks the mutex and starts working with data. The following code demonstrates how we can solve the problem of a race condition using a mutex:

```
#include <mutex>
...
std::mutex locker;
void inc()
{
    locker.lock();
```

```
        global = global + 1;
        locker.unlock();
    }
    ... std::thread t1{inc};
    std::thread t2{inc};
```

When `t1` starts executing `inc()`, it locks a mutex, which stops any other thread from accessing the global variable unless the original thread doesn't unlock the next thread.

C++17 introduced the `std::lock_guard` class, which provides us with a convenient way to guard a mutex and ensure that it has been unlocked properly. In the given code snippet, a `std::mutex` class named `locker` is declared as the synchronization primitive for protecting the shared data:

```
std::mutex locker;
void inc()
{
    std::lock_guard g(locker);
    global = global + 1;
}
```

The `inc()` function demonstrates the usage of `std::lock_guard`. When this function is called, a lock guard object, `g`, is created, with the mutex locker as its argument. The lock guard automatically locks the mutex upon its creation, ensuring that only one thread can access the critical section at a time.

While utilizing language-provided guards such as `std::lock_guard` can help mitigate race conditions, it is crucial to understand potential pitfalls that can arise when dealing with multithreaded applications, such as deadlocks.

Hence, if possible, it's always better to use language-provided guards.

Avoiding deadlocks

New problems arise with mutexes, such as **deadlocks**. A deadlock is a condition of multithreaded code when two or more threads lock a mutex and wait for the other to unlock another.

The most common piece of advice to avoid deadlocks is to always lock two or more mutexes in the same order. C++ provides the `std::lock()` function, which serves the same purpose.

The following code illustrates the `swap` function, which takes two arguments of the X type. Suppose that X has a member, `mt`, which is a mutex. The implementation of the `swap` function locks the mutex of the left object first, then locks the mutex of the right object:

```
void swap(X &left, X &right)
{
    std::lock(left.mt, right.mt);
    std::lock_guard<std::mutex> lock1(left.mt,
```

```
      std::adopt_lock);
   std::lock_guard<std::mutex> lock2(right.mt,
     std::adopt_lock);
   // do the actual swapping
}
```

To avoid deadlocks in general, avoid nested locks. That said, don't acquire a lock if you are already holding one. If this is not the case, then acquire locks in a fixed order. This fixed order will allow you to avoid deadlocks.

Designing concurrent code

Project complexity rises drastically when concurrency is introduced. It's much easier to deal with sequentially executing synchronous code compared to concurrent counterparts. Many systems avoid using multithreading at all by introducing event-driven development concepts, such as event loops. The point of using an event loop is to introduce a manageable approach to asynchronous programming. To take this concept further, imagine any application providing a **graphical user interface** (**GUI**). Whenever the user clicks on any GUI component, such as buttons, types in fields, or even moves the mouse, the application receives so-called events regarding the user action. Whether it's button_press, button_release, mouse_move, or any other event, it represents a piece of information for the application to use to react properly. A popular approach is to incorporate an event loop to queue any event that occurred during user interaction.

While the application is busy with its current task, the events produced by user actions are queued to be processed in the future. This processing involves calling handler functions attached to each event. They are called in the order they were put into the queue.

Introducing multithreading into the project brings additional complexity. You should now take care of race conditions and proper thread handling, maybe even using a thread pool to reuse thread objects. In sequentially executed code, you care for the code and only the code. When using multithreading, you now care a little bit more about how the very same code is executed. For example, a simple design pattern, such as the singleton, behaves differently in a multithreading environment. The classic implementation of a singleton looks like this:

```
class MySingleton
{
public:
    static MySingleton* get_instance() {
    if (instance_ == nullptr) {
    instance_ = new MySingleton();
}
return instance_;
}
// code omitted for brevity
```

```
private:
    static inline MySingleton* instance_ = nullptr;
};
```

The following code starts two threads, both using the `MySingleton` class:

```
void create_something_unique()
{
    MySingleton *inst = MySingleton::get_instance();
    // do something useful
}
void create_something_useful()
{
    MySingleton *anotherInst = MySingleton::get_instance();
    // do something unique
}
std::thread t1{create_something_unique};
std::thread t2{create_something_useful};
t1.join();
t2.join();
// some other code
```

The `t1` and `t2` threads both call the `get_instance()` static member function of the `MySingleton` class. `t1` and `t2` may both pass the check for the empty instance and both execute the new operator. We have a race condition here. The resource – in this case, the class instance – should be protected from such a scenario. Here's an obvious solution that uses a mutex:

```
class MySingleton
{
public:
    static MySingleton *get_instance()
    {
        std::lock_guard lg{mutex_};
        if (instance_ == nullptr)
        {
            instance_ = new MySingleton();
        }
        return instance_;
    }
// code omitted for brevity
private:
    static std::mutex mutex_;
    static MySingleton *instance_;
}
```

Using a mutex will solve this problem, but it will make the function work more slowly because each time a thread requests an instance, a mutex will be locked instead (which involves additional operations by the OS kernel). The proper solution would be using what is known as the **double-checked locking pattern**. Its basic idea is this:

1.   Lock the mutex after `instance_` check.

2.   Check `instance_` again after the mutex has been locked; another thread might have passed the first check and waited for the mutex to unlock.

See the following code for details:

```cpp
static MySingleton *get_instance()
{
    if (instance_ == nullptr)
    {
        std::lock_guard lg{mutex_};
        if (instance_ == nullptr)
        {
            instance_ = new MySingleton();
        }
    }
    return instance_;
}
```

Several threads may pass the first check and one of them will lock the mutex. Only one thread will make it to the new operator call. However, after unlocking the mutex, the threads that have passed the first check will try to lock it and create the instance. The second check is there to prevent this. The preceding code allows us to reduce the performance overhead of the synchronized code. The approach we provided here is one of the ways to prepare yourself for concurrent code design.

Concurrent code design is very much based on the capabilities of the language itself. The evolution of C++ is marvelous. In its earliest versions, it didn't have built-in support for multithreading. Now, it has a well-stocked thread library and the new C++20 standard provides us with even more powerful tools, such as coroutines.

Introducing coroutines

We discussed an example of asynchronous code execution when speaking about GUI applications. GUI components react to user actions by firing corresponding events, which are pushed into the event queue. This queue is then processed, one by one, by invoking the attached handler functions. This process happens in a loop; that's why we usually refer to the concept as the event loop.

Asynchronous systems are really useful in input/output (I/O) operations because any I/O operation blocks the execution at the point of an I/O call. For example, the following pseudocode reads a file from a directory and then prints a welcome message to the screen:

```
auto f = read_file("filename");
cout << "Welcome to the app!";
process_file_contents(f);
```

Attached to the synchronous execution pattern, we know that the `Welcome to the app!` message will only be printed after the `read_file()` function finishes executing. `process_file_contents()` will be invoked only after `cout` completes. When dealing with asynchronous code, all we know about code execution starts to behave like something unrecognizable. The following modified version of the preceding example uses the `read_file_async()` function to read the file contents asynchronously:

```
std::future<std::string> p = read_file_async("filename");
cout << "Welcome to the app!";
process_file_contents(p);
// we shouldn't be able to do this.
```

Considering `read_file_async()` is an asynchronous function, `Welcome to the app!` will be printed sooner than the file's contents. The very nature of asynchronous execution allows us to invoke functions to be executed in the background, which provides us with non-blocking **I/O**.

However, there is a slight change in the way we treat the return value of the function. If we deal with an asynchronous function, its return value is considered something called a **promise** or a **promise object**. This is the way the system notifies us when the asynchronous function has been completed. The promise object has three states:

- Pending

- Rejected

- Fulfilled

> **Note**
>
> A promise object is said to be fulfilled if the function is done and the result is ready to be processed. In the event of an error, the promise object will be in the rejected state. If the promise is not rejected or fulfilled, it is pending.

C++20 introduced coroutines as an addition to the classic asynchronous functions. Coroutines move the background execution of the code to the next level; they allow a function to be paused and resumed when necessary. Imagine a function that reads file contents and stops in the middle, passes the execution context to another function, and then continues reading the file to its end. So, before diving deeper, consider a coroutine as a function that can be as follows:

- Started

- Paused

- Resumed

- Finished

To make a function a coroutine, you can use the `co_await`, `co_yield`, or `co_return` keyword. `co_await` is a construct that tells the code to wait for asynchronously executing code. This means that the function can be suspended at that point and its execution can be resumed when a result is ready. For example, the following code requests an image from the network using a socket:

```
task<void> process_image()
{
    image i = co_await request_image("url");
    // do something useful with the image
}
```

Since the network request operation is also considered an I/O operation, it might block the execution of the code. To prevent blocking, we can use asynchronous calls. The line that uses `co_await` in the preceding example is a point where the function's execution could be suspended. In simpler words, when the execution reaches the line with `co_await`, the following happens:

1. It quits the function for a while (until there isn't ready data).

2. It continues executing from where it was before `process_image()` was called.

3. It comes back again to continue executing `process_image()` at the point where it left it.

To achieve this, a coroutine (the `process_image()` function is a coroutine) is not handled the way regular functions are handled in C++. One of the interesting or even surprising features of coroutines is that they are **stackless**. We know that functions can't live without the stack. That's where the function pushes its arguments and local variables before even executing its instructions. Coroutines, on the other hand, instead of pushing anything to the stack, save their state in the heap and recover it when resumed.

> **Tip**
> This is tricky because there are stackful coroutines as well. Stackful coroutines, also referred to as **fibers**, have a separate stack.

Coroutines are connected to callers. In the preceding example, the function that calls `sprocess_image()` transfers execution to the coroutine and is then paused by the coroutine (also known as **yielding**), which transfers the execution back to the caller. As we stated, the heap is used to store the state of the coroutine, but the actual function-specific data (arguments and local variables) are stored on the caller's stack. That's it – the coroutine is associated with an object that is stored on the caller function's stack. The coroutine lives as long as its object.

Coroutines might give the wrong impression of adding redundant complexity to the language, but their use cases are great in improving applications that use asynchronous I/O code (as in the preceding example) or lazy computations. That said, when we have to invent new patterns or introduce complexities into projects to handle, for instance, lazy computations, we can improve our experience by using coroutines in C++.

Please note that asynchronous I/O or lazy computations are just two examples of coroutine applications. There are many more out there.

Summary

In this chapter, we discussed the concept of concurrency and showed how it is different from parallelism. We learned about the difference between a process and a thread – the latter being of interest. Multithreading allows us to manage a program so that it's more efficient, though this also brings additional complexity. To handle data races, we can use synchronization primitives such as mutexes. A mutex is a way to lock the data used by one thread to avoid invalid behavior being produced by simultaneously accessing the same data from several threads.

We also covered the idea that an I/O operation is considered blocking and that asynchronous functions are one of the ways to make it non-blocking. Coroutines, as part of asynchronously executing code, were introduced in C++20.

Finally, we learned how to create and start a thread. More importantly, we learned how to manage data between threads. In the next chapter, we will dive into data structures that are used in concurrent environments.

Questions

Answer the following questions to test your knowledge of this chapter:

1. What is concurrency?
2. What is the difference between concurrency and parallelism?
3. What is a process?
4. What's the difference between a process and a thread?
5. Write code to start a thread.

6. How could you make the singleton pattern thread-safe?

7. Rewrite the `MySingleton` class so that it uses `std::shared_ptr` for the returned instance.

8. What are coroutines and what is the `co_await` keyword used for?

Further reading

To learn more about the topics that were covered in this chapter, take a look at the following resource:

- *Anthony Williams, C++ Concurrency in Action*: `https://www.amazon.com/C-Concurrency-Action-Anthony-Williams/dp/1617294691/`

10

Designing Concurrent Data Structures

In the previous chapter, we touched on the basics of concurrency and multithreading in C++. One of the biggest challenges in concurrent code design is properly handling data races. The concepts of thread synchronization and orchestration are not easy to grasp. However, they are essential. While we can use synchronization primitives such as mutexes in all places where data races may occur, that practice has costs and side effects, which must be considered.

A better way of designing concurrent code is to avoid locks at all costs. That would not only increase the performance of the application but also make it much safer than before. Easier said than done – lock-free programming is a challenging topic, which we will introduce in this chapter. In particular, we will go further into the fundamentals of designing lock-free algorithms and data structures. This is a complex topic being continuously researched by many outstanding developers. We will touch on the basics of lock-free programming, which will give you an idea of how to construct your code efficiently. After reading this chapter, you will be better able to picture problems with data races and acquire the basic knowledge needed to design concurrent algorithms and data structures. It might also be helpful for your general design skills to build fault-tolerant systems.

The following topics will be covered in this chapter:

- Understanding data races and lock-based solutions
- Using atomics in C++ code
- Designing lock-free data structures

Technical requirements

The g++ compiler with the -std=c++2a option is used to compile the examples in this chapter. You can find the source files used in this chapter at https://github.com/PacktPublishing/Expert-CPP.

Thread safety

Thread safety is a crucial idea in computer science and programming. In the current world, where applications can run in parallel both locally and remotely, being able to write code that multiple processes can execute simultaneously plays a crucial role in software development.

Imagine a C++ first-person platform game with functions that allow the player to perform actions such as moving and jumping, computer-generated characters that can attack the player, and a user interface that keeps the player updated with the most relevant information about the status of the game (i.e., points, health, etc.). In this context, all those functions must be thread-safe. If the functions are not thread-safe, the game can behave unpredictably. For example, the player could end up interacting with a piece of a computer-generated object that is not in that spot anymore, or they may see a status of their actions that is outdated or incorrect.

This example includes the main concerns regarding thread safety. The most likely cause of the player trying to interact with an object that is not there is known as a **race condition**. A race condition occurs when two processes, in this case, the player's movement and the computer updating their character's location, occur simultaneously. Given that both can't happen simultaneously, there needs to be a synchronization mechanism that determines how the character's location is updated. On top of causing immediate issues, race conditions can have longer-term side effects. One of those side effects is known as data corruption. Data corruption occurs when data is modified by multiple threads and left in a state that would not occur if the modifications happened sequentially. A synchronization mechanism can also help address this issue.

The solution to the problems mentioned involves implementing synchronization mechanisms. These mechanisms can have side effects and cause problems. The most common issues are deadlocks. The synchronization mechanism is implemented so that two or more processes may wait to access a resource forever. This usually happens when the synchronization mechanism consists of locking, and a resource user never unlocks it. On top of this, synchronization mechanisms add overhead to the execution of the program, which can cause performance problems and lead to the program running too slow for its expected use.

We can use a mechanism known as concurrent data structures to address the need for thread-safe operations to reduce the chances of causing one of the side effects mentioned. These data structures are implemented in a multi-threaded environment without manually implementing synchronization. This allows the structures to provide both thread safety and better performance. The most common concurrent data structures include Concurrent Queues, Concurrent Hash Tables, Concurrent Sets, and Concurrent Stacks.

Lock-based concurrent data structures

Lock-based concurrent data structures are a type of concurrent structure. They are called lock-based because they use synchronization-locking mechanisms such as mutexes to ensure that only one thread can access the underlying data.

A thread-safe singleton pattern

In the previous chapter, we discussed deadlocks and ways to avoid them. The last example we used was implementing a thread-safe singleton pattern. We will expand on that in this section. Imagine that we want to use a class for creating database connections. We will name that class `connection_manager`.

Here's a simple pattern implementation that tracks down the connections to the database. Keeping a separate connection whenever we need access to the database is not a good practice. Instead, we will re-use the existing connection to query the database from different parts of the program:

```cpp
#include <memory>

namespace db_utils {

class connection_manager {

private:
  static std::shared_ptr< connection_manager> instance_;

public:
  static std::shared_ptr<connection_manager> get_instance() {
    if (instance_ == nullptr) {
      instance_.reset(new connection_manager());
    }
    return instance_;
  }
}; // class connection_manager

std::shared_ptr<connection_manager> connection_manager::instance_ =
nullptr;

} // namespace db_utils
```

The goal of implementing the singleton pattern is to ensure that we only have one connection to the database that all threads use instead of having multiple connections. However, the implementation shown here is not thread-safe. To understand why, let's look at the following function:

```cpp
static std::shared_ptr<connection_manager> get_instance() {
  if (instance_ == nullptr) {
    instance_.reset(new connection_manager());
  }
  return instance_;
}
```

Let's imagine that `thread1` and `thread2` are running this function. One potential execution sequence is as follows:

Thread 1	Thread 2
→if (instance_ == nullptr) {	
→ instance_.reset(new ConnectionManager());	
→return instance_;	
	→if (instance_ == nullptr) {
	instance_.reset(new ConnectionManager());
	→return instance_;

The arrows indicate the lines of code that get executed in each thread. As we can see, Thread 1 will see no connection and create one, while Thread 2 will see a connection and re-use the existing one.

Now, let's look at the following execution sequence:

Thread 1	Thread 2
→if (instance_ == nullptr) {	
	→if (instance_ == nullptr) {
à instance_.reset(new ConnectionManager());	
→return instance_;	
	→ instance_.reset(new ConnectionManager());
	→return instance_;

As we can see, in this case, both Thread 1 and Thread 2 see the instance as null, and both proceed to create a connection. Each thread returns its connection. However, the connection created by Thread 1 will be lost as soon as Thread 1 stops using it, as the pointer to the connection held by the singleton class is now pointing to the connection created by Thread 2. Even worse than that, let's look at this sequence:

Thread 1	Thread 2
→if (instance_ == nullptr) {	
	→if (instance_ == nullptr) {
→ instance_.reset(new ConnectionManager());	
	→ instance_.reset(new ConnectionManager());
→return instance_;	
	→return instance_;

In this case, the connection generated by Thread 1 is leaked immediately after Thread 2. The preceding issue is that Thread 2 resets `instance_` after it has already been set. This is because even though we perceive `get_instance()` as a single operation, it consists of several instructions, each executed sequentially by a thread. The function shouldn't consist of more than one instruction for two threads so that they don't interfere with each other. When the operation consists of more than one instruction, data races appear. A solution to this problem is to use a synchronization primitive, such as a mutex. The following code modification uses a mutex and the double-checked locking pattern discussed in the previous chapter to solve this problem:

```
#include <memory>
#include <mutex>

namespace db_utils {

class connection_manager {

private:
  static std::shared_ptr<connection_manager> instance_;
  static std::mutex mutex_;

public:
  static std::shared_ptr<connection_manager> get_instance() {
    // lock the Mutex
    std::lock_guard lg { mutex_ };
    if (instance_ == nullptr) {
      instance_.reset(new connection_manager());
    }
    return instance_;
  }

}; // class connection_manager

std::shared_ptr<ConnectionManager> ConnectionManager::instance_ =
nullptr;
std::mutex ConnectionManager::mutex_;

} // namespace db_utils
```

Note the use of `std::lock_guard`. This class creates a mechanism that establishes a lock when the class is created and releases the lock when the class goes out of scope. This is very convenient to avoid leaving a Mutex locked.

Now, let's take a look at the scenarios from before with the mutex in place:

Thread 1	Thread 2
→`std::lock_guard lg { mutex_ };`	
à`if (instance_ == nullptr) {`	
→ `instance_.reset(new ConnectionManager());`	
→`return instance_;`	
	→`std::lock_guard lg { mutex_ };`
	→`if (instance_ == nullptr) {`
	`instance_.reset(new ConnectionManager());`
	→`return instance_;`

This scenario continues to work as before, with the overhead of locking and unlocking the mutex. This is an example of the extra cost of using synchronization mechanisms. The second scenario now looks like this:

Thread 1	Thread 2
→`std::lock_guard lg { mutex_ };`	
→`if (instance_ == nullptr) {`	→`std::lock_guard lg { mutex_ };`
→ `instance_.reset(new ConnectionManager());`	
→`return instance_;`	
	→`if (instance_ == nullptr) {`
	→ `instance_.reset(new ConnectionManager());`
	→`return instance_;`

Notice that Thread 2 has to stop once it tries to get the lock as Thread 1 has it. This prevents the problems mentioned in the previous parts. The third scenario also looks this way: Thread 2 always has to stop if Thread 1 has the lock.

As seen in the mutex running on the first scenario, the synchronization mechanism causes an overhead every time the connection is requested under this implementation. There is an optimization that solves that problem and looks as follows:

```
private:
  static std::shared_ptr<ConnectionManager> instance_;
  static std::mutex mutex_;
```

```
public:
  static std::shared_ptr<ConnectionManager> get_instance() {
    if (instance_ == nullptr) {
      // lock the Mutex
      std::lock_guard lg { mutex_ };
      if (instance_ == nullptr) {
        instance_.reset(new ConnectionManager());
      }
    }
    return instance_;
  }
}
```

As you can see in this code, the mutex is only acquired in the case in which it may be needed, that is, when the connection is currently `null`. Because this optimization requires checking twice the condition. It is called double-checked locking.

As a rule of thumb, when dealing with operations with multiple lines of code, we should always consider the possibility of those lines running in an interleaved way and see what could happen.

Synchronized counters

Another typical example of thread safety is the synchronized counter. That is a counter that multiple threads can use simultaneously to keep a common count. An example of the code is as follows:

```
#include <thread>
#include <iostream>
int counter = 0;
void foo() { counter++; }

int main() {
  std::thread A { foo };
  std::thread B { foo };
  std::thread C {[] { foo(); } };
  std::thread D {[] {
    for (int i = 0; i < 10; ++i) {
      foo();
    }
  }};
  std::cout << "Count: " << counter;
}
```

Note that when running this code, the output tends to be a random number, sometimes 3, sometimes 13, and sometimes a number in between. This issue is due to a combination of problems: thread safety and synchronization issues.

The thread safety issue is that even though the `counter++` operation seems to be thread-safe, however, it is not, as it is the combination of two operations:

```
counter = counter + 1
```

This can be read as follows (in pseudo-code):

```
temp = counter
temp = temp + 1
counter = temp
```

Let's analyze the execution of these by two threads:

Thread 1	Thread 2
àtemp = counter	
	→temp = counter
→temp = temp + 1	
	→temp = temp + 1
→counter = temp	
	→counter = temp

As we can see from this sequence, the end of the execution of the thread counter will be incremented only by one, even though it should have been incremented by two.

We can use the same technique as the singleton example and add a blocking mutex to solve this problem:

```
std::mutex m;
void foo(){
    std::lock_guard g{m};
    counter++;
}
```

Looking at the execution sequence from before, Thread 2 will be locked from adding to the counter until Thread 1 has finished adding, as seen here:

Thread 1	Thread 2
→std::lock_guard g{m};	
→temp = counter	→std::lock_guard g{m};
→temp = temp + 1	
→counter = temp	
	→temp = counter
	→temp = temp + 1
	→counter = temp

As we saw in these examples, the main drawback to locking is performance. Theoretically, we use threads to speed up program execution, specifically data processing. In the case of big collections of data, using multiple threads might increase the program's performance drastically. However, in a multi-threaded environment, we take care of concurrent access first because accessing the collection with multiple threads might lead to its corruption.

Concurrent stacks

In *Chapter 6, Digging into Data Structures and Algorithms in STL*, we learned about stacks. In this section, we will implement a thread-safe version of the Lock-Based Concurrent version of a stack using locks. A stack has two primary operations, push and pop. Both of them modify the state of the container. The stack is not a container itself; it's an adapter that wraps a container and provides an adapted interface to access it. We will wrap `std::stack` in a new class by incorporating thread safety. Besides constructors and destructors, `std::stack` offers the following functions:

Operation	Functionality
`top()`	Accesses the top element of the stack
`empty()`	Returns true if the stack is empty
`size()`	Returns the current size of the stack
`push()`	Inserts a new item into the stack (at the top)
`emplace()`	Constructs an element in place at the top of the stack
`pop()`	Removes the top element of the stack
`swap()`	Swaps the contents with another stack

We will focus on thread safety to simplify the implementation rather than making a powerful, full-featured stack. With this in mind, we will look at functions that modify the underlying data structure. These are the `push()` and `pop()` functions. These functions might corrupt the data structure if several threads try to execute them simultaneously. So, the following declaration is the class representing a thread-safe stack:

```cpp
#include <mutex>
#include <stack>
#include <memory>

template <typename T> class safe_stack {

private:
  std::stack<T> wrappee_;
  mutable std::mutex mutex_;

public:
  safe_stack();
```

```
    safe_stack(const safe_stack &other);
    void push(T value);
    std::shared_ptr<T> pop();


    bool empty() const;
};
```

We declared `Mutex_` as `mutable` because we locked it in the `empty() const` function. It's arguably a better design choice than removing the `const`-ness of `empty()`. However, you should know by now that using a mutable for any data member suggests we have made bad design choices. Anyway, the client code for `safe_stack` won't care much about the inner details of the realization; it doesn't even know that the stack uses a mutex to synchronize concurrent access.

Let's now look at the implementation of its member functions, along with a short description starting with the copy constructor:

```
template <typename T> safe_stack<T>::safe_stack(const safe_stack<T>
&other) {
  std::lock_guard<std::mutex> lock(other.mutex_);
  wrappee_ = other.wrappee_;
}
```

Note that this operation requires locking `Mutex` of the other stack. This ensures that the other stack's underlying data won't get modified while we make a copy of it.

Next, let's look at the implementation of the `push()` function. Similar to the previous one, we need to lock the mutex and push the data into the underlying stack:

```
template<typename T>
void safe_stack<T>::push(T value) {
    std::lock_guard<std::mutex> lock(mutex_);
    wrappee_.push(value);
}
```

Note that the remaining functions also similarly incorporate thread synchronization:

- Locking the mutex
- Performing the task
- Unlocking the mutex

This ensures that only one thread is accessing the data at any time.

> **Tip**
>
> If you are not a fan of typing long C++ type names such as `std::lock_guard<std::mutex>`, use the `using` keyword to make short aliases for types, for example, using `locker = std::lock_guard<std::mutex>;`.

Continuing with the implementations, we can now write the `pop()` function. We can implement it so that `pop()` directly returns the value at the top of the stack. We do this mainly because we don't want someone to access the top of the stack (with a reference) and then pop that data from within another thread. The implementation is as follows:

```
template<typename T>
std::shared_ptr<T> safe_stack<T>::pop() {
    std::lock_guard<std::mutex> lock(mutex_);
    if (wrappee_.empty()) {
        return nullptr;
    }
    else {
        return std::make_shared<T>(wrappee_.pop());
    }
}
```

In this section, we looked at mutex implementations of thread-safe structures, particularly thread-safe stacks. As we mentioned, adding mutexes to the code has performance consequences, as well as possibly causing unintended locks and deadlocks. In the next section, we'll discuss a solution to the problem, which is the use of lock-free concurrent structures.

Lock-free concurrent data structures

As mentioned in the previous sections, lock-based data structures have some drawbacks. Among them, the reduction in performance is caused by the need to check the synchronization structures and the possibility of introducing problems such as deadlocking. A possible solution to this problem is to use lock-free concurrent data structures.

Unlike lock-based functions, where one thread can block another, and both might wait for some condition before making progress, a lock-free state ensures progress is made by at least one of the threads. We say that algorithms and data structures using data synchronization primitives are blocking. That is, a thread is suspended until another thread acts. That means the thread can't progress until the block is removed (typically unlocking a mutex). Our interest lies in data structures and algorithms that don't use blocking functions. We call some of them lock-free, although we should make a distinction between the types of non-blocking algorithms and data structures.

Using atomic types

Earlier in this chapter, we introduced the use of multiple separate lines of code as one reason for data races. Whenever you have an operation with more than one instruction, those instructions may interleave when run by multiple parallel threads. Very few functions can be implemented without multiple instructions, so the solution to this problem must come from the language. In the case of C++, it provides atomic types.

First, let's understand why the word atomic is used. In general, we understand atomic to mean something that can't be broken down into smaller parts. That is, an atomic operation is an operation that can't be partially performed: either it's fully executed or it isn't. An example of an atomic operation is the assignment of an integer:

```
num = 37;
```

If two threads access this line of code, neither can encounter it partially executed. In other words, there are no gaps where other threads could interfere with this operation between assignments. Of course, the same statement might have a lot of gaps if num represents a complex object with a user-defined assignment operator. On the other hand, a non-atomic operation might end up being partially executed. As shown before, a way to deal with this problem is to use a mutex:

```
#include <mutex>

std::mutex mutex_;

void foo() {
  mutex_.lock();
  int a{41};
  int b{a + 1};
  mutex_.unlock();
}
```

> **Note**
>
> In Greek, *a* means *not,* and *tomo* means to *cut.* The word *atom* comes from the Greek *atomos,* which translates to *uncuttable.* Therefore, atomic means indivisible units. We use atomic types and operations to avoid gaps between instructions.

To simplify this process and reduce the need to add blocking mechanisms manually, C++ provides atomic types. An atomic type guarantees that all operations performed on them are also atomic. That means we can write thread-safe operations with atomic types.

The difference between an operation that uses an atomic type and a manual locking mechanism is that the first doesn't require specified mechanisms. That's a big help as it reduces the performance hits and possibilities for errors. In most cases, this is achieved by leveraging lower-level mechanisms to ensure the independent and atomic execution of instructions. However, atomic types might also use internal locking. All atomic types in the standard library expose the `is_lock_free()` function to ensure they don't use internal locking. The standard atomic types are defined in the `<atomic>` header.

The `obj.is_lock_free()` function returns `true` if operations on `obj` are done directly with atomic instructions, and it returns `false` if any means of internal locking is used.

> **Note**
>
> The only atomic type that doesn't have the `is_lock_free()` member function is `std::atomic_flag`. The operations of this type are required to be lock-free. It's a Boolean flag mainly used as a base to implement other lock-free types.

The implementation of lock-free mechanisms sometimes depends on the hardware. To check for this, the static `constexpr` function, `is_always_lock_free()`, returns `true` if the atomic type is lock-free for all supported hardware. The function is `constexpr`, so we can define whether the type is lock-free at compile time.

We use specializations for atomic types, for example, `std::atomic<long>`; however, you can refer to the following table for more convenient names for atomic types. The left-hand column of the table contains the atomic type, and the right-hand column contains its specialization:

Atomic type	Specialization
`atomic_bool`	`std::atomic<bool>`
`atomic_char`	`std::atomic<char>`
`atomic_schar`	`std::atomic<signed char>`
`atomic_uchar`	`std::atomic<unsigned char>`
`atomic_int`	`std::atomic<int>`
`atomic_uint`	`std::atomic<unsigned>`
`atomic_short`	`std::atomic<short>`
`atomic_ushort`	`std::atomic<unsigned short>`
`atomic_long`	`std::atomic<long>`
`atomic_ulong`	`std::atomic<unsigned long>`

`atomic_llong`	`std::atomic<long long>`
`atomic_ullong`	`std::atomic<unsigned long long>`
`atomic_char16_t`	`std::atomic<char16_t>`
`atomic_char32_t`	`std::atomic<char32_t>`
`atomic_wchar_t`	`std::atomic<wchar_t>`

The preceding table represents basic atomic types. The fundamental difference between regular and atomic types is the operations we can apply to them. Let's now discuss atomic operations in more detail.

Operations on atomic types

Recall that the primary goal of atomic types is to remove the opportunity for different threads to run separate instructions in incorrect orders. To achieve this, atomic types either eliminate gaps between instructions or provide operations that combine several instructions wrapped as a single instruction. The following are operations on atomic types.

Operation	Functionality
`load()`	Loads and returns the value of the atomic variable.
`store()`	Replaces the value of the atomic variable with the provided non-atomic argument.
`exchange()`	Stores a new value in the variable and returns the previous value.
`compare_exchange_weak()`	Performs compare and swap (CAS). Stores a new value in the variable if the variable currently contains a specific value. This operation is marked weak because it is not thread-safe.
`compare_exchange_strong()`	Implements the thread-safe version of CAS.
`wait()`	Waits for a change in the value of the variable.
`notify_one()`	Notifies one of the threads waiting that the variable has changed.
`notify_all()`	Notifies all threads that are waiting that the variable has changed.

Both `load()` and `store()` are similar to regular read and assign operations for non-atomic variables. Whenever we access the value of an object, we execute a read instruction. For example, see the following use of `int`:

```
#include <iostream>

void function() {
```

```
    int i = 1;
    std::cout << i;
}
```

It can be re-written using `atomic int` as follows:

```
#include <iostream>
#include <atomic>

void function() {
    std::atomic_int i;
    i.store(1);
    std::cout << i.load();
}
```

As we can see, even though both pieces of code achieve similar results, accessing atomic variables should be done through atomic operations. The following code shows the definitions of `load`, `store`, and `exchange` in the GCC compiler:

```
#include <atomic>

std::atomic<int> atomic_value{42};

int load_impl(std::atomic<int>* atomic_ptr) {
    int value;
    __asm__ __volatile__("movl %1, %0 ; lock; addl $0, %0"
                        : "=r"(value)
                        : "m"(*atomic_ptr));
    return value;
}

void store_impl(std::atomic<int>* atomic_ptr, int value) {
    __asm__ __volatile__("movl %1, %0 ; lock; addl $0, %0"
                        : "=m"(*atomic_ptr)
                        : "r"(value)
                        : "memory");
}
int exchange_impl(std::atomic<int>* atomic_ptr, int value) {
    __asm__ __volatile__("xchgl %0, %1"
                        : "=r"(value), "=m"(*atomic_ptr)
                        : "0"(value), "m"(*atomic_ptr)
                        : "memory"),
    return value;
}
```

As we can see, the implementations have to be written directly in assembly to avoid using lock operations. Similarly, here is the implementation of `exchange`:

```
int __sync_lock_test_and_set(std::atomic<int>* atomic_ptr, int value)
{
    __asm__ __volatile__("lock; xchg %0, %1"
                        : "=r"(value), "=m"(*atomic_ptr)
                        : "0"(value), "m"(*atomic_ptr)
                        : "memory");
    return value;
}

int exchange_impl(std::atomic<int>* atomic_ptr, int value) {
    int previous_value =
        __sync_lock_test_and_set(atomic_ptr, value);
    return previous_value;
}
```

The `compare_exchange_weak()` and `compare_exchange_strong()` functions work similarly. They compare the first argument (`expected_value`) with the atomic variable, and if they are equal, they replace the variable with the second argument (`target_value`). Otherwise, they atomically load the value into the first argument (that's why it is passed by reference). The difference between weak and robust exchanges is that `compare_exchange_weak()` can fail incorrectly (a spurious failure). That is, even when `expected_value` is equal to the underlying value, the function treats them as not equal. That's done because, on some platforms, it leads to increased performance.

The `wait()`, `notify_one()`, and `notify_all()` functions have been added since C++20. The `wait()` function blocks the thread until the value of the atomic object modifies. It takes an argument to compare with the value of the atomic object. If the values are equal, it blocks the thread. To manually unblock the thread, we can call `notify_one()` or `notify_all()`. The difference is that `notify_one()` unblocks at least one blocked operation, while `notify_all()` unblocks all such operations.

Lock-free stacks

A critical feature of a stack is ensuring that another thread can safely access values pushed by one thread. In a previous section, we implemented a lock-based stack that wrapped `std::stack`. A stack is not a real data structure but an adapter. Usually, when implementing a stack, we choose either a vector or a linked list as its underlying data structure. Let's look at an example of a lock-free stack based on a linked list. Pushing a new element into the stack involves creating a new list node, setting its next pointer to the current head node, and then setting the head node to point to the newly inserted node.

> **Note**
>
> If you are confused by the terms head or next pointer, revisit *Chapter 6, Digging into Data Structures and Algorithms in STL*, where we discussed linked lists in detail.

In a single-threaded context, the steps described are fine; however, if there is more than one thread modifying the stack, we should start worrying. Let's find the pitfalls of the push() operation. Here are the three main steps happening when a new element is pushed into the stack:

```
void push(T data) {
    node *new_elem = new node(data);
    new_elem->next_ = head_;
    head_ = new_elem;
}
```

In the first step, we declare the new node that will be inserted into the underlying linked list. The second step describes that we are inserting it at the start of the list – that's why the new node's next pointer points to head_. Finally, as the head_ pointer represents the starting point of the list, we should reset its value to indicate the newly added node, as done in *step 3*.

The node type is the internal structure used in the stack to represent a list node. Here's how it is defined:

```
#include <atomic>

template <typename T>
class lock_free_stack {
private:

struct node {
    T data_;
    node* next_;
    node(const T& data) : data_{ data } {}
};
node* head_;

std::atomic<std::shared_ptr<node>> top;

// The rest of the body is omitted for brevity
};
```

When looking at the code, we can see a race condition as shown in this table:

Thread 1	Thread 2
→ node *new_elem = new node(data);	
	→ node *new_elem = new node(data);
→ new_elem->next_ = head;	
→ head_ = new_elem;	
	→ new_elem->next_ = head;
	→ head_ = new_elem;

As you can see in the table, one thread at *step 2* sets the next pointer of the new element to point to head_. The other thread makes `head_` point to the other new element. This leads to data corruption. This race condition can be solved by using locking. However, in this case, we want to solve it in a non-locking way, so instead, we'll use an atomic type. The code then looks like this:

```cpp
#include <atomic>
#include <memory>

template <typename T>
class lock_free_stack {
private:
    struct node {
        T data_;
        std::shared_ptr<node> next_;

        node(T value) : data_(std::move(value)),
          next_(nullptr) {}
    };

    std::atomic<std::shared_ptr<node>> head_;
public:
    void push(T data) {
        std::shared_ptr<node> new_elem =
          std::make_shared<node>(data);

        new_elem->next_ = head_.load();
        while (!std::atomic_compare_exchange_weak(&head_,
          &new_elem->next_, new_elem)) {
            new_elem->next_ = head_.load();
        }
    }
};
```

We use `compare_exchange_weak()` to ensure that `head_` pointer has the same value as we stored in new_elem->next. If it is, we set it to new_elem. Once `compare_exchange_weak()` succeeds, we are sure the node has been successfully inserted into the list.

Now, we are accessing nodes using atomic operations. The atomic form of a pointer of type T – `std::atomic<shared_ptr<T>>` – provides the same interface. Besides that, `std::atomic<shared_ptr<T>>` provides a pointer to the `fetch_add()` and `fetch_sub()` arithmetic operations. They do atomic addition and subtraction on the stored address.

Finally, we will implement `pop()` to complete the implementation of the stack:

```cpp
std::shared_ptr<T> pop() {
    std::shared_ptr<node> old_head = head_.load();
```

```
        while (old_head &&
            !std::atomic_compare_exchange_weak(&head_,
            &old_head, old_head->next_)) {
            old_head = head_.load();
        }

        return (old_head ? std::make_shared<T>(
            std::move(old_head->data_)) : nullptr);
    }
```

We applied almost the same logic in the preceding code as with the push() function.

A lock-free queue

Similar to the way we implemented stack, we can implement a lock-free version of the queue using atomics:

```
#include <atomic>
#include <memory>
#include <iostream>

template<typename T>
class lock_free_queue {
private:
    struct node {
        T data;
        std::atomic<node*> next;
        node(const T& value): data(value), next(nullptr) {}
    };

    std::atomic<node*> head;
    std::atomic<node*> tail;

public:
    lock_free_queue(): head(new node(T())),
        tail(head.load()) {}

    void push(const T& value) {
        node* new_node = new node(value);
        node* old_tail = tail.exchange(new_node,
            std::memory_order_acq_rel);
        old_tail->next = new_node;
    }

    bool pop(T& value) {
```

```
            node* old_head = head.load(
              std::memory_order_relaxed);
            while (true) {
                node* next = old_head->next.load(
                  std::memory_order_acquire);
                if (!next) {
                    return false;
                }
                if (head.compare_exchange_weak(old_head, next,
                  std::memory_order_release)) {
                    value = next->data;
                    delete old_head;
                    return true;
                }
            }
        }
    }
};

int main() {
    lock_free_queue<int> q;
    q.push(1);
    q.push(2);
    q.push(3);

    int value;
    while (q.pop(value)) {
        std::cout << "Popped value: " << value
          << std::endl;
    }

    return 0;
}
```

A lock-free hashtable

We can also implement a lock-free hashtable as shown here:

```
#include <iostream>
#include <atomic>

template<typename K, typename V, std::size_t N>
class lock_free_hash_table {
private:
    struct Node {
        K key;
```

```cpp
        V value;
        Node* next;
        Node(const K& k, const V& v) : key(k), value(v),
          next(nullptr) {}
    };

    std::atomic<Node*> buckets[N];

public:
    lock_free_hash_table() {
        for (std::size_t i = 0; i < N; ++i) {
            buckets[i].store(nullptr);
        }
    }

    bool insert(const K& key, const V& value) {
        std::size_t hash = std::hash<K>()(key) % N;
        Node* newNode = new Node(key, value);
        while (true) {
            Node* head = buckets[hash].load();
            newNode->next = head;
            if (buckets[hash].compare_exchange_weak(head,
              newNode)) {
                return true;
            }
            // if compare_exchange_weak fails, head is
            // updated to the new value
            // we need to update the next pointer of
            // newNode and try again
            newNode->next = nullptr;
        }
    }

    bool find(const K& key, V& value) {
        std::size_t hash = std::hash<K>()(key) % N;
        Node* node = buckets[hash].load();
        while (node != nullptr) {
            if (node->key == key) {
                value = node->value;
                return true;
            }
            node = node->next;
        }
        return false;
    }
```

```
};

int main() {
    lock_free_hash_table<int, std::string, 100> hashTable;
    hashTable.insert(1, "one");
    hashTable.insert(2, "two");
    hashTable.insert(3, "three");

    std::string value;
    if (hashTable.find(2, value)) {
        std::cout << "Found value: " << value << std::endl;
    } else {
        std::cout << "Value not found." << std::endl;
    }

    return 0;
}
```

A lock-free set

Finally, we will take a look at a lock-free set:

```
#include <iostream>
#include <atomic>

template<typename T>
class lock_free_set {
private:
    struct Node {
        T value;
        Node* next;
        Node(const T& v) : value(v), next(nullptr) {}
    };

    std::atomic<Node*> head;

public:
    lock_free_set() : head(nullptr) {}

    bool insert(const T& value) {
        Node* newNode = new Node(value);
        while (true) {
            Node* curHead = head.load();
            newNode->next = curHead;
            if (head.compare_exchange_weak(curHead,
```

```
                newNode)) {
                    return true;
                }
                newNode->next = nullptr;
            }
        }

    bool contains(const T& value) {
        Node* curNode = head.load();
        while (curNode != nullptr) {
            if (curNode->value == value) {
                return true;
            }
            curNode = curNode->next;
        }
        return false;
    }
};

int main() {
    lock_free_set<int> set;
    set.insert(1);
    set.insert(2);
    set.insert(3);

    if (set.contains(2)) {
        std::cout << "Set contains 2." << std::endl;
    } else {
        std::cout << "Set does not contain 2."
            << std::endl;
    }

    return 0;
}
```

More operations on atomics

In the previous section, we used `std::atomic<>` on a pointer to a user-defined type. That is, we declared the following structure for the list node:

```
struct node {
    T data_;
    std::shared_ptr<node> next_;

    node(T value) : data_(std::move(value)),
```

```
            next_(nullptr) {}
    };
```

The `node` struct is a user-defined type. Although in the previous section, we instantiated `std::atomic<std::shared_ptr<node>>`, in the same way, we can instantiate `std::atomic<>` for almost any user-defined type, that is, `std::atomic<T>`. However, you should note that the interface of `std::atomic<T>` is limited to the following operations:

- `load()`
- `store()`
- `exchange()`
- `compare_exchange_weak()`
- `compare_exchange_strong()`
- `wait()`
- `notify_one()`
- `notify_all()`

On top of these, some operations are specifically available for atomics based on their underlying type.

`std::atomic<>` instantiated with an integral type (such as an integer or a pointer) has the following operations, along with the ones we listed previously:

- `fetch_add()`
- `fetch_sub()`
- `fetch_or()`
- `fetch_and()`
- `fetch_xor()`

On top of increment (`++`) and decrement (`--`), the following operators are also available: `+=`, `-=`, `|=`, `&=`, and `^=`.

Finally, there is a special atomic type called `atomic_flag` with two available operations:

- `clear()`
- `test_and_set()`

You should consider `std::atomic_flag` with atomic operations. The `clear()` function clears it by setting the flag to `false`, while `test_and_set()` changes the value to `true` and returns the previous value.

C++ 20 added more new member functions as indicated here:

- `test()` – atomically returns the value of the flag.
- `wait()` – blocks the thread until notified and the atomic value changes.
- `notify_one()` – notifies at least one thread waiting on the atomic object.
- `notify_all()` – notifies all threads blocked waiting on the atomic object.

Summary

In this chapter, we introduced a simple example of a stack design. There are more complex examples to research and follow. When we discussed designing a concurrent stack, we looked at two versions, one representing a lock-free stack. Unlike lock-based solutions, lock-free data structures and algorithms are the ultimate goals for programmers, as they provide mechanisms to prevent data races without synchronizing the resources.

We also introduced atomic types and operations, which you can use in your projects to ensure instructions are indivisible. If you remember to use atomic types when using multithreading, it is unnecessary to worry about synchronization. We strongly suggest you continue researching the topic and build more robust, complex lock-free data structures. In the next chapter, we will see how to design world-ready applications.

Questions

1. What is the advantage of checking whether the instance is null in the multi-threaded singleton implementation?
2. What is the purpose of using a mutex in implementing a lock-based stack's copy constructor?
3. What are atomic types, and what are their basic operations?
4. What operations do the `load()` and `store()` functions perform in atomic types?
5. What additional operations are supported on `std::atomic<int>` compared to `std::atomic<>`?

Further reading

- *Concurrent Patterns and Best Practices* by Atul Khot, at `https://www.packtpub.com/application-development/concurrent-pattern s-and-best-practices`
- *Mastering C++ Multithreading* by Maya Posch, at `https://www.packtpub.com/application-development/mastering-c-multithreading`

11

Designing World-Ready Applications

Using a programming language in production-ready projects is a new step in learning the language itself. Sometimes, the examples in this book may take a different approach than the equivalent version used in real-world programs. When theory meets practice is when you learn a language. C++ is not an exception. Learning syntax, solving book problems, and understanding examples in books are stepping stones toward creating real-world applications. However, in the real world, we face an extra set of challenges.

In this chapter, we will go over the basics of practical programming with C++. This will help you tackle real-world applications better. Complex projects require a lot of thinking and designing. Sometimes, programmers must completely rewrite a project and start from scratch because they have made bad design choices at the beginning of development. This chapter addresses some common design ideas that will help prevent errors and write world-ready applications.

The chapter will cover the following topics:

- Design patterns
- Applying design patterns
- Domain-driven design
- An example of a real-world project (an Amazon clone)

Technical requirements

The g++ compiler with the -std=c++2a option is used to compile the examples in this chapter. You can find the source files used in this chapter at https://github.com/PacktPublishing/Expert-C-2nd-edition.

Design patterns

Design patterns are a set of well-studied solutions to commonly occurring design situations. These patterns provide mechanisms to solve complex problems in a structured and reusable way. Design patterns were first introduced by Christopher Alexander, who was an architect and design theorist. In 1977, he published a book titled *A Pattern Language: Towns, Buildings, Construction*. His work was later adapted by programmers and developers to organize their work, which led to the creation of software design patterns. This eventually led to the publication of *Design Patterns: Elements of Reusable Object-Oriented Software* by the *Gang of Four*. The Gang of Four includes Erich Gamma from Eclipse, IBM, and Microsoft, Richard Helm from IBM, Ralph Johnson from Xerox, and John Vissides from IBM.

Design patterns are important in software design, as they provide a common language for designers to refer to their ideas and proposed solutions. Design patterns allow designers to use ideas already tried and produce reproducible code. Being able to do this reduces the time it takes to make code and the chances of the code having errors. Design patterns are categorized into creational, structural, and behavioral.

As the name suggests, creational design patterns are used during object creation. The most common creational patterns include Singleton, which ensures that only one instance of a class is created, and Factory, which allows for a superclass to create objects while allowing subclasses to change the type of the object being made.

Structural patterns center on ways to combine classes to create larger structures. This group includes the Adapter pattern, which allows incompatible classes to work together, and the Composite pattern, which allows objects to be combined in tree-shaped structures.

Behavioral patterns focus on the communication between objects and ways to delegate responsibilities. This group includes the Observer pattern, which allows for notifications from one object to others, and the Command pattern, which separates requests from actions and their execution.

As discussed, design patterns are an essential consideration during the design and implementation of software in a way that is maintainable and reliable.

Singleton

The Singleton pattern is a creational design pattern that guarantees that a class has only one instance across a system. That instance can then be used as a single point of access. Singleton is one of the most well-known and used design patterns.

Many times in a system, having only one instance of a class becomes necessary. This occurs, for example, when the class represents a resource of which there is only one instance – a device attached to the computer. In this scenario, having multiple instances of this class would lead to potential conflicts as they try to interact with the resource.

The Singleton pattern attempts to maintain this single instance by ensuring that only one class instance can be created and that any component using that `class` will be redirected to that instance. This is done in effect by making the `class` constructor private and using a `static` method to access the instance, as shown in the `Chapter11/ch11-1.cpp`.

In code, when the first request for an instance of `class` is made, the `getInstance` method creates a new instance. After that instance is created, all future calls to `getInstance` will return the existing class instance. In line with this, the constructor is made private to prevent others from creating an instance. The copy constructor and copy assignment operators are deleted to prevent an accidental copy from happening there.

The Singleton pattern can be beneficial. However, it has some drawbacks, such as introducing a global state that can make code harder to understand. Similarly, the implementation presented here is not thread-safe. A thread-safe implementation of Singleton does exist.

Factory

The Factory pattern is a creational design pattern that provides mechanisms to create an object without explicitly calling out the class of the object that needs to be created. This pattern is helpful in scenarios where the class of the object to be created is unknown until the code is executed or when the logic needed to create the object is complex, so the code should be abstracted into its own class.

A factory pattern consists of a `Creator` class, the class that creates the objects, and `Product` classes, which are the classes of the objects to be created. The `Creator` class provides mechanisms to create `Product` objects without specifying the class of the created object.

The factory patterns have many positive effects, such as reducing the coupling between classes and increasing flexibility and extensibility. This comes from the fact that `Product` classes can be added later without changing the code in the `Creator` class.

On top of this, the factory pattern is also helpful when the logic to create an object is complex, and encapsulating it in a separate class can simplify the process of modifying and maintaining that logic. This works especially well when complex calculations or external dependencies are present.

The code in `Chapter11/ch11-5.cpp` shows an implementation of the `Factory` pattern to create two types of objects, used to calculate the factorial of a number.

The `AbstractFactorial` class is the base class for all factorial implementations in this code. Recursive and iterative factorials are different implementations of the function. `FactorialFactory` is the `Factory` class, and it creates a class that calculates a factorial based on the parameter sent to the constructor – I for iterative and R for recursive.

While the factory pattern is an excellent tool to address the aforementioned situations, it also has some drawbacks. Those drawbacks include the following:

- Increasing code complexity, as the code's creation now requires multiple classes and methods

- Increasing the coupling, as client classes now need to know about the factory class
- Reducing performance by dynamically creating new objects that could have been created statically

Adapter

The Adapter pattern is a structural pattern used to convert an interface into another so that the interface user can still connect through it. This idea is analogous to that of an electrical adapter.

In software systems, especially legacy ones, it is common to see classes developed in the past that cannot be modified. These classes sometimes need to be used by newer pieces of software that require a different interface than the ones these classes provide. Given the impossibility of modifying the original class, the Adapter pattern can connect the class and the new client.

To help to solve any given problem, the adapter pattern has three components – the original interface, the target interface, and the adapter. The original interface is the interface provided by the class, the target interface is the interface that is expected, and the adapter is the intermediary between the two.

Adapters can be implemented in two ways – as a class and as an object. A class adapter inherits from both interfaces simultaneously, allowing the adapter to override the original interface. An object adapter contains an instance of the original class that can call the original interface as needed.

The code in `Chapter11/ch11-2.cpp` shows an implementation of a class adapter that adapts the `Adaptee::sum` function to the expected `TargetInterface::add` function:

As shown here, the adapter pattern can be used in situations where interfaces need to be adapted without permanent changes being made to the original interface. This problem appears when adapting legacy or third-party interfaces.

Composite

The Composite pattern is a structural design pattern where individual objects and groups of objects can be treated similarly. This pattern is useful when a hierarchy of objects and operations must consistently be performed over these objects. For example, this pattern can be observed when grouping objects in a drawing.

For example, the following diagram shows a hierarchy of objects – a rectangle is an object, group 1 contains a rectangle, and a triangle is another object. Group 2, which includes the previous group and the hexagon, is another object. All these objects have a common set of operations. If we operate group 2 (i.e., move or delete), that operation must be run on all objects inside the group.

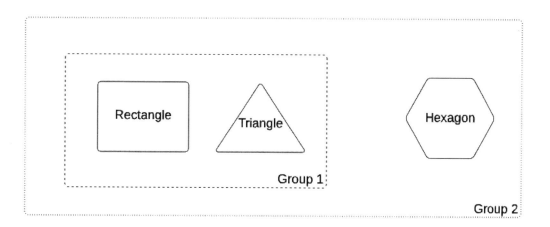

Figure 11.1 – A composite pattern example

As shown in the preceding diagram, the main idea for the composite pattern is to create nested composites of objects that can contain objects or composites of other objects. All the objects in this hierarchy share common interfaces. These interfaces allow the user to perform operations consistently across the whole composite.

The composite pattern can be used to improve flexibility and extensibility. The hierarchical representation allows us to add or remove objects without changing the rest of the code. This pattern can be particularly convenient when a hierarchy needs to be created at runtime.

Another positive effect of the composite pattern is to make code more readable and maintainable, as some of the code needed to perform the operations can be simplified and abstracted.

The code in `Chapter11/ch11-6.cpp` shows an implementation of the shape grouping composite pattern.

In this code, there are two shapes, `Rectangle` and `Triangle`, which can be composed in a `CompositeShape` that contains `Shapes`. The `CompositeShape` type also inherits from a shape, meaning that `CompositeShapes` can contain `CompositeShapes` inside of it.

Even though the composite pattern has many positive effects, it also has some drawbacks. These include potentially making code more complex if the objects in the hierarchy are very different, and hence, the hierarchy adds more complexity than it can simplify. Similarly, understanding how an individual object works can be harder if the code is too abstracted, as it may depend on how the hierarchy operates.

Observer

The Observer pattern is a behavioral design pattern that can establish a one-to-many connection among objects. When one object changes, all the other objects are notified of the change so that they can take action. This pattern is also known as Publish-Subscribe and Event-Listener.

When designing software, it is common to find dependencies where changes in one object require other objects to perform tasks. This configuration can be seen in scenarios such as the mouse moving on the screen, the user pressing a button, or a printer showing an error. The observer pattern shows a mechanism to create these relationships.

To achieve this goal, the observer pattern has two main kinds of participants – subject and multiple observers. The subject is the object that needs to be observed, and the observers are the objects that need to be notified.

Under the observer pattern, the subject keeps a collection of all the observers by providing mechanisms for the observers to add themselves to the collection or remove themselves from it. Once in the collection, the observer is notified when the subject state changes.

The code in `Chapter11/ch11-4.cpp` implements the observer pattern for a mouse move operation. In this code, `MouseMoveSubject` collects and notifies all the objects interested in being informed when the mouse is moved. `MouseEvent` includes the necessary information to understand the move that happened.

Command

The Command design pattern is a behavioral pattern that encapsulates requests so that the object that requests the operation is decoupled from the object that operates. This mechanism allows for the use of different request mechanisms, such as queues or logs, and supports operations that can be undone.

The command pattern has four components – `Command`, `Receiver`, `Invoker`, and `Client`. The `Command` component implements the request to act and serves as a common interface for all clients. `Receiver` implements the actual execution of the action. The Invoker creates and runs commands. The `Client` uses the invoker the `run` commands.

The code in `Chapter11/ch11-7.cpp` shows an example of the command pattern used to implement the open and save file operations. The command pattern can support implementations of features such as undo, as it can store a history of the executed commands. However, it can also have some drawbacks, including adding complexity to code if there are too many commands or they are already too complex.

Applying design patterns

Design patterns are powerful solutions that can be used to solve common software problems. Given the amount of study that has gone into them, they can produce scalable, maintainable, and flexible code. Despite this, they must be applied appropriately for the patterns to be useful. The following are some considerations to make sure that patterns are applied appropriately.

The problem

When applying a design pattern, it is essential to consider the problem at hand and all the requirements involved. Once understood, they must be contrasted with the patterns being considered and the problem they are designed to resolve. Patterns are general solutions, so they may or may not match the precise requirements of the problem at hand.

Trade-offs

Each pattern has a series of positive effects and also some drawbacks. When applying a pattern, it is important to consider the trade-offs related to code complexity and potential performance issues.

Systemwide impact

When considering patterns, it's essential to consider the local problem being solved and the higher-level system being implemented. Particularly, the pattern implementation should fit the overall design and not incorporate new complexities, new dependencies, or unnecessary dependencies, given that other dependencies are already needed in the system.

Users

The system user and the code being written should be considered when considering patterns. Patterns tend to make things simpler. However, they can make them more challenging if not implemented correctly. Understanding the level of complexity that users will face after implementing a pattern is essential when deciding which pattern to use or whether to use one at all.

Using domain-driven design

Domain-Driven Design (**DDD**) is an approach to building software that makes it reflect its real-life applications' domain structure. To be able to do this, the approach emphasizes learning about and understanding the domain in which the software will exist and using that knowledge to create the data structures and algorithms. Eric Evans describes this strategy in the book *Domain-Driven Design: Tackling Complexity in the Heart of Software*.

As mentioned, DDD focuses on understanding the domain. This understanding can come from multiple sources, the most common of which is working with domain experts. The theory is that once developers have a solid understanding of the domain, they can write software that supports the real-life scenarios required in the business. This understanding can, in turn, produce software that delivers more value to users and causes less dissatisfaction.

Another advantage of DDD is producing more modular, less coupled, and more cohesive code. That is because a thorough understanding of the domain can help develop structures that contain only the necessary information and are only connected with the objects relevant to its function.

As DDD requires interaction between domain experts and development teams, both groups must have a common language. This way, both experts and developers can reduce misunderstandings and streamline communications. These languages are known as **Domain Specific Languages** (**DSLs**). Under this language, concepts such as bounded context can be defined. Bounded contexts are areas of a domain that are self-contained and have their own rules and behaviors. This bounded context results in more modular codes that are easier to evolve and maintain over time.

DDD also puts focus on domain models. Domain models abstract the real-world concepts in a domain. Using these abstractions, it is possible to model the domain more straightforwardly so that experts and developers can understand it.

Even though DDD can be an excellent approach to software development, it can also be complex. The interactions between experts and developers can lead to more complex models than needed, resulting in more complex and challenging code maintenance. Given this, balancing the need to understand domain details with writing simpler, durable code over time is essential.

An example of a real-world project

To help ground the ideas of design patterns and DDD, we will discuss the implementation of an Amazon clone in C++.

Using DDD, the first step is to understand the domain. In this scenario, the domain is e-commerce. The idea, then, is to create a piece of software that models electronic commerce and supports users buying products online.

As previously mentioned, using bounded context is an essential component of DDD. In this case, we can identify the following ones – product management, order processing, and payment processing. Each has its own set of rules and constraints and can be considered a separate part of the system.

To begin with, let's focus on the product management domain. This area includes product listings, inventory tracking, and customer feedback processing. Those concepts can be modeled using product, inventory, and review.

Let's start with the product. Since product addition and removal happens frequently, we can model each product as a class. The code for this class is shown in `Chapter11/ch11-8.cpp`.

This code shows how products, electronics, and TV are valid representations of their corresponding entities in the domain – that is, each of them seems to have the appropriate properties. However, this is a problematic implementation, as it requires the creation of a new class each time a product is added, which involves recompilation and redeployment. Instead of this, we need to find a more extensible solution. Luckily, this is a well-known problem that has already been studied, and there is a design pattern that provides a solution – the builder design pattern. The following code shows a rewrite of the previous code using the builder pattern.

Let's start with the include as in the previous part:

```
#include <string>
#include <iostream>
```

The Product class has the name, description, price, and inventoryLevel properties:

```
class Product {
    private:
        std::string name;
        std::string description;
        double price;
        int inventoryLevel;
```

The constructor once again initializes the properties:

```
    public:
        // Constructor
        Product(std::string name, std::string description,
          double price, int inventoryLevel)
            : name(name), description(description),
            price(price), inventoryLevel(inventoryLevel) {}
```

The class has the corresponding getters and setters:

```
        // Getters
        std::string getName() {
            return name;
        }
        std::string getDescription() {
            return description;
        }
        double getPrice() {
            return price;
        }
        int getInventoryLevel() {
            return inventoryLevel;
        }
};
```

We now create the builder class that includes the necessary properties:

```
class ProductBuilder {
    private:
        std::string name;
        std::string description;
```

```
        double price;
        int inventoryLevel;
```

The product builder also contains getters and setters to manipulate those properties:

```cpp
    public:
        ProductBuilder() {}

        ProductBuilder& setName(std::string name) {
            this->name = name;
            return *this;
        }

        ProductBuilder& setDescription(std::string
          description) {
            this->description = description;
            return *this;
        }

        ProductBuilder& setPrice(double price) {
            this->price = price;
            return *this;
        }

        ProductBuilder& setInventoryLevel(int
          inventoryLevel) {
            this->inventoryLevel = inventoryLevel;
            return *this;
        }
```

Finally, the product builder contains a `build` method that takes the values in the product builder and uses them to create a product object:

```cpp
        Product build() {
            return Product(name, description, price,
              inventoryLevel);
        }
};
```

Now, let's try creating a product using the product builder. As shown in this code, the way to do that is to create a product builder, set all its properties, and then use the `build` method. Once built, the product can be used as usual:

```cpp
int main() {
    Product product = ProductBuilder()
```

```
        .setName("Samsung TV")
        .setDescription("A 55-inch 4K smart TV from
          Samsung.")
        .setPrice(899.99)
        .setInventoryLevel(10)
        .build();

    // Use the Product object
    std::cout << "Product name: " << product.getName() <<
      std::endl;
    std::cout << "Product description: " <<
      product.getDescription() << std::endl;
    std::cout << "Product price: $" << product.getPrice()
      << std::endl;
    std::cout << "Product inventory level: " <<
      product.getInventoryLevel() << std::endl;

    return 0;
}
```

As shown in the code, the builder pattern is designed to create complex objects using a step-by-step approach that allows for objects of different configurations and variations. In this case, the product object can have these multiple configurations.

Now that we have an implementation for the product, let's implement an inventory. Implementing an inventory in this system may seem simple, as an inventory is a collection of products and their availability. However, this can be complex in an e-commerce system, as multiple users interact with the system and may try to buy the same product. This problem is then a good candidate to use the observer pattern. In this case, we can use an observer to help update the inventory. The implementation of this is shown as follows.

Let's start with the necessary includes:

```
#include <string>
#include <vector>
#include <iostream>
#include <algorithm>
```

Then, we can create a class product that will be observed. We'll only declare it at this point and then implement it:

```
class Product;
```

Now that we have a product, we can create an `Observer` class that can be inherited by classes that need to observe the product. This class contains a single abstract method used to report updates on the product:

```cpp
class Observer {
public:
    virtual void update(Product* product) = 0;
protected:
    static std::vector<Product*> products;
};
std::vector<Product*> Observer::products;
```

Now, we can implement the product class, which has the usual properties (name, description, price, and inventory level) and a list of observers:

```cpp
class Product {
    private:
        std::string name;
        std::string description;
        double price;
        int inventoryLevel;
        std::vector<Observer*> observers;
```

The product class also includes a constructor to initialize the properties:

```cpp
    public:
        // Constructor
        Product(std::string name, std::string description,
          double price, int inventoryLevel) {
            this->name = name;
            this->description = description;
            this->price = price;
            this->inventoryLevel = inventoryLevel;
        }
```

There is also a series of getters and setters:

```cpp
        // Getters and setters
        std::string getName() {
            return name;
        }
        void setName(std::string name) {
            this->name = name;
        }
        std::string getDescription() {
```

```
                return description;
        }
        void setDescription(std::string description) {
            this->description = description;
        }
        double getPrice() {
            return price;
        }
        void setPrice(double price) {
            this->price = price;
        }
        int getInventoryLevel() {
            return inventoryLevel;
        }
        void setInventoryLevel(int inventoryLevel) {
            this->inventoryLevel = inventoryLevel;
            notify();
        }
```

And the operations attach and detach, allowing observers to list themselves as necessary updates and remove themselves from the list:

```
        //observer pattern methods
        void attach(Observer* observer) {
            observers.push_back(observer);
        }
        void detach(Observer* observer) {
            observers.erase(std::remove(observers.begin(),
              observers.end(), observer), observers.end());
        }
```

Finally, the product includes a notify function, called by the setters, and it reaches the update function on all the observers:

```
        void notify() {
            for (auto observer : observers) {
                observer->update(this);
            }
        }
};
```

Now, let's implement a couple of observers. The first one is Cart, which is defined as a class that inherits from the observer and contains a list of products:

```
  class Cart : public Observer {
```

```
    private:
        std::vector<Product*> products;
    public:
        void addProduct(Product* product) {
            products.push_back(product);
            product->attach(this);
        }
```

As the cart is an observer, it must implement the update method. In this case, the cart removes from itself any product that has become unavailable:

```
        void update(Product* product) {
            // Check if the product is in the cart and
            // remove it if inventory level reaches zero
            for (auto it = products.begin(); it !=
              products.end(); it++) {
                if ((*it) == product && product->
                  getInventoryLevel() == 0) {
                    products.erase(it);
                    break;
                }
            }
        }
        size_t size() {
            return products.size();
        }
};
```

We can also implement a second observer, the checkout. The checkout includes a list of products and the total price:

```
class Checkout : public Observer {
    private:
        double totalPrice;
        std::vector<Product*> products;
```

When a product is updated, the checkout recalculates the total price using the new prices of the products:

```
    public:
        void update(Product* product) {
            // Recalculate total price when inventory level
            // changes
            totalPrice = 0;
            // Loop through all products in the cart and
            // recalculate the total price
```

```
                    // This assumes that the cart is already
                    // populated with products
                    for (auto product : products) {
                        totalPrice += product->getPrice();
                    }
                }
            void addProduct(Product* product) {
                products.push_back(product);
                product->attach(this);
                update(product);
            }
            double getTotalPrice() {
                return totalPrice;
            }
    };
```

Now, let's try the code. Let's create some products:

```
int main() {
    // Create a product with an initial inventory level of
    // 10
    Product product = Product ("Samsung TV", "A 55-inch 4K
      smart TV from Samsung.", 899.99, 10);
```

Add the products to the cart and checkout:

```
    // Create a shopping cart and add the product to the
    // cart
    Cart cart = Cart();
    cart.addProduct(&product);

    // Create a checkout object and add it as an observer
    // of the product
    Checkout checkout = Checkout();
    product.attach(&checkout);
```

Finally, we can modify the product's inventory level to see the effect of the cart size and the total price:

```
    // Reduce the inventory level of the product and
    // observe the effect on the cart and checkout
    product.setInventoryLevel(9);
    std::cout << "Cart size: " << cart.size() << std::endl;
    std::cout << "Total price: $" <<
      checkout.getTotalPrice() << std::endl;
```

```
    // Reduce the inventory level of the product to zero
    // and observe the effect on the cart and checkout
    product.setInventoryLevel(0);
    std::cout << "Cart size: " << cart.size() << std::endl;
    std::cout << "Total price: $" <<
      checkout.getTotalPrice() << std::endl;

    return 0;
}
```

We'd have to continue going through the bounded context while implementing the Amazon clone. For example, we can focus on the context of orders, including address, payment, and status. The domain customer should include information, payment methods, and subscriptions. We can also look at domain payments, including payment methods such as credit cards, debit cards, and bank transfers. Each domain has its own complexities and is interesting to explore. Once the domains have been defined and the problems inherited from each are identified, we can consider using design patterns if the issues are well known.

Summary

Software development requires meticulous design. In this chapter, we looked at using design patterns to help us identify well-known solutions to already-studied problems. We looked at creational, structural, and behavioral patterns. Creational patterns allow us to create objects more flexibly. Structural designs help us organize things and classes, and behavioral patterns help us manage interactions between objects.

On top of this, we looked at a technique used to facilitate the design of our entities, known as DDD. This approach uses domain expertise to model the real-world entities needed to perform operations that a system needs to support. This knowledge is usually acquired by interacting with domain experts. DDD promotes the use of domain areas so that we can create less coupled and more cohesive entities.

Finally, we showed a partial implementation of an Amazon clone, where we used DDD to identify the entities involved. Then, we used design patterns to implement them in a consistent and extensible manner.

In the next chapter, we will continue working on incorporating design patterns in C++ programs, including game development, data-intensive applications, and enterprise applications.

Questions

1. What are the benefits of using design patterns?

2. What is the purpose of creational patterns?

3. What is the purpose of structural patterns?

4. What is the purpose of behavioral patterns?

5. What is the purpose of DDD?

6. Which entities would you identify in the bounded domain payment from the Amazon clone example?

7. Which pattern would you use to create different payment methods?

Further reading

For further information, refer to the following:

- *Object-Oriented Analysis and Design with Applications* by Grady Booch: `https://www.amazon.com/Object-Oriented-Analysis-Design-Applications-3rd/dp/ 020189551X/`

- *Design Patterns: Elements of Reusable Object-Oriented Software* by Erich Gamma et al: `https://www.amazon.com/Design-Patterns-Elements-Reusable-Object-Oriented/dp/0201633612/`

- *Code Complete: A Practical Handbook of Software Construction* by Steve McConnel: `https://www.amazon.com/Code-Complete-Practical-Handbook-Con struction/dp/0735619670/`

- *Domain-Driven Design: Tackling Complexity in the Heart of Software* by Eric Evans: `https://www.amazon.com/Domain-Driven-Design-Tackling- Complexity-Software/dp/0321125215/`

12

Incorporating Design Patterns in C++ Applications

As the previous chapter showed, design patterns are reusable solutions to common problems that developers encounter while developing software. Using design patterns, we can make code more modular, flexible, and easier to maintain. C++ is commonly used to develop high-performance applications. Incorporating design patterns can be beneficial, as they can help make coding more efficient, easier to maintain, and less error-prone.

Several design patterns can be used in C++ applications, including creational, structural, and behavioral. **Creational patterns** can be used to make code more efficient and flexible. **Structural patterns** can make coding more organized and better structured. **Behavioral patterns** can be used to implement communication between objects and classes.

In this chapter, we will analyze examples of using design patterns in C++ applications in the following areas:

- Design patterns in game development
- Design patterns in data-intensive applications
- Design patterns in enterprise applications

Technical requirements

The g++ compiler with the -std=c++2a option is used to compile the examples in this chapter. You can find the source files used in this chapter at https://github.com/PacktPublishing/Expert-C-2nd-edition/tree/main/Chapter12.

Design patterns in game development

This section will discuss common uses of design patterns in game development. We will explore using some of the patterns from the previous chapter, combined with the introduction of two new patterns (the **flyweight pattern** and the **state pattern**).

For this purpose, we'll implement a hybrid of an action and strategy game, where the player controls a group of agents fighting another group of agents. As part of this game, we will use the following patterns:

- **Singleton**: The singleton pattern can be used to manage global resources across the game, such as the game manager, the audio system, and the input system.

- **Factory pattern**: The factory pattern can create different game objects, such as agents, weapons, and ammunition.

- **Flyweight pattern**: The flyweight pattern can manage game assets, such as terrain, textures, and animation.

- **Observer pattern**: The observer pattern can be used to monitor player actions and produce the appropriate reactions from the remaining elements in the game.

- **State pattern**: The state pattern can be used to manage the different stages of the game and ensure that the elements respond appropriately. This includes menus, gameplay, and game-over screens.

The singleton pattern

Let's get started with the implementation of this game:

1. We'll start by using the singleton pattern to create a game manager. First, we'll add the include statements:

    ```
    #include <iostream>
    #include <unordered_map>
    ```

2. Then, we can implement the GameManager class with operations controlling the game. Most infrastructures in which the game will run (i.e., a PC or a console) keep the player in one game at a time, so it makes sense for GameManager to be a singleton. Given that, we can implement it as follows. We will declare GameManager as a private instance of itself and a private contractor:

    ```
    class GameManager {
    private:
        static GameManager* instance; // singleton
                                       // instance
        GameManager() {} // private constructor to prevent
                         // direct instantiation
    ```

3. We then implement the `getInstance` method as required by the singleton pattern:

```cpp
public:
    static GameManager* getInstance() {
        if (instance == nullptr) {
            instance = new GameManager(); // create
                // singleton instance if it doesn't exist
        }
        return instance;
    }
```

4. Finally, we add some functions to manipulate the game, such as start, pause, resume, and end:

```cpp
    void startGame() {
        std::cout << "Starting the game...\n";
    }

    void pauseGame() {
        std::cout << "Pausing the game...\n";
    }

    void resumeGame() {
        std::cout << "Resuming the game...\n";
    }

    void endGame() {
        std::cout << "Ending the game...\n";
    }
};
```

5. Now that the class is ready, we can try it by adding a `main` method that accesses the game manager and starts, pauses, resumes, and ends the game:

```cpp
GameManager* GameManager::instance = nullptr; // initialize
singleton instance to null
int main() {
    GameManager* gameManager =
        GameManager::getInstance(); // get singleton
                                    // instance
    gameManager->startGame(); // start the game
    gameManager->pauseGame(); // pause the game
    gameManager->resumeGame(); // resume the game
    gameManager->endGame(); // end the game

    return 0;
}
```

The execution of this code produces the following:

```
Starting the game...
Pausing the game...
Resuming the game...
Ending the game...
```

The factory pattern

We can now use the Factory pattern to create a weapon:

1. To do this, we will create a `Weapon` class that includes a name:

```cpp
class Weapon {
private:
    std::string name;
public:
    Weapon(std::string name) : name(name) {}

    void use() {
        std::cout << "Using " << name << "!\n";
    }
};
```

2. We then use a factory to create new weapons. Note that this is a very simplified version of the factory pattern, used this way to reduce the amount of code needed:

```cpp
class WeaponFactory {
public:
    static Weapon* createWeapon(std::string name) {
        return new Weapon(name);
    }
};
```

3. We can also modify the start of the game to include the creation of the weapon:

```cpp
void startGame() {
    std::cout << "Starting the game...\n";
    Weapon* weapon =
      WeaponFactory::createWeapon("Sword");
    weapon->use();
    delete weapon;
}
```

The execution of the program now looks as follows:

```
Starting the game...
Using Sword!
Pausing the game...
Resuming the game...
Ending the game...
```

We can now use the flyway pattern to create a target. Since this is a pattern we haven't discussed before, let's do so now before using it.

The flyway pattern

The **flyway pattern** is a structural design pattern used to minimize resource utilization and improve performance by sharing information among multiple objects. This is achieved by dividing the information of an object into two – the intrinsic (invariant) information, which is the same for all instances of the object, and the extrinsic (variable) information. This means that the intrinsic information is shared by all the objects, while the extrinsic information changes with each one.

A traditional example of the pattern is using characters in a word processing application. In this context, each character has two sets of properties. The intrinsic ones are the font, size, and color, and the extrinsic ones are the position in the document. In a game context, targets can be implemented using this pattern. Many properties of the targets, such as the shape and color, are shared among all targets, while each target's position is individual:

1. To implement this pattern, we can use a factory that stores all previous instances of the object with the same intrinsic properties and returns them, while creating new models when they don't exist. Let's look at an implementation in the context of our game.

   The `Target` class contains a property named `texture` that describes its texture:

   ```cpp
   class Target {
   private:
       std::string texture; // intrinsic state
   ```

2. The class also includes a constructor and a function that draws the target on the screen:

   ```cpp
   public:
       Target(std::string texture) : texture(texture) {}

       void draw(int x, int y) {
           std::cout << "Drawing target at (" << x << ",
             " << y << ") with texture: " << texture <<
             std::endl;
       }
   };
   ```

```
//Then a factory class includes a set of existing //targets for
use if needed.
class TargetFactory {
private:
    static std::unordered_map<std::string, Target*>
      targets; // flyweight pool
```

3. The factory then uses the texture as intrinsic and no properties as extrinsic. This means the first instance is returned if a second target with the same texture is requested. If no target with that texture exists, a new one is created:

```
public:
    static Target* getTarget(std::string texture) {
        if (targets.count(texture) == 0) {
          // check if target exists in pool
            targets[texture] = new Target(texture);
              // create new target if it doesn't exist
        }
        return targets[texture];
          // return existing or newly created target
    }
};
```

4. Finally, we initialize the pool as empty:

```
std::unordered_map<std::string, Target*> TargetFactory::targets
= {}; // initialize flyweight
                                    // pool
```

5. Now that we have the target, we can modify the Weapon class so that targets appear once the weapon is used:

```
void use() {
    Target* target =
      TargetFactory::getTarget("red");
    target->draw(10, 10);
    std::cout << "Using " << name << "!\n";
}
```

With all these modifications in place, the program produces the following output:

```
Starting the game...
Drawing target at (10, 10) with texture: red
Using Sword!
Pausing the game...
Resuming the game...
Ending the game...
```

As mentioned at the beginning of the section, we can continue adding patterns such as observer for the reactions and state for better state management. Other patterns can also be useful, depending on the requirements of the game.

Design patterns in data-intensive applications

This section will discuss the common uses of design patterns in data-intensive applications. We will not select patterns from those in the previous section to show as many patterns as possible. However, the patterns included in the previous section can have applications in data-intensive applications.

In this context, we will explore a data-intensive application that provides a real-time stock process and allows users to perform buy and sell operations. The system uses a database to store information and a C++ API to allow users to perform the operations. The performance of this application is key, as a small time difference can result in big monetary losses. To implement this application, we'll consider five design patterns:

- **Proxy pattern**: The proxy pattern can limit access to information. For example, it can be used to check users' permissions and return results based on the customer level of access, from live data to a proxy date with a time delay.

- **Decorator pattern**: The decorator pattern can add information to stock objects. This information can include historical performance, forecasting, currency exchanges, and so on.

- **Iterator pattern**: The iterator pattern can be used to iterate over sets of values and perform operations such as calculating the total value of a portfolio.

- **Adapter pattern**: The adapter pattern can provide a uniform interface for multiple sources of stock information – for example, the different interfaces provided by other markets and financial institutions.

- **Command pattern**: The command pattern can be used to encapsulate the steps needed to perform the buy and sell operations in a way that they can be undone as needed.

The proxy pattern

Let's start by using the proxy pattern to cache the stock and reduce the need to access the database. The proxy pattern is another new one, so let's discuss it before using it.

The **proxy pattern** is a structural pattern that provides a placeholder for another object to control access to it. The proxy, then, acts as an intermediary between the user of the object and the actual object. This allows the proxy to provide additional or restricted functionality compared to accessing the object directly.

This pattern helps protect objects that can be expensive or need to be protected from access. It can also be added to provide functionality, such as logging access to the object or caching the results. In the context of the stock application, we will use the proxy to cache and restrict access to the information. The following is a reference implementation:

1. Let's start by adding the necessary `include` statements:

```cpp
#include <iostream>
#include <string>
#include <unordered_map>
#include <vector>
```

2. Then, we define a class that contains the symbols and stock prices. This class will be an interface for any source providing stock information:

```cpp
// Subject Interface
class StockData {
public:
    virtual ~StockData() {}
    virtual std::vector<std::string> getSymbols() = 0;
    virtual float getPrice(const std::string& symbol)
      = 0;
};
```

3. Now that we have the interface, we will implement the real subject – in this case, a MySQL database that contains the live data, but it is expensive to access and can experience performance degradation if too many clients access it simultaneously:

```cpp
// Real Subject
class MySQLDatabase : public StockData {
```

This class contains the SQL operations needed to get the symbols available:

```cpp
public:
    std::vector<std::string> getSymbols() override {
        // Query the database for the list of symbols
        // here
        std::vector<std::string> symbols = {"AAPL", "MSFT"};
        return symbols;
    }
```

It also contains a method to return the price of a given symbol:

```cpp
    float getPrice(const std::string& symbol) override {
        // Query the database for the stock price here
        std::cout << "Retrieving stock price for " <<
        symbol << " from MySQL database" << std::endl;
        float price = 0.0f;
        // ...
```

```
        return price;
    }
};
```

4. Now that we have the interface and object we want to protect using a proxy, we can define it. The proxy implements the same interface as the main object, which is supposed to provide equivalent functionality:

    ```
    // Proxy
    class StockDataProxy : public StockData {
    ```

    This proxy will be used to cache the stock data, so it has a reference to the main object if the data is unavailable and a map to cache the already available data:

    ```
    private:
        StockData* realSubject;
        std::unordered_map<std::string, float> cache;

    public:
        StockDataProxy(StockData* realSubject) :
          realSubject(realSubject) {}
    ```

    For example, we'll assume that the symbols can be updated, so when a client requests all the symbols, the proxy returns them from the main object:

    ```
    std::vector<std::string> getSymbols() override {
        return realSubject->getSymbols();
    }
    ```

5. On the other hand, when the client requests price information, the proxy tries to access the information from the cache. If the price is present in the cache, the proxy returns it. If the information is not cached, it's retrieved from the main object and stored in the cache. A more advanced implementation of this idea would include an expiration for the cache to ensure the price information doesn't become stale. We won't add that here to simplify the code:

    ```
    float getPrice(const std::string& symbol) override {
        // Check if the stock price is in the cache
        auto it = cache.find(symbol);
        if (it != cache.end()) {
            std::cout << "Retrieving stock price for "
              << symbol << " from proxy cache" <<
              std::endl;
            return it->second;
        }

        // If the stock price is not in the cache,
        // forward the request to the real subject
    ```

```
        float price = realSubject->getPrice(symbol);
        cache[symbol] = price;   // Update the proxy
                                 // cache
        return price;
    }
};
```

6. Now that we have all the pieces in place, we can use the proxy to obtain the information needed:

```
// Client
int main() {
    StockData* stockData = new StockDataProxy(new
      MySQLDatabase());

    // Retrieve the price of MSFT twice
    std::cout << "Price of MSFT: " << stockData->
      getPrice("MSFT") << std::endl;
    std::cout << "Price of MSFT: " << stockData->
      getPrice("MSFT") << std::endl;

    delete stockData;
    return 0;
}
```

This program should return the following:

```
Price of MSFT: Retrieving stock price for MSFT from MySQL
database
0
Price of MSFT: Retrieving stock price for MSFT from proxy cache
0
```

As shown in the output, the first time the client requests the price for MSFT, it's returned from the database, and the second time, it's returned from the cache in the proxy.

Let's move on to the next pattern.

The decorator pattern

In this example, we will use the decorator pattern to provide stock information in euros instead of dollars. Before implementing it, let's discuss the decorator pattern.

The **decorator pattern** is a structural design pattern used to dynamically extend the functionality of objects without the need to modify the original code. This causes the objects to acquire extra behaviors at runtime. To achieve this, a decorator class is created. The decorator wraps the original and adds the new functionality while delegating the functions that the original object can perform back to it. Let's implement this in the context of the stock application:

1. As usual, let's start with the `include` statements:

```cpp
#include <iostream>
#include <string>
```

2. We will reuse the previous part's simplified version of the `StockPrice` interface. This interface now allows for the return of a stock price:

```cpp
// Component Interface
class StockPrice {
public:
    virtual ~StockPrice() {}
    virtual float getPrice(const std::string& symbol)
      = 0;
};
```

3. For this example, we'll return the prices directly instead of simulating access from a database to get an actual number of the given stocks:

```cpp
// Concrete Component
class StockPriceData : public StockPrice {
public:
    float getPrice(const std::string& symbol) override {
        // Get the stock price from a data store or
        // web service here
        float price = 0.0f;
        if (symbol == "AAPL") {
            price = 134.16f;
        } else if (symbol == "MSFT") {
            price = 252.46f;
        } else if (symbol == "GOOG") {
            price = 2362.01f;
        }
        return price;
    }
};
```

4. Now, let's implement the `ExchangeRate` interface. This interface will represent objects that can return the exchange rate between two currencies:

```cpp
// Component Interface
class ExchangeRate {
public:
```

```
    virtual ~ExchangeRate() {}
    virtual float getRate(const std::string&
    fromCurrency, const std::string& toCurrency) = 0;
};
```

5. We can create a class that implements the exchange rate functionality with that interface. To simplify the code, we will hardcode an exchange rate of 1.5. A full implementation would consider the from and to currencies and use a service to obtain the exchange rate:

```
// Concrete Component
class ExchangeRateData : public ExchangeRate {
public:
    float getRate(const std::string& fromCurrency,
        const std::string& toCurrency) override {
        // Query the external API for the exchange
        // rate here
        std::cout << "Retrieving exchange rate for "
            << fromCurrency << " to " << toCurrency <<
            " from external API" << std::endl;
        float rate = 1.5f;
        // ...
        return rate;
    }
};
```

6. We have the functionality now, so we can obtain the stock price and exchange rate. Using a decorator, we can augment the stock price calculation to include exchange rates. The decorator inherits from StockPrice, as it implements the ability to return a stock price when given a symbol:

```
// Decorator
class StockPriceDecorator : public StockPrice {
```

7. The decorator includes an instance of the original stock price calculator, as it still needs to use it to obtain the prices:

```
protected:
    StockPrice* component;

public:
    StockPriceDecorator(StockPrice* component) :
        component(component) {}

    float getPrice(const std::string& symbol) override {
        return component->getPrice(symbol);
```

```
        }
    };
```

8. With the decorator interface available, we can create a concrete implementation that inherits from the decorator (and, hence, also from `StockPrice`):

```
// Concrete Decorator
class StockPriceExchangeRateConverter : public
StockPriceDecorator {
```

9. When calculating the stock price, the decorator uses the main object combined with the exchange rate calculator and augments the result, returning the value in euros instead of dollars:

```
public:
    StockPriceExchangeRateConverter(StockPrice*
    component, ExchangeRate* exchangeRate)
        : StockPriceDecorator(component),
          exchangeRate(exchangeRate) {}

    float getPrice(const std::string& symbol) override {
        float price = component->getPrice(symbol);
        float rate = exchangeRate->getRate("USD",
          "EUR"); // Convert to EUR
        float convertedPrice = price * rate;
        return convertedPrice;
    }

private:
    ExchangeRate* exchangeRate;
};
```

10. With all the pieces in place, we can now run the code to obtain the price of AAPL and MSFT in euros:

```
int main() {
    StockPrice* stockPrice = new
      StockPriceExchangeRateConverter(new
      StockPriceData(), new ExchangeRateData());

    std::cout << "Price of AAPL in EUR: " <<
      stockPrice->getPrice("AAPL") << std::endl;
    std::cout << "Price of MSFT in EUR: " <<
      stockPrice->getPrice("MSFT") << std::endl;

    delete stockPrice;
```

```
      return 0;
}
```

This code returns the following:

```
Retrieving exchange rate for USD to EUR from external API
Price of AAPL in EUR: 201.24

Retrieving exchange rate for USD to EUR from external API
Price of MSFT in EUR: 378.69
```

This, as expected, is the stock prices in euros.

The iterator pattern

Finally, we'll show an example of using the iterator pattern in the app. The **iterator pattern** is a behavioral design pattern that can access collection elements without exposing the underlying mechanism to obtain the values. This means that the transversal is separated from the implementation of the data storage, allowing for different transversal methods to be used on the same collection. In the context of the stocks app, we could combine the stock price between cached and not cached data, or return the data by combining different sources, such as markets. To simplify the implementation, we will represent the stocks in an array to focus the code on the iterator pattern. The code for this implementation can be found in `Chapter12/Iterator.cpp` on GitHub.

This code outputs the following:

```
Price of AAPL: 134.16
Price of MSFT: 252.46
Price of GOOG: 2362.01
```

This is the list of stocks and prices stored in the underlying structure.

Design patterns in enterprise applications

This section will discuss common uses of design patterns in enterprise applications. We will again explore different patterns to those mentioned before, even though those patterns can also have applications in this domain. For this section, we'll use a **Customer Relationship Management** (**CRM**) application to create and manage user accounts, as a driving example. In this context, let's consider the following five patterns:

- **Service-Oriented Architecture** (**SOA**): The SOA pattern separates responsibilities for different tasks. Each task is implemented by an independent, reusable object that is easier to deploy and reuse.

- **Dependency Injection (DI)**: The DI pattern can manage object dependencies. Objects are created using a container that can inject dependencies and manage their life cycle, making it easier to orchestrate complex operations and test complex systems.

- **Model-View-Controller (MVC)**: The MVC pattern can be used to separate the data layers (model), the user interface (view), and the management of inputs and outputs (controller).

- **Event-Driven Architecture (EDA)**: The EDA pattern can manage customer creation or deletion events. These events are used by different systems that need to take action based on the actual event. This pattern allows for looser coupling and more effortless scalability.

- **Repository**: The repository pattern can be used to encapsulate access to data. This allows an application to access data without being tied to a particular data source or technology.

SOA

This pattern is more complex and requires multiple components to be implemented, making them hard to represent in simple code. For that reason, we'll use one example in this section, which can be found in `Chapter12/SOA.cpp`.

The output of this program is as follows:

```
Customer Account for johndoe@example.com
```

Note how all the operations in this application are independent of each other. Each service is loosely coupled, which means they can be used by other applications as needed.

Summary

In this chapter, we discussed the application of design patterns to three main scenarios – games, data-intensive applications, and enterprise applications. As mentioned in the previous chapter, design patterns play a key role in performant, scalable applications that will be easy to modify in the future. As we saw in the different sections, some patterns are used in some areas more than others, and some require more complex implementations than others.

Given the extensive number of patterns and situations that can apply, we studied the application of eight patterns to eight different scenarios across the three domains. As you continue learning about patterns and domains, consider reviewing how patterns can apply to those.

In the next chapter, we will move to a new aspect of software development – networking and security. There, we will discuss ways to make your program work across different computers and how to write applications that keep information safe and systems protected from malicious actors.

Questions

1. What design patterns can be used in games?

2. What design patterns can be used in data-intensive applications?

3. What design patterns can be used in enterprise applications?

4. How can the flyweight pattern be used to reduce resource consumption?

5. How can the proxy pattern be used to cache data?

6. How can the decorator pattern be used to augment the functionality of an object?

7. What is the purpose of **SOA**?

8. What are the components of the **MVC** pattern?

Further reading

For further information, refer to the following:

- *Object-Oriented Analysis and Design with Applications* by Grady Booch: `https://www.amazon.com/Object-Oriented-Analysis-Design-Applications-3rd/dp/020189551X/`

- *Design Patterns: Elements of Reusable Object-Oriented Software* by Erich Gamma et al: `https://www.amazon.com/Design-Patterns-Elements-Reusable-Object-Oriented/dp/0201633612/`

- *Code Complete: A Practical Handbook of Software Construction* by Steve McConnel: `https://www.amazon.com/Code-Complete-Practical-Handbook-Construction/dp/0735619670/`

- *Domain-Driven Design: Tackling Complexity in the Heart of Software* by Eric Evans: `https://www.amazon.com/Domain-Driven-Design-Tackling-Complexity-Software/dp/0321125215/`

13

Networking and Security

Network programming continues to become more and more popular. Most computers are connected to the internet, and more and more applications now rely on being connected. From simple program updates that might require an internet connection to applications that depend on a stable internet connection, network programming is necessary for application development.

Designing a network application is an excellent addition to your skillset as a programmer. This chapter will discuss the standard networking extension and see what is needed to implement networking-supported programs. We will focus on the main principles of networking and the protocols driving communication between devices.

Once an application uses a network, one of the significant challenges developers face is keeping the application secure. Whether it's related to the input data being processed or coding with proven patterns and practices, the application's security must be the top priority. This chapter will also visit the techniques and best practices used to write secure C++ programs.

We will cover the following topics in this chapter:

- Introduction to networks, the OSI model, and network programming using sockets
- Understanding network protocols
- Designing an echo server
- Securing applications
- Securing network applications

Technical requirements

The g++ compiler with the -std=c++2a option is used to compile the examples in this chapter. You can find the source files used in this chapter at the following GitHub repository: https://github.com/PacktPublishing/Expert-C-2nd-edition/tree/main/Chapter13

Introduction to networks, the OSI model, and network programming using sockets

Two or more computers can interact using networks. For example, computers connect to the internet using a hardware component called a network adapter or a **network interface controller** (**NIC**). The operating system installed on the computer provides drivers to work with the network adapter—that is, to support network communications. The computer must have a network adapter installed with an OS that supports the networking stack.

By *stack*, we mean the layers of modifications the data goes through when traveling from one computer to another. For example, opening a website on a browser renders data gathered through the network. That data is received as a sequence of zeros and ones and then transformed into a more intelligible form for the web browser. Layering is essential in networking. Network communication as we know it today consists of several layers conforming to the **Open Systems Interconnection** (**OSI**) model we'll discuss here. The NIC is a hardware component that supports the physical and data link layers of the OSI model.

The OSI model

The OSI model aims to standardize communication functions between various devices that differ in structure and organization. These standards are needed for both hardware and software. For example, a smartphone using an Intel CPU running on Android differs from a MacBook computer running on macOS. The difference is not the names and companies behind the aforementioned products but the structure and organization of hardware and software. A set of standardized protocols and intercommunication functions is proposed as the OSI model to account for differences in network communication. The layers that we mentioned earlier are presented here:

- Application layer
- Presentation layer
- Session layer
- Transport layer
- Network layer
- Data-link layer
- Physical layer

A more simplified model includes the following four layers:

- **Application**: This processes the details of the particular application
- **Transport**: This provides data transmission between two hosts
- **Network**: This handles the transfer of packets around the network

- **Link**: This includes the device driver in the operating system and the network adapter inside the computer

The link (or data-link) layer consists of the device driver in the operating system and the network adapter in the computer.

Suppose you use a desktop messaging application such as Skype or Telegram to understand these layers. When you type in a message and hit the **Send** button, the message goes through the network to its destination. In this scenario, let's suppose you are sending a text message to your friend with the same application installed on their computer. This process might seem simple from a high-level perspective, but it is sophisticated, and even the most straightforward message undergoes many transformations before reaching its destination. First, when you hit the **Send** button, the text message gets converted into binary form. The network adapter operates with binaries. Its basic function is to send and receive binary data through the medium. Besides the actual data sent over the network, the network adapter should know the destination address of the data.

The destination address is one of many properties appended to user data. By user data, we mean the text you typed and sent to your friend. The destination address is the unique address of your friend's computer. The typed text is packaged with the destination address and other information necessary to be sent to its target.

Your friend's computer (including the network adapter, OS, and messaging application) receives and unpackages the data. The messaging application renders the text in that package on the screen.

Almost every OSI layer mentioned at the beginning of this chapter adds its specific header to the data sent over the network. The following diagram depicts how the data from the application layer gets stacked with headers before it's moved to its destination:

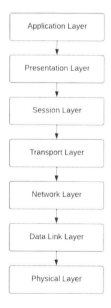

Figure 13.1 – OSI model

Look at the first segment (the application layer) in the preceding diagram. The data is the text you've typed into the messaging application to send to your friend. The data is packaged with headers specific to each OSI model layer in each layer, down to the physical layer. On the other side, the computer receives and retrieves the packaged data. Each layer removes the header specific to that layer and moves the rest of the package to the next layer. Finally, the data reaches your friend's messaging application.

As programmers, we are mostly concerned with writing applications that can send and receive data over a network without delving into the details of layers. However, we need a minimal understanding of how layers augment higher-level data with headers. Let's learn how a network application works in practice.

Network applications under the hood

A network application on a device communicates with other applications installed on different devices through the network. In this chapter, we'll discuss applications working together through the internet. A high-level overview of this communication can be seen in the following diagram:

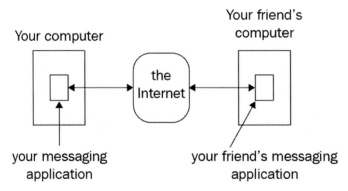

Figure 13.2 – Network applications

At the lowest level of communication is the physical layer, which transmits bits of data through the medium. In this case, a medium is the network cable (consider Wi-Fi communication too). The user application abstracts from the lower levels of network communication. The operating system provides everything a programmer needs. The operating system implements the low-level details of the network communication, such as the **Transmission Control Protocol/Internet Protocol (TCP/IP)** suite.

Whenever an application needs to access the network, whether a **local area network (LAN)** or the internet, it requests the operating system to provide an access point. The OS offers a gateway to the network by utilizing a network adapter and specific software that speaks to the hardware.

Here's a more detailed illustration of what this looks like:

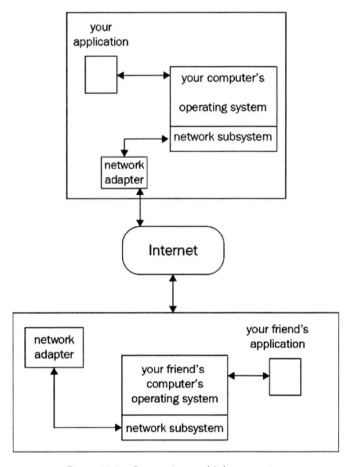

Figure 13.3 – Connecting multiple computers

The operating system provides an API to work with its networking subsystem. The main abstraction that programmers should care about is the socket. We can treat a socket as a file that sends its contents through the network adapter. Sockets are the access points that connect two computers via the network, as depicted in the following diagram:

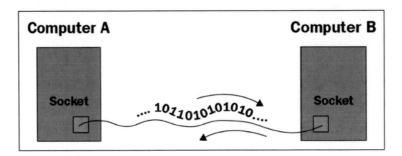

Figure 13.4 – Sockets

From the programmer's perspective, the socket is a structure that allows us to implement data through the network in applications. The socket is a connection point that either sends or receives data; that is, an application receives data via sockets too. The operating system provides a socket for the application upon request. An application can have more than one socket. Client applications in the client-server architecture usually operate with a single socket. Now, let's delve into socket programming in detail.

Programming network applications using sockets

As we mentioned previously, a socket is an abstraction over network communication. We treat them as regular files—everything written to a socket is sent via the network to its destination by the operating system. Everything received via the network is written into the socket by the operating system. This way, the OS provides two-way communication for network applications.

Let's suppose that we run two different applications working with the network. For example, we open a web browser to surf the web and use a messaging application (such as Skype) to chat with friends. The web browser represents a client application in a client-server network architecture. In this case, the server is the computer that responds to the requested data. For example, we type an address into the web browser's address bar and see the resulting web page on the screen. The web browser requests a socket from the operating system whenever we visit a website. In terms of coding, the web browser creates a socket using the API provided by the OS. We can describe the socket with a more specific prefix: a client socket. For the server to process client requests, the web server's computer must listen for incoming connections; the server application creates a server socket to listen to connections.

Whenever a connection is established between the client and server, data communication can proceed. The following diagram depicts a web browser request to facebook.com:

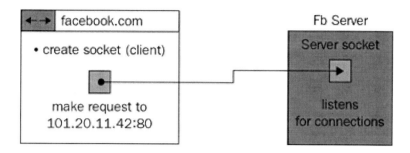

Figure 13.5 – Browser requests

Pay attention to the group of numbers in the preceding diagram. This is called an IP address. The IP address is the location we need to transfer data to the device. There are billions of devices connected to the internet. Each device exposes a unique numeric value representing its address to make a unique distinction between them. A connection is established using the IP protocol, which we call an IP address. An IP address consists of four groups of 1-byte-length numbers. Its dotted-decimal representation is in the form XXXX, where X is the 1-byte number. The values at each position range from 0 to 255. More specifically, it's a version 4 IP address. Modern systems use a version 6 address, a combination of numbers and letters, providing a wider range of available address values.

When creating a socket, we assign the IP address of the local computer to it; that is, we're binding the socket to the address. When using the socket to send data to another device in the network, we should set its destination address. Another socket on that device holds the destination address. To create a connection between two devices, we use two sockets. Reasonable questions might arise—*What if several applications run on the device? What if we run several applications, each creating a socket for itself? Which one should receive the incoming data?*

To answer these questions, take a good look at the preceding diagram. You should see a number after the colon at the end of the IP address. That's called the **port number**. A port number is a 2-byte-length number assigned to the socket by the operating system.

Because of the 2-byte length limit, the OS cannot assign more than 65,536 unique port numbers to sockets; you cannot have more than 65,536 simultaneously running processes or threads communicating via the network (however, there are ways to reuse sockets). Apart from that, port numbers are reserved for specific applications. These ports are called *well-known ports* and range from 0 to 1023. They are reserved for privileged services. For example, the **Hyper-Text Transfer Protocol** (**HTTP**) server's port number is 80. That doesn't mean it can't use other ports.

Understanding network protocols

A network protocol is a collection of rules and data formats that define intercommunication between applications. For example, a web browser and server communicate via HTTP. HTTP is more like a set of rules than a transport protocol. Transport protocols are at the base of every network communication. An example of a transport protocol would be TCP. When we mentioned the TCP/IP suite, we meant the implementation of TCP over IP. We can consider the IP protocol as the heart of internet communications.

It provides host-to-host routing and addressing. Everything we send or receive online is packaged as an IP packet. The following diagram shows what an IPv4 packet looks like. In this context, an octet refers to a group of 8 bits equivalent to 1 byte:

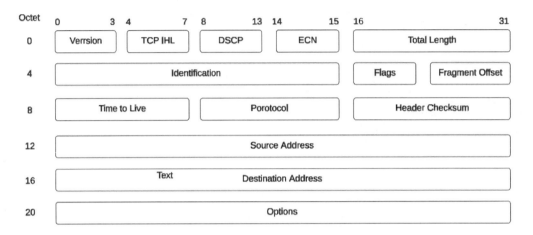

Figure 13.6 – IP packet

The IP header weighs 20 bytes. It combines necessary flags and options for delivering a packet from the source address to the destination address. In the domain of the IP protocol, we usually call a packet a datagram. Each layer has its specific terms for packets. More careful specialists talk about encapsulating TCP segments into IP datagrams. It's totally fine to call them packets.

Each protocol at the higher level appends meta-information to data that is sent and received via the network; for example, TCP data is encapsulated in an IP datagram. Besides this meta-information, the protocol also defines the underlying rules and operations that should be performed to complete a data transfer between two and more devices.

> **Tip**
> You can find more detailed information in specific documents called **Requests for Comments (RFCs)**. For example, RFC *791* describes the IP protocol, while RFC *793* describes TCP.

Many popular applications—file transfer, email, web, and others—use TCP as their primary transport protocol. For example, the HTTP protocol defines the format of messages transferred from the client to the server and vice versa. The actual transfer happens using a transport protocol—in this case, TCP. However, the HTTP standard doesn't limit TCP to being the only transport protocol.

The following diagram illustrates the TCP header being appended to data before passing it to the lower level:

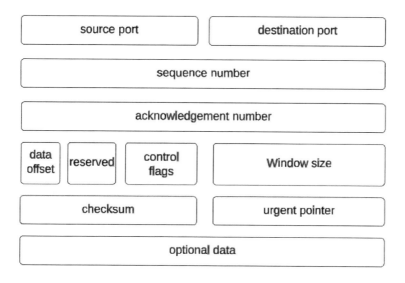

Figure 13.7 – TCP header

Pay attention to the source port number and destination port number. Those are the unique identifiers that differentiate between running processes in operating systems. Also, take a look at the sequence and acknowledgment numbers. They are TCP-specific and used for transmission reliability.

In practice, TCP is used due to its following features:

- Retransmission of lost data
- In-order delivery
- Data integrity
- Congestion control and avoidance

IP is not reliable. It doesn't care for lost packets, so TCP handles the retransmission. It marks each packet with a unique identifier that the other transmission side should acknowledge. If the sender does not receive an **acknowledgment code** (**ACK**) for a packet, the protocol will resend the packet (a few times). It is also crucial to receive packets in the proper order. TCP reorders received packets to represent correctly ordered information. That's why, when listening to music online, we don't listen to the end of the song at its beginning.

Retransmission of packets might lead to another problem known as network congestion. This happens when a node doesn't manage to send packets fast enough. Packets get stuck for a while, and unnecessary retransmission increases their number. Various implementations of TCP employ algorithms for congestion avoidance.

TCP maintains a congestion window—a factor determining how much data can be sent out. TCP slowly increases the congestion window after initializing the connection using the slow-start mechanism. Though the protocol is described in the corresponding RFC, operating systems implement many mechanisms differently.

On the other side of the fence is the **User Datagram Protocol (UDP)**. The main difference between these two is that TCP is reliable. This means that, in the case of lost network packets, it resends the same packet until it reaches its designated destination. Because of its reliability, data transmissions via TCP are considered to take longer than UDP. UDP doesn't guarantee we can deliver packets properly and without losses. Instead, developers should resend, check, and verify the data transmission. Applications that require fast communication tend to rely on UDP. For example, a video call application or an online game uses UDP because of its speed. Even if a couple of packets get lost during the transmission, it won't affect the user experience. It's better to have small glitches while playing a game or talking to a friend in a video chat than to wait seconds for the next frame of the game or video.

Designing an echo server

For this example, we will implement an echo server. An echo server is a network server that echoes back any data it receives from a client. In other words, when a client sends a message to an echo server, the server returns the same message to the client. The purpose of an echo server is to demonstrate basic communication between a client and a server. The echo server operates based on a simple request-response model. When a client connects to the server, it establishes a communication channel with the server. The client can then send a message to the server over this channel. The server receives the message, processes it, and sends the same message back to the client. The client can then receive and display the echoed message. Echo servers are commonly used for testing network connectivity, troubleshooting, and verifying the integrity of network communication. They allow developers to check whether the network functions properly by verifying that the data sent and received remains intact during transmission.

Additionally, echo servers can serve as a starting point for building more complex server applications. They provide a foundation for understanding the basics of socket programming. They can be expanded to handle more sophisticated tasks, such as processing and responding to specific requests or implementing protocols such as HTTP or the **File Transfer Protocol (FTP)**.

We start by including the necessary header files, such as `iostream` for input/output operations, `string` for string handling, `cstring` for string manipulation functions, `sys/socket.h` for socket programming, `arpa/inet.h` for manipulating IP addresses, and `unistd.h` for closing sockets:

```
#include <iostream>
#include <string>
#include <cstring>
```

```
#include <sys/socket.h>
#include <arpa/inet.h>
#include <unistd.h>
```

We define two constants—BUFFER_SIZE to specify the buffer size for receiving and sending data, and PORT to specify the port number on which the server will listen for incoming connections:

```
const int BUFFER_SIZE = 1024;
const int PORT = 8080;
```

The main function begins. We declare variables to store the server socket, client socket, server address, client address, and a buffer for receiving and sending data:

```
int main() {
    int serverSocket, clientSocket;
    sockaddr_in serverAddress, clientAddress;
    char buffer[BUFFER_SIZE];
```

We create a socket using the socket system call. The function takes three arguments—the address family (AF_INET for IPv4), the socket type (SOCK_STREAM for TCP), and the protocol (0 for the default protocol). If the socket creation fails, we print an error message and return 1:

```
    // Create socket
    serverSocket = socket(AF_INET, SOCK_STREAM, 0);
    if (serverSocket == -1) {
        std::cerr << "Failed to create socket." << std::endl;
        return 1;
    }
```

Next, we set up the server address structure. We set the address family to AF_INET, the IP address to INADDR_ANY (which means the server will bind to all available network interfaces), and the port number to the one specified in the PORT constant:

```
    // Set up the server address
    serverAddress.sin_family = AF_INET;
    serverAddress.sin_addr.s_addr = INADDR_ANY;
    serverAddress.sin_port = htons(PORT);
```

We bind the socket to the server address using the bind system call. If the binding fails, we print an error message and return 1:

```
    // Bind socket to address
    if (bind(serverSocket, (struct sockaddr*)
      &serverAddress, sizeof(serverAddress)) < 0) {
```

```
        std::cerr << "Failed to bind socket." << std::endl;
        return 1;
    }
```

The server enters the listening state using the `listen` system call. We pass the server socket and the maximum number of connections that can be waiting (5 in this case):

```
// Listen for incoming connections
listen(serverSocket, 5);
```

We print a message indicating that the server is listening on the specified port:

```
std::cout << "Server listening on port " << PORT <<
    std::endl;
```

The server waits for an incoming connection using the `accept` system call. It blocks until a client connects to the server. Once a client connection is established, a new socket is created for communication with that client. If the `accept` call fails, we print an error message and return `1`:

```
// Accept incoming connection
socklen_t clientAddressLength = sizeof(clientAddress);
clientSocket = accept(serverSocket, (struct
    sockaddr*)&clientAddress, &clientAddressLength);
if (clientSocket < 0) {
    std::cerr << "Failed to accept a connection." <<
        std::endl;
    return 1;
}
```

We print a message indicating that a client has connected, along with the client's IP address:

```
std::cout << "Client connected: " <<
    inet_ntoa(clientAddress.sin_addr) << std::endl;
```

The server enters a loop to receive data from the client and send it back. We use the `recv` system call to receive data from the client into the buffer. The function returns the number of bytes received, `0` if the client disconnects, or `-1` if an error occurs. If data is received successfully, we use the `send` system call to return the received data to the client. We also print the number of bytes received and sent:

```
// Receive and send data back to the client
ssize_t bytesRead;
while ((bytesRead = recv(clientSocket, buffer,
    BUFFER_SIZE, 0)) > 0) {
    send(clientSocket, buffer, bytesRead, 0);
    std::cout << "Received and sent " << bytesRead << "
        bytes." << std::endl;
```

```
    }
```

We check the return value of `recv` outside the loop. If it's 0, the client has disconnected, so we print a corresponding message. If it's -1, it indicates an error, so we print an error message and return 1:

```
    if (bytesRead == 0) {
        std::cout << "Client disconnected." << std::endl;
    } else if (bytesRead == -1) {
        std::cerr << "Error in receiving data." <<
            std::endl;
        return 1;
    }
```

Finally, we close the client and server sockets using the `close` system call:

```
    // Close the sockets
    close(clientSocket);
    close(serverSocket);

    return 0;
}
```

This completes the code for the echo server. Note that this is a basic example and does not extensively handle multiple concurrent connections or error handling. It is recommended to add appropriate error handling and enhance the server based on your specific requirements.

Note that we've kept each component independent from the others to make it easier to try separately. A full implementation would require using one component inside another to achieve full functionality.

Securing applications

Compared to many languages, C++ is a little harder to master regarding secure coding. Plenty of guidelines provide advice regarding how to and how not to avoid security risks in C++ programs. One of the most popular issues discussed in *Chapter 1, Building C++ Applications*, is using preprocessor macros. The example we used had the following macro:

```
#define DOUBLE_IT(arg) (arg * arg)
```

Improper use of this macro leads to logic errors that are hard to spot. In the following code, the programmer expects to get 16 printed to the screen:

```
int res = DOUBLE_IT(3 + 1);
std::cout >> res >> std::endl;
```

The output is 7. The issue here is with the missing parentheses around the `arg` parameter; that is, the preceding macro should be rewritten as follows:

```
#define DOUBLE_IT(arg) ((arg) * (arg))
```

Although this example is popular, we strongly suggest avoiding macros as much as possible. C++ provides many constructs that can be processed at compile time, such as `constexpr`, `consteval`, and `constinit`—even if statements have a `constexpr` alternative. Use them if you need compile-time processing in your code.

Although we don't want you to become paranoid about security issues, you should be careful almost everywhere. Learning the language's quirks and oddities will avoid most of these issues. Also, a good practice would be to use the newest features that replace or fix the disadvantages of previous versions. For example, consider the following `create_array()` function. Remember not to return pointers or references to local variables:

```
double* create_array()
{
double arr[10] = {0.0};
return arr;
}
```

The caller of the `create_array()` function is left with a pointer to the non-existing array because `arr` has an automatic storage duration. We can replace the preceding code with a better alternative if required:

```
#include <array>;
std::array<double> create_array()
{
    std::array<double> arr;
    return arr;
}
```

Strings are treated as character arrays and are the reason behind many buffer overflow issues. One of the most frequent issues is writing data into a string buffer while ignoring its size. The `std::string` class is a safer alternative to C strings in that regard. However, when supporting legacy code, you should be careful when using functions such as `strcpy()`, as shown in the following example:

```
#include <cstdio>
#include <cstring>
int main()
{
    char small_buffer[4];
    const char* long_text = "This text is long enough to
      overflow small buffers!";
```

```
    strcpy(small_buffer, long_text);
}
```

Given that, legally, `small_buffer` should have a null terminator at the end of it, it will only cope with the first three characters of the `long_text` string. However, the following happens after calling `strcpy()`:

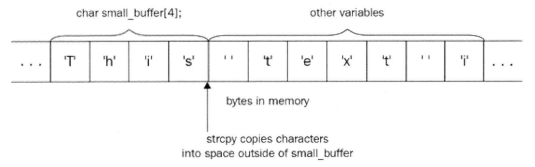

Figure 13.8 – strcopy

It would help if you were even more careful when implementing network applications. Most data coming from client connections should be handled properly, and buffer overflows are not rare. Let's learn how to make network applications more secure.

Securing network applications

In the previous section of this book, we designed a network application that receives client data using socket connections. Besides the fact that most viruses that penetrate the system are from the outside world, network applications have this natural tendency to open the computer to various threats on the internet. First, an open port exists when running a network application. Someone who knows the same port your application listens to can intrude by faking protocol data. We will mostly discuss the server side of network applications here; however, some topics also apply to client applications.

One of the first things you should do is incorporate client authorization and authentication. These are two terms that are easy to confuse. Be careful not to use them interchangeably; they are different, as detailed here:

- Authentication is the process of validating client access. This means that not every incoming connection request is served right away. Before transferring data to and from the client, the server application must be sure that the client is known. In almost the same way we access a social network platform by typing in our email and password, the authentication of a client defines whether the client has the right to access the system.

- Authorization, on the other hand, defines what precisely the client can do in the system. It's a set of permissions that are provided to specific clients. For instance, the client application we discussed in the previous section can upload files to the system. Sooner or later, you might want to incorporate paid subscriptions and provide paying clients with a broader range of features; for example, by allowing them to create folders to organize their files. So, when a client requests a folder's creation, we might want to authorize the request to discover whether the client has the right to do so.

When the client application initiates a connection with the server, all the server gets is the connection details (IP address, port number). To let the server know who is behind the client application (the actual user), the client application sends over the user's credentials. Usually, this process involves sending the user a unique identifier (such as a username or an email address) with the password to access the system. The server then checks these credentials against its database and verifies whether it should grant access to the client.

This communication between the client and the server might be a simple text or formatted object transfer. For example, the protocol that's defined by the server might require the client to send a **JavaScript Object Notation (JSON)** document in the following form:

```
{
  "email": "myemail@example.org," "password": "notSoSIMPLEp4s8"
}
```

The response from the server allows the client to proceed further or update its UI to let the user know the result of the operation. When signing in, you might have encountered several cases while using any web or network application. For example, a wrongly typed password might lead to an *Invalid username or password* error being returned by the server.

Besides this first necessary step, it is wise to validate every piece of data coming from the client application. A buffer overflow might be easily avoided if the email field is checked for size. For example, when intentionally trying to break the system, the client application might send a JSON object with a large value for its fields. That check is on the server's shoulders. Preventing security flaws starts with data validation.

Another form of security attack is making too many requests per second from single or multiple clients. For example, a client application making hundreds of authentication requests in 1 second causes the server to intensively process those requests and waste resources trying to serve them all. It would be better to check the rate of client requests—for example, limiting them to a single request per second.

These forms of attacks (intentional or unintentional) are called **Denial-of-Service (DOS)** attacks. The more advanced version of a DOS attack takes the form of making a huge number of requests to the server from multiple clients. This form is called a **Distributed DOS (DDOS)** attack. A simple approach might be to blacklist IP addresses trying to crash the system by making multiple requests per second. As a programmer of network applications, you should consider all the issues described here and many others outside the scope of this book when developing your applications.

Summary

In this chapter, we introduced designing network applications in C++. We started by introducing the basics of networking. Understanding networking completely takes a lot of time, but there are several foundational concepts that every programmer must know before implementing an application in any way related to the network. Those foundational concepts include layering in the OSI model and different kinds of transport protocols, such as TCP and UDP. Understanding the differences between TCP and UDP is necessary for any programmer. As we learned, TCP makes reliable connections between sockets, the next thing a programmer encounters when developing network applications. Those are the connection points of two instances of applications. Whenever we need to send or receive data through a network, we should define a socket and work with it almost as usual with a regular file.

All the abstractions and concepts we use in application development are handled by the OS and, in the end, by the network adapter. This is a device that's capable of sending data through a network medium. Receiving data from the medium doesn't guarantee safety. The network adapter receives anything coming from the medium. To ensure we handle incoming data correctly, we should also ensure application security. The last section of this chapter was about writing secure code and validating the input to make sure no harm will be done to the program. Securing your program is a good step in ensuring high-quality programs. One of the best approaches to developing programs is testing them thoroughly. In *Chapter 11, Designing World-Ready Applications*, you may recall that we discussed software development steps and explained that one of the most important steps explained testing the program once the coding phase was complete. After testing it, you will most probably discover a lot of bugs. Some of these bugs are hard to reproduce and fix, and that's where debugging comes to the rescue.

The next chapter is all about testing and debugging your programs correctly.

Questions

1. List all seven layers of the OSI model.
2. What's the point of port numbers?
3. Why should you use sockets in network applications?
4. Describe the sequence of operations you should perform on the server side to receive data using a TCP socket.
5. What are the differences between TCP and UDP?
6. Why shouldn't you use macro definitions in your code?
7. How would you differentiate between different client applications when implementing a server application?

Further reading

For further information, refer to the following resources:

- *TCP/IP Illustrated, Volume 1: The Protocols*, by R. Stevens and K.R. Fall: `https://www.amazon.com/TCP-Illustrated-Protocols-Addison-Wesley-Professional/dp/0321336313/`

- *Networking Fundamentals*, by Gordon Davies: `https://www.packtpub.com/cloud-networking/networking-fundamentals`

14

Debugging and Testing

Testing and debugging play a crucial part in the pipeline of the software development process. While debugging fixes problems, testing assists in problem detection. But many possible flaws can be avoided if we adhere to specific guidelines throughout the implementation stage. In addition, since testing is expensive, it would be beneficial if we could use tools to automatically examine software before human testing became necessary. Furthermore, it's crucial to consider when, how, and which software tests we should conduct.

In this chapter, we will cover the following topics:

- Understanding the root cause of an issue
- Debugging programs
- Static and dynamic analysis
- Testing, **test-driven development** (**TDD**), and **behavior-driven development** (**BDD**)

This chapter describes the analysis of a software defect, the use of the **GNU Debugger** (**GDB**) tool to debug a program, and the use of tools to automatically analyze software. The concepts of unit testing, TDD, and BDD, as well as how to use them practically during the software engineering development process, will also be covered.

Technical requirements

The g++ compiler with the -std=c++2a option is used to compile the examples throughout the chapter. You can find the source files used in this chapter in the GitHub repository for this book at https://github.com/PacktPublishing/Expert-C-2nd-edition/tree/main/Chapter14.

Understanding the root cause of an issue

In medicine, a good doctor needs to understand the difference between treating the symptoms and curing the condition. For instance, prescribing medications to a patient with a broken arm will just soothe the symptoms; surgery is likely the best option to help bones to heal. **Root cause analysis**

(RCA) is a systematic process that's used to identify the fundamental cause of a problem. It tries to determine the root of the problem's fundamental cause by following a predetermined sequence of procedures with the use of the appropriate tools. Thus, we may ascertain the following:

- What happened?

- How did it happen?

- Why did it happen?

- What appropriate measures should be taken to stop it from happening again or to lessen its impact?

According to RCA, an action in a particular place triggers another action in another place, and so on. We can determine the origins of the problem and how it evolved into the symptom we have by tracing the action chain back to the beginning. Aha! This is exactly the procedure we should use to eliminate or decrease software defects. We will learn about the fundamental RCA processes, how to apply the RCA method to find software defects, and what guidelines a C++ developer should follow to avoid such errors from appearing in software in the following subsections.

RCA overview

An RCA procedure typically consists of five phases, listed as follows:

1. **Define the problem**: We may discover answers to the following questions at this stage: *What is going on? What are the signs of a problem? In what environment or conditions is the problem occurring?*

2. **Gather data**: We need to collect enough data to create a causal factor chart. This phase might be costly and time-consuming.

3. **Create a causal factor chart**: A causal factor chart provides a visual structure for organizing and analyzing the obtained data. The causal factor chart is nothing more than a sequence diagram with logic tests that describes the events leading up to the occurrence of a symptom. This charting process should drive the data collection process until the investigators are satisfied with the thoroughness of the chart.

4. **Identify the root causes**: Using the causal factor chart, we can create a decision diagram known as the root cause map to determine the underlying cause or reasons.

5. **Recommend and implement solutions**: Once a root cause or multiple causes have been identified, the answers to the following questions can help us find a solution: *what can we do to avoid this from happening again? How will a solution be implemented? Who will be held accountable for it? What are the expenses and risks of implementing the solution?*

One of the most common factor diagrams used in the software engineering industry is the RCA tree diagram. The following diagram provides an example of its structure:

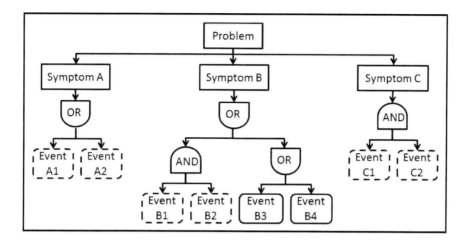

Figure 14.1 – Example of an RCA tree diagram

Let's assume we have a problem that has **A**, **B**, and **C** symptoms. Symptom **A** can be caused by events **A1** or **A2**, symptom **B** can be caused by either events **B1** and **B2** or events **B3** and **B4**, and symptom **C** is caused by events **C1** and **C2**. After data collection, we found that symptoms **A** and **C** never appeared and that we only have symptom **B**. Further analysis shows that events **B1** and **B2** are not involved when the problem occurs, so we can identify that the root cause of this problem is happening because of event **B3** or event **B4**.

If the software has a defect, rather than simply fixing it at the point of failure, we should use RCA to investigate the original fundamental root cause(s) of the problem. Then, the root cause(s) of the problem can be traced back to the requirements, the design, the implementation, the verification, and/or the test planning and input data. When the underlying issues are identified and resolved, the software's quality may be improved, and therefore maintenance costs can be dramatically lowered.

We've just learned how to identify the root cause of a problem but keep in mind that *the best defense is a good offense*. So, instead of analyzing and fixing a problem, what if we can prevent it from happening?

Prevention is better than cure – good coding behavior

According to an IBM study, if the overall cost of requirements and design is 1X, the implementation and coding process will take 5X, unit and integration tests will take about 10X, comprehensive customer beta test costs will take about 15X, and costs to fix bugs in the post-product release stage will take about 30X! As a result, reducing code defects is one of the most efficient strategies to reduce production costs.

Although the generic methodology for determining the root causes of software defects is critical, it would be even better if we could avoid some defects during the implementation stage. To achieve this, we need to have good coding behavior, which implies following a particular set of rules. These rules are divided into two categories: low and high. The low-level rules may cover the following items:

- Uninitialized variables

- Integer divisions

- Mistakenly using = instead of ==

- Potentially assigning a signed variable to an unsigned variable

- Missing `break` in `switch` statements

- Side effects in compound expressions or function calls

When it comes to the high-level rules, we have topics related to the following:

- Interfaces

- Resource management

- Memory management

- Concurrency

B. Stroustrup and H. Sutter have proposed adopting these guidelines in their live document, *C++ Core Guidelines (Release 0.8)*, which emphasizes static type safety and resource safety. They also underline the benefits of using range checking to avoid dereferencing `null-ptr`, dangling pointers, and the systematic usage of exceptions. If a developer follows these principles, their code will be statically type-safe with no resource leaks. Furthermore, it will not only catch a greater number of programming logic errors but it will also run faster. Because of page limitations, we will only look at a few examples of this in this subsection. If you want to look at more examples, please go to `https://isocpp.github.io/CppCoreGuidelines/`.

The uninitialized variable problem

An uninitialized variable is one of the most common mistakes a programmer can make. When we declare a variable, a certain amount of continuous memory will be allocated to it. If it is not initialized, it still has some value, but there is no deterministic way of predicting it. Consequently, unpredictable behavior shows up when we execute the program, which you can find at `https://github.com/PacktPublishing/Expert-C-2nd-edition/blob/main/Chapter14/ch14_rca_uninit_variable.cpp`.

In the code at the preceding link, when x is declared, the OS will assign 4 bytes of unused memory to it, which means that the value of x is whatever value was residing in that memory. Every time we run this program, both the address and value of x might be different. Additionally, some compilers, such as Visual Studio, will initialize the value of x as 0 in the debug version but keep it uninitialized in the release version. In that case, we have a totally different output in the debug and release versions.

Side effects in compound expressions

When an operator, expression, statement, or function has finished being evaluated, it may be prolonged or may continuously exist inside its compound. This continuous existence has some side effects that may lead to some undefined behaviors. Let's have a look at the code at `https://github.com/PacktPublishing/Expert-C-2nd-edition/blob/main/Chapter14/ch14_rca_compound.cpp` to understand this.

Because of the undefined behavior of the evaluation order of operands, the result of the preceding code could be either `16` or `12`.

Mixed signed and unsigned problems

Typically, binary operators (`+`, `-`, `*`, `/`, `%`, `<`, `<=`, `>`, `>=`, `==`, `!=`, `&&`, `||`, `!`, `&`, `|`, `<<`, `>>`, `~`, `^`, `=`, `+=`, `-=`, `*=`, `/=`, and `%=`) require both side operands to be of the same type. If the two operands are of different types, one will be promoted to the same type as the other. Roughly speaking, there are three C standard conversion rules given in *subclause 6.3.1.1 [ISO/IEC 9899:2011]*:

* When we mix types of the same rank, the signed one will be promoted to an unsigned type

* When we mix types of a different rank, the lower-ranked one will be promoted to the higher-ranked type if all the values of the lower-ranked side can be represented by the higher-ranked side

* If none of the values of the lower-ranked type can be represented by the higher-ranked type in the preceding case, then the unsigned version of the higher-ranked type will be used

Now, let's take a look at the traditional signed integer minus unsigned integer problem at `https://github.com/PacktPublishing/Expert-C-2nd-edition/blob/main/Chapter14/ch14_rca_mix_sign_unsigned.cpp`.

In the code example at the preceding link, the signed `int` value will be automatically converted into an unsigned `int` value, and the result will be `uint32_t z = -10`. On the other hand, because `-10` cannot be represented as an unsigned `int` value, its hexadecimal value, `0xFFFFFFF6`, will be interpreted as `UINT_MAX - 9` (that is, `4294967286`) on two's complement machines.

Order of evaluation problem

The following example is concerned with the initialization order of class members in a constructor. Since the initialization order is the order in which the class members appear in the class definition, it's a good practice to separate the declaration of each member into different lines, as demonstrated at `https://github.com/PacktPublishing/Expert-C-2nd-edition/blob/main/Chapter14/ch14_rca_order_of_evaluation.cpp`.

Now, let us write the main function where we are going to create objects of the classes declared previously, and based on those objects, we are going to explain how the initialization order works:

```
int main()
{
A a(10);
B b1(10), b2(3.0f);
a.print(); //v1=10,v2=10,v3=10 for both debug and release
b1.print(); //v1=10, v2=10 for both debug and release
b2.print(); //v1=-858993460,v2=3 for debug; v1=0,v2=3 for
            //release.
}
```

In class A, although the declaring order is v1 -> v2, putting them in one line confuses other developers. In the first constructor of class B, v1 will be initialized as x, then v2 will be initialized as v1 because its declaration order is v1->v2. However, in its second constructor, v1 will be initialized as v2 first (at this point, v2 is not initialized yet!), then v2 will be initialized by x. This causes the different output values of v1 in debug and release versions.

Compile-time checking versus runtime checking

The following example shows that runtime checking the (number of bits for an integer-type cloud variable) can be replaced by compile-time checking:

```
//check # of bits for int
//courtesy:https://isocpp.github.io/CppCoreGuidelines/
CppCoreGuidelines
int nBits = 0; // don't: avoidable code
for (int i = 1; i; i <<= 1){
++nBits;
}
if (nBits < 32){
cerr << "int too small\n";
}
```

Since int can be either 16 or 32 bits, depending on the OS, this example fails to achieve what it is trying to achieve. We should use int32_t or just replace it with the following:

```
static_assert(sizeof(int) >= 4); //compile-time check
```

Another example is concerned with reading the max number of n integers into a one-dimensional array:

```
void read_into(int* p, int n); // a function to read max n
                               // integers into *p
...
int v[10];
read_into(v, 100); //bad, off the end, but the compile
                   //cannot catch this error.
```

This can be fixed using span<int>:

```
void read_into( span<int> buf); // read into a range of integers
...
int v[10];
read_into(v); //better, the compiler will figure out the
              //number of elements
```

The general rule here is to do the analysis at compile time as much as possible and not postpone it until runtime.

Avoiding memory leaks

A memory leak means that the allocated dynamic memory can never be freed. In C, we use malloc() and/or calloc() to allocate memory and free() to release it. In C++, the new operator and the delete or delete[] operators are used to manage memory dynamically. Although the risks of memory leaks can be reduced with the help of smart pointers and **Resource Acquisition Is Initialization (RAII)**, there are still some rules we need to follow if we wish to build high-quality code.

First, the easiest memory management way is the memory you never allocated by your own code. For example, whenever you can write T x;, don't write T* x = new T(); or shared_ptr<T> x(new T());.

Next, do not manage the memory using your own code, as shown here:

```
void f_bad(){
T* p = new T() ;
...             //do something with p
delete p ;      //leak if throw or return before reaching
                //this line
}
```

Instead, try to use RAII, as follows:

```
void f_better()
{
std::auto_ptr<T> p(new T());      //other smart pointers is
                                  //ok also
...                               //do something with p
//will not leak regardless of whether this point is reached or not
}
```

Then, use unique_ptr to replace shared_ptr unless you need to share its ownership, as follows:

```
void f_bad()
{
```

```
shared_ptr<Base> b = make_shared<Derived>();
...
} //b will be destroyed at here
```

Since b is locally used without copying it, its refcount value will be always 1. This means we can use a unique_ptr instance to replace it, like so:

```
void f_better()
{
unique_ptr<Base> b = make_unique<Derived>();
... //use b locally
} //b will be destroyed at here
```

Finally, even if you really need to dynamically manage the memory by yourself, don't manually allocate the memory if there is an std container library class available.

In this section, we learned how to locate a problem using RCA and how to prevent a problem by following coding best practices. Next, we'll learn how to use a debugger tool to control the line-by-line execution of a program and examine the values of variables and expressions during its running time.

Debugging programs

Debugging is the process of locating and fixing program bugs or problems. Interactive debugging, data/control flow analysis, and unit and integration testing are all examples of this. We will only cover interactive debugging in this part, which is the process of executing your source code line by line with breakpoints while displaying the values of the variables being used and corresponding memory addresses.

Tools for debugging a C/C++ program

There are several tools accessible in the C++ community, depending on your development environment. The following is a list of the most popular ones across various platforms:

- *Linux/Unix*:

  - **GDB**: A free open source **command-line interface** (CLI) debugger.

  - **Eclipse**: A free open source **integrated development environment** (IDE). It supports not only debugging but also compiling, profiling, and smart editing.

  - **Valgrind**: Another open source dynamic analysis tool; it is good for debugging memory leaks and threading bugs.

  - **Affinic**: A commercial **graphical user interface** (GUI) tool built for the **GDB**, **Low-Level Debugger** (LLDB), and **Low-Level Virtual Machine** (LLVM) debuggers.

- **Data Display Debugger (DDD)**: An open source data display debugger for **GDB**, **DBX**, the **Java Debugger** (**JDB**), **Extended Debugger** (**XDB**), and **Python**; it displays data structures as graphs.

- **GDB in Emacs mode**: An open source GUI tool that uses GNU Emacs to view and edit source code when debugging with GDB.

- **KDevelop**: A free and open source IDE and debugger tool for programming languages such as C/C++, Objective-C, and so on.

- **Nemiver**: An open source tool that works well in the **GNOME** desktop environment.

- **SlickEdit**: A good tool for debugging multithreaded and multiprocessor code.

- *Windows*:

  - **Visual Studio**: A commercial tool with a GUI that's free for community versions

  - **GDB**: This can run in Windows as well with the help of **Cygwin** or **MinGW**

  - **Eclipse**: Its **C++ Development Tooling** (**CDT**) project can be installed on Windows with the MinGW **GNU Compiler Collection** (**GCC**) compiler in the toolchains

- *macOS*:

  - **LLDB**: This is the default debugger in **Xcode** on macOS and supports C/C++ and Objective-C on desktop and iOS devices and their simulators

  - **GDB**: This CLI debugger is also used on macOS and iOS systems

  - **Eclipse**: This free IDE using GCC works for macOS

Since GDB can be run on all platforms, we will show you how to use GDB in the following subsections.

GDB overview

GDB allows a developer to examine what is happening within another program while it is running or what another program was doing when it crashed. GDB can do the following four main things:

- Start a program and specify anything that might affect its behavior.

- Make a program stop when certain conditions are met.

- Investigate what happened when a program was terminated.

- Change the values of variables while a program is executing. This implies we can experiment with something to reduce the impacts of one problem and/or learn about the side effects of another.

It is important to note that two programs or executable files are involved: GDB and the program that needs to be debugged. Because these two programs can run on the same or different machines, we can divide debugging into three categories:

- **Native debugging**: Both programs run on the same machine
- **Remote debugging**: GDB runs on a host machine, while the debugged program runs on a remote machine
- **Simulator debugging**: GDB runs on a host machine, while the debugged program runs on a simulator

Based on the latest release (GDB v8.3) at the time of writing this book, the languages supported by GDB include C, C++, Objective-C, Ada, Assembly, D, Fortran, Go, OpenCL, Modula-2, Pascal, and Rust.

Because GDB is a cutting-edge debugging tool that is complex and has many functions, it will be impossible to cover all its features in this section. Instead, we'll look at examples to learn about the most helpful aspects.

Examples of GDB

Before practicing these examples, we need to check whether GDB has been installed on our system by running the following code:

```
~wus1/chapter-13$ gdb -help
```

If the following kind of information is displayed, we will be ready to start:

```
This is the GNU debugger. Usage:
gdb [options] [executable-file [core-file or process-id]]
gdb [options] --args executable-file [inferior-arguments ...]


Selection of debuggee and its files:
--args Arguments after executable-file are passed to inferior
--core=COREFILE Analyze the core dump COREFILE.
--exec=EXECFILE Use EXECFILE as the executable.
...
```

Otherwise, we need to install it. Let's go over how we can install it on the different OSes:

- For Debian-based Linux, run the following command:

  ```
  ~wus1/chapter-13$ sudo apt-get install build-essential
  ```

- For Red Hat-based Linux, run the following command:

  ```
  ~wus1/chapter-13$sudo yum install build-essential
  ```

- For macOS, run the following command:

```
~wus1/chapter-13$brew install gdb
```

Windows users can install GDB through MinGW distributes. macOS will need a taskgated configuration.

Then, type gdb --help again to check whether it was successfully installed.

Setting breakpoints and inspection variable values

In the following example, we will learn how to set breakpoints, continue, step into, or step over a function, print values of variables, and how to use help in gdb. The source code is available at https://github.com/PacktPublishing/Expert-C-2nd-edition/blob/main/Chapter14/ch14_gdb_1.cpp.

Let's build this program in debug mode, as follows:

```
~wus1/chapter-13$ g++ -g ch14_gdb_1.cpp -o ch14_gdb_1.out
```

Note that for g++, the -g option means the debugging information will be included in the output binary file. If we run this program, it will show the following output:

```
x=10.000000, y=20.000000, x*y = 30.000000
```

Now, let's use gdb to see where the bug is. To do that, we need to execute the following command line:

```
~wus1/chapter-13$ gdb ch14_gdb_1.out
```

By doing this, we will see the following output:

```
GNU gdb (Ubuntu 8.1-0ubuntu3) 8.1.0.20180409-git
Copyright (C) 2018 Free Software Foundation, Inc.
License GPLv3+: GNU GPL version 3 or later
http://gnu.org/licenses/gpl.html
This is free software: you are free to change and redistribute it.
There is NO WARRANTY, to the extent permitted by law. Type "show
copying" and "show warranty" for details.
This GDB was configured as "aarch64-linux-gnu".
Type "show configuration" for configuration details.
For bug reporting instructions, please see:
<http://www.gnu.org/software/gdb/bugs/>.
Find the GDB manual and other documentation resources online at:
<http://www.gnu.org/software/gdb/documentation/>.
For help, type "help".
Type "apropos word" to search for commands related to "word"...
Reading symbols from a.out...done.
(gdb)
```

Now, let's have a look at the various commands in detail:

- break and run: If we type b main or break main and press *Enter*, a breakpoint will be inserted into the main function. Then, we can type run or r to start debugging the program. The following information will be shown in a Terminal window. Here, we can see that our first breakpoint is at the sixth line in the source code and that the debugged program has been paused in order to wait for a new command:

```
(gdb) b main
Breakpoint 1 at 0x8ac: file ch14_gdb_1.cpp, line 6.
(gdb) r
Starting program: /home/nvidia/wus1/Chapter-13/a.out
[Thread debugging using libthread_db enabled]
Using host libthread_db library "/lib/aarch64-linuxgnu/
libthread_db.so.1".
Breakpoint 1, main () at ch14_gdb_1.cpp:6
6 float x = 10, y = 20;
```

- next, print, and quit: The n or next command will go to the next line of the code. If the line calls a subroutine, it does not enter the subroutine; instead, it steps over the call and treats it as a single source line. If we want to show the value of a variable, we can use the p or print command, followed by the variable's name. Finally, if we want to exit from gdb, the q or quit command can be used. Here is the output from the Terminal window after running these operations:

```
(gdb) n
7 float z = multiple(x, y);
(gdb) p z
$1 = 0
(gdb) n
8 printf("x=%f, y=%f, x*y = %f\n", x, y, z);
(gdb) p z
$2 = 30
(gdb) q
A debugging session is active.
Inferior 1 [process 29187] will be killed.
Quit anyway? (y or n) y
~/wus1/Chapter-13$
```

- step: Now, let's learn how to step into the multiple() function and find the bug. To do that, we need to start over by using the b, r, and n commands to reach *line 7* first. Then, we can use the s or step command to step into the multiple() function. Next, we use the n command to reach *line 14* and p to print the value of the ret variable, which is 30. At this point, we've figured out that by using aha the bug is at line 14!:, instead of x*y, we have a typo—that is, x+y. The following code block shows the corresponding outputs from these commands:

```
~/wus1/Chapter-13$gdb ch14_gdb_1.out
...(gdb) b main
Breakpoint 1 at 0x8ac: file ch14_gdb_1.cpp, line 6.
(gdb) r
The program being debugged has been started already.
Start it from the beginning? (y or n) y
Starting program: /home/nvidia/wus1/Chapter-13/a.out
[Thread debugging using libthread_db enabled]
Using host libthread_db library "/lib/aarch64-linuxgnu/
libthread_db.so.1".
Breakpoint 1, main () at ch14_gdb_1.cpp:6
6 float x = 10, y = 20;
(gdb) n
7 float z = multiple(x, y);
(gdb) s
multiple (x=10, y=20) at ch14_gdb_1.cpp:14
14 float s = x + y;
(gdb) n
15 return s;
(gdb) p s
$1 = 30
```

- `help`: Lastly, let's learn about the `help` command to end this small example. When gdb is launched, we can use the `help` or `h` command to get the usage information of a particular command in its command input line. For instance, the following Terminal window summarizes what have we learned so far:

```
(gdb) h b
Set breakpoint at a specified location
break [PROBE_MODIFIER] [LOCATION] [thread THREADNUM] [if
CONDITION]
PROBE_MODIFIER shall be present if the command is to be placed
in
a
probe point. Accepted values are `-probe' (for a generic,
automatically
guessed probe type), `-probe-stap' (for a SystemTap probe) or
-probe-dtrace' (for a DTrace probe).
LOCATION may be a linespec, address, or explicit location as
described
below.
....
```

```
(gdb) h r
Start debugged program.
You may specify arguments to give it.
Args may include "*", or "[...]"; they are expanded using the
shell that will start the program (specified by the "$SHELL"
environment
variable). Input and output redirection with ">", "<", or ">>"
are also allowed.

(gdb) h s
Step program until it reaches a different source line.
Usage: step [N]
Argument N means step N times (or till program stops for another
reason).

(gdb) h n
Step program, proceeding through subroutine calls.
Usage: next [N]
Unlike "step", if the current source line calls a subroutine,
this command does not enter the subroutine, but instead steps
over
the call, in effect treating it as a single source line.
(gdb) h p
Print value of expression EXP.
Variables accessible are those of the lexical environment of the
selected
stack frame, plus all those whose scope is global or an entire0
file.
(gdb) h h
Print list of commands.
(gdb) h help
Print list of commands.
(gdb) help h
Print list of commands.
(gdb) help help
Print list of commands.
```

At this point, we have learned about a few basic commands we can use to debug a program. These commands are break, run, next, print, quit, step, and help. We will learn about functions and conditional breakpoints, the watchpoint, and the continue and finish commands in the next subsection.

A detailed explanation of `gdb`'s function breakpoints, conditional breakpoints, watchpoint, and the continue and finish commands can be found at `https://github.com/PacktPublishing/Expert-C-2nd-edition/blob/main/Chapter14/Function%20Breakpoints%2C%20Conditional%20Breakpoints%2C%20Watchpoint%2C%20and%20the%20Continue%20and%20Finish%20Commands.pdf`, while an explanation of logging `gdb` into a text file can be found at `https://github.com/PacktPublishing/Expert-C-2nd-edition/blob/main/Chapter14/Logging%20GDB%20Into%20a%20Text%20File.pdf`.

Practical debugging strategies

Since debugging is the costliest stage in the software development life cycle, finding bugs and fixing them isn't feasible, especially for large, complex systems. However, certain strategies can be used in practical processes, some of which are listed here:

- **Use printf() or std::cout**: This is the old-fashioned way of doing things. By printing some information to the Terminal, we can check the values of variables and perform where-and-when kinds of log profiles for further analysis.

- **Use a debugger**: Although learning to use a GDB kind of debugger tool is not an overnight thing, it can save lots of time. So, try to become familiar with it step by step and gradually.

- **Reproduce bugs**: Whenever a bug is reported in the field, make a record of the running environment and input data.

- **Dump log files**: An application program should dump log messages into a text file. When a crash happens, we should check the log files as the first step to see whether an abnormal event occurred.

- **Have a guess**: Roughly guess a bug's location and then prove whether it was right or wrong.

- **Divide and conquer**: Even in the worst scenario where we do not have any idea of what bugs there are, we still can use the **binary search** strategy to set breakpoints and then narrow down and eventually locate them.

- **Simplify**: Always start from the most simplified scenario and gradually add peripherals, input modules, and so on until the bug can be reproduced.

- **Source code version controlled**: If a bug has suddenly appeared on a release but it ran fine previously, do a source code tree check first. Someone may have made a change!

- **Don't give up**: Some bugs are hard to locate and/or fix, especially for complex and multi-team involved systems. Put them aside for a while and rethink it on your way home—the *aha moment* may reveal itself eventually.

So far, we've learned about macro-level problem localization using RCA, as well as good coding practices to prevent problems. Furthermore, by using a cutting-edge debugger tool such as GDB, we can control the execution of a program line by line, allowing us to analyze and fix problems at the micro level. All these activities are programmer-centralized and manual. Can any automatic tools help us diagnose the potential defects of a program? We'll take a look at static and dynamic analysis in the next section.

Static and dynamic analysis

In the previous sections, we learned about the RCA process and how to use GDB to debug a defect. This section will discuss how to analyze a program with and without executing it. The former is called **dynamic analysis**, while the latter is called **static analysis**.

Static analysis

Static analysis is used to evaluate the quality of a computer program without executing it. Although this can usually be accomplished through the use of automatic tools and code reviews/inspections, we will only focus on automatic tools in this section.

Automatic static code analysis tools are intended to compare a set of code to one or more sets of coding standards or guidelines. Typically, the terms *static code analysis*, *static analysis*, and *source code analysis* are used interchangeably. We may uncover many potential issues before the testing phases by scanning the whole code base with every conceivable code execution path. However, it has several limitations, which are set out here:

- It can produce false positive and false negative alarms
- It only applies the rules that were implemented inside the scanning algorithm, and some of them may be subjectively interpreted
- It cannot find vulnerabilities that were introduced in a runtime environment
- It can provide a false sense of security that everything is being addressed

There are about 30 automatic C/C++ code analysis tools under both commercial and free open source categories. The names of these tools include Clang, CLion's built-in code analysis tool, Cppcheck, Eclipse, Visual Studio, and GNU g++, just to name a few.

Details on `-Wall`, `-Weffcc++`, and `-Wextra` options, which are built into the g++ GNU compiler, can be found at `https://github.com/PacktPublishing/Expert-C-2nd-edition/blob/main/Chapter14/Introducing%20-Wall%2C%20-Weffcc%2B%2B%20and%20-Wextra.pdf`.

Dynamic analysis

Dynamic analysis is a shortened form of dynamic program analysis, which examines the performance of a software program by running it on a real or virtual processor. Dynamic analysis, as with static analysis, can be performed automatically or manually. Unit tests, integration tests, system tests, and acceptance tests, for example, are often human-involved dynamic analytical procedures. Memory debugging, memory leak detection, and profiling tools, on the other hand, such as IBM Purify, Valgrind, and Clang sanitizers, are examples of automated dynamic analysis tools. In this section, we will concentrate on automatic dynamic analysis tools.

The stages in a dynamic analysis process include preparing the input data, running a test program, gathering the relevant parameters, and analyzing the output. In general, dynamic analysis tools employ code instrumentation and/or a simulation environment to conduct tests on the analyzed code as it executes. We can interact with a program in the following ways:

- **Source code instrumentation**: A special code segment is inserted into the original source code before compilation.

- **Object code instrumentation**: A special binary code is added directly into the executable file.

- **Compilation stage instrumentation**: A checking code is added through special compiler switches. It doesn't change the source code. Instead, it uses special execution stage libraries to detect errors.

Dynamic analysis has the following pros:

- There are no false positive or false negative results because an error will be detected that isn't predicted from a model

- It does not need source code, which means the proprietary code can be tested by a third-party organization

The cons of dynamic analysis are set out here:

- It only detects defects on the routes related to the input data. Other defects may not be found.

- It can only check one execution path at a time. To obtain a complete picture, we need to run the test as many times as possible. This requires a significant amount of computational resources.

- It cannot check the correctness of the code. It is possible to get the correct result from the wrong operation.

- Executing incorrect code on a real processor may have unanticipated results.

- A detailed explanation of the usage of Valgrind can be found at `https://github.com/PacktPublishing/Expert-C-2nd-edition/blob/main/Chapter14/Usage%20of%20Valgrind.pdf`.

Testing, TDD, and BDD

In the previous section, we learned about automatic static and dynamic program analysis. This section will concentrate on human-involved (test code preparation) tests, which are a subset of dynamic analysis. Unit testing, TDD, and BDD are examples.

Unit testing presumes that if we already have a single unit of code, we must develop a test driver and prepare input data to see whether the output is right. Following that, we perform integration tests to test multiple units at once, followed by acceptance tests to test the entire application. Because integration and acceptance tests are more difficult to maintain and more project-related than unit tests, covering them in this book is extremely difficult. Those of you who are interested can find out more by going to `https://www.iso.org/standard/45142.html`.

In contrast to unit tests, TDD believes that we should have test code and data first, develop some code and make it pass quickly, and finally refactor until the customer is happy. On the other hand, BDD has the philosophy that we should not test the implementation of a program and instead test its desired behavior. To this end, BDD emphasizes that a communication platform and language among people involved in software production should be set up as well.

Unit testing

A unit is a component that is part of a larger or more complicated application. A unit, such as a function, a class, or an entire module, often has its own user interface. Unit testing is a type of software testing used to determine whether a unit of code behaves as expected in terms of its design criteria. The following are the primary characteristics of unit testing:

- It is small and simple, quick to write and run, and, as a result, it finds problems in the early development cycle; hence, problems can be fixed easily.

- Since it is isolated from dependencies, each test case can be run in parallel.

- Unit test drivers help us understand the unit interface.

- It greatly helps integration and acceptance tests when tested units are integrated later.

- It is normally prepared and performed by developers.

While we can write a unit test package from scratch, there are a lot of **Unit Test Frameworks (UTFs)** already being developed in the community. Boost.Test, CppUnit, GoogleTest, Unit++, and CxxTest are the most popular ones. These UTFs typically offer the following features:

- They only require a minimal amount of work for setting up a new test.

- They depend on standard libraries and support cross-platform, which means they are easy to port and modify.

- They support test fixtures, which allow us to reuse the same configuration for objects for several different tests.

- They handle exceptions and crashes well. This means that a UTF can report exceptions but not crashes.

- They have good assert functionalities. Whenever an assertion fails, its source code location and the values of the variables should be printed.

- They support different outputs, and these outputs can be conveniently analyzed either by humans or other tools.

- They support test suites, and each suite may contain several test cases.

Now, let's take a look at an example of the Boost UTF (since **v1.59.0**). It supports three different usage variants: the single-header-only variant, the static library variant, and the shared library variant. It includes four types of test cases: test cases without parameters, data-driven test cases, template test cases, and parameterized test cases.

It also has seven types of check tools: `BOOST_TEST()`, `BOOST_CHECK()`, `BOOST_REQUIRE()`, `BOOST_ERROR()`, `BOOST_FAIL()`, `BOOST_CHECK_MESSAGE( )`, and `BOOST_CHECK_EQUAL()`. It supports fixtures and controls the test output in many ways as well. When writing a test module, we need to follow these steps:

1. Define the name of our test program. This will be used in output messages.

2. Choose a usage variant: header-only, link with a static, or as a shared library.

3. Choose and add a test case to a test suite.

4. Perform correctness checks on the tested code.

5. Initialize the code under test before each test case.

6. Customize the ways in which test failures are reported.

7. Control the runtime behavior of the built test module, which is also called runtime configuration.

For example, the following example covers *steps 1-4*. If you are interested, you can get examples of *steps 5-7* at `https://www.boost.org/doc/libs/1_70_0/libs/test/doc/html/index.html`.

To build the code at `https://github.com/PacktPublishing/Expert-C-2nd-edition/blob/main/Chapter14/ch14_unit_test1.cpp`, we may need to install Boost, as follows:

```
sudo apt-get install libboost-all-dev
```

Then, we can build and run it, as follows:

```
~/wus1/Chapter-13$ g++ -g ch14_unit_test1.cpp
~/wus1/Chapter-13$ ./a.out
```

The preceding code results in the following output:

```
Running 3 test cases...
ch14_unit_test1.cpp(13): error: in "my_suite/test_case1": check x ==
'b'
has failed ['a' != 'b']
ch14_unit_test1.cpp(25): error: in "my_suite/test_case3": check false
```

```
has
failed
*** 2 failures are detected in the test module "my_test"
```

Here, we can see that there are failures in `test_case1` and `test_case3`. In `test_case1`, the value of `x` is not equal to `b`, and obviously, a false check cannot pass the test in `test_case3`.

TDD

As shown in the following diagram, a TDD process starts by writing failing test code and then adds/modifies the code to let the test pass. After that, we refactorize the test plan and code until all the requirements are satisfied:

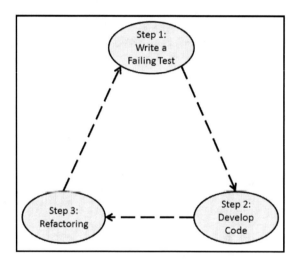

Figure 14.2 – TDD process

Step 1 is to write a failing test. Instead of developing code first, TDD starts to write test code initially. Because we do not have code yet, we know that if we run the test, it will fail. During this stage, the test data format and interface are defined, and the code implementation details are imagined.

The goal of **Step 2** is to make the test pass as quickly as possible with minimal development effort. We don't want to implement everything perfectly; we only want it to pass the test. Once it goes green, we will have something to show and tell the customer, at which point the customer may refine the requirement after seeing the initial product. Then, we move on to the next phase.

The third phase is refactoring. During this stage, we may go in, look at, and see what we would like to change and how to change it.

For traditional developers, the most difficult thing about TDD is the mindset change from the coding then testing pattern to the testing then coding pattern. To get a vague idea of a test suite, J. Hartikainen suggested that a developer considers the following five steps to start:

1. Decide the inputs and outputs first.

2. Choose class/function signatures.

3. Decide on only one tiny aspect of the functionality to test.

4. Implement the test.

5. Implement the code.

Once we've finished this iteration, we can gradually refactor it until the overall comprehensive goal is achieved.

BDD

The most difficult part of software development is communicating with business participants, developers, and the quality analysis team. A project can easily exceed its budget, miss deadlines, or fail completely because of misunderstood or vague requirements, technical arguments, and slow feedback cycles.

BDD is an agile development process with a set of practices that aims to reduce communication gaps/barriers and other wasteful activities. It also encourages team members to continuously communicate with real-world examples during the production life cycle.

BDD contains two main parts: deliberate discovery and TDD. To let people in different organizations and teams understand the right behavior of the developed software, the deliberate discovery phase introduces an *example mapping* technique to make people in different roles have conversations through concrete examples. These examples will become automated tests and living documentation of how the system behaves later. In its TDD phase, BDD specifies that the tests for any software unit should be specified in terms of the desired behavior of the unit.

There are several BDD framework tools (JBehave, RBehave, FitNesse, Cucumber, and so on) for different platforms and programming languages. Generally speaking, these frameworks perform the following steps:

1. Read a specification format document that's been prepared by a business analyst during the deliberate discovery phase.

2. Transform the document into meaningful clauses. Each individual clause is capable of being set into test cases for **quality assurance** (**QA**). Developers can implement source code from the clause as well.

3. Execute the test for each clause scenario automatically.

As shown in the following diagram, the traditional V-shape model emphasizes the pattern of *requirement | design | coding | testing*. TDD believes a development process should be driven by testing, while BDD adds communication between people from different backgrounds and roles into the TDD framework and focuses on behavior testing:

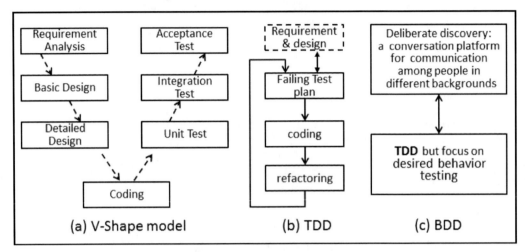

Figure 14.3 – V-shaped, TDD, and BDD models in comparison with each other

Moreover, unit testing emphasizes testing individual components when coding is complete. TDD focuses more on how to write tests before writing code, and then adding/modifying code through next-level test plans. BDD encourages collaborations between customers, business analysts, developers, and QA analysts. Although we can use each one individually, we really should combine them for the best results in this agile software development era.

To learn about incorporating TDD and BDD, refer to our GitHub repository at the following link: `https://github.com/PacktPublishing/Expert-C-2nd-edition/blob/main/Chapter14/Incorporating%20TDD%20and%20BDD.pdf`.

Summary

In this chapter, we discussed testing and debugging in the context of the software development process. Testing uncovers problems, while RCA assists in discovering a problem at the macro level. However, good programming practices can help to prevent software defects in the early stages. Furthermore, the CLI debugging tool known as GDB can help us set breakpoints and execute a program line by line while printing variable values during program execution.

We also discussed automatic analysis tools and human-assisted testing processes. Static analysis evaluates a program's performance without running it. Dynamic analysis tools, on the other hand, can detect flaws by simply running the program. Finally, we learned about the tactics for incorporating testing into a software development pipeline, including what, when, and how. When the coding is finished, unit testing focuses on testing individual components. TDD focuses more on how to write tests before developing code and then reiterates this process through a next-level test plan. BDD encourages collaborations between customers, business analysts, developers, and QA analysts.

Further reading

- *J. Rooney* and *L. Vanden Heuvel. Root Cause Analysis For Beginners. Quality Progress, July 2004, p.45-53.*

- *T. Kataoka, K. Furuto,* and *T. Matsumoto. The Analyzing Method of Root Causes for Software Problems. SEI Tech. Rev. no. 73, p. 81, 2011.*

- *K. A. Briski et al.. Minimizing code defects to improve software quality and lower development costs. IBM Rational Software Analyzer and IBM Rational PurifyPlus software.*

- `https://www.learncpp.com/cpp-programming/eight-c-programming-mistakes-the-compiler-wont-catch/`

- *B. Stroustrup* and *H. Sutter. C++ Core Guidelines.* (`https://isocpp.github.io/CppCoreGuidelines/`)

- `https://www.sourceware.org/gdb/`

- `https://www.fayewilliams.com/2014/02/21/debugging-for-beginners/`

- `https://www.perforce.com/blog/sca/what-static-analysis`

- `https://linux.die.net/man/1/g++`

- `https://www.embedded.com/static-vs-dynamic-analysis-for-secure-code-development-part-2/`

- *ISO/IEC/IEEE 29119-1:2013: Software and systems engineering – Software testing*

- `https://www.boost.org/doc/libs/1_70_0/libs/test/doc/html/index.html`

- *K. Beck. Test-Driven Development by Example,* published by *Addison Wesley, ISBN 978-0321146533.*

- *H. Erdogmus* and *T. Morisio. On the Effectiveness of Test-first Approach to Programming. Proc. of the IEEE Trans. on Software Engineering, 31(1). January 2005.*

- `https://codeutopia.net/blog/2015/03/01/unit-testing-tdd-and-bdd/`

- `https://cucumber.io/blog/bdd/intro-to-bdd-and-tdd/`

- *D. North. Introducing BDD.* (`https://dannorth.net/introducing-bdd/`) (*March 2006*)

- *D. North, E. Keogh, et al.,* `https://jbehave.org/`, *May 2019.*

15

Large-Scale Application Design

The demand for scalable and efficient systems has increased as more organizations have embraced technology. As more and more businesses start using digital technologies, the need to handle large volumes of data, support growing user bases, and ensure application performance becomes key. This chapter focuses on large-scale applications in C++, focusing on crucial aspects such as organization and scaling.

In this context, we will analyze the ideas behind horizontal and vertical scaling. Scaling is used to improve application performance in two primary ways – via horizontally and vertically scaling. This chapter examines the benefits and considerations associated with each approach. The chapter also discusses the specific challenges and techniques in scaling C++ applications. C++ has long been a popular programming language for its performance and flexibility, but scaling C++ applications to handle large-scale projects can present unique obstacles. We will explore strategies to optimize and distribute workloads, leverage parallelism and concurrency, and employ scalable data structures.

One type of large-scale application is data-intensive applications. With exponential data, processing, and storage growth, designing applications that can efficiently handle massive data volumes has become critical. This chapter will discuss the practices behind building data-intensive applications. The chapter also explores data partitioning, replication, caching, and data flow optimization. By understanding these principles, we can design robust and scalable applications that can handle the demands of large-scale data processing.

In summary, we will cover the following topics in this chapter:

- The introduction of large-scale, cross-platform project organization
- Horizontal and vertical scaling
- Scaling C++ applications
- Designing data-intensive applications

Technical requirements

The g++ compiler with the -std=c++2a option is used to compile the examples in this chapter. You can find the source files used in this chapter at https://github.com/PacktPublishing/ Expert-C-2nd-edition/tree/main/Chapter15.

The introduction of large-scale, cross-platform project organizing

Large-scale, cross-platform project organizing in C++ refers to implementing a comprehensive system that facilitates managing and coordinating multiple projects across different platforms, using the C++ programming language. It involves the development of a robust framework that enables seamless integration, communication, and resource sharing between diverse projects. By leveraging the power and versatility of C++, this approach provides a scalable and efficient solution to organize and execute large-scale projects on various platforms.

Large-scale, cross-platform project organization in C++

Large-scale, cross-platform projects in C++ pose unique challenges in organization and management. These projects involve developing software applications that can run on multiple operating systems or platforms, such as Windows, macOS, and Linux. This article will explore the key aspects and considerations involved in organizing a large-scale, cross-platform project in C++, along with examples to illustrate the concepts discussed.

Cross-platform project organization refers to the structure and management practices that ensure efficient software application development, maintenance, and deployment across different operating systems or platforms. It involves handling platform-specific code, libraries, and dependencies and ensuring compatibility and performance on each target platform.

A modular architecture is crucial for large-scale, cross-platform projects. Breaking down a project into smaller, independent modules offers several benefits, including code reusability, maintainability, and ease of testing. Each module can encapsulate platform-specific functionality, such as user interfaces or system integrations. Consider a cross-platform project that involves developing a media player application. The project can be divided into modules – core functionality, UI components, media playback, and file management. Each module can have platform-specific implementations while the core logic remains platform-agnostic.

Abstraction layers provide a way to isolate platform-specific code and provide a unified interface for the rest of an application. This allows developers to write portable code seamlessly, adapting to different platforms without extensive modifications. Suppose you are developing a cross-platform graphics application that utilizes different rendering APIs, such as DirectX on Windows and OpenGL on macOS and Linux. By implementing an abstraction layer, you can encapsulate the platform-specific rendering code within separate modules and expose a common interface for the rest of the application. This ensures that the core logic remains independent of the underlying rendering technology.

Utilizing platform-independent libraries can significantly simplify cross-platform development. These libraries provide pre-built functionality that can be seamlessly integrated into a project, reducing the need to write platform-specific code. Examples of such libraries include Boost, Qt, and SDL, which offer cross-platform support for various tasks, such as networking, user interfaces, and multimedia. For instance, you can leverage Boost if you develop a networking component for a cross-platform project. It provides a consistent API for network operations, abstracting the platform-specific details and enabling the application to communicate over different operating systems.

Large-scale, cross-platform projects require robust build systems and **continuous integration** (**CI**) practices – build systems that automate compiling, linking, and packaging applications for different platforms. Popular build systems such as CMake and Make can handle complex dependencies and generate platform-specific scripts. CI tools, such as Jenkins or Travis CI, facilitate automated testing, deployment, and integration of code changes across multiple platforms. They ensure that the project remains stable and functional on all supported platforms.

Thorough testing and debugging are critical in large-scale, cross-platform projects. Verifying an application's behavior on different platforms is essential, ensuring compatibility, stability, and optimal performance. Tools such as Google Test and CppUnit assist in creating unit tests, while platform-specific debugging tools aid in identifying and resolving platform-specific issues.

A large-scale, cross-platform project in C++

Organizing a large-scale, cross-platform project in C++ requires careful planning and consideration of various factors. These projects involve developing software applications that can run on multiple operating systems or platforms. Understanding the target platforms' specific requirements is crucial for effective project organization. Each platform may have unique capabilities, constraints, and APIs that must be considered during development. By thoroughly researching and documenting these requirements, developers can design an architecture that accommodates the specific needs of each platform. For example, if developing a cross-platform mobile application in C++, developers need to consider different screen sizes, input methods, and performance characteristics across platforms such as iOS and Android. Considering these platform-specific requirements upfront, they can design a flexible architecture that efficiently adapts to different screen resolutions and leverages platform-specific APIs.

Abstraction layers are crucial in decoupling platform-specific code from the core application logic. Developers can write portable code agnostic to the underlying platform using abstraction layers and interfaces. This approach simplifies maintenance, reduces code duplication, and promotes cross-platform compatibility.

Despite efforts to abstract platform-specific code, some scenarios may require direct interaction with platform-specific APIs or libraries. In such cases, developers should carefully handle platform-specific code and avoid cluttering the code base with numerous conditionals. Using conditional compilation directives, such as preprocessor directives or C++11's `constexpr if`, allows developers to isolate platform-specific code sections without cluttering the main code base. This approach helps maintain code readability and reduces the chances of introducing bugs due to conditional logic.

The section below the preprocessor directives in the following code block represents the cross-platform code, which can be shared code that does not depend on any specific platform. This code can be executed on all platforms, ensuring a project's cross-platform compatibility. This code snippet demonstrates two key considerations when organizing a large-scale, cross-platform project in C++. We will utilize preprocessor directives (`#ifdef`, `#elif`, and `#endif`) to include platform-specific code based on the current platform. This example defines platform-specific code for Windows, macOS, and Linux. You can add more platform-specific sections as needed:

```cpp
// main.cpp - Entry point of the cross-platform project

#include <iostream>

// Define platform-specific code using preprocessor
// directives
#ifdef _WIN32
    #define PLATFORM_NAME "Windows"
    // Include platform-specific headers and code
    #include <windows.h>
#elif __APPLE__
    #define PLATFORM_NAME "macOS"
    // Include platform-specific headers and code
    #include <CoreFoundation/CoreFoundation.h>
#elif __linux__
    #define PLATFORM_NAME "Linux"
    // Include platform-specific headers and code
    #include <unistd.h>
#endif

int main() {
    std::cout << "Running on " << PLATFORM_NAME << std::endl;

    // Cross-platform code
    // ...

    return 0;
}
```

When you compile and run this code, it will display the name of the platform it runs on. The platform-specific code sections can contain any platform-specific functionality or API calls required for your project.

Please note that this is a simplified example demonstrating the concept of platform-specific and cross-platform code organization. In a real-world, large-scale, cross-platform project, you would have more complex structures, additional modules, and various platform-specific functionalities integrated into the overall project organization.

Clear and comprehensive documentation is essential for large-scale, cross-platform projects. Documenting a project's architecture, design decisions, APIs, and platform-specific considerations allows developers to understand the project's structure and functionality. Additionally, well-documented code helps new team members quickly get up to speed and facilitates collaboration. Collaboration is crucial in cross-platform projects, especially when multiple teams or developers are involved. Establishing effective communication channels, such as regular meetings, shared project documentation, and version control systems, helps ensure everyone is aligned and working toward the same goals. Collaboration tools such as Git and project management platforms such as Jira can aid in tracking progress, assigning tasks, and resolving issues efficiently.

Cross-platform projects often require performance optimization to ensure a smooth operation on different platforms. Developers should profile and analyze an application's performance on each target platform, identifying bottlenecks and platform-specific optimizations. For example, if a cross-platform project involves real-time audio processing, developers may need to consider different audio libraries or adjust buffer sizes based on platform-specific latency characteristics. By fine-tuning the application's performance on each platform, developers can provide a consistent user experience across different operating systems.

Handling errors and exceptions in a cross-platform project requires consideration of platform-specific behaviors and conventions. Different operating systems may have unique error codes, exception-handling mechanisms, or APIs for error reporting. Developers should carefully handle errors and exceptions, ensuring that an application gracefully handles platform-specific exceptions and communicates errors effectively to the user. Adopting a consistent error-handling strategy across platforms improves an application's reliability and user experience.

Best practices and strategies for managing a large-scale, cross-platform project in C++

Managing a large-scale, cross-platform project in C++ requires careful planning, coordination, and adherence to best practices. These projects involve developing software applications that run seamlessly on multiple operating systems or platforms. In this article, we will explore the best practices and strategies that can help efficiently manage and coordinate large-scale, cross-platform projects in C++, ensuring compatibility, maintainability, and successful project delivery.

Defining clear project goals and scope is vital to managing large-scale, cross-platform projects. Determine the specific platforms to target, the desired functionality, and the project's expected outcomes. Communicate these goals to the development team to align everyone's efforts and ensure a shared understanding of the project's scope.

Agile development methodologies, such as Scrum or Kanban, offer significant benefits to manage large-scale, cross-platform projects. These methodologies emphasize iterative development, frequent communication, and adaptive planning. By breaking a project into smaller, manageable sprints and conducting regular team meetings, developers can address challenges, adapt to changing requirements, and deliver incremental value.

Effective version control and collaboration tools are crucial to managing large-scale, cross-platform projects involving multiple team members. Utilize version control systems such as Git to track changes, manage branches, and facilitate collaboration. Collaboration tools such as project management platforms (e.g., Jira and Trello) and communication platforms (e.g., Slack and Microsoft Teams) foster effective communication, task tracking, and issue resolution.

Implementing a robust **continuous integration/continuous delivery (CI/CD)** pipeline is essential to managing large-scale, cross-platform projects. CI automates the process of building, testing, and integrating code changes across different platforms. CD ensures that an application is always in a deployable state. By adopting CI/CD practices, developers can detect and resolve issues early, streamline the release process, and maintain high software quality.

Developing and adhering to cross-platform development guidelines is critical to maintaining code consistency, readability, and portability. Establish coding conventions, naming conventions, and design patterns that promote cross-platform compatibility. Document these guidelines and ensure that all team members are familiar with them to facilitate collaboration and maintain a unified code base.

Maintain a continuous feedback loop throughout a project to monitor progress, identify issues, and gather stakeholder feedback. Regularly review project milestones, performance metrics, and user feedback to make informed decisions and iterate on the project's direction. Actively seek feedback from team members, end users, and stakeholders to ensure the project meets their expectations and needs.

Horizontal and vertical scaling

Horizontal and vertical scaling are architectural strategies that can be applied in various domains, including software development in C++. Although scaling primarily refers to managing infrastructure and resources, it can affect software design and development.

Horizontal and vertical scaling are two fundamental approaches to handling increased demands or improving performance in computing systems. These concepts apply to various domains, including software development, databases, and server infrastructure. Let's delve into horizontal and vertical scaling, understanding their differences, advantages, and use cases.

Horizontal scaling

Horizontal scaling, or scaling out, involves adding more instances or nodes to distribute a workload across multiple machines. In this approach, a system's capacity is increased by expanding horizontally rather than enhancing the resources of individual devices.

The advantages of horizontal scaling include the following:

- **Improved scalability**: Horizontal scaling allows for easy scalability by adding more machines to a system. It provides the flexibility to accommodate increased user demand or data processing requirements.

- **Enhanced fault tolerance**: By distributing a workload across multiple machines, horizontal scaling enhances fault tolerance. If one machine fails, the others can continue handling the load, ensuring high availability.

- **Cost-effectiveness**: Horizontal scaling can be cost-effective since it involves adding commodity hardware or virtual instances, which are generally more affordable than investing in high-end machines.

Horizontal scaling is well suited to scenarios involving the following:

- **High-traffic websites**: Distributing web traffic across multiple servers can efficiently handle many concurrent user requests

- **Big data processing**: Distributing data processing tasks across multiple nodes allows for parallel processing, improving performance

- **Load balancing**: Horizontal scaling works well in load-balanced environments, where multiple servers can distribute requests evenly

Vertical scaling

Vertical scaling, or scaling up, involves increasing a single machine's resources (such as CPU, memory, or storage) to handle increased workloads or improve performance. In this approach, the capacity of a machine is expanded by enhancing its capabilities.

The advantages of vertical scaling include the following:

- **Simplicity**: Vertical scaling involves upgrading or replacing existing hardware resources without requiring significant software or system architecture changes.

- **Efficient resource utilization**: Vertical scaling allows for the efficient utilization of resources within a single machine. It can be more effective for applications that require significant processing power or memory access.

- **Reduced complexity**: Since a system is contained within a single machine, managing multiple instances or nodes is typically less complex.

Vertical scaling is beneficial in the following scenarios:

- **Applications with single-threaded performance requirements**: Some applications, such as certain scientific computations or simulations, may benefit from increased processing power on a single machine
- **Memory-intensive applications**: Vertical scaling can be effective for applications that heavily rely on memory, such as in-memory databases or complex data analytics

It is important to note that horizontal and vertical scaling are not mutually exclusive and can be combined, based on the specific needs of a system. A hybrid approach, known as diagonal scaling, combines the advantages of both strategies.

Scaling C++ applications

Scaling C++ applications refers to optimizing and expanding C++ code bases to handle increased workloads and accommodate growing user demands. It involves analyzing performance bottlenecks, identifying areas of improvement, and implementing scalable solutions such as parallelization, distributed computing, and load balancing. By scaling C++ applications, developers can ensure that their software can efficiently handle larger data volumes, higher user concurrency, and increased processing demands, resulting in improved performance and a better user experience.

Horizontal scaling in C++

Horizontal scaling in C++ involves distributing a workload across multiple machines or instances to handle increased demand or achieve better performance. This can be achieved through techniques such as load balancing and distributed computing.

In a horizontally scaled C++ application, different instances or nodes can handle other parts of the workload concurrently. This approach can improve the application's overall throughput, scalability, and fault tolerance. For example, horizontal scaling in a web application written in C++ can involve deploying multiple instances of an application server behind a load balancer to distribute incoming requests evenly.

To facilitate horizontal scaling in C++, designing the application with a modular architecture and loose coupling is essential. This allows different instances to work independently and communicate effectively. Technologies such as message queues or distributed databases can also ensure data consistency across instances.

Vertical scaling in C++

Vertical scaling, or scaling up, involves increasing a single machine's resources (such as CPU, memory, or storage) to handle increased workloads or improve performance. This can be achieved by upgrading the hardware or provisioning more powerful virtual machines.

Vertical scaling can also involve using advanced techniques such as vectorization or parallel programming to leverage specialized hardware features such as **Single Instruction, Multiple Data (SIMD)** instructions or **Graphics Processing Unit (GPU)** acceleration.

Choosing between horizontal and vertical scaling depends on the specific requirements and constraints of an application. Horizontal scaling offers better scalability and fault tolerance, while vertical scaling can provide a cost-effective solution for applications with lower demands or resource constraints.

It is worth noting that scaling considerations in C++ often extend beyond just managing infrastructure. Designing an application with scalability in mind, utilizing efficient algorithms and data structures, and leveraging parallelism can contribute to the ability to scale effectively in both horizontal and vertical directions.

Designing data-intensive applications

Designing data-intensive applications in C++ involves considering various aspects, including data storage, data processing, and efficient utilization of system resources. This section will list some key considerations and best practices for designing data-intensive applications in C++.

To begin with, some best practices for data modeling and storage are listed as follows:

- **Identify the nature and structure of the data**: Analyze the data requirements and determine the appropriate data model, such as relational, NoSQL, or a combination of both, based on the application's needs.

- **Choose efficient data storage solutions**: Select appropriate data storage technologies, such as databases (MySQL, PostgreSQL, and MongoDB) or distributed filesystems (Hadoop HDFS and Apache Cassandra), based on factors such as scalability, performance, and data integrity requirements.

- **Optimize data access and retrieval**: Employ techniques such as indexing, caching, and query optimization to enhance data retrieval performance. Utilize appropriate data structures and algorithms to store and retrieve data efficiently.

We should consider the following in terms of concurrency and parallelism:

- **Leverage multi-threading**: Utilize multithreading to parallelize data processing tasks and improve overall performance. Use synchronization mechanisms such as locks or mutexes to ensure data consistency and avoid race conditions.

- **Utilize parallel algorithms and libraries**: Use similar computing libraries such as Intel **Threading Building Blocks (TBBs)** or OpenMP to parallelize computationally intensive operations. These libraries provide abstractions and utilities for efficient parallel processing.

The following applies to efficient memory management:

- **Minimize memory overhead**: Design data structures and algorithms that minimize memory usage, avoiding unnecessary duplication or excessive object creation. Use memory-efficient containers, such as `std::vector` or `std::deque`, and manage dynamic memory allocation carefully.

- **Utilize memory pooling**: Implement custom memory pooling techniques to reduce the overhead of frequent memory allocation and deallocation, especially in scenarios with high object creation rates.

See these suggestions for stream processing and pipelining:

- **Employ stream processing techniques**: Utilize frameworks such as Apache Kafka or RabbitMQ for real-time data ingestion and processing. Stream processing enables efficient data processing as it arrives, facilitating real-time analytics and response.

- **Implement data pipelines**: Design data processing pipelines to transform and manipulate data efficiently. Break down processing tasks into smaller stages or modules, ensuring scalability and maintainability.

Apply the following to your performance optimization:

- **Profile and identify bottlenecks**: Use profiling tools and techniques to identify performance bottlenecks in data-intensive operations. Optimize critical sections of code by applying appropriate algorithms, data structures, or parallelization techniques.

- **Utilize SIMD instructions**: Use SIMD instructions, such as Intel SSE or AVX, to perform data-parallel operations efficiently. SIMD instructions can significantly improve performance in numerical and vectorized computations.

These practices align with data security and integrity:

- **Ensure data privacy and protection**: Implement appropriate security measures, such as encryption, access control, and authentication, to safeguard sensitive data. Follow best practices for secure coding and handling of user input to prevent security vulnerabilities.

- **Implement data validation and error handling**: Validate input data to ensure its integrity and reliability. Handle exceptions and errors gracefully, providing informative error messages and robust recovery mechanisms.

By considering and incorporating these best practices into the design and implementation of data-intensive applications in C++, developers can create efficient, scalable, and robust systems that effectively handle large volumes of data and deliver optimal performance.

This example shows a simple data-intensive application, demonstrating data storage, processing, and management:

```cpp
#include <iostream>
#include <vector>
#include <algorithm>
```

Data structure

We define a `Record` structure to represent individual records. Each record has an ID, name, and age associated with it:

```cpp
// Data structure for storing records
struct Record {
    int id;
    std::string name;
    int age;
};
```

Data processing

The `processData` function takes a vector of `Record` objects as input and performs various data processing operations. In this case, we sort the records based on age using the `std::sort` algorithm, with a lambda function as the comparison criterion. Then, we print the sorted records:

```cpp
// Function to process records
void processData(const std::vector<Record>& records) {
    // Sort records by age
    std::vector<Record> sortedRecords = records;
    std::sort(sortedRecords.begin(), sortedRecords.end(),
      [](const Record& a, const Record& b) {
        return a.age < b.age;
    });

    // Print sorted records
    std::cout << "Sorted Records by Age:\n";
    for (const auto& record : sortedRecords) {
        std::cout << "ID: " << record.id << ", Name: " <<
          record.name << ", Age: " << record.age <<
          std::endl;
    }

    // Perform data processing operations
```

```
    // ...
}
```

The main function

In the `main` function, we create a sample dataset with multiple records. We pass this dataset to the `processData` function to perform the data processing operations.

This is a simplified example, but it demonstrates how data structures can be used to store records and how data processing operations can be performed on them. In real-world data-intensive applications, you typically have more complex data structures, advanced algorithms, and additional functionality to handle large datasets efficiently:

```cpp
int main() {
    // Create a sample dataset
    std::vector<Record> records = {
        {1, "John", 35},
        {2, "Alice", 28},
        {3, "Michael", 42},
        {4, "Emily", 32},
        {5, "David", 40}
    };

    // Process the data
    processData(records);

    return 0;
}
```

Summary

This chapter covered several essential aspects of large-scale software development, providing insights into organizing cross-platform projects, implementing scaling strategies, scaling C++ applications, and designing efficient data-intensive applications.

This introduction to large-scale, cross-platform project organization highlights the complexity of developing software applications that can seamlessly run across multiple operating systems or platforms. It emphasizes key considerations such as modular architecture, abstraction layers, platform-independent libraries, build systems, testing practices, documentation, and collaboration. By understanding and implementing these practices, developers can effectively manage the intricacies of large-scale, cross-platform projects.

The discussion on horizontal and vertical scaling explored two fundamental approaches to handling increased demands and enhancing performance in computing systems. Horizontal scaling involves distributing a workload across multiple machines or instances, providing benefits such as improved scalability, fault tolerance, and cost-effectiveness. On the other hand, vertical scaling focuses on enhancing the resources of a single machine, simplifying management, and ensuring efficient resource utilization. Understanding each scaling approach's advantages, use cases, and considerations is crucial to optimizing system performance and handling growing workloads.

The information covered on scaling C++ applications delved into the specific techniques and strategies to scale applications written in C++. It covers multithreading, parallel computing, memory management, and efficient resource utilization. Leveraging the capabilities of C++ language features, libraries, and optimization techniques can significantly enhance the scalability and performance of C++ applications in diverse environments.

Designing data-intensive applications in C++ involves crucial data storage, processing, and resource management considerations. Key areas covered include data modeling and storage selection, concurrency and parallelism, efficient memory management, stream processing and pipelining, performance optimization, and data security and integrity. By following best practices and implementing efficient design patterns, developers can create data-intensive applications that handle large volumes of data, optimize performance, and ensure data integrity and security.

Understanding and incorporating these concepts into software development processes enable developers to tackle the challenges associated with large-scale projects efficiently. Developers can achieve optimal performance, scalability, and maintainability in their software systems by organizing cross-platform projects, implementing appropriate scaling strategies, optimizing C++ applications, and designing efficient data-intensive applications. The next chapter will look at using C++ for machine learning tasks.

Questions

1. What are the key considerations for organizing a large-scale cross-platform project in C++?

2. What are the differences between horizontal and vertical scaling, and what are their respective advantages and use cases?

3. How can C++ applications be scaled effectively, considering multithreading, parallel computing, and efficient resource utilization?

4. What are the important factors to consider when designing data-intensive applications in C++, including data storage, processing, and memory management?

5. How can modular architecture and abstraction layers be leveraged in large-scale cross-platform projects to ensure scalability and maintainability?

6. What are the best practices to optimize performance and ensure data integrity and security in data-intensive applications developed in C++?

7. How would you differentiate between different client applications when implementing a server application?

Further reading

For further information, refer to the following:

- *Lessons from Building and Scaling LinkedIn*: `https://www.infoq.com/presentations/linkedin-architecture-stack/`
- *High-Performance Computing: Modern Systems and Practices* by Thomas Sterling, Matthew Anderson, and Maciej Brodowicz: `https://www.sciencedirect.com/book/9780124201583/high-performance-computing`

Part 3:
C++ in the AI World

This part is an overview of recent advances in AI and machine learning. You will learn how to tackle machine learning tasks using C++, and even designing a dialog-based search engine. This part has the following chapters:

- Chapter 16, Understanding and Using C++ in Machine Learning Tasks

- Chapter 17, Using C++ in Data Science

- Chapter 18, Designing and Implementing a Data Analysis Framework

16

Understanding and Using C++ in Machine Learning Tasks

This book aims to provide you with a comprehensive guide to leveraging the power of C++ in the field of **machine learning** (**ML**). Whether you're a beginner exploring the realms of **artificial intelligence** (**AI**) or an experienced developer looking to expand your skill set, this book will equip you with the knowledge and tools necessary to apply C++ effectively to ML tasks. ML has become a fundamental discipline in the realm of AI, enabling computers to learn from data and make predictions or decisions without explicit programming. As the demand for intelligent systems continues to grow, so does the need for robust programming languages that can handle the computational complexities of ML algorithms. This is where C++ shines. So, whether you're a researcher, a data scientist, or simply a curious learner, we hope this book will serve as your roadmap to mastering C++ in the realm of ML. We invite you to dive in, experiment, and unlock the immense potential that C++ brings to the world of intelligent systems.

AI and ML have become more and more popular recently. From simple food delivery websites to complex industrial robots, AI has been declared as one of the main features powering software and hardware. While, most of the time, the terms are used to make the product look more serious, some companies are intensively researching and incorporating AI into their systems. Before we go further, take into account the fact that this chapter is a gentle introduction to ML from a C++ programmer's perspective. For more comprehensive literature, refer to the list of books in the *Further reading* section. In this chapter, we will introduce the concepts of AI and ML. While it is preferred that you have a mathematical background, we will barely use any math in this chapter. If you are planning to enlarge your skill set and dive into ML, you must consider studying mathematics first.

Besides introducing the concepts, this chapter also provides examples of tasks in ML. We are going to implement them and give you a basic idea of how you should research and move forward with solving more complex tasks.

We will cover the following topics in the chapter:

- Introduction to AI and ML in general
- Categories and applications of ML
- Designing a C++ class for calculations
- Neural network structure and implementation
- Regression analysis and clustering

Technical requirements

The g++ compiler with the `-std=c++2a` option was used to compile the examples in this chapter. You can find the source files that were used in this chapter at `https://github.com/PacktPublishing/Expert-C-2nd-edition`.

Introduction to AI

The simplest definition of AI is robots acting like humans. It is the intelligence demonstrated by machines. And this is where the discussion around the definition of intelligence comes in: how can we define it for machines, and at what level should we shout out loud that we are dealing with an intelligent machine?

If you are not familiar with the different tests we can use to verify the intelligence of a machine, one of the popular ways to do so is the Turing test. The idea is to have an interrogator asking questions to two people, one of them being a machine and the other a human. If the interrogator can't make a clear distinction between those two, the machine should be considered intelligent.

> **Note**
>
> The Turing test is named after Alan Turing. The test was introduced in his paper, *Computing Machinery and Intelligence*, in 1950. He proposed using the imitation game to determine whether a machine thinks like a human.

The people being interrogated are behind a wall so that the interrogator can't see them. The interrogator then asks several questions to both participants. The following diagram demonstrates how the interrogator communicates with the human and the machine, but can't physically see them:

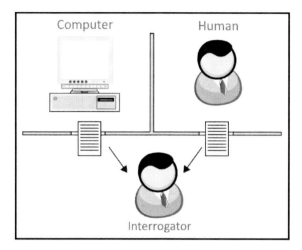

Figure 16.1 – Interrogator

When you start diving into the field of AI, the definition of intelligence gets more and more vague. Questions can be asked to a machine in any form: in text, in audio, in visual form, and so on. Numerous things might never be available in machines, such as the look on their faces. Sometimes, people understand each other's moods by the look on their faces. You can't be sure whether a robot will understand or will even be able to imitate the mood on its face. No one taught us to look angry when we are angry. No one taught us to have emotions. They are just there. It's hard to tell whether someday, something similar might be achieved for machines.

When speaking about AI, most of the time, we presume it's about a robot that talks and behaves similarly to humans. But when you try to dissect it as a programmer, you come across a lot of sub-fields, each of which takes a lot of time to understand. Many of the fields have a lot of tasks in progress or are in the early research phase. Here are some of the sub-fields in AI that you might be interested in focusing on in your career:

- **Computer vision**: This involves designing algorithms for visual object recognition and understanding objects by analyzing their visual representation. It's easy for humans to spot a familiar face in the crowd, but implementing similar functionality for machines might take a lot of time to gain accuracy equal to humans.

- **Natural language processing** (**NLP**): A linguistic analysis of text by machines. It has applications in various segments, such as machine translation. Imagine that the computer completely understands human written text so that we can tell it what to do instead of spending months learning a programming language.

- **Knowledge reasoning**: This might seem the obvious goal for machines to behave intelligently. Knowledge reasoning is concerned with making machines reason and provide solutions based on the information they have; for example, providing a diagnosis by examining medical conditions.

- **ML**: A field of study of algorithms and statistical models used by machines to perform tasks without explicit instructions. Instead of direct instructions, ML algorithms rely on patterns and inference. That said, ML allows machines to do the job on their own, without human involvement.

Let's discuss the preceding sub-fields separately and then concentrate on ML.

Computer vision

Computer vision is a comprehensive field of study and has a lot of ongoing research projects. It is concerned with almost everything related to visual data processing. It has wide applications in various areas; for example, face recognition software processing data from various cameras spread over the city to find and determine criminal suspects, or optical character recognition software that produces text from images containing it. Combined with some **augmented reality** (**AR**) technologies, the software can translate text in images into a language familiar to the user.

Studies in this field are making progress by the day. Combined with AI systems, computer vision is the field that makes machines perceive the world as we do. A simple task for us, however, is challenging to implement in terms of computer vision. For example, when we see an object in an image, we can easily spot its dimensions. For example, the following figure represents the front view of a bicycle:

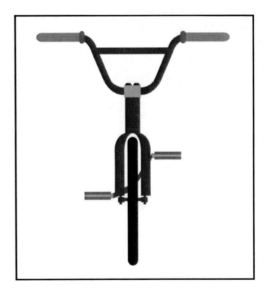

Figure 16.2 – Front view of a bicycle

Even if we don't mention that it's a bicycle, it's not so hard for a human to determine it. It's obvious to us that the black bold line at the bottom center is the front wheel of the bicycle. It's hard to tell the computer to understand that this is a wheel. All the computer sees is a collection of pixels, some of which are the same color:

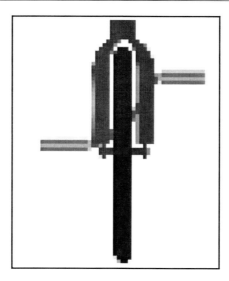

Figure 16.3 – Collection of pixels

Besides understanding the wheel of the bicycle, it should also deduce that this bicycle must have another wheel that is not visible in the figure. And again, we might guess the approximate size of the bicycle, whereas this is a comprehensive task for the computer to determine from the image. That said, this simple thing from our perspective might become a real challenge in computer vision.

> **Important**
>
> We suggest using the OpenCV (https://opencv.org/) library for computer vision tasks. It is a cross-platform library written in C and C++. OpenCV represents a set of functions aimed at real-time computer vision, including, but not limited to, facial recognition, gesture recognition, motion understanding, motion tracking, and other features.

Typical tasks in computer vision include object recognition, identification, and detection:

- **Object recognition**: Object recognition refers to the ability to classify or categorize an object based on its general characteristics or features. It involves determining the class or category to which an object belongs. In our example, object recognition is the understanding that the object in the preceding figure is a vehicle. It involves recognizing the overall characteristics and features that define an object as a vehicle, such as its shape, size, and general appearance.

- **Object identification**: Object identification, on the other hand, goes beyond recognizing the general class or category of an object. It involves pinpointing or specifically identifying an individual instance or part of an object. In our example, object identification would involve recognizing and isolating a specific part of the vehicle, such as identifying the wheel of the bicycle in the preceding figure. It focuses on identifying specific details or components that distinguish one instance or part of an object from others.

- **Object detection**: Object detection tasks for bicycles might include identifying specific components or regions of interest, such as handlebars, pedals, the saddle, or wheels. These tasks aim to locate and label the different parts of the bicycle within an image, enabling a comprehensive understanding of its structure and attributes.

Now, let's look at NLP.

NLP

Another interesting field of study is NLP. NLP makes efforts to make computers understand human languages. A more generalized approach is automatic speech recognition and natural language understanding, which are key features of virtual assistants. Today, it's not magic anymore to talk to your phone and ask it to search for something on the web, for example. The entire process is powered by complex algorithms in speech and text analysis. The following diagram shows a high-level view of the process that happens within the conversational agents:

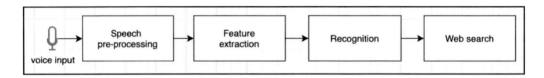

Figure 16.4 – NLP

Furthermore, in addition to virtual assistants, there are numerous chat-like programs (ChatGPT, Bard, and others) and language models that have emerged, offering assistance and providing valuable information to users. These programs, much like the one you are currently interacting with, utilize advanced NLP techniques to understand user input, generate relevant responses, and assist with a wide range of queries.

Many language processing tasks are related to the web. A search engine processing the user input to search millions of documents on the web is one of the top applications of NLP. In the next chapter, we will dive a lot deeper into search engine design and implementation. One of the main concerns in search engine design is processing the text data. The search engine cannot just store all the websites and respond to the user for the first match for the query. Numerous tasks in NLP have complex implementations. Suppose that we are designing a program that is fed with a text document and we need to output sentences within the document. Recognizing the beginning and the end of a sentence is one of its complex tasks. The following sentence is a simple example:

```
I love studying C++. It's hard, but interesting.
```

The program will output two sentences:

```
I love studying C++.
It's hard, but interesting.
```

In terms of a coding task, we just search for the . (dot) character at the end and make sure the first word starts with a capital letter. How would the program behave if one of the sentences had the following form?

```
I love studying C++!
```

As there is an exclamation point at the end of the sentence, we should revisit our program to add another rule for recognizing the ending of a sentence. What if a sentence ends like this?

```
It's hard, but interesting...
```

One by one, more and more rules and definitions are introduced so that we have a fully functional sentence extractor. Leveraging ML moves us in a smarter direction when solving NLP tasks.

Another language-related task is machine translation, which automatically translates a document from one language into another. Also, note that building a comprehensive NLP system will benefit other fields of study, such as knowledge reasoning.

Knowledge reasoning

Knowledge reasoning involves making computers think and reason in a similar way to humans. Imagine having a conversation with a machine that starts like this:

```
[Human] Hello
[Machine] Hello
```

We can program the machine to answer specific questions or understand complex text input given by the user, but it's a lot harder to make the machine reason based on previous experience. For example, the following reasoning is one of the goals of the study:

```
[Human] I was walking yesterday and it was raining.
[Machine] Nice.
[Human] I should dress warmer next time.
[Machine] OK.
[Human] I think I have a temperature.
[Machine] Did you should be a cold yesterday?
[Human] I guess so.
```

While it might seem easy to spot the connection between catching a cold and the rain, it takes a lot of effort for the program to deduce it. It must associate the rain with cold and having a temperature with catching a cold. It also needs to remember the previous input so that it can intelligently keep the dialog.

All of the aforementioned fields of study are exciting areas for a programmer to dive deeper into. Finally, ML in general is something that sits at the fundament for all other fields in terms of designing algorithms and models for each specific application. We are fortunate to live in an era where the boundaries between humans and machines are blurring, thanks to breakthroughs in NLP and related fields. Now, let's embark on a journey to unravel the intricacies of NLP and harness the power of C++ in creating intelligent language-based applications.

ML

ML takes us to a whole new level of making machines execute tasks the way humans do, maybe even better. Compared to the fields we introduced previously, the goal of ML is to build systems that can do things without specific instructions. In the journey of inventing artificially intelligent machines, we should take a closer look at human intelligence. When a child is born, they don't express intelligent behavior; instead, they start to slowly become familiar with the surrounding world. There is no recorded evidence of any 1-month-old child solving differential equations or composing music. In the same way that a child learns and discovers the world, ML is concerned with building the foundational models that directly perform the tasks and learning how to do them. That's the fundamental difference between setting up a system to carry out predefined instructions and letting it figure it out on its own.

When a child starts walking, taking things, talking, and asking questions, they are gaining knowledge about the world step by step. They take a book, taste it, and sooner or later stop chewing books as they realize they're not edible. Years pass and the child now opens the pages of the book and looks for images in it and the little figures comprising the text. A few more years pass and the child starts to read them. Over the years, the child's brain becomes more and more complicated and creates more and more connections between its neurons. The child becomes an intelligent human being.

Imagine a system that has some magical algorithms and models in it. After feeding it a bunch of data, it will be able to understand more and more, the same way a child gets to know the world by processing the input data in the form of visual data (looking through their eyes), smell, or flavor. Later on, by developing a way to ask questions, the child gets to understand words and associates those words with objects in the real world, and even intangible concepts. ML systems act almost in the same way. They process the input data and produce some output that conforms to the results expected by us. The following diagram illustrates this idea:

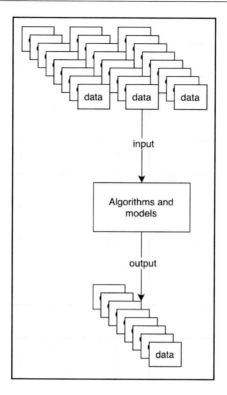

Figure 16.5 – The ML system

Now, let's dive deeper into ML. As always, the best way to understand something new is to try to implement it first.

Understanding ML

ML is a big field of study with a lot of research in progress and is expanding rapidly. To understand ML, we should first understand the nature of learning. Thinking and reasoning are the key concepts that make us – humans – special. The core of ML is to make the system learn and use that knowledge to act upon tasks. You might recall your first steps in studying programming. We are sure it wasn't easy. You had to learn new concepts, build abstractions, and make your brain understand what's going on under the hood of program execution. After that, you were supposed to build complex systems using those small building blocks described in primers as keywords, instructions, conditional statements, functions, classes, and so on.

However, an ML program differs from the programs we usually create. Take a look at the following code:

```
int calculate()
{
    int a{14};
```

```
    int b{27};

    int c{a + b};

    return c;
}
```

This simple program does what we instructed it to do. It contains several simple instructions that lead to the c variable representing the sum of a and b. We can modify this function to take user input, as follows:

```
int calculate(int a, int b)
{    int c{a + b}; return c;
}
```

The preceding function will never gain any intelligence. It doesn't matter how many times we call the calculate() function. It also doesn't matter what numbers we provide as its input. The function represents a collection of instructions. We might say even a collection of hardcoded instructions – that is, the function will never modify its instructions to behave differently based on the input. However, we can introduce some logic; let's say we make it return 0 every time it receives negative numbers:

```
int calculate(int a, int b)
{    if (a < 0 && b < 0) {
    return 0;
    }    int c{a + b}; return c;
}
```

The conditional statement introduced the simplest form of a decision that the function makes based on its input. We can add more and more conditionals so that the function will grow and have a complex implementation. However, no number of conditional statements will make it smarter because it is not something that the code comes up with on its own. And here comes the limit that we face when dealing with programs: they don't think; they act as we programmed them to act. We are the ones who decide how they must behave. And they always obey. Well, so long as we didn't introduce bugs.

Now, imagine an ML algorithm in action. Suppose the calculate() function has some magic in it so that it returns a value based on the input. Let's say it has the following form:

```
int calculate(int a, int b)
{    // some magic
    // return value
}
```

Now, suppose that we are calling `calculate()` and passing 2 and 4 as its arguments, hoping that it will calculate their sum and return 6. Also, imagine that we can somehow tell whether the result is what we expected. After a while, the function behaves such that it understands how to use those input values and return their sum. The class that we will build in the next section represents our first steps toward understanding ML.

Designing an algorithm that learns

The following class represents a calculation machine. It comprises four arithmetic operations and expects that we provide examples of how it should calculate the input values:

```
classExample
{
public:
int input1;
int input 2;
int output;
};
class CalculationMachine
{
public:
using Examples = std::vector<Example>;
// pass calculation examples through the setExamples() void
setExamples(const Examples& examples);
// the main function of interest
// returns the result of the calculation int calculate(int a, int b);
private:
// this function pointer will point to // one of the arithmetic
functions below int (*fptr_)(int, int) = nullptr;
private:
// set of arithmetic functions
static int sum(int, int);
static int subtract(int, int);
static int multiply(int, int);
static int divide(int, int);
};
```

Before using the `calculate()` function, we should provide a list of examples for the `setExamples()` function. Here's a sample of the examples that we provide to `CalculationMachine`:

```
3 4 7
2 2 4
5 5 10
4 5 9
```

The first two numbers in each line represent the input arguments; the third number is the result of the operation. The `setExamples()` function is how `CalculationMachine` learns how to use the correct arithmetic function. In the same way that we can guess what's going on from the preceding examples, `CalculationMachine` tries to find the best fit for its operations. It goes through examples and defines which of the functions it should use when `calculate()` is called. The implementation is similar to the following:

```
void CalculationMachine::setExamples(const Examples &examples)
{int sum_count{0};
int sub_count{0};
int mul_count{0};
int div_count{0};
for (const auto &example : examples)
{if (CalculationMachine.sum(example.input1, example.input2) ==
example.output)
{++sum_count;
}if (CalculationMachine.subtract(example.input1, example.input2) ==
example.output)
{++sub_count;
}// the same for multiply() and divide()
}// the function that has the maximum number of correct
// output results
// becomes the main function for called by calculate()
// fptr_ is assigned the winner arithmetic function
}
```

As you can see from the preceding example, the function calls all the arithmetic functions and compares their return value with the example output. Every time the result is correct, it increases the count of correct answers for the specific function. Finally, the function with the maximum number of correct answers is assigned to `fptr_`, which is used by the `calculate()` function, as follows:

```
int CalculationMachine::calculate(int a, int b)
{// fptr_ points to the sum() function
return fptr_(a, b);
}
```

With that, we have devised a simple learning algorithm. The `setExamples()` function might be renamed `setDataSet()`, `trainWithExamples()`, or something similar. The point of this example with `CalculationMachine` is that we define a model and algorithm that works with it; we can call this ML. It learns from data. Or, even better, it learns from experiences. Each record in the vector of examples that we provided to `CalculationMachine` can be regarded as an experience. We say that the performance of the calculation improves with experience – that is, the more we provide examples, the more it becomes confident in choosing the right function to perform the task. And the task is calculating the value based on two input arguments. The process of learning itself is not a task.

Learning is what leads to performing the task. Tasks are usually described as how the system should process an example, where an example is a collection of features. However, in ML terms, an example is represented as a vector (mathematical), where each entry is another feature; the choice of the vector data structure is just a coincidence. As one of the fundamental principles is training the system, ML algorithms can be categorized as supervised or unsupervised. Let's examine their differences and then establish various applications of ML systems.

Categories of ML

Categorizing ML algorithms depends on the kind of experience they have during the learning process. We usually call this collection of examples a dataset. Some books also use the term data points. A dataset is a collection of data representing anything useful to the target system. It might include measurements of weather for certain periods, a list of prices for the stock of some company or companies, or any other set of data. While the dataset might be unprocessed or so-called raw, some datasets contain additional information for each contained experience. In the CalculationMachine example, we used a raw dataset, although we already programmed the system to recognize that the first two values were the operands of the operation and the third value was its result. As already mentioned, we categorize ML algorithms into supervised and unsupervised:

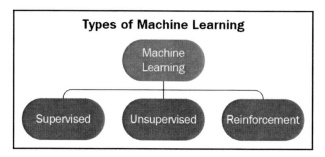

Figure 16.6 – Categorization of ML

Supervised learning algorithms learn from labeled datasets; that is, each record contains additional information describing the data. CalculationMachine is an example of a supervised learning algorithm. Supervised learning is also known as training with an instructor. The instructor teaches the system using the dataset:

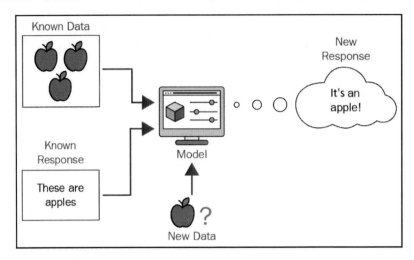

Figure 16.7 – Supervised learning

A good example of an application of a supervised learning algorithm is the spam filter in email applications. Users label emails as spam or not and the system then tries to find patterns in new incoming emails to detect potential spam emails.

The example with `CalculationMachine` is another case of supervised learning. We fed it the following dataset:

```
3 4 7
2 2 4
5 5 10

4 5 9
```

We programmed `CalculationMachine` to read the first two numbers as input arguments, and the third number as the output produced by a function applied to the input. This way, we provided the necessary information on what exactly the system should get as a result.

Unsupervised learning algorithms are even more complex – they process the dataset, which contains a bunch of features, and then try to find useful properties of these features. Unsupervised learning algorithms are mostly left alone to define what's in the dataset. In terms of intelligence, an unsupervised learning approach meets the description of an intelligent creature more than supervised learning algorithms. In contrast, supervised learning algorithms try to predict which input values map to the output values, while unsupervised algorithms perform several operations to discover patterns in a dataset. Following the same association in the preceding diagram, the following diagram describes an unsupervised learning algorithm:

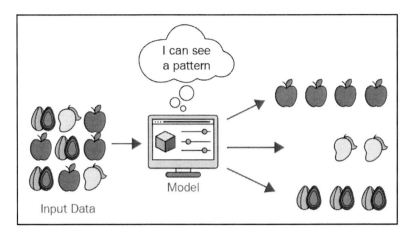

Figure 16.8 – Unsupervised algorithm

Examples of applications of unsupervised learning algorithms are recommendation systems. We will discuss one in the next chapter, where we will design a web search engine. Recommendation systems analyze user activity to recommend similar data, such as movie recommendations.

As shown in *Figure 16.6*, reinforcement learning is also an option. This is a category of algorithms that learn from mistakes. There is a feedback loop between the learning system and its experiences so that reinforcement learning algorithms interact with an environment. They might make a lot of mistakes in the beginning and, after processing the feedback, correct and improve themselves. The learning process becomes part of task execution. Imagine that `CalculationMachine` receives only input numbers but not the result of the calculation. For each experience, it will produce a result by applying one of the arithmetic operations and then receive feedback. Let's say it subtracts the numbers and then modifies itself to calculate the sum based on the feedback.

Applications of ML

Understanding the different categories of ML helps us apply it better to various kinds of tasks. There is a wide range of tasks that can be solved with ML. We have already mentioned classification as one of the tasks that can be solved with ML algorithms. Classification is the process of filtering and ordering the input to specify the categories the input belongs to. Solving classification with ML usually means that it produces a function that maps input to a specific output. Outputting a probability distribution over classes is also a type of classification task. One of the best examples of a classification task is object recognition. The input is a set of pixel values (in other words, an image) and the output is a value that identifies the object in the image. Imagine a robot that can recognize different kinds of tools and deliver them to workers on command – for example, a mechanic working in a garage has an assistant robot that can recognize a screwdriver and bring it on command.

Something more challenging is classification with missing inputs. In the preceding example, it's similar to asking the robot to bring something to screw the bolts. When some of the input is missing, the learning algorithm must operate with more than one function to achieve a successful result. For example, the assistant robot might bring pliers first and then come up with a screwdriver as the correct solution.

Similar to classification is regression, where the system is asked to predict a numerical value, given some input that is provided. The difference is the format of the output. An example of a regression task is predicting the future prices of stocks. These and other applications of ML are making it grow rapidly as a field of study. Learning algorithms are not just a list of conditional statements, which is what they might feel like at first. They are based on more comprehensive constructs modeled after human brain neurons and their connections. This leads us to the next section, where we will cover **artificial neural networks (ANNs)**.

Neural networks

Neural networks are designed to recognize patterns. They are modeled after the human brain; more specifically, we speak about neurons of the brain and their artificial counterparts – artificial neurons. A neuron in the human brain is illustrated in the following diagram:

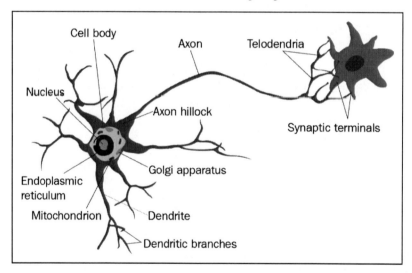

Figure 16.9 – A neuron in the human brain

A neuron communicates with other neurons via synapses. The basic functionality of a neuron is processing a portion of data and producing signals based on that data. In programming terms, a neuron takes a set of inputs and produces an output.

That's why the following diagram makes it clear why an artificial neuron is similar to the human brain's neuron structure:

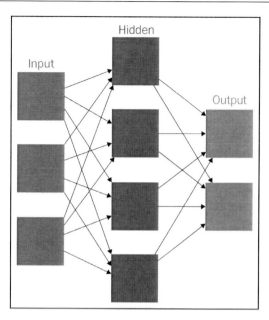

Figure 16.10 – The human brain's neuron structure

ANNs consist of interconnected artificial neurons or nodes organized in layers, and they are primarily used for ML and pattern recognition tasks. They leverage mathematical algorithms and optimization techniques to learn and make predictions based on input data. An ANN represents a group of interconnected nodes, with each node representing a model after a neuron. Each node connection can transmit signals similar to synapses in biological brain neurons. Neural networks are a set of algorithms that helps cluster and classify. As you can see from the preceding diagram, the neural network consists of three layers:

- Input layer
- Hidden layer
- Output layer

The input and output layers speak for themselves; the initial inputs are external data, such as images, audio, or text files. The output is the task's accomplishment, such as classifying the text's content or the objects that were recognized in images. The hidden layer is what makes the network produce reasonable results. The transition of input to output goes through the hidden layer, which does the heavy analyzing, processing, and modifications necessary to produce the output.

Consider the preceding diagram; it shows that a neuron can have multiple input and output connections. Usually, each connection has a weight that specifies the importance of the connection. The layering in the preceding diagram tells us that neurons in each layer are connected to neurons of the immediately preceding and immediately following layers. You should note that there might be several hidden layers between the input and output layers. While the primary purpose of input and output layers is reading external data and returning calculated (or deduced) output, the purpose of hidden layers is to adapt by learning. Learning also involves adjusting connections and weights to improve the output's accuracy. This is the part where ML comes into play. So, if we create a complex neural network with several hidden layers ready to learn and improve, we get an AI system. In the next section, we'll examine the clustering problem before covering regression analysis.

Clustering

Clustering is concerned with grouping a set of objects to distribute them into groups of similar objects. Also known as **cluster analysis**, this is a set of techniques and algorithms that intends to group similar objects, producing clusters. The simplest illustrative introduction would be grouping a set of colored objects into different groups consisting of objects of the same color, as follows:

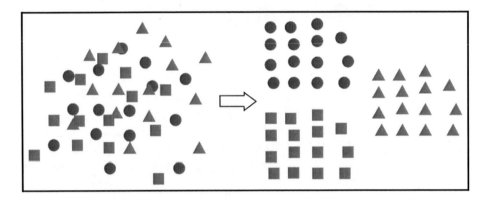

Figure 16.11 – Clustering

Although we are discussing AI tasks in this chapter, we suggest that you first try to solve problems with the knowledge base that you have so far. Let's think about how we would categorize objects by similarity. First of all, we should have a basic idea of what the object will look like. In the preceding example, we are looking at an object's shape, color, dimensions (the width and height of a 2D object), and so on. Without going much deeper, a basic representation of an object might look like this:

```
classObject
{
public:
int color;
int shape;
int width;
int height;
};
```

Let's consider the fact that the values for `color` and `shape` are in a range of predefined values. We could use enumerations for better readability. Clustering analysis involves analyzing objects to categorize them somehow. The first thing that comes to mind is having a function that accepts a list of objects. Let's try to define one:

```
using objects_list = std::vector<Object>;
using categorized_table = std::unordered_map<int, objects_list>;
categorized_table clusterize(const objects_list &objects)
{
// categorization logic
}
```

Think for a moment about the implementation details. We need to define the clustering points. These might be the color and the type of the shape. The challenging thing is that they might be unknown. That said, to cover everything just in case, we will categorize objects for every property, as follows:

```
categorized_table clusterize(const objects_list &objects)
{
categorized_table result;
for (const auto &obj : objects)
{result[obj.color].push_back(obj);
result[obj.shape].push_back(obj);
}return result;
}
```

Objects with a similar color or shape are grouped in a hash table. While the preceding code is rather simple, it bears the basic idea of grouping objects by some similarity criterion. What we did in the previous example is more likely to be described as hard clustering, where an object either belongs to a cluster or it doesn't. On the contrary, soft clustering (also known as **fuzzy clustering**) describes an object that belongs to a cluster to a certain degree.

For example, the similarity of objects for the `shape` property could be defined by the result of a function applied to the objects – that is, the function defines whether object A and object B have a similar shape if, let's say, object A's shape is a square and object B's shape is a rhombus. This means we should update the logic in the previous example to compare objects against several values and define their shape as a group. By developing this idea further, sooner or later, we will arrive at different strategies and algorithms of clustering, such as K-means clustering.

Regression analysis

Regression analysis is concerned with finding the deviations for one value from another. The simplest way of understanding regression analysis is through the graphs for functions in mathematics. You might recall the graph for the $f(x) = y$ function:

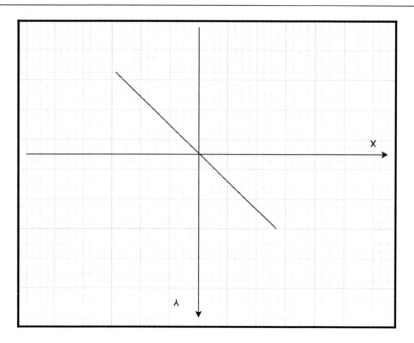

Figure 16.12 – Graph for the f(x) = y function

For every value of x, the function results in a fixed value for y. Regression analysis is somewhat similar to the preceding graph as it is concerned with finding a relationship between variables. More specifically, it estimates relationships between a dependent variable and several independent variables. The dependent variable is also known as an **outcome**, while the independent variables are also referred to as **features**. The number of features might be 1.

The most common form of regression analysis is linear regression. It looks similar to the preceding graph. Here's an example representing the relationship between hours spent on testing programs and the number of bugs discovered in the release version:

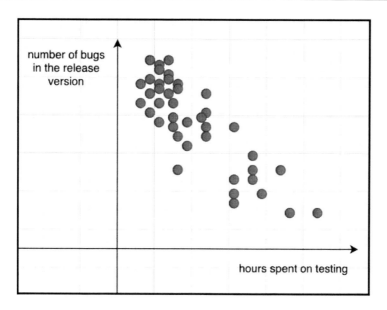

Figure 16.13 – Linear regression

In ML, regression analysis is used as a way of forecasting. You might develop a program to predict an outcome based on the values for dependent variables. As you have probably already guessed so far, ML is a big field with a wide range of topics. Although programmers tend to use math as little as possible, ML makes it impossible. You still need to grasp some of the math subjects to get the most out of ML. Regression analysis strongly depends on math statistics.

C++ and ML

It's now no longer a secret that ML is more about math than programming. Computer science has its roots in mathematics and, in the early years, computer scientists were mathematicians first. You might be familiar with several eminent scientists, including Alan Turing, John von Neuman, Claude Shannon, Norbert Wiener, Niklaus Wirth, Donald Knuth, and many others. All of them are mathematicians with a special love for technology. During its development, computer programming became a more friendly field to newcomers. In the last two or three decades, computer programmers stopped being forced to learn math before developing useful programs. Languages evolved into more and more high-level tools that allow almost everyone to code.

There are plenty of frameworks that make this job easier for programmers. It now takes a matter of weeks to grasp some framework or a high-level programming language and create a new program. Programs, however, tend to repeat themselves. It's not so hard to build something nowadays because there are a lot of patterns and best practices that help us along the way. The role of mathematics has been pushed back and more and more people become programmers without even the slightest need to use math. That's not an issue; it's more like a natural flow for the technology to evolve. In the end, technology aims to make human living more comfortable. The same relates to engineers. While, back in the 1960s, engineers at NASA made calculations using computers, they were not computers as we know them today. Those were real human beings with this specialty called being a computer, although being a computer meant being great at mathematics and solving equations much faster than others.

Now, we are part of the new age in computer science, where mathematics is back again. ML engineers are now using mathematics the same way mathematicians used programming languages in the 1970s or 1980s. It's now not enough to know a programming language or a framework to devise a new algorithm or incorporate ML into your applications. You should also be good at least in some sub-fields of mathematics, such as linear algebra, statistics, and probability theory.

Almost the same logic applies to C++. Modern languages provide a wide range of functionality out of the box, while C++ developers are still striving to design flawless programs with manual memory management. If you do some quick research into the field of ML, you will find that most of the libraries or examples out there use Python. At first, this might be seen as the default language to use in ML tasks. However, ML engineers are starting to touch a new threshold in evolution – performance. This threshold is not new; lots of tools out there still use C++ in parts where they need performance. Game development, operating systems, mission-critical systems, and many other fundamental areas use C++ (and C) as the de facto standard. It's now time for C++ to conquer a new area. Our best advice would be to study both ML and C++ because it is slowly becoming critical for ML engineers to incorporate C++ to get the best performance out there.

Summary

In this chapter, we introduced ML, alongside its categories and applications. It is a rapidly growing field of study that has numerous applications in building intelligent systems. We categorized ML into supervised, unsupervised, and reinforcement learning algorithms. Each of these categories has its applications in solving tasks, such as classification, clustering, regression, and machine translation.

Then, we implemented a simple learning algorithm that defines a calculation function based on experiences provided as input. We called this a dataset and used it to train the system. Training with datasets (called **experiences**) is one of the key properties of ML systems.

Finally, we introduced and discussed ANNs and applied them to recognize patterns. ML and neural networks go hand in hand in solving tasks. This chapter provided you with a necessary introduction to this field, along with several examples of tasks, so that you can spend some time diving into the topic. This will help you have a general idea of AI and ML since it's becoming increasingly necessary for engineers in real-world application development. In the next chapter, we will learn how to implement a dialog-based search engine.

Questions

Answer the following questions to test your knowledge of this chapter:

1. What is ML?

2. What are the differences between the supervised and unsupervised learning algorithms?

3. Give some examples of ML applications.

4. How would you modify the `CalculationMachine` class to change its behavior after training it with a different set of experiences?

5. What is the purpose of neural networks?

Further reading

To learn more about the topics that were covered in this chapter, take a look at the following resources:

- *Artificial Intelligence and Machine Learning Fundamentals*: `https://www.packtpub.com/product/artificial-intelligence-and-machine-learning-fundamentals/9781789801651`

- *Machine Learning Fundamentals*: `https://www.packtpub.com/product/machine-learning-fundamentals/9781789803556`

- *Hands-On Machine Learning for Algorithmic Trading*: `https://subscription.packtpub.com/search?query=hands%20machine%20learning%20algorithmic%20trading`

- *OpenCV*: `https://opencv.org/`

17
Using C++ in Data Science

C++ is widely used in many fields, including data science. Data scientists typically choose Python because of its simplicity and breadth of libraries, but C++ offers some advantages that make it an effective tool for data analysis. This chapter explains why C++ can be used in the data science industry and how it makes it possible. C++ is fast and efficient. In C++, code is compiled into machine code before execution. This compilation enables C++ programs to execute significantly faster than an interpreted language such as Python. C++ can perform well when dealing with extensive data or computationally intensive tasks. C++ algorithms can use lower memory management and better code execution to process data faster.

Additionally, C++ provides extensive support for parallel computing. The language offers libraries such as OpenMP and MPI, allowing developers to standardize their code and use multicore processors and distributed systems. Parallel computing is beneficial when processing complex data, which can be broken down into smaller independent tasks. Using the parallel capabilities of C++, data scientists can speed up their calculations and improve productivity.

C++ offers many advantages for data science, including the ability to interface with other languages and programs. With its robust interfaces, C++ makes it easy to interface with libraries written in other languages, such as Python and R. This interface allows data scientists to take advantage of the vast ecosystem of available libraries and tools old while gaining the advantage of differing performance advantages by combining the strengths of programming languages, data scientists can create powerful and efficient data processing pipelines.

In addition, C++ provides many data structures and algorithms well suited for data science projects. The **Standard Template Library** (**STL**) provides a comprehensive set of streams and algorithms, including vectors, maps, aggregation, sorting, and search functions. These data structures and algorithms are highly customized and manage large amounts of data. In addition, C++ allows developers to create custom data structures and algorithms for specific data analysis needs. This increases flexibility and control over their data processing pipeline.

While C++ may require more effort and expertise than Python for the data science industry, its speed, efficiency, parallel computing, connectivity, and data manipulation make it a solid choice for certain applications. In particular, C++ shines for business needs, such as extensive datasets, processing resources, implementing complex algorithms, and optimizing resources.

In this chapter, we will cover the following topics:

- Introduction to data science
- Data capturing and manipulation
- Data cleansing and processing
- Applying machine learning algorithms
- Data visualization

Technical requirements

The `g++` compiler with the `-std=c++2a` option is used to compile the examples in this chapter. You can find the source files used in this chapter at `https://github.com/PacktPublishing/Expert-C-2nd-edition/tree/main/Chapter17`.

Introduction to data science

Data science is a set of disciplines that combines statistical analysis, machine learning, and domain knowledge to extract insights and informed decisions from large complex datasets. It involves collecting, processing, and analyzing data to reveal patterns, trends, and relationships, which are predictive models that can be used to drive business decisions.

The essence of data science is the process of analyzing and pre-processing data. This involves understanding the structure and quality of the data, identifying missing values, outliers, and anomalies, and transforming the data into a format suitable for analysis to facilitate subsequent analytical procedures such as data cleaning. Feature engineering and dimensionality reduction are better and more efficient.

After pre-processing the data, data scientists use statistical and machine learning techniques to extract insights and build models. They use statistical techniques such as hypothesis testing, regression analysis, and time-series analysis to understand relationships between variables and make predictions based on historical data. Using machine learning algorithms with decision trees, random forests, support vector machines, and neural networks includes use for tasks such as classification, clustering, and regression. They also learn to respect and predict or identify patterns in other unseen data.

In recent years, big data and technological advances have opened up new opportunities in data science. Large amounts of data from social media, sensors, and **Internet of Things** (**IoT**) devices present challenges and opportunities. Data scientists now access more information but face the challenge of such mass production working well and analyzing information. Technologies such as distributed computing, cloud computing, and parallel processing have emerged to address these challenges and enable scalable data analysis.

Data visualization is essential in data science because it helps communicate insights and patterns more effectively. Data scientists can present their findings to stakeholders and decision-makers meaningfully and impactfully by visualizing data with charts, graphs, and interactive dashboards. Visualization helps tell a story and detect and identify hidden patterns or outliers that are not obvious from raw data analysis alone.

Ethics and privacy are essential considerations in data science. While working with sensitive personal information, data scientists must ensure that data is used responsibly and ethically. Protecting individual privacy, ensuring data security, and addressing bias and impartiality in samples are important aspects of ethical data science practice. Organizations and data scientists must be compliant with guidelines such as the **General Data Protection Regulation (GDPR)** to ensure ethical data handling.

C++ example

As a first example, the following code calculates the most basic statistic for a set of numbers, the average. The code uses only the standard library and does all the calculations by hand:

```cpp
#include <iostream>
#include <vector>

// Function to calculate the average of a vector of numbers
double calculateAverage(const std::vector<double>& data) {
    if(data.size() == 0) {
        return 0.0;
    }
    double sum = 0.0;
    for (double value : data) {
        sum += value;
    }
    return sum / data.size();
}

int main() {
    // Create a vector of numbers
    std::vector<double> numbers = {1.2, 2.5, 3.7, 4.1, 5.6};

    // Calculate the average using the calculateAverage
    // function
    double average = calculateAverage(numbers);

    // Print the average to the console
    std::cout << "The average of the numbers is: " <<
```

```
        average << std::endl;


    return 0;
}
```

Given these functions' complexity, libraries have been developed to implement them, allowing programmers to build on those to calculate more complex results. For example, the following code calculates the covariance matrix using the Eigen/Dense library. The Eigen library can be downloaded from this link: https://eigen.tuxfamily.org/index.php?title=Main_Page.

This example was written using version 3.4.0:

```cpp
#include <iostream>
#include <Eigen/Dense>


Eigen::MatrixXd calculateCovarianceMatrix(const Eigen::MatrixXd& data)
{
    int numVariables = data.cols();
    int numSamples = data.rows();

    // Calculate centered data
    Eigen::MatrixXd centeredData = data.rowwise() -
      data.colwise().mean();

    // Calculate covariance matrix
    Eigen::MatrixXd covarianceMatrix =
      (centeredData.transpose() * centeredData) /
      (numSamples - 1);

    return covarianceMatrix;
}


int main() {
    // Create a data matrix with 5 samples and 3 variables
    Eigen::MatrixXd data(5, 3);
    data << 1.2, 2.3, 3.4,
            2.5, 3.6, 4.7,
            3.7, 4.8, 5.9,
            4.1, 5.2, 6.3,
            5.6, 6.7, 7.8;

    // Calculate the covariance matrix
    Eigen::MatrixXd covarianceMatrix =
      calculateCovarianceMatrix(data);
```

```
    // Print the covariance matrix
    std::cout << "Covariance Matrix:\n" << covarianceMatrix
      << std::endl;

    return 0;
}
```

Now that we have some understanding of the overall process, let's take a look at each of the steps involved.

Data capturing and manipulation

Data capturing and manipulation are critical areas of data science. They involve the acquisition, extraction, transformation, and processing of data so that it is helpful for analysis and decision-making. These techniques are important in gaining meaningful insights and taking advantage of large, complex datasets. In this article, we will explore the importance of data capture and manipulation and discuss the basic concepts and techniques of these techniques.

Data capture refers to collecting and retrieving data from various sources. This can include structured data from databases, spreadsheets, or APIs and unstructured data from text, images, and social media sources. The data capture phase involves identifying the right start, extracting data, and converting it into a format suitable for analysis. Techniques such as web scraping, data extraction tools, and data integration frameworks are often used to capture and aggregate data from various sources.

Once captured, the data must be processed and transformed to make it useful for analysis. Data processing involves cleaning, filtering, and pre-processing data to ensure quality, integrity, and accuracy. Typical tasks in this category include dealing with missing values, eliminating duplicates, correcting errors, standardizing data, transforming data into suitable proxies for analysis, and procedures such as data cleaning management, statistical techniques, and data wrangling tools to be used to ensure data is dependable and valuable.

Data manipulation also includes feature engineering, which involves creating or modifying existing data to extract relevant information and improve predictive models. This process can consist of techniques such as scaling, normalization, encoding categorical variables, creating interaction terms, and deriving features based on domain knowledge. Engineering can improve the efficiency and accuracy of machine learning models and enable better insights from data.

Data capture and processing must consider data privacy and security. Organizations must comply with regulations and standards to protect sensitive information and ensure data privacy. Anonymization, data masking, encryption, and access control mechanisms protect data during storage and processing. Handling data ethically and securely is essential, especially when dealing with **Personally Identifiable Information (PII)** or sensitive business data.

Effective data capture and use requires careful planning and consideration of data needs and research objectives. Defining clear data capture methods, identifying appropriate data sources, and establishing data quality standards is important. Organizations should also establish data governance practices to ensure consistency, documentation, and version control.

Moreover, automation and advanced technologies play a key role in data capture and manipulation. Machine learning algorithms, natural language processors, and computer vision techniques can automate data extraction and pre-processing tasks, reducing manual effort and improving productivity. Tools and assemblies have advanced, such as data integration software **Extract, Transform, and Load (ETL)** pipelines, and data preparation systems. They will be able to handle large amounts of data and simplify the conversion process.

C++ example

Let's look at an example:

```
#include <iostream>
#include <curl/curl.h>
```

In this example, we use cURL to retrieve data from the specified URL (`https://letsusedata.com/data/cpp_sample.txt`):

```
// Callback function to receive data from cURL
size_t WriteCallback(void* contents, size_t size, size_t nmemb,
std::string* data) {
    size_t totalSize = size * nmemb;
    data->append(static_cast<char*>(contents), totalSize);
    return totalSize;
}
```

The received data is stored in the `responseData` string. The `WriteCallback` function is a callback function assigned to cURL. It adds the received data to the data set. In the main function, we use `curl_easy_init()` to initialize the cURL. If possible, we configure the URL to retrieve the data using `curl_easy_setopt()`. We provide the `WriteCallback` function to get the data as a callback and set the `responseData` string to write data. Then, we use `curl_easy_perform()` to execute the request. If the request is successful, we print the retrieved data to the console. Finally, we clean up the cURL using `curl_easy_cleanup()`. The cURL library can be downloaded from `https://curl.se/`.

To use the cURL library, it needs to be linked. The linking command can be platform-specific; for example, the library can be linked by using `g++ -o app main.cpp -std=c++20 -lcurl`:

```
int main() {
    // Initialize cURL
    CURL* curl = curl_easy_init();
    if (curl) {
```

```cpp
        std::string url =
          "https://letsusedata.com/data/cpp_sample.txt";
        std::string responseData;

        // Set the URL to retrieve data from
        curl_easy_setopt(curl, CURLOPT_URL, url.c_str());

        // Provide the callback function to receive the
        // data
        curl_easy_setopt(curl, CURLOPT_WRITEFUNCTION,
          WriteCallback);
        curl_easy_setopt(curl, CURLOPT_WRITEDATA,
          &responseData);

        // Perform the request
        CURLcode res = curl_easy_perform(curl);
        if (res != CURLE_OK) {
            std::cerr << "cURL failed: " <<
              curl_easy_strerror(res) << std::endl;
        }
        else {
            // Data retrieval successful
            std::cout << "Data retrieved successfully:" <<
              std::endl;
            std::cout << responseData << std::endl;
        }

        // Clean up cURL
        curl_easy_cleanup(curl);
    }
    else {
        std::cerr << "cURL initialization failed." <<
          std::endl;
    }

    return 0;
}
```

Now that we have looked at how to capture data, we'll review how to clean and process data in the next section.

Data cleansing and processing

Data cleaning and processing is a key step in the data science industry, where unstructured data is processed and used to improve its quality, integrity, and usability. These processes play a key role in ensuring that the data used for assessment and decision-making is accurate, precise, and dependable. This section will explore the importance of data cleansing and processing and discuss these processes' basic concepts and techniques.

Data cleaning, also known as data cleaning or data scrubbing, refers to the process of identifying, correcting, or removing errors, inconsistencies, and anomalies from a data structure. Raw data often contain missing values, anomalies, records duplicates, inconsistent characters, or other abnormalities that are biased if not dealt with or may produce inaccurate results. Data cleansing aims to address these issues and improve data collection.

However, using the information to make the data relevant to analysis requires cleansing and processing This includes storing, filtering, organizing, integrating, or transforming data to derive useful insights. Data processing techniques derive meaningful information, reveal patterns, and interpret data in a manageable way.

The following are the basic steps and procedures for data cleansing and processing:

1. **Data validation**: Data validation ensures the data complies with predetermined rules or constraints. It is about ensuring the data's integrity, accuracy, and correctness. Validation methods include data type checking, range verification, and consistency checks between related data fields.

2. **Handling missing data**: Missing data is common in datasets. Methods of handling missing data include imputation, where missing values are replaced by estimated or estimated values, or deletion, where rows or columns of missing data are explicitly removed. Different imputation methods, such as mean imputation, regression imputation, or model-based imputation, can be used.

3. **Outlier identification**: An outlier is a data point that deviates significantly from a typical pattern or value in a dataset. Outliers can adversely affect data analysis and modeling. Techniques such as statistical methods, visualization, and machine learning algorithms can be used to detect and deal with abnormalities appropriately.

4. **Removal of duplicate data**: Duplicate records can corrupt analysis and produce biased results. Identifying and removing duplicate records ensures data integrity. Methods include eliminating duplicate entries by comparing records based on key fields or similarity measures.

5. **Standardization and normalization**: Standardization and normalization of data is the conversion of data into a consistent format or scale. This step ensures that different data sources or variables are comparable. Scaling, z-score normalization, or min-max normalization transform the data.

6. **Feature engineering**: Feature engineering involves creating or modifying new features to extract meaningful information and improve predictive models. These steps include encoding

categorical variables, creating interaction terms, and finding new dependent features, domain knowledge, or statistical methods.

7. **Data integration**: Data integration combines data from multiple sources into an integrated dataset. This includes resolving inconsistencies, setting up data structures, and ensuring data consistency.

8. **Data reduction**: Data reduction techniques aim to reduce the size or scope of a data set while preserving its important characteristics. This step is especially useful when working with large datasets. Techniques such as sampling, feature selection, or dimensionality reduction techniques such as **principal component analysis** (**PCA**) can be used to reduce the size and complexity of the data.

Effective data cleaning and processing requires domain expertise, statistical methods, and programming skills. It is important to understand dataset characteristics, analyze the data, and make informed decisions based on the specific goals and needs of the analysis. Also, advanced automation and technology, such as data cleansing tools and wrangling platforms, or machine learning algorithms, improve data cleansing and make things much easier.

C++ example

The following code shows how to use C++ to remove duplicates, normalize the data, and manage missing values:

```cpp
#include <iostream>
#include <vector>
#include <algorithm>
#include <numeric>

// Function to remove duplicates from a vector
template <typename T>
void removeDuplicates(std::vector<T>& data) {
    std::sort(data.begin(), data.end());
    data.erase(std::unique(data.begin(), data.end()),
        data.end());
}

// Function to normalize data between 0 and 1
template <typename T>
void normalizeData(std::vector<T>& data) {
    T minVal = *std::min_element(data.begin(), data.end());
    T maxVal = *std::max_element(data.begin(), data.end());
    T range = maxVal - minVal;
    std::transform(data.begin(), data.end(), data.begin(),
```

```
            [minVal, range](T val) { return (val - minVal) /
                range; });
}

int main() {
    // Create a vector with some duplicate values and
    // missing data
    std::vector<double> values = { 1.2, 2.5, 3.7, 4.1, 2.5,
        5.6, -1.0, 6.7, 4.1, 7.8 };

    // Remove duplicates from the vector
    removeDuplicates(values);

    // Handle missing data by removing -1 values
    values.erase(std::remove(values.begin(), values.end(),
        -1.0), values.end());

    // Normalize the data between 0 and 1
    normalizeData(values);

    // Display the unique values after data cleansing and
    // normalization
    std::cout << "Unique values (after data cleansing and
        normalization):\n";
    for (const auto& value : values) {
        std::cout << value << std::endl;
    }

    return 0;
}
```

Now that we have completed the data preparation component, let's look at how machine learning algorithms can be applied.

Applying machine learning algorithms

Machine learning algorithms are central to data science and artificial intelligence. They use mathematical models and statistical techniques to train computers to learn from data and make predictions or perform informal actions. Machine learning algorithms enable you to extract insights and patterns from large, complex datasets and inform decisions, automatically processing and improving predictive capabilities. Let us examine and discuss some commonly used algorithms.

Machine learning algorithms can be classified into three categories: supervised learning, unsupervised learning, and reinforcement learning.

Supervised learning algorithms learn from labeled training data, where each data point is associated with a corresponding goal or outcome. These algorithms aim to generalize from the training data and make predictions about unseen data. Commonly used supervised learning algorithms include linear regression, decision trees, support vector machines, and neural networks.

Unsupervised learning algorithms work with unlabeled data, where the goal is to discover hidden patterns, clusters, or patterns in the data. These algorithms search for the underlying structure of the data without a predefined target variable. Examples of unsupervised learning algorithms are clustering algorithms such as k-means and hierarchical clustering and dimensionality reduction techniques such as **principal component analysis (PCA)** and t-SNE.

Reinforcement learning algorithms involve training an agent to interact with the environment, learn from its actions, and improve its decision-making through trial and error. These algorithms use rewards or punishments to determine the agent's actions toward a specific goal. Reinforcement learning has applications in robotics, sports games, and autonomous systems.

Implementing machine learning algorithms includes data pre-processing, feature selection or extraction, model training, analysis, and deployment. This requires thoroughly understanding the problem domain, carefully selecting appropriate algorithms, and developing model parameters well to get what you want.

Machine learning algorithms have wide applications in various industries, including healthcare, finance, marketing, image and speech recognition, natural language processing, recommendation systems, and so on. They support applications such as customer segmentation, fraud identification, sensitivity analysis, predictive monitoring, and personalization to deliver business recommendations.

It is important to note that the choice of algorithm depends on the specific problem, the nature of the data, and the desired results. Different algorithms have different strengths and weaknesses, and their performance can vary depending on the context. Therefore, it is essential to implement different algorithms, evaluate their performance, and iterate to improve the results.

Machine learning algorithms enable data scientists and researchers to use data for prediction, insight, and decision-making. With so many available frameworks, choosing the most appropriate one is important based on the problem, data characteristics, and preferences. By effectively implementing machine learning algorithms, organizations can unlock the potential of their data to innovate in different areas.

C++ example

This example demonstrates the application of a supervised learning algorithm, linear regression, to predict housing prices based on input features. You can modify and extend this code to include additional features, use different regression models, or incorporate more complex algorithms to tackle a variety of prediction tasks in different domains:

```cpp
#include <iostream>
#include <vector>
#include <numeric>
#include <cmath>
```

In this example, we have a dataset of house sizes (`houseSizes`) and their corresponding prices (`prices`).

We use the `calculateMean` function to compute the input features' meaning and the target variable's mean:

```cpp
// Function to calculate the mean of a vector
template <typename T>
T calculateMean(const std::vector<T>& data) {
    T sum = std::accumulate(data.begin(), data.end(), 0.0);
    return sum / data.size();
}
```

Then, the `calculateLinearRegression` function is used to calculate the coefficients of the linear regression model. This function estimates the slope and intercept of the regression line best fitting the given data:

```cpp
// Function to calculate the linear regression coefficients
template <typename T>
std::pair<T, T> calculateLinearRegression(const
  std::vector<T>& x, const std::vector<T>& y) {
    T xMean = calculateMean(x);
    T yMean = calculateMean(y);

    T numerator = 0.0;
    T denominator = 0.0;

    for (size_t i = 0; i < x.size(); i++) {
        numerator += (x[i] - xMean) * (y[i] - yMean);
        denominator += std::pow(x[i] - xMean, 2);
    }

    T slope = numerator / denominator;
```

```
    T intercept = yMean - slope * xMean;

    return std::make_pair(slope, intercept);
}
```

Finally, using the calculated regression coefficients, we use the `predictPrice` function to predict the price for a new house size (`newHouseSize`):

```
// Function to predict the housing price using linear
// regression
template <typename T>
T predictPrice(const std::pair<T, T>& coefficients, T x) {
    return coefficients.first * x + coefficients.second;
}

int main() {
    // Input features (house sizes)
    std::vector<double> houseSizes = { 1000, 1500, 2000,
      2500, 3000 };

    // Corresponding housing prices
    std::vector<double> prices = { 300000, 450000, 500000,
      600000, 700000 };

    // Calculate the linear regression coefficients
    std::pair<double, double> regressionCoefficients =
      calculateLinearRegression(houseSizes, prices);

    // Predict the price for a new house size
    double newHouseSize = 1800;
    double predictedPrice =
      predictPrice(regressionCoefficients, newHouseSize);

    // Display the results
    std::cout << "Linear Regression Equation: y = " <<
      regressionCoefficients.first << "x + " <<
      regressionCoefficients.second << std::endl;
    std::cout << "Predicted price for a house of size " <<
      newHouseSize << " sq. ft.: " << predictedPrice <<
      std::endl;

    return 0;
}
```

Now that we have used machine learning on the data, we can help users understand the results using data visualization.

Data visualization

Data visualization is the visual representation of data and information. It requires visual representations such as charts, diagrams, and maps to communicate complex issues and examples to a large audience effectively. Data visualization is important in exploratory data analysis, insight presentation, and decision-making processes. This section will examine data visualization's importance and discuss some key features and techniques.

One of the key benefits of data visualization is the ability to simplify complex data and make it more meaningful and accessible. Patterns, trends, and relationships can be quickly identified by visually presenting information, allowing participants to gain insight and make appropriate decisions. Visual representations recognizing them makes it easier to identify notable features, differences, and anomalies in the data.

Data visualization can take many forms, including bar charts, line graphs, scatter plots, histograms, and heat maps. The choice of image depends on the nature of the data and the specific insights or comparisons to be provided. Each model has strengths and is appropriate for different data types and research objectives.

Several considerations need to be considered in effective data visualization. Considerations such as choosing the right visual style, choosing the right colors and fonts, providing a clear headline and legend, and ensuring proper scale are important. The graphic design should focus on the information and a clear, simple, and logical representation of the underlying data.

Advancements in technology and the availability of data visualization tools and libraries have made it easier for individuals and organizations to create visualizations. Popular tools include Python libraries such as Matplotlib and Seaborn, JavaScript libraries such as D3.js and Plotly, and data visualization software such as Tableau and Power BI.

Data visualization has numerous applications across various fields. It is widely used in business analytics, finance, healthcare, marketing, and social sciences. Visualization aids in communicating insights, monitoring key performance indicators, presenting trends and forecasts, and engaging stakeholders.

C++ example

In this code, the input features (house sizes) are stored in the houseSizes vector, and the corresponding housing prices are stored in the prices vector. We create a data file named data.dat and write the house sizes and prices to the file.

Next, we generate a gnuplot script file named `script.plt`. The script sets the *x*-axis label to `House Size (sq. ft.)`, the *y*-axis label to `Price`, and plots the data points using the `with points` option.

Finally, we execute the gnuplot command using `system()` to plot the data. The generated plot will display the house sizes on the *x* axis and the corresponding prices on the *y* axis.

The gnuplot command can be downloaded from `http://www.gnuplot.info/`:

```cpp
#include <iostream>
#include <fstream>
#include <vector>

int main() {
    // Input features (house sizes)
    std::vector<double> houseSizes = { 1000, 1500, 2000,
     2500, 3000 };

    // Corresponding housing prices
    std::vector<double> prices = { 300000, 450000, 500000,
      600000, 700000 };

    // Create a data file for plotting
    std::ofstream dataFile("data.dat");
    for (size_t i = 0; i < houseSizes.size(); i++) {
        dataFile << houseSizes[i] << " " << prices[i] <<
          std::endl;
    }
    dataFile.close();

    // Generate the gnuplot script for plotting
    std::ofstream scriptFile("script.plt");
    scriptFile << "set xlabel 'House Size (sq. ft.)'" <<
      std::endl;
    scriptFile << "set ylabel 'Price'" << std::endl;
    scriptFile << "plot 'data.dat' with points" <<
      std::endl;
    scriptFile.close();

    // Execute the gnuplot command
    std::string command = "gnuplot -persist script.plt";
    if (std::system(command.c_str()) != 0) {
        std::cerr << "Failed to execute gnuplot command."
            << std::endl;
```

```
        return 1;
    }


    return 0;
}
```

The addition of data visualization completes the data analysis steps.

Summary

Data science is an interdisciplinary field that utilizes statistical methods, machine learning algorithms, and data visualization to extract insights from large volumes of data. It involves programming skills, mathematical expertise, and domain knowledge to explore, transform, and model data for informed decision-making and predictions.

The first step in the data science pipeline is data capturing and manipulation. This process involves collecting and organizing data from various sources into a structured format. Data scientists work with large datasets, employing efficient methods to manipulate and transform the data. This includes merging datasets, filtering out irrelevant information, and handling missing or inconsistent data, ensuring a solid foundation for analysis.

Data cleansing and processing are crucial to enhancing data quality. Data scientists address anomalies and errors by identifying and handling missing values, outliers, and inconsistencies. They use imputation, outlier detection, and data transformation to clean and pre-process the data. They create a reliable dataset for further analysis and modeling by eliminating noise and ensuring data integrity.

Applying machine learning algorithms is a key aspect of data science. These algorithms learn patterns and relationships in the data to make predictions or classifications. Data scientists select suitable algorithms based on the problem and data at hand. They train models using historical data and apply them to new, unseen data for predictions. Machine learning algorithms range from simple regression and classification methods to complex techniques such as neural networks and ensemble methods.

Data visualization plays a crucial role in data science by transforming complex data into intuitive representations. Data scientists create charts, graphs, and interactive visualizations to communicate insights effectively. Visualization tools and libraries help explore the data, identify trends, and uncover relationships between variables. Presenting data visually makes complex information accessible and understandable, enabling stakeholders to make data-driven decisions.

In summary, data science combines statistical methods, machine learning algorithms, and data visualization to extract insights from data. The process involves capturing and manipulating data, cleansing, and processing it, applying machine learning algorithms, and visualizing the results. By harnessing the power of data, data scientists drive innovation and make informed decisions across various domains.

Questions

1. What are some features of C++ that make it suitable for data analysis and manipulation?

2. Is there a way to read data from an external source, such as a database or file in C++, and manipulate it?

3. What are the common methods and libraries in C++ for data cleaning, processing, and normalization tasks?

4. In C++, how can you implement popular machine learning algorithms such as linear regression?

5. How can you display and analyze your data effectively with interactive and attractive data visualizations in C++?

Further reading

For further information, refer to the following:

*   *Data Science for Business* by Foster Provost and Tom Fawcett

*   *C++ Data Structures and Algorithm Design Principles* by Pavel A. Pevzner and Michael S. Sanders

*   *Mastering OpenCV 4 with C++* by Daniel Lélis Baggio, David Millán Escrivá, Khvedchenia Ievgen, and Naureen Mahmood

18

Designing and Implementing a Data Analysis Framework

Designing and implementing data analysis programs in C++ requires careful consideration of various factors. C++ is known for its efficiency and functionality, which makes it the best choice for dealing with large amounts of data. This chapter will explore the basic steps of building a complex data analysis program using C++. Defining the goals and requirements of the program is an important first step. This helps guide the design and implementation process, ensuring that the process meets specific research requirements.

Data governance is critical to the data analysis process. C++ provides robust data structures and libraries for efficient data processing. Choosing an appropriate data structure, such as arrays or vectors, is important for proper data storage and processing. Preliminary data processing and cleaning play an important role in ensuring data quality. C++ provides string manipulation capabilities to handle formatting, outliers, and missing values. Implementing an algorithm for data preprocessing before performing the analysis is important.

Dealing with multiple data sources often requires data transformation and integration. C++ provides libraries and functions for simple data processing and integration. C++ libraries such as Boost and Eigen provide a wide range of mathematical functions, linear algebra functions, machine learning algorithms, and so on for analysis and modeling.

Visualization and reporting are essential for effective communication of data. C++ libraries such as Qt and OpenGL allow developers to create interactive diagrams, charts, and graphs. Performance improvements are important for large datasets and tasks requiring computer processing. C++ features such as multithreading and parallel computation can improve the framework's performance.

Data security and privacy should be addressed through encryption, secure data management, and regulatory compliance. Proper documentation ensures system longevity and maintainability. In conclusion, designing and implementing data analysis systems in C++ requires careful consideration of data management, preprocessing, transformation, analysis, visualization, optimization, security, and documentation. Using the power and strength of C++, developers can build robust systems to facilitate effective data analysis and informed decision-making.

In this chapter, we will cover the following topics:

- Using and processing statistical data types
- Working with tabular and rectangular data
- A complete ETL pipeline design strategy

Technical requirements

The `g++` compiler with the `-std=c++2a` option is used to compile the examples in this chapter. You can find the source files used in this chapter at `https://github.com/PacktPublishing/Expert-C-2nd-edition/tree/main/Chapter18`.

Using and processing statistical data types

In C++, information is typically represented using standard C++ types, including integers, floating-point numbers, and strings. When running statistical data in C, it is vital to consider an appropriate information type for a selected analysis or calculation.

- **Categorical variables**: They represent qualitative records falling into unique classes or classes. In C++, these variables are typically defined with the aid of strings. Developers can use standard string manipulation functions and strategies in C++ to manage this data and perform operations such as frequency counts.

- **Numerical variables**: Numerical variables represent quantitative facts and can be continuous or discrete. C++ includes multiple numerical data types, including integers (int, long, and short), floating-point numbers (float and double), and other types (`std::fixed` and `std::decimal`). These types make it possible to create estimates and perform statistical and mathematical operations.

- **Ordinal Variables**: Ordinal variables represent data with a natural order or ranking. In C++, developers can use integers or enumerations to represent ordinal variables. By assigning numeric values to different categories or ranks, C++ allows for comparisons, sorting, and other operations on ordinal variables.

To process statistical data types in C++, developers can leverage various libraries and frameworks specifically designed for statistical analysis. For example, the Boost C++ libraries provide statistical algorithms, random number generators, and probability distributions that facilitate advanced statistical calculations. Additionally, developers can use C++ libraries such as Eigen, Armadillo, or OpenCV for linear algebra operations, matrix manipulations, and numerical computations required in statistical modeling and analysis.

Visualization of statistical data in C++ can be accomplished using graphics libraries such as Qt, OpenGL, or Matplotlib (with C++ bindings). These libraries enable developers to create charts, graphs, and visual representations of data to aid in data exploration and interpretation.

In summary, while C++ does not have dedicated data types labeled explicitly as "statistical data types," developers can utilize standard C++ data types and libraries to effectively manage and process categorical, numerical, and ordinal variables. By leveraging the power and flexibility of C++ and relevant libraries, statistical analysis and calculations can be performed efficiently and accurately.

C++ example

This example demonstrates the processing of numerical, categorical, and ordinal data:

```
#include <iostream>
#include <vector>
#include <algorithm>
#include <map>
```

We calculate the median using the same approach as before for numerical data. We sort the `numericalData` vector and calculate the median based on size and values:

```
int main() {
    // Numerical Data
    std::vector<double> numericalData = {4.5, 2.3, 1.8,
      3.2, 5.1};

    // Calculating the median
    std::sort(numericalData.begin(), numericalData.end());
    size_t size = numericalData.size();
    double median;
    if (size % 2 == 0) {
        median = (numericalData[size / 2 - 1] +
          numericalData[size / 2]) / 2.0;
    } else {
        median = numericalData[size / 2];
    }
    std::cout << "Numerical Median: " << median <<
      std::endl;
```

For categorical data, we count the frequency of each category using an `std::map` variable called `categoryCounts`. By iterating over the `categoricalData` vector, we increment the count for each category in the map. Finally, we print the category counts to the console:

```
    // Categorical Data
    std::vector<std::string> categoricalData = {"Apple",
```

```
    "Orange", "Banana", "Apple", "Grape"};

// Counting the frequency of each category
std::map<std::string, int> categoryCounts;
for (const auto& category : categoricalData) {
    categoryCounts[category]++;
}
// Print the category counts
std::cout << "Category Counts:" << std::endl;
for (const auto& pair : categoryCounts) {
    std::cout << pair.first << ": " << pair.second <<
        std::endl;
}
```

For ordinal data, we count the frequency of each value using an `std::map` variable called `ordinalCounts`. By iterating over the `ordinalData` vector, we increment the count for each value in the map. Then, we identify the mode (the most frequent value) by finding the value with the highest count. Finally, we print the mode to the console:

```
// Ordinal Data
std::vector<int> ordinalData = {2, 1, 3, 2, 2, 1, 3};

// Calculating the mode (most frequent value) of the
// ordinal data
std::map<int, int> ordinalCounts;
for (const auto& value : ordinalData) {
    ordinalCounts[value]++;
}

int mode = 0;
int maxCount = 0;
for (const auto& pair : ordinalCounts) {
    if (pair.second > maxCount) {
        mode = pair.first;
        maxCount = pair.second;
    }
}
std::cout << "Ordinal Mode: " << mode << std::endl;

return 0;
}
```

This example highlights numerical, categorical, and ordinal data processing using C++. You can expand upon these techniques, incorporate more advanced statistical calculations, or use specialized libraries for more complex analyses.

Working with tabular and rectangular data

Working with tabular and rectangular data in C++ is fundamental to data analysis and manipulation. Tabular data, or rectangular data, is structured in rows and columns, resembling a table or spreadsheet. C++ provides various techniques and libraries that enable efficient handling and processing of such data. This section will explore the key concepts and approaches for working with tabular and rectangular data in C++.

To represent tabular data in C++, the most common approach is to use two-dimensional arrays or vectors. Arrays provide a straightforward way to store data in a grid-like structure, where each element represents a specific cell in the table. Alternatively, vectors of vectors can be used to create a more flexible and resizable structure, allowing for dynamic manipulation of the tabular data.

When working with tabular data, it is essential to consider techniques for data input and output. C++ provides various mechanisms to read and write tabular data from files, such as **CSV** (**comma-separated values**) files. Libraries such as the **Standard Template Library** (**STL**) or external libraries such as Boost can efficiently simplify the process of reading and writing tabular data.

Once the tabular data is loaded into the program, C++ offers powerful data manipulation and analysis capabilities. Developers can iterate over rows and columns of the tabular data structure, perform calculations, apply transformations, and filter or select specific subsets of the data.

When dealing with large tabular datasets, optimizing performance becomes crucial. C++ provides techniques to improve efficiency, such as using efficient algorithms, employing parallel computing techniques, or leveraging libraries such as Intel's **Threading Building Blocks** (**TBB**) or OpenMP for parallelization.

In addition to core C++ functionality, various libraries and frameworks offer specialized tools for working with tabular data. For example, the Eigen library provides efficient matrix operations and linear algebra functionality, making it suitable for advanced data manipulations and computations on tabular data. The Qt library offers GUI-based solutions for interactive visualization and manipulation of tabular data.

Furthermore, C++ provides opportunities for data analysis and statistical calculations on tabular data. Libraries such as Boost and **GNU Scientific Library** (**GSL**) offer statistical functions, probability distributions, and regression analysis capabilities that enable developers to derive valuable insights and perform advanced statistical computations on tabular data.

Visualizing of tabular data is crucial for gaining a deeper understanding of the data patterns and relationships. C++ offers several options for data visualization, including libraries such as Qt, OpenGL, or Matplotlib (with C++ bindings). These libraries allow developers to create plots, charts, and graphs that present the tabular data in a visually appealing and interpretable way.

Data validation and error handling are essential aspects of working with tabular data. C++ provides mechanisms for data validation, such as checking for missing or inconsistent values, handling errors during data processing, and implementing robust error-handling tools to ensure the integrity and reliability of the tabular data.

In conclusion, working with tabular and rectangular data in C++ involves leveraging the language's core features, libraries, and external tools. C++ provides powerful capabilities for loading, manipulating, analyzing, and visualizing tabular data efficiently. Developers can process and analyze tabular data effectively by employing the right techniques and libraries, extracting meaningful insights, and making informed decisions.

C++ example

We define a sample tabular data structure using vector vectors (`tabularData`) in this example. Each inner vector represents a row in the table, and each element within the inner vectors represents a cell. We then display the tabular data by iterating over the rows and cells using nested `for` loops. The elements are printed to the console, with tabs (`\t`) used to separate the values and new lines (`std::endl`) to move to the next row.

Next, we calculate the sum of each row in the tabular data. We iterate over the rows and cells, accumulating the sum for each row. The row sums are stored in a separate vector (`rowSums`). Finally, we display the calculated row sums by iterating over the `rowSums` vector and printing each value to the console. This example demonstrates basic operations on tabular data, such as displaying the data and performing calculations on specific rows. You can extend these techniques to include more complex data manipulations and analyses based on the requirements of your particular use case:

```cpp
#include <iostream>
#include <vector>

int main() {
    // Sample tabular data
    std::vector<std::vector<int>> tabularData = {
        {1, 2, 3},
        {4, 5, 6},
        {7, 8, 9}
    };

    // Display the tabular data
    for (const auto& row : tabularData) {
```

```cpp
        for (const auto& cell : row) {
            std::cout << cell << '\t';
        }
        std::cout << std::endl;
    }

    // Calculate the sum of each row
    std::vector<int> rowSums;
    for (const auto& row : tabularData) {
        int rowSum = 0;
        for (const auto& cell : row) {
            rowSum += cell;
        }
        rowSums.push_back(rowSum);
    }

    // Display the row sums
    std::cout << "Row Sums:" << std::endl;
    for (const auto& sum : rowSums) {
        std::cout << sum << std::endl;
    }

    return 0;
}
```

In this second example, we define a rectangular data structure using vector vectors (`rectangularData`). Each inner vector represents a row in the rectangular structure, and each element within the inner vectors represents an element in that row. We demonstrate accessing and modifying elements of the rectangular data. For example, we access the element at index `[1][2]` using `rectangularData[1][2]` and print its value to the console. We also modify the element at index `[2][1]` to a new value (`100`) using `rectangularData[2][1] = 100`.

Next, we iterate over the rectangular data using nested for loops. We traverse each row and element within the row, printing the elements to the console. Tabs (`\t`) are used to separate the values, and new lines (`std::endl`) are used to move to the next row. Finally, we display the rectangular data structure with the modified element and the corresponding row and column indexes.

This example highlights basic operations on rectangular data in C++, including accessing and modifying specific elements and iterating the entire data structure. You can expand upon these techniques to perform more complex operations and manipulations on rectangular data based on your specific needs:

```cpp
#include <iostream>
#include <vector>
```

```cpp
int main() {
    // Rectangular data represented as a vector of vectors
    std::vector<std::vector<int>> rectangularData = {
        {1, 2, 3},
        {4, 5, 6},
        {7, 8, 9},
        {10, 11, 12}
    };

    // Accessing and modifying rectangular data
    int element = rectangularData[1][2];  // Accessing a
      specific element
    std::cout << "Element at [1][2]: " << element <<
      std::endl;

    rectangularData[2][1] = 100;  // Modifying an element
    std::cout << "Modified element at [2][1]: " <<
      rectangularData[2][1] << std::endl;

    // Iterating over rectangular data
    std::cout << "Rectangular Data:" << std::endl;
    for (const auto& row : rectangularData) {
        for (const auto& element : row) {
            std::cout << element << '\t';
        }
        std::cout << std::endl;
    }

    return 0;
}
```

A complete ETL pipeline design strategy

Designing a complete **Extract, and Transform, Load** (**ETL**) pipeline in C++ involves careful planning and considering various components to ensure efficient and reliable data integration and processing. An ETL pipeline encompasses extracting data from multiple sources, transforming it according to business rules or requirements, and loading it into a target system or database. This section will explore a comprehensive ETL pipeline design strategy in C++.

1. **Data Extraction**: The first step in an ETL pipeline is extracting data from diverse sources. C++ offers various techniques for data extraction, including reading from files (such as CSV or JSON), connecting to databases using SQL, or integrating with APIs for real-time data retrieval—libraries such as Boost.Asio or cURL can aid in handling network-based data extraction.

2. **Data Transformation**: Once the data is extracted, it often requires transformation to ensure its quality, consistency, and compatibility with the target system. C++ provides powerful tools for data manipulation, such as string parsing, regular expressions, and algorithms from the STL. Additionally, libraries such as Boost and Eigen offer advanced data manipulation capabilities, including matrix operations and statistical transformations.

3. **Data Validation and Cleansing**: Data quality is vital for reliable analysis and decision-making, performing data validation on C++ facilities, and cleansing through data type checks, range validation, and handling missing or erroneous values. Custom validation functions and algorithms can be implemented to verify data integrity and enforce data quality rules.

4. **Data Aggregation and Enrichment**: In some cases, data needs to be aggregated or enriched with additional information before loading it into the target system. C++ allows developers to perform complex aggregations, merging, and joining operations using algorithms from the STL or custom implementations. Integration with external services or databases can enhance data enrichment capabilities.

5. **Target System Loading**: C++ offers multiple approaches to loading transformed data into the target system or database. Depending on the requirements, developers can use direct database connections and execute SQL statements, use **object-relational mapping** (**ORM**) frameworks such as ODB or SOCI, or leverage third-party libraries such as Apache Kafka or RabbitMQ for streaming or message-based data loading.

6. **Error Handling and Logging**: Robust error handling and logging mechanisms are crucial for an ETL pipeline. C++ provides exception-handling constructs, such as try-catch blocks, to handle runtime errors effectively. Logging libraries such as Boost.Log or `spdlog` can record detailed information about the ETL process, including errors, warnings, and informational messages.

7. **Performance Optimization**: Optimizing the performance of the ETL pipeline is vital when dealing with large datasets or complex transformations. C++ provides various techniques for performance optimization, such as parallel processing using multithreading or multiprocessing, utilizing efficient algorithms, and optimizing memory management. Profiling tools such as Valgrind or `gperftools` can aid in identifying performance bottlenecks.

8. **Scalability and Flexibility**: An effective ETL pipeline design should be scalable and flexible to accommodate future growth and changes in data sources or requirements. By following modular design principles and adhering to good software engineering practices, such as encapsulation, abstraction, and decoupling, developers can build an ETL pipeline that is easy to maintain, extend, and adapt to evolving needs.

In conclusion, designing a complete ETL pipeline in C++ involves a thoughtful approach to data extraction, transformation, validation, loading, error handling, and performance optimization. By leveraging the power, flexibility, and extensive libraries available in C++, developers can create robust, efficient, and scalable ETL pipelines that effectively integrate and process data, enabling organizations to derive valuable insights and make informed decisions.

C++ example

In this example, assume we have a CSV file (`data.csv`) with customer and sales columns:

```
#include <iostream>
#include <fstream>
#include <sstream>
#include <vector>
#include <map>
#include <sqlite3.h>
```

We will extract the data from the CSV file, transform it by calculating the total sales for each customer, and load the transformed data into an SQLite database.

The `split` function is used to split a string based on a delimiter (in this case, a comma). This function parses each CSV file line into individual data elements:

```cpp
// Function to split a string based on a delimiter
std::vector<std::string> split(const std::string& str, char delimiter)
{
    std::vector<std::string> tokens;
    std::stringstream ss(str);
    std::string token;
    while (std::getline(ss, token, delimiter)) {
        tokens.push_back(token);
    }
    return tokens;
}
```

The `transformData` function takes the extracted data and calculates the total sales for each customer using an `std::map` variable. Each row of the data is processed, and the sales value is accumulated for each customer:

```cpp
// Function to transform the data
std::map<std::string, double> transformData(const
std::vector<std::vector<std::string>>& data) {
    std::map<std::string, double> transformedData;
    for (const auto& row : data) {
        std::string customer = row[0];
        double sales = std::stod(row[1]);
        transformedData[customer] += sales;
    }
    return transformedData;
}
```

Using the SQLite C++ API, the `loadIntoDatabase` function establishes a connection to the SQLite database (`sales.db`). It creates a `sales` table if it does not already exist. Then, it prepares an `INSERT` query statement and binds the customer name and total sales values for each transformed data entry. The prepared statement is executed, and the bindings are cleared and reset for the next entry. Finally, the database connection is closed:

```cpp
// Function to load transformed data into the database
void loadIntoDatabase(const std::map<std::string, double>&
transformedData) {
    sqlite3* db;
    sqlite3_open("sales.db", &db);

    std::string createTableQuery = "CREATE TABLE IF NOT
      EXISTS sales (customer TEXT PRIMARY KEY, total_sales
      REAL);";
    sqlite3_exec(db, createTableQuery.c_str(), nullptr,
      nullptr, nullptr);

    std::string insertQuery = "INSERT INTO sales (customer,
      total_sales) VALUES (?, ?);";
    sqlite3_stmt* stmt;
    sqlite3_prepare_v2(db, insertQuery.c_str(), -1, &stmt,
      nullptr);

    for (const auto& pair : transformedData) {
        sqlite3_bind_text(stmt, 1, pair.first.c_str(), -1,
          SQLITE_STATIC);
        sqlite3_bind_double(stmt, 2, pair.second);
        sqlite3_step(stmt);
        sqlite3_clear_bindings(stmt);
        sqlite3_reset(stmt);
    }

    sqlite3_finalize(stmt);
    sqlite3_close(db);
}
```

In the `main` function, we open the input file (`data.csv`) and read its contents line by line. Each line is split into individual data elements using the `split` function, and the resulting rows are stored in the data vector. Next, the `transformData` function is called, passing the data vector. It calculates the total sales for each customer and returns an `std::map` variable containing the transformed data:

```cpp
int main() {
    std::ifstream inputFile("data.csv");
```

```
    if (!inputFile) {
        std::cout << "Failed to open input file." <<
          std::endl;
        return 1;
    }

    std::vector<std::vector<std::string>> data;
    std::string line;
    while (std::getline(inputFile, line)) {
        std::vector<std::string> row = split(line, ',');
        data.push_back(row);
    }

    inputFile.close();

    std::map<std::string, double> transformedData =
      transformData(data);
```

The loadIntoDatabase function is then called, passing the transformed data. It loads the transformed data into the SQLite database by establishing a connection, creating the table (if necessary), and inserting the customer's name and total sales values. Finally, a success message indicates that the ETL pipeline has been executed successfully:

```
    loadIntoDatabase(transformedData);

    std::cout << "ETL pipeline executed successfully." <<
      std::endl;

    return 0;
}
```

To run this example, ensure the SQLite and libsqlite3-dev libraries are installed and linked correctly. Also, provide a valid data.csv file in the same directory as the executable, containing customer and sales data separated by commas.

This example provides a basic framework for an ETL pipeline in C++, where data is extracted, transformed, and loaded into a target database. You can expand and enhance this pipeline to handle more complex data transformations, validation, error handling, and other tasks per your specific requirements.

Summary

In C++, you can work with statistical data types, process tabular data, and design a complete ETL pipeline strategy using various libraries and techniques. Here's a brief overview of how you can accomplish each of these tasks in C++.

Using and processing statistical data types in C++ involves utilizing the built-in data types for numerical data, such as integers (`int`, `long`, `float`, and `double`) and characters (`char`). These data types allow you to perform basic statistical computations and calculations. However, you can leverage libraries such as Boost, Armadillo, or Eigen for more advanced statistical analysis. These libraries provide extensive functionality for working with statistical data types, including statistical modeling, regression analysis, hypothesis testing, and data manipulation.

To work with tabular and rectangular data in C++, you can use the container classes provided by the standard library, such as `std::vector` or `std::array`. These classes allow you to represent rows and columns of data in a structured manner. The STL also offers algorithms and functions specifically designed for sorting, searching, and efficiently transforming tabular data. These utilities enable you to manipulate and analyze the tabular structure's data effectively.

Designing a complete ETL pipeline in C++ involves utilizing various libraries and tools that facilitate different stages of the pipeline. One popular library for building ETL pipelines in C++ is Apache Kafka. Kafka provides a distributed streaming platform that allows you to process and transform data in real time. You can use it for the pipeline's extraction and loading phases, enabling efficient and scalable data transfer. Also, libraries such as Apache Avro or Protocol Buffers can define data schemas and serialize/deserialize data during extraction and loading.

For the transformation phase, libraries such as Apache Spark or TensorFlow can be employed, depending on the transformations' complexity. These libraries offer powerful tools for data manipulation, machine learning, and distributed processing, allowing you to perform advanced data transformations on large datasets. Moreover, C++ provides database connectors such as ODBC or JDBC, which enable you to connect to different data sources and load data into a target database or data warehouse. These connectors facilitate the loading phase of the ETL pipeline, ensuring efficient and reliable data storage.

In conclusion, by leveraging the capabilities of C++ and various libraries, you can effectively work with statistical data types, process tabular and rectangular data, and design a complete ETL pipeline. C++ provides a versatile and powerful programming environment for handling data, and by utilizing appropriate libraries and tools, you can perform complex statistical analysis, manipulate tabular data efficiently, and automate the extraction, transformation, and loading of data in your projects.

Questions

1. What are some advantages of using statistical data types in data analysis, and how can C++ facilitate their processing?

2. How can C++ effectively handle and process tabular and rectangular data? What are some techniques and libraries available for this purpose?

3. What are the key components and considerations in designing a complete ETL pipeline? How does C++ enable the implementation of an efficient and reliable ETL pipeline?

Further reading

C++ for Data Science by Cristiano L. Fontana (`https://opensource.com/article/20/2/c-data-science`)

Index

`Packtpub.com`

Subscribe to our online digital library for full access to over 7,000 books and videos, as well as industry leading tools to help you plan your personal development and advance your career. For more information, please visit our website.

Why subscribe?

- Spend less time learning and more time coding with practical eBooks and Videos from over 4,000 industry professionals

- Improve your learning with Skill Plans built especially for you

- Get a free eBook or video every month

- Fully searchable for easy access to vital information

- Copy and paste, print, and bookmark content

Did you know that Packt offers eBook versions of every book published, with PDF and ePub files available? You can upgrade to the eBook version at `packtpub.com` and as a print book customer, you are entitled to a discount on the eBook copy. Get in touch with us at `customercare@packtpub.com` for more details.

At `www.packtpub.com`, you can also read a collection of free technical articles, sign up for a range of free newsletters, and receive exclusive discounts and offers on Packt books and eBooks.

Other Books You May Enjoy

If you enjoyed this book, you may be interested in these other books by Packt:

C++ High Performance - Second Edition

Björn Andrist, Viktor Sehr

ISBN: 978-1-83921-654-1

- Write specialized data structures for performance-critical code
- Use modern metaprogramming techniques to reduce runtime calculations
- Achieve efficient memory management using custom memory allocators
- Reduce boilerplate code using reflection techniques
- Reap the benefits of lock-free concurrent programming
- Gain insights into subtle optimizations used by standard library algorithms
- Compose algorithms using ranges library
- Develop the ability to apply metaprogramming aspects such as constexpr, constraints, and concepts
- Implement lazy generators and asynchronous tasks using C++20 coroutines

Modern C++ Programming Cookbook - Second Edition

Marius Bancila

ISBN: 978-1-80020-898-8

- Understand the new C++20 language and library features and the problems they solve
- Become skilled at using the standard support for threading and concurrency for daily tasks
- Leverage the standard library and work with containers, algorithms, and iterators
- Solve text searching and replacement problems using regular expressions
- Work with different types of strings and learn the various aspects of compilation
- Take advantage of the file system library to work with files and directories
- Implement various useful patterns and idioms
- Explore the widely used testing frameworks for C++

Packt is searching for authors like you

If you're interested in becoming an author for Packt, please visit `authors.packtpub.com` and apply today. We have worked with thousands of developers and tech professionals, just like you, to help them share their insight with the global tech community. You can make a general application, apply for a specific hot topic that we are recruiting an author for, or submit your own idea.

Share Your Thoughts

Now you've finished *Expert C++, 2nd edition*, we'd love to hear your thoughts! Scan the QR code below to go straight to the Amazon review page for this book and share your feedback or leave a review on the site that you purchased it from.

`https://packt.link/r/1804617830`

Your review is important to us and the tech community and will help us make sure we're delivering excellent quality content.

Download a free PDF copy of this book

Thanks for purchasing this book!

Do you like to read on the go but are unable to carry your print books everywhere? Is your eBook purchase not compatible with the device of your choice?

Don't worry, now with every Packt book you get a DRM-free PDF version of that book at no cost.

Read anywhere, any place, on any device. Search, copy, and paste code from your favorite technical books directly into your application.

The perks don't stop there, you can get exclusive access to discounts, newsletters, and great free content in your inbox daily

Follow these simple steps to get the benefits:

1. Scan the QR code or visit the link below

https://packt.link/free-ebook/9781804617830

1. Submit your proof of purchase
2. That's it! We'll send your free PDF and other benefits to your email directly

Made in United States
North Haven, CT
16 December 2023

45941598R10330